Praise for
The Price of Democracy

"I love this book. American democracy has always been based on the right of the people to tax themselves to create a state that serves their needs—and oligarchs determined to destroy that state have always fought taxes. A colorful and interesting trip through American history, *The Price of Democracy* makes a convincing case that we must take back the power of taxation to restore our democracy. The history of taxes has never been more interesting or more important than it is right now, and in Williamson's hands, it comes alive."

—Heather Cox Richardson, *New York Times*–
bestselling author of *Democracy Awakening*

"Readable, entertaining, and astute, Vanessa Williamson's new book offers a fresh look at the politics of U.S. taxation from the original Tea Party to the present. Rich and poor may clash over who pays for government and how, but many Americans have always realized their stakes in paying enough in legitimate ways to make democracy work. Going far beyond the usual platitudes about how 'Americans hate taxes,' this book shows us why some levies are more popular and effective than others for sustaining democratically responsive government. As America's tax battles flare anew, *The Price of Democracy* has valuable lessons for citizens and analysts alike."

—Theda Skocpol, coauthor of *The Tea Party and the*
Remaking of Republican Conservatism

"Taxes are not just the lifeblood of government. They are the wellspring of democracy. That is the revelatory message of Vanessa Williamson's propulsive, panoramic history. Compelling, original, and beautifully written, *The Price of Democracy* is an essential antidote to the anti-tax extremism that threatens our democracy."

—Jacob S. Hacker, coauthor of *Let Them Eat Tweets*

"Deeply researched and magnificently written, this book reminds us of a profound truth: that taxation and democracy are inextricably linked. At a time when democracy is under attack, look no further than taxes to see both the battleground and the war. An absolute must-read."

—Gabriel Zucman, author of *The Hidden Wealth of Nations*

"Vanessa Williamson has synthesized recent research to tell a gripping story about the contested history of taxation in the United States. Written with style and verve, this book should appeal to everyone interested in this always central but too often arcane aspect of the American story."

—Robin Einhorn, University of California, Berkeley

THE
PRICE OF
DEMOCRACY

ALSO BY VANESSA S. WILLIAMSON

Read My Lips: Why Americans Are Proud to Pay Taxes

The Tea Party and the Remaking of Republican Conservatism (coauthor)

THE PRICE OF DEMOCRACY

THE REVOLUTIONARY POWER OF TAXATION IN AMERICAN HISTORY

VANESSA S. WILLIAMSON

BASIC BOOKS

New York

Basic Books
Hachette Book Group
1290 Avenue of the Americas, New York, NY 10104
www.basicbooks.com

Printed in the United States of America

First Edition: November 2025

Published by Basic Books, an imprint of Hachette Book Group, Inc. The Basic Books name and logo is a registered trademark of the Hachette Book Group.

The Hachette Speakers Bureau provides a wide range of authors for speaking events. To find out more, go to hachettespeakersbureau.com or email HachetteSpeakers@hbgusa.com.

Basic books may be purchased in bulk for business, educational, or promotional use. For more information, please contact your local bookseller or the Hachette Book Group Special Markets Department at special.markets@hbgusa.com.

The publisher is not responsible for websites (or their content) that are not owned by the publisher.

Additional copyright/credits information is on page 255.

Print book interior design by Amy Quinn

Library of Congress Control Number: 2025002910

ISBNs: 9781541606111 (hardcover), 9781541606128 (ebook)

LSC-C

Printing 1, 2025

Contents

Introduction

I n the still of a cold winter evening in 1773, a young man named George
Robert Twelves Hewes slipped into a blacksmith's shop and smeared
his face with soot. Suitably disguised, he made his way to Griffin's Wharf,
where he met up with dozens of like-minded colonists. Some were dressed
as Mohawk Indians. Some, like Hewes, had covered their faces with coal
dust. Others had donned women's gowns. They carried axes and clubs,
and they called themselves the "Sons of Liberty."

Hewes was a poor man, a shoemaker. His fellows in the Sons of Liberty
were mostly young artisans and mechanics, not famous or wealthy men. Historians today are still unsure of their names. But as part of Samuel Adams's
paramilitary patriot organization, these men were about to board three ships
docked in Boston Harbor and challenge the most powerful empire the world
had ever known.

After politely but firmly demanding the keys and some lanterns from the
ships' crews, the men worked in teams to haul hundreds of chests from the
ships' holds, split them open, and dump their contents into the ocean. Though
there was almost no moonlight, a crowd of Bostonians gathered silently and
watched. Three hours later, ninety thousand pounds of tea had been dis-
patched into the water.

The cargo was worth a small fortune, but careful discipline ensured
that the tea was not looted and resold. When Hewes saw another man, a

Captain Charles O'Connor, slipping packets of valuable tea into his coat lining, he tore the coat from O'Connor's back, raised his fist, and suggested that O'Connor had better write his will. The captain fled, empty-handed. Later, when tea floated to shore with the rising tide, sailors rowed out in small boats to sink anything that might otherwise be salvageable.[1] This was not robbery. It was rebellion.

The Boston Tea Party, as it is now known, is commonly recalled as evidence that Americans have always been reflexively antitax opponents of "big government."[2] There is just one problem with the familiar story: It is utterly untrue.

In fact, the patriots who threw the tea into Boston Harbor were opposing not a tax hike but a corporate tax *cut*. The British government wanted to lower the duties on tea as part of a bailout for the floundering East India Company. In addition to providing a massive £1.4 million government loan to the company and allowing it to sell tea directly to American retailers, the Tea Act eliminated the English import duties on tea that was resold to America. It was a measure intended to prop up a struggling corporation believed to be "too big to fail."[3]

Though they recognized that the act would make their tea cheaper, the Sons of Liberty rabidly opposed this corporate bailout and tax break. In a letter to Benjamin Franklin, Samuel Adams denounced the act as "introductive to Monopolies," which he viewed as "dangerous to Publick Liberty," particularly when "under the direction and Influence of Government." The "destruction of the tea," as it was known in the early nineteenth century, was a direct-action attack on private property to resist government-abetted corporate power.[4]

When American colonists did object to British taxes, their protests were not about the taxes themselves, but about who did the taxing. The colonists wanted taxation with representation by their own local elected officials, not the distant Parliament. In 1765, the Virginia House of Burgesses protested the Stamp Act, Parliament's new tax on colonial documents, by insisting that "Taxation of the People by themselves, or by Persons chosen by themselves to represent them" is the "distinguishing Characteristick of British Freedom." Liberty, for colonial Americans, was not freedom from taxation but the power to impose their own taxes—at first within the British Empire, and then, when Britain would not agree, as an independent nation.[5]

So committed were the colonists of Massachusetts to taxpaying that, even as they flouted British authority, they kept collecting revenue locally. Dozens of towns held meetings in 1774 in which they decided to stop sending their taxes to Harrison Gray, the loyalist treasurer of the colony. But rather than pocket the money, the colonists voted to send "moneys which they then had, or in future might have in their hands, belonging to the Province" to one Henry Gardner. Gardner, a trusted patriot, would eventually become treasurer of the new state of Massachusetts. To the extent the American Revolution was about taxation, it was about the desire of Americans to *tax themselves*: to take on the legitimate burdens of a government in which they had a voice.[6]

Setting the record straight here is no minor matter. The falsehood that our nation was born in opposition to taxation has limited our vision of what America can be. It suggests that we cannot, as a country, have nice things because we cannot, as a country, agree to pay for them. It is the ready-made excuse for why America does such a bad job of caring for our children and for our poor. It implies that those seeking to raise taxes or to spend more on social investments are un-American. And the slur "Americans hate taxes" has for decades propped up a reactionary antitax political movement, allowing a radically right-wing politics to pass itself off as traditional even as it has come to threaten the most basic functioning of our democracy.

If the history we have been told is wrong, there must be another explanation for why taxes show up over and over at our country's most consequential moments, for why taxation is bound up with representation, and for why a rich country leaves so many people poor and struggling. There is a different explanation. It can be found in the history I will share in this book.

FREE COUNTRIES ARE HIGH-TAX COUNTRIES

Before we get started, let us clear away one other conservative trope about taxation that is utterly unsupported by the historical record. It is a cliché of right-wing fulmination to equate taxation with "tyranny."[7] Much like the histories describing the Boston Tea Party as an antitax rebellion, these diatribes get the facts backward. In reality, tyrants are bad at raising taxes, and elected officials are good at it.

Historically and cross-nationally, authoritarian governments collect less in taxes, and where taxes are heavier, democratic practices are more vibrant. In Europe in the Middle Ages, for instance, systems of representation developed where taxes were higher, and as those representative institutions grew stronger, tax revenue continued to rise.[8] The nations that collect the most tax revenue today—like Sweden and Norway—also score at the top of international measures of democratic practices.[9] When taxation begets representation and representation legitimates taxation, a virtuous cycle can create more effective and accountable government. Free countries are high-tax countries.

Why? Governments that are dependent on taxation have reason to listen to their citizens.[10] The effective imposition of taxes relies in part on the compliance of the citizenry. When citizens see the state as legitimate, and when they can use the levers of government to influence policymaking, they are more inclined to foot the resulting bill, making tax collection significantly easier. To appear worthy to their taxpaying citizens, regimes respond to the citizens' needs and demands.

Those incentives disappear in states that do not rely on tax revenue. Consider countries with large deposits of valuable fossil fuels or minerals, lands often described as bearing a "resource curse." These nations are rich, but their governments are authoritarian, and little of the country's wealth makes its way to the people. If leaders can extract wealth from the ground, they do not need to tax it from their people. Unconstrained by the need for tax revenue, they do not have to make themselves answerable to their citizens by adopting democratic practices or developing competent government institutions. The resource curse is, in other words, the curse of low taxation. Declines in taxation can even lead to declines in representation. When revenues from the *tributum*, a wealth tax paid by Roman citizens to support the military, were replaced with spoils from Rome's foreign conquests, the Roman elite were no longer fiscally beholden to the citizenry and had a freer hand to rule more autocratically.[11]

Taxation gives governments an incentive to provide what their citizens desire and also makes governments more capable of doing so. Taxes provide the revenue to pay for the citizens' demands, of course. But serious levels of taxation also require an effective bureaucracy to administer the system, and an effective bureaucracy enables all kinds of government action. In Britain, for example, the need for literate and numerate tax collectors helped spur the growth of public education.[12]

Tax bureaucracy can also improve government competency through more indirect means. Imagine a tax as simple as a toll on a bridge. To apply that tax consistently, you will need tax collectors. You'll want those collectors to be honest and able, so you need to put in place a system to hire qualified people, train them, and pay them competitively. And you'll want to know how much money the toll will raise, so you might decide to assess traffic levels and estimate revenue. With the oversight that comes from tax collection, you might recognize that potholes are reducing traffic and therefore revenue, and with your local bureaucracy in place, you would be able to organize a system of road repair. In other words, effective tax collection requires planning, systematization, competence, and professionalism—and project management skills, as we say these days, are transferrable.

Taxes are a key ingredient in the recipe for successful representative government; leave them out and democracy struggles to rise, even if people can vote. It is not enough to hold elections. A government also needs the resources and the organization to fulfill the demands of the voters.[13] Thus it is taxes that make democracy *consequential*. It is for this reason that, as we will see, so many opponents of democracy in the United States have fought against both fair elections and strong tax systems.

TAX FIGHTS ARE FIGHTS OVER DEMOCRACY

In 1776, as John Adams helped organize a revolution from his seat in the Continental Congress, his beloved wife, Abigail, wrote to him from Boston. The new government had better "Remember the Ladies" and protect their rights, Abigail lightly suggested, or women might make a revolution of their own. In his reply, John feigned shock. The American struggle, he said, had been blamed for loosening "the bands of Government every where.

That Children and Apprentices were disobedient—that schools and Colleges were grown turbulent—that Indians slighted their guardians and Negroes grew insolent to the Masters. But your Letter was the first Intimation that another Tribe more numerous and powerfull than all the rest were grown discontented."[14]

Adams was joking, but the fear that the revolution would destabilize the social order was both widespread and entirely plausible. It is dangerous to assert that "all men are created equal" within the hearing of the lower orders. They might take you at your word.[15] Even narrowly representative institutions carry within them the potential for expansion. Letting some people vote raises the question of why others should not.

The American Revolution swept away centuries-old justifications for a hierarchical society and popularized the radical notions that all men are born free and equal in rights.[16] Even the most casual student of American history knows that the resulting political order did not make good on that promise; instead, it balanced white freedom on Black subjugation and Native expropriation. For the 250 years since, we have been fighting over what it means to be equal and what it means to be free.

What is less commonly recognized is that the battles over the breadth of our democracy are, with a startling regularity, fights about taxes. Relatively few Americans know, for example, that the impetus for the US Constitution—the reason that leading lights of the founding generation met and designed the government we live under today—was that small farmers had been (in the eyes of America's elite) too successful in resisting regressive tax policies in the states. The states were too democratic, the framers decided, so they needed to shift power to a federal government that would be *much less accountable to the people.* Tax and monetary powers were the issue of the day; the Bill of Rights was a literal afterthought. (The Constitutional Convention did not write one. It was added later to ensure popular ratification of the new government framework.) As we will see in Part One of this book, our federal government was designed by elites afraid that the American people had too much authority over the public purse.

The effects of the founders' fiscal concerns are still being felt today. If, for example, you have heard that a national wealth tax would be unconstitutional, it is because, as part of the framers' compromises to protect slavery, the Constitution included a limit on the federal government's ability to directly tax property. Infamously, the Gilded Age Supreme Court in 1895 reinterpreted the direct taxation clause to declare unconstitutional a new federal income tax. The only reason we have a federal income tax today is thanks to the Sixteenth Amendment, passed after a twenty-year campaign led by Populist farmers. But the Sixteenth Amendment says nothing about wealth taxes, so it would do nothing to prevent the conservative Supreme Court of our contemporary Gilded Age from declaring a wealth tax unconstitutional.

Taxes were also the vital subject during our nation's second founding in the years after the Civil War. For many newly emancipated people, real freedom meant access to an education and to a homestead; they wanted to work for themselves and send their children to school. During this period of Radical Reconstruction, freedmen voted into office state legislators who tried to shift taxes onto wealthy plantation owners, both to pay for universal public schooling and to encourage land sales. White resistance to those taxes was a key part of the violent campaign that overthrew the Reconstruction governments and reinstituted white supremacist rule, the most monumental defeat for racial justice in American history.

Many of the antidemocratic fiscal limitations enacted after Reconstruction are still in effect today. In 2019, when 58 percent of voters in the school district of Leland, Mississippi, voted for a bond issue to rebuild their schools, it was not enough to overcome the 60 percent threshold required for passage. The children in this rural, majority-Black county were left in buildings with leaking roofs, unreliable air-conditioning, and a heating system that failed so regularly in winter that students brought blankets to class.[17] All because white supremacists more than one hundred years ago rewrote the voting rules so that taxes cannot go up, even when most citizens want them to.

One might think that the tax limitations imposed by the Constitution and in the post-Reconstruction era are simply evidence that taxes have always been extremely contentious. But this is not the case. In the mid-twentieth century, federal tax policy did not feature prominently in the political platform of either the Democratic or the Republican Party.[18]

Similarly, in early and mid-Victorian Britain, taxation was not a subject of much dispute; it was seen as an important but rather boring function of government.[19] That is not to say there were no debates over taxes during this period, but such disputes tended to focus on the details: rates and exemptions, exactly how much revenue was needed, and how precisely it should be raised. These two periods of fiscal consensus collapsed, not coincidentally, when the franchise expanded and new, poorer groups sought access to public goods—in Britain, as the working class gained suffrage rights, and in America, after the civil rights movement restored voting power to Black people. *Public revenue is contested most fiercely when the scope of the public is itself disputed.*

The recurring dynamic is this: When poorer groups of Americans have increased their political power, they have called for higher taxes on the wealthy and more spending on public goods. In response, elites have attempted, and often succeeded, in curtailing the state's tax powers or making government less accountable to the public, or both. Particularly when they could play on racial animus, American elites have won these antitax and antidemocratic victories by exploiting the issue of taxation—both rhetorically, by casting themselves as the victims of a corrupt fiscal regime, and substantively, by promising lower taxation to poorer whites in exchange for their support. These deals were bad ones; the white masses have regularly traded their power for very little gain.

Note that what has been unacceptable to the wealthy and the powerful is the *combination* of mass representation and state capacity: a democratic government with strong tax powers. An effective tax apparatus is generally acceptable to the wealthy when they are confident in their grip on power and can arrange the fiscal system to reinforce their privileges. Indeed, the very word *privilège*, meaning "private law," referred to the special immunity nobles and the clergy had from paying taxes that fell heavily on commoners before the French Revolution.[20] But elites become suspicious of the state's tax powers when poorer people seem plausibly capable of gaining some additional leverage in government. As the sociologist Rudolf Goldscheid put the point, only the "poor State can calmly be allowed to fall into the hands of the people."[21]

It might seem obvious why the ruling elite would oppose democratic taxation. In the words of archconservative Lord Salisbury, the late nineteenth-century British prime minister who once sardonically described constituents as "vermin" for which he wished he had insecticide powder, wider suffrage rights would mean "the rich shall pay all the taxes, and the poor shall make all the laws."[22] But as with the real history of the Boston Tea Party, the truth is perhaps not what you think—and in this case, it is liberal shibboleths, not conservative ones, that have been misleading.

THE THREAT OF DEMOCRATIC TAXATION

American liberals care a lot about tax progressivity.[23] The primary standard by which Democrats today assess tax policy is whether a tax is paid especially or exclusively by the rich. Candidates typically promise to raise federal income taxes, or increase tax enforcement, only on those making hundreds of thousands of dollars a year. Everyone else is promised tax cuts. Don't get me wrong: Taxing the rich is vitally important. But when we understand the egalitarian power of taxation only in terms of tax progressivity, we miss seeing the full egalitarian potential of a democracy's power to tax. And without that broader understanding, the history of taxation and democracy in America does not make much sense.

Let's start with the obvious part: Progressive taxation can directly reduce inequality. For decades after the Second World War, income and estate taxation prevented extreme wealth concentration. The rollback of those taxes led to our contemporary oligarchy.[24] Between 1976 and 2023, the top 0.01 percent of US households saw their share of national wealth more than quadruple, to more than 10 percent of total US wealth.[25] The US tax code has also reduced poverty. The Earned Income Tax Credit and the Child Tax Credit supplement the incomes of lower-income families, lifting millions of Americans above the poverty line. An expansion of the child tax credit during the COVID-19 pandemic cut the child poverty rate *in half*. But income requirements, discriminatory audit rates, and predatory paid tax preparers substantially reduce the effectiveness of tax breaks aimed at the poor, and the expanded Child Tax Credit was allowed to expire at the end of 2021. Child poverty rates quickly rebounded.[26]

So taxes directly affect how poor and how rich Americans are. Taxes are also used to pay for (or, in the case of the federal government, to partially offset) public spending.[27] This might seem too obvious to mention, except that this aspect of taxation is sometimes ignored by those purporting to explain how the economy works. In contemporary introductions to economics, the equation introducing the effect of taxation treats "the collection of taxes as though it were only a common disaster—as though the tax money once collected were thrown into the sea."[28] Perhaps the most popular economics textbook in America informs undergraduates that taxes "are costly to market participants" because "taxes transfer resources from those participants to the government."[29] Upon arrival at "the government," those dollars are never to be heard from again, it seems. Presumably, none of the "market participants" were public school teachers or firefighters, none of the markets were accessed by public roads, none of the contracts resulted in a legal dispute, and none of the transactions involved money.[30]

In reality, an enormous fraction of the economy passes through public hands. Including federal, state, and local expenditures, government accounted for a third of the US gross domestic product in 2023. This figure is low by international standards; in Sweden in 2023, public spending made up about 47 percent of GDP, and in the United Kingdom, 40 percent.[31] Our budget looks smaller than it is, however, because the United States gives tax breaks where other countries spend money directly. Many US tax provisions attempt to encourage the private provision of goods—such as housing, retirement savings, and health insurance—that in other countries are subsidized or provided by government spending. America's expensive tax breaks disproportionately benefit the white and the well-off, so they exacerbate inequality and miss many of the people who most need them. America has far higher rates of poverty than other wealthy nations.[32]

Even with our comparatively ineffectual welfare state, however, public investments in the United States substantially reduce poverty. Prior to the introduction of Social Security, for instance, about half of senior citizens were poor, compared to about 9 percent today.[33] Social Security allows millions of older Americans to live much more comfortable and dignified lives. Those senior citizens are also more *free*—free from reliance on charity, free from feeling themselves a burden on their children, free from having to work until they die.

So social spending can be *emancipatory*. Conservatives have for so long enlisted the language of liberty to defend their preferred economic institutions that it can be easy to overlook market subjugation. Without government spending, the economy is a strict and capricious master. Unless you are lucky enough to be born in a rich family, your survival is always contingent on your ability to do the kind of work the market rewards, and you have little control over the availability of or compensation for that work. Necessities like housing and health care are dependent on forces far outside an individual's control. And when the market fails to provide, the only backstop is charity, leaving the poor dependent on the fickle benevolence of the rich. By contrast, when governments ensure that the essentials of life are available to the citizenry by right, they provide, as economist Mike Konczal has said, *freedom from the market*.[34]

The emancipatory capacity of social spending not only liberates people from market forces; it can empower them to act as citizens. Before Social Security, old people were less likely to participate in politics than younger Americans. For people living on whatever meager savings they had managed to accrue, or struggling to continue working as they aged, getting involved in political affairs could feel like a luxury. Today, older people are the most reliable voting bloc in the US. By providing older Americans (and especially the elderly poor) with the resources, the time, and the incentive to care about politics, government pensions "made citizens," as political scientist Andrea Campbell has demonstrated.[35]

It is worth noting that Social Security and Medicare are not funded by progressive taxation; they are funded by payroll taxes that fall heavily on working people. Similarly, and perhaps surprisingly to many American liberals, European governments with robust social spending programs also rely more heavily on regressive taxes than the United States does.[36] If we judge taxes exclusively on a progressivity standard, it obscures the vital consideration of how much money the tax raises and where that money goes. As we will see in Chapter 4, some states in the slaveholding South had comparatively progressive tax systems. But these systems did not reduce wealth concentration or fund big investments in public goods because the overall revenue levels were so low.

The fact that taxes and tax-funded programs can redistribute wealth might seem like enough to explain why taxes become controversial when the poor are enfranchised. Yet this can't be the whole story, since taxes and spending are far from the only government policies that determine the allocation of wealth. Billions of dollars hang in the balance when the US government decides what is legal business (like marijuana sales or stock buy-backs), what can be owned and how (like a patent or an emissions credit), or which owners deserve protection from the vagaries of the market (like corporate investors or depositors at failed banks). Indeed, the three largest redistributions of wealth in American history—the genocidal seizure of the land of Native nations, the defense of chattel slavery, and emancipation—involved the creation and destruction of entire forms of property through law and military force. The redistributive effects of the income tax start to look puny by comparison.

Though conservatives commonly treat taxation and welfare spending as uniquely dangerous interventions in an otherwise self-regulating, natural economy, this is bosh.[37] Taxes and markets are, in fact, part of a single system of political economy; historically, money itself developed because rulers wanted to systematize tax payments, and all markets of any size or scope are dependent on the tax-funded legal and monetary system.[38] Governments intervene in the market in the same way your skeleton intervenes in your body; it is the organizing structure, not an external force. All economic allocations, from the greatest fortunes to the deepest poverty, are political products. Taxes are only an especially salient version of the government's economic authority.

What is distinct about taxation is not, then, that it somehow changes distributional outcomes more than other government policies. But taxes are unique in two ways: First, they are the exaction that supports the state, and second, they seem to apply after an initial distribution. Let's consider each point in turn.

As British statesman and philosopher Edmund Burke put it, the "revenue of the state is the state."[39] This is not the same as saying that taxes can be used to pay for social spending. The government is not merely a series of funnels and tubes directing money between various private pockets. It is an entity with a power of its own. Taxes make the very existence of government possible.

The power of the state holds the space, both metaphorically and literally, for public life to occur. The public portion of our lives occurs on the sidewalks, parks, and other common spaces we maintain with public money. Taxes also support the public venues—the courts, the schools, the town halls, the voting booths, and the government offices—where people are, at least in principle, given equal standing and protected from private domination. These are places where it is not supposed to matter if you are rich or poor, Black or white, immigrant or native-born.

Of course, our government institutions fail to deliver on this promise, perhaps most egregiously in our schools and in our criminal justice system. But it remains the case that your boss (or your landlord, parent, or spouse) cannot look over your shoulder in the voting booth. The people who might have power over you in a private capacity are not supposed to be able to dictate your public choices. Similarly, few Americans, after failing their driver's test, would attempt to buy their license by bribing the DMV agent. There is a standard, not always met and sometimes shamefully disregarded, that in public places, private forms of influence stop at the door.

Taxes make possible those public spaces, those limits on private forms of influence. And this, too, makes taxes threatening to those who have large stocks of private power—particularly because those limits are paid for by an exaction on private property. And this is the second salient fact about taxation.

With taxation, the state agrees that something is yours and then takes part of it away. In part because people value things much more once they have them—a phenomenon that psychologists refer to as the "endowment effect"—the post hoc structure of taxation encourages taxpayers' sense that they have a stake in government. It also provokes frustration and resistance when the state fails to concern itself with whether a tax is affordable, whether the payment process is reasonable, or whether public money is being well spent.[40] This is one of the key reasons taxation and representation reinforce each other: The incentive to get re-elected encourages representatives to implement fiscal structures that work better for their constituents—though, as we will see in the coming chapters, elections certainly do not immunize politicians against adopting wholly misbegotten tax policies.

Taxes feel as if they occur after an initial distribution of wealth, but the idea that taxes are an "after the fact" policy is misleading at best. An economist would point out that since taxes are generally predictable, they affect decision-making before the tax is applied. For example, high income taxes, when effectively enforced, reduce the incentive for corporate boards to overpay executives. When seven-tenths of each additional dollar would go to Uncle Sam, board members think twice before approving a big salary increase for a mediocre CEO. With lower tax rates, boards are more willing to reward their friends in the executive suite, independent of the CEO's actual contributions to the company's bottom line.[41]

More fundamentally, there is no such thing as an income that is truly "pretax," because taxes fund the state that defines and defends property rights in the first place. As the philosophers Liam Murphy and Thomas Nagel point out, what most of us would earn absent taxation is nothing, because most of us would struggle to survive in a government-free state of nature.[42] Whether you prefer to imagine a gentle life as a forest hermit or a nasty, brutish, and short existence in a *Mad Max*–style postapocalyptic hellscape, worlds without governments (that is, worlds without taxation) do not allow for much property accumulation.

Philosophers and economists can say what they will, but taxes take money out of your pocket, or at least it feels that way. You can calculate how much more money you would have if, for some reason, you (alone) didn't have to pay taxes on this paycheck or that purchase. Taxes therefore seem to have an obvious cost—and they also have an obvious cause. The government is the reason my taxes are high; it is far harder to trace the reasons why my wages are low or my rent has gone up. Other economic policies, even if they have larger effects, operate at greater remove.

Taxes thus provide a prominent reminder that private property, legitimately held, can be directed to public purposes. Taxes are the only money in the economy allocated according to the democratic process, a daily demonstration that private gain is subordinate to the public interest. What is more, taxes suggest that this fundamental primacy of the public interest is utterly ordinary. Whereas fines and forfeitures are premised on the putative misbehavior of the payer, most taxes (barring "sin" taxes) are applied to activities that are deemed respectable: legal ways of acquiring, selling, and owning. Taxes wield the everyday power of the polity over the economy, and therefore *normalize* the reassignment of private property to the state. Taxes are not just radical and boring; they are radical because they are boring.

So the subversive power of democratic taxation is far more than simply the possibility of raising taxes on the rich. Yes, progressive taxes can directly prevent the concentration of wealth, a vital backstop against plutocracy. But taxes do not need to be graduated by income to be egalitarian in their effects. Broad-based taxes can fund the public goods that free people from market subjugation. Taxation is the strength of the state and therefore can empower a democratic government. Above all, taxes demonstrate that the polity—in a democracy, the people—have ultimate authority over the economic order. This is why elites seek to keep the power of the purse in their own hands. This is why taxes are so inextricably tied to representation, and why increases in the political power of the poor cause taxes to become controversial. This is why the great fights over taxation are contests over suffrage, and why battles over the breadth of a democracy are fought on fiscal grounds.

The jurist Oliver Wendell Holmes Jr. once described taxation as the price we pay for civilized society, and this is true; taxes fund the myriad legal, political, social, and economic systems that hold our complex, interconnected modern world together. But even more, taxes are the price of *democracy*. Taxes empower the state and make that state responsive to the citizens.

All too often, democracy is something the rich do not want to buy. The most powerful forces resisting taxation in America have also been the country's most antidemocratic elements, ready to support suffrage restrictions, malapportionment of legislative seats, minority rule, and sometimes direct intimidation and violence to keep fiscal power in elite hands. The same antidemocratic, reactionary movements have also fought to undermine the state's fiscal powers, starving the government and thereby curtailing the consequences of mass enfranchisement. When it comes to contestation over democracy, taxes are *both* the battleground and the war.

•-•

At the time I am writing this, the teaching of history has become increasingly controversial. The censors are right: History is dangerous. It threatens the self-justifying nostalgia and mythmaking of those who benefit from the status quo. The stories in the coming pages resonate closely, and sometimes all too closely, with our nation's contemporary challenges. It may well be a matter of temperament whether, on balance, readers will find it more reassuring or disheartening to know that "we have been this way before." In either case, the book is intended as an act of reorientation, a finding of our bearings. Travelers should know the roads they have taken.

The book traces the three great arcs of contestation over taxation and representation in America. The first part, "Taxation for a Republic," follows the revolutionary generation as they consider a vital question: How do free people tax themselves? Early Americans agreed that a republican form of government required a rough economic equality among the citizenry; if people were dominated economically, they could not be free to act politically. Conservatives concluded that political participation must therefore be limited to the economic elite. But democrats proposed the opposite—that a republican government must ensure, through its taxation and its spending, that the people had the economic independence necessary to exercise their political rights. It is a contention that remains radical to this day.

The second part, "Taxation for Black Liberation," demonstrates how the cause of Black freedom has always been bound up in the cause of democratic taxation. Fear of abolition by taxation led slaveholders to hobble democratic institutions and the government's fiscal capacity. After the Civil War, Radical Reconstruction governments sought to break the planter class's hold on economic power by taxing land fairly and funding a public school system. In their campaign to overthrow the Reconstruction governments, the plantation elite reconstituted themselves as "taxpayers," a rhetoric that materially aided their cause by unifying Southern elites and poorer white farmers and legitimating white supremacist violence in the eyes of wealthy Northern observers. In the following decades, the white supremacist regimes that kept Black people and poor whites from voting also developed new policies to ensure that, even if in the minority, the white elite could prevent the taxation of wealth.

The final part, "Taxation for the General Welfare," describes the development of a more egalitarian federal fiscal state during racial apartheid, and the assault on that system, and on democracy itself, that came as a part of the long reaction to the civil rights movement. The modern federal income tax and the welfare programs of the mid-twentieth century were not achieved easily; these egalitarian policies always had natural enemies among the rich. It was with successes of the civil rights movement, however, that the antitax elite found new allies. The return of multiracial democracy in America led to the resurgence of the war against taxation. The last forty-plus years have seen an increasingly extreme conservatism that echoes the politics of Reconstruction's opponents. There is, at the time of this writing, the serious possibility that an antitax, antidemocratic regime will consolidate power in the United States.

As President Franklin Delano Roosevelt once said, a "sure way to determine the social conscience of a Government is to examine the way taxes are collected and how they are spent."[43] What kind of government we are funding is a choice that Americans have made and remade throughout our history. How taxation influenced those decisions is the story of the pages to come.

Part One

Taxation for a Republic

1

THE STAMP ACT

Taxation, Slavery, and Representation

The grand Right to tax ourselves.

—New York General Assembly, 1764 petition to Parliament

A fearsome, snake-eyed dragon lurked on the edge of a cliff, baring its teeth. With a saber held high, ready to strike the dragon's throat, a gentleman in a tricorn hat reaches forward to seize a precious scroll clutched in the dragon's claws. Behind him stand men ready with muskets and swords, and a woman armed with a pole.

An asterisked footnote to this 1765 cartoon by Paul Revere informs the reader that the dragon Tyrant is the Stamp Act, Britain's effort to tax colonial documents and paper goods. From this terrifying beast, the American colonists are attempting to save the ancient English charter, Magna Carta, long hallowed as a foundation of British political freedom.

The original Magna Carta was issued in 1215 in an unsuccessful effort to secure peace between the profligate and despised King John and a group of rebellious barons. Alongside obscurities about the placement of fish weirs on the Thames, the parchment includes civil rights, like the right to a trial by

21

A cartoon by Paul Revere, adapted from an English print, portrays the Stamp Act as a dragon threatening Magna Carta. (Credit: Collection of the Massachusetts Historical Society)

jury, that still look familiar today, and, most significantly, a new principle of community consent to taxation.

King John's imposition of heavy and arbitrary duties, which raised substantially more revenue than those imposed by his predecessors, motivated the nobles to demand this revolutionary new system.[1] Under Magna Carta, the imposition of an extraordinary tax (called an "aid" or "scutage") requires "the general consent of the realm."[2] To obtain such consent, the document demanded "the archbishops, bishops, abbots, earls, and greater barons to be summoned individually by letter . . . to come together on a fixed day (of which at least forty days' notice shall be given) and at a fixed place," a system of authorization that was to be organized and defended by an elected council.[3] In requiring taxes to be regular and subject to a system of consent, Magna Carta drew a line between taxation and extortion.

But Magna Carta was not merely an effort to constrain the king. The proposed system also bound the taxpayers. An individual baron could not simply refuse to pay; instead, he was obliged to participate in a collective process of decision-making and to live by the results.[4] Centuries before the modern conception of individual rights, there was nascent within the regularization of taxation a radical idea: that power was *both bounded and legitimated* by the rule of law and public consent.

In 1215, Magna Carta was an abject failure; it did not bring peace and its terms were not implemented. But later kings issued new versions of the charter. Henry III did so in 1225, for instance, when he badly needed new tax revenue.[5] By the fourteenth century, an institution had developed much like that proposed in Magna Carta: English kings assembled representative councils to approve their tax impositions. Over time, that assembly evolved into the modern British Parliament.[6] This system of representative consent made tax collection easier and more productive. The early Parliaments' assent to the king's decisions lent a new authority to his demands, and so began a self-reinforcing cycle of taxation and representation. In the following centuries, England's unusually effective tax capacity would underwrite its military strength.[7]

Had the English nobles been powerful enough to simply refuse to pay the king, the trajectory of English government might have looked more like France's.[8] The French Estates-General failed to develop into an effective legislative body like Parliament, and so France possessed neither any institutional limit on the king's demands nor any commitment mechanism to encourage nobles' compliance. Nominally, the French kings' power was absolute, but in practice they struggled to raise revenues.[9] Then as today, regimes tended to have either representation and high taxes, or despotism and low taxes.

England's greater fiscal capacity was critical to defeating France in the Seven Years' War (1756–1763). Ironically, that victory would soon reveal the geographic limits of Parliament's tax powers, as the cost of England's expanded empire motivated Parliament to attempt to tax its North American colonies. British North Americans, like their peers in the mother country, had been raised to love their Magna Carta and believed that free people could be taxed only with the consent of their elected representatives.[10] Because there were no seats in Parliament for the colonies—and anyway, a legislature an ocean away could not provide meaningful representation—many colonists believed that the local colonial assemblies could impose taxes but Parliament could not.[11] And, as Paul Revere's cartoon suggests, some of the colonists were ready to fight about it.

The war for American independence was not primarily motivated by taxation. Where the Declaration of Independence listed the abuses of King

George III, only one—the seventeenth of twenty-seven grievances—referred to taxation: "imposing Taxes on us without our Consent."[12] American colonists disliked Britain's monopolistic trade laws, procreditor monetary policies, and limits on white settlements in Native territory as much as if not more than parliamentary taxation.[13]

But taxes reframed resistance to British rule as a matter of principle, rather than simple self-interest. Because taxation was inextricably linked, in the colonists' minds, to the right of representation, and because taxation without representation was understood as a violation akin to slavery, the fight for American independence was imbued from its very start with the most profound questions of what it meant to be free.

SUGAR AND STAMPS

Prior to the 1760s, England had been dependent on colonial support for its perennial wars with France, and Parliament could not afford to risk alienating the colonies by squeezing their pocketbooks. But in the Seven Years' War, France had lost its American territory east of the Mississippi, and Britain needed money to pay down its debt and secure its new colonial holdings. Thus began an authoritarian shift in colonial policy: Along with new strictures on trade, political institutions, and monetary policy, Parliament applied new colonial taxes.[14] Or, at least, it tried to.

First, in 1764, Parliament passed the American Duties Act, better known as the Sugar Act, which applied a tariff on molasses, wine, and other important commodities in the colonial trade economy. Technically, a tariff on foreign molasses had been in place since 1733, but this earlier tax was not intended to produce revenue. Instead, the exorbitant tax was simply meant to deter colonials from purchasing foreign molasses, thus securing England a monopoly on the molasses trade in the colonies. The tariff had, however, been widely evaded, and American merchants lobbied for the tax to be allowed to expire after thirty years, as scheduled. Instead, Parliament reduced the tax rate on molasses, imposed new taxes on other goods, and stepped up enforcement. And in contrast to the earlier tariff, Parliament intended these duties to raise revenue—making the American Duties Act, at least by some lights, a tax rather than a trade regulation.[15]

This distinction between a tax and a trade regulation might seem the quibble of a policy wonk. If so, a striking number of Americans were wonks in the 1760s. One was a Massachusetts lawyer named James Otis, who is sometimes credited with coining the slogan "no taxation without representation."[16] What Otis actually said, in a July 1764 pamphlet opposing the American Duties Act, was less pithy: "Taxes are not to be laid on the people, but by their consent in person, or by deputation."[17] Otis was careful to differentiate between taxes and laws, asserting that "the parliament of Great-Britain has an undoubted power and lawful authority to make acts for the general good." What Parliament cannot do, Otis argued, was extract revenue from the people without their consent. This distinction between taxes and other laws was common; in its 1764 petition to Parliament, New York's General Assembly agreed that Britain had the right to regulate colonial trade but insisted upon "the grand Right to tax ourselves."[18]

Leaders in Parliament, fixated on the immense cost of running Britain's global empire, paid little heed to the petitions of the colonists. When British Prime Minister George Grenville proposed the American Duties Act, he also suggested that a stamp tax might go into effect the following year. The Stamp Act would tax colonial documents and paper goods, from legal instruments to newspapers to playing cards, by requiring those materials to be printed on officially stamped paper. If there was uncertainty about whether Parliament was taxing the colonies under the American Duties Act or merely regulating trade, the Stamp Act was an indisputable act of taxation and ignited a firestorm of opposition.

This resistance cannot be explained in terms of its total expense. Overall, taxes in British North America were only a fifth of those paid in England, and the stamp rates proposed for the colonies were only two-thirds of the equivalent English tax.[19] There is little evidence that the cost of the Stamp Act was a major source of colonial frustration; in fact, several colonies asked that, in place of a parliamentary stamp tax, Parliament inform the colonial legislatures what revenue was needed so that the legislatures could apply their own taxes and remit the money to Britain.[20]

The Stamp Act did, however, have a particularly maladroit design. As Virginia's petition to the House of Lords politely put it, Parliament was not "best acquainted" with the "least burthensome Mode of taxing" the colonies.[21] Parliament's stamp taxes would raise the cost of land purchases in a country of small farmers, would increase court costs that already fell heavily on poor debtors, and would cripple the newspaper industry.[22] Parliament did not seem to understand this local context; indeed, Grenville's administration had been obliged to write to the colonies to inquire what legal documents they used, so that the documents could be included in his stamp tax.[23]

Even more vexing than the target of the tax was how Parliament imagined it would be paid. Stamped paper was to be bought with silver coin, but the colonists hardly had any. British North America was suffering a serious economic slump and hard currency shortage. Silver coins were so rare as to be almost unheard of outside the major American ports, and many observers doubted whether there was enough silver coin in the colonies to cover even one year of taxation. In demanding payment in silver, an agent for the Massachusetts Bay Colony observed, the Stamp Act might as well have "ordained, that every man in the colonies should be seven foot high."[24] (As we will see, the lack of money would cause persistent problems with tax collection both before and after independence.)

For many colonists, the Stamp Act also had troubling political implications. The taxes would pay for a standing army of ten thousand redcoats on American soil. If a large force were stationed in town, soldiers might feel themselves above the local civilian law. On the frontier, the army might restrain white settlers from squatting on valuable Indian lands. Neither of these possibilities was acceptable to the average American colonist. In addition, violations of the Stamp Act were to be tried in admiralty courts, abridging colonists' rights to trial by a jury of their peers (who were notably less likely to convict their neighbors of smuggling).

Saddled with a tax they could not pay to fund an army they did not want, colonists had little official recourse. Instead, the colonies engaged in widespread resistance. Colonial assemblies sent a flurry of petitions. Delegates from nine colonies met to coordinate a response, and this Stamp Act Congress issued a declaration of rights and directed petitions to the king, the House of Lords, and the House of Commons. Courts closed rather than use stamped paper, while ports operated in flagrant violation of the new law.

In Boston, mobs rioted, burning effigies and occasionally the homes of those seen as supporters of the British taxes. Royal tax collectors were forced to renounce their positions. Merchants were pressured to cease importation of British goods.

Facing formidable opposition in the colonies and among the British merchant class, Parliament repealed the Stamp Act after only a few months. But the rapid reversal could not undo the erosion of colonial trust in Parliament or the new networks of coordination between political radicals from Massachusetts to South Carolina. The colonies' ties to the empire frayed still further in 1767, when Parliament, wrongly believing that the colonists objected only to direct internal taxation and not to tariffs, applied new duties on the importation of glass, lead, paints, paper, and tea as part of the Townshend Acts.[25]

The opposition to parliamentary taxation did not just spark intercolonial unity or anti-Parliament sentiment, however. The tax fights of the 1760s helped to define how the coming war for independence would be understood by the American people. First, Americans consistently framed their opposition to British taxes as resistance to *slavery*. Second, the opposition to the Stamp Act crystalized for the first time the difference between the British and the American conception of *representation*.

"TAXATION WITHOUT REPRESENTATION" AS SLAVERY

In July 1768, Pennsylvania lawyer John Dickinson wrote what he described as "a song for American freedom." Intended to be sung to the tune of the Royal Navy anthem, "Heart of Oak," the chorus to Dickinson's poem demands taxation with representation:

> *In FREEDOM we're BORN, and in FREEDOM we'll LIVE,*
> *Our Purses are ready,*
> *Steady, Friends, Steady,*
> *Not as SLAVES, but as FREEMEN our Money we'll give.*

A martial paean to taxpaying might challenge the most gifted of poets, and as Dickinson himself admitted in a shy letter sharing the poem with his friend James Otis, "I have long since renounced poetry." Whatever its artistic merits, however, Dickinson's song found popular success and was sung at patriotic gatherings throughout the colonies.[26]

The publication of Dickinson's poem followed only a few months after his famous condemnations of the Townshend Acts, *Letters of a Farmer in Pennsylvania*. These were, until Thomas Paine wrote *Common Sense* in 1776, the most widely read political documents in the thirteen colonies. Like his poem, Dickinson's letters described taxation without representation as slavery. His seventh missive concludes, "We are taxed without our own consent, expressed by ourselves or our representatives. We are therefore—SLAVES." In his ninth letter, Dickinson asked his readers if it was "possible to form an idea of a slavery more *compleat*, more *miserable*, more *disgraceful*" than taxation without representation. He should not have needed to look far for an answer; he personally enslaved dozens of people and was at one time among the largest slaveowners in the Delaware Valley.[27]

In a society where slavery was anything but metaphorical, colonial opponents of parliamentary taxation regularly insisted that that British policy was tantamount to enslavement. Three years earlier, James Otis had asserted, in his protest of the Sugar Act, that taxation without representation "makes me a slave." Maryland lawyer Daniel Dulany, in his 1765 pamphlet *Considerations on the Propriety of Imposing Taxes in the British Colonies*, argued that those stripped of the right of consent to taxation "are at the same Time deprived of every Privilege distinguishing Free-Men from Slaves." The slaveholding opponents of parliamentary taxation were apparently utterly immune to irony. A meeting of the Sons of Liberty in Norfolk, Virginia, a colony where two-fifths of the population was held in chattel slavery, resolved that they were "unwilling to rivet the shackles of slavery and oppression on ourselves, and millions yet unborn" by submitting to the Stamp Act. Virginian Richard Henry Lee organized a protest of the Stamp Act that featured George Grenville hung in effigy wearing a sign reading "the infamous projector of AMERICAN SLAVERY." Lee could be assured of a good crowd for the event because he forced the people he enslaved to participate.[28]

The colonists' persistent references to slavery were not just ill-considered hyperbole. As sociologist Orlando Patterson explains, leading American patriots "really did see their condition as one of enslavement—not merely metaphorical, but real enslavement."[29] Taxation without representation exemplified the seizure of a man's property without consent. This was not an argument against taxation in general; where taxpayers were represented, taxes were sometimes described as a "free gift" to the government.[30] But to be compelled to part with one's property via taxes to which one had not consented was the equivalent of being forced to work for another's gain, a violation of the right to the fruits of one's labor.[31]

If taxation without representation was wrong because it was a form of slavery, how did the colonists justify their society built upon the forced labor of hundreds of thousands of Black people? Or as the English essayist Samuel Johnson famously put it in *Taxation No Tyranny*, his 1775 pamphlet mocking the American rebellion, "How is it that we hear the loudest yelps for liberty among the drivers of Negroes?"

One explanation is that the colonists were not objecting to slavery as such, but were merely claiming that parliamentary taxation enslaved *the wrong people*: English people.[32] In their petition against the Stamp Act, Virginians demanded their "just and undoubted Rights as Britons," because they were "descended from Britons." Similarly, when the wealthy Boston patriot John Hancock condemned the Stamp Act, he insisted, "I will not be a Slave, I have a right to the Libertys & privileges of the English Constitution, & as an Englishman will enjoy them." If self-taxation was the "distinguishing Characteristick of British Freedom," that freedom might not apply to others.[33]

Basing one's rights upon one's Englishness, however, requires those in England to accept the premise. The experience of the Stamp Act provoked in many colonists the horrifying realization that England did not see them as English anymore. They were, instead, "Americans," a lesser sort within the British Empire. As one English critic of colonial tax resistance exclaimed, "All the Americans, all the people of the West-Indies and the East-Indies to have representatives! What sort of parliament must that be?" In his estimation, North American colonists were no more British than the people of India.[34]

The racial implication of the Americans' second-class status within the empire did not escape white colonists. Daniel Dulany, for instance, asks what "a strange Animal must a North-American appear to be" to those in England, and suggests Britons would be surprised to learn "that he may be neither black, nor tawny." John Adams, writing an anti–Stamp Act diatribe under the name Humphrey Ploughjogger, proclaimed, "We won't be their negroes." The colonists' almost obsessive references to slavery during the Stamp Act crisis could therefore be read as an effort by white North Americans to rebuild their self-regard by distinguishing themselves from their supposed inferiors. Their superficially antislavery rhetoric could reinforce an increasingly rigid racial hierarchy: White freedom could be defined by and based upon its opposite.[35]

But the colonists' claims were not exclusively couched in language about Magna Carta, the glorious English constitution, or the rights of Britons. During the 1760s, it became increasingly popular in the colonies to discuss their grievances in terms of natural and universal rights.[36] James Otis—who was extremely unusual among white American patriots in claiming that "the colonists, black and white, born here, are free born British subjects, and entitled to all the essential civil rights of such"—also encouraged his readers to look beyond Magna Carta for the source of their rights. To tax someone's hard-earned property without their consent was, for Otis, "a breach of the law of nature," and "no law of society can make it just." To expropriate a man's labor is not wrong because the man is British. It is wrong because he is a man.

Slaves and free Blacks seized upon the patriots' rhetoric and transformed the language of the revolution into a call for Black freedom. In 1777, a group of enslaved people in Massachusetts petitioned the state legislature, demanding their freedom based on their "natural and unalienable" rights and "every principle from which America has acted in the course of her unhappy difficulties with Great-Britain." Only through an act of universal emancipation would Massachusetts be "no longer chargeable with the inconsistancy of acting, themselves, the part which they condemn and oppose in others."[37] Whether white American patriots meant their antislavery eloquence as a declaration of universal rights or simply as special pleading, they were pressured to assert a *general* antipathy to slavery at a time when they desperately wanted the moral high ground.[38]

Few white people were willing to make this intellectual and moral leap, but some did.[39] In 1773, Pennsylvania patriot Benjamin Rush wrote in an antislavery tract, "If domestic Slavery is agreeable to the Will and Laws of God, political Slavery is much more so. Then it follows, that . . . the Right of the British Parliament to tax the American colonies, is unlimited and indisputable."[40] Either a man's labor was his own or it was not. There was no defense of slavery that did not undermine the patriot cause, Rush argued, and no rationale for opposition to parliamentary taxation that did not also demand emancipation.

Over the course of the revolutionary period, an increasing number joined Rush and Otis in concluding that the ideals of the revolution were incompatible with slavery. Some Northern states instituted slow processes of gradual emancipation during the revolutionary period, and some American patriots, including Benjamin Franklin and John Jay, eventually freed their slaves.[41] So did John Dickinson, the "Farmer in Pennsylvania" who so famously declared himself a slave to parliamentary taxation. But for most of the revolutionary generation, their antislavery commitments rarely went beyond words or outlasted the revolutionary moment. It is no coincidence that most Black men who fought in the Revolutionary War chose the British side.[42] The colonial debates over parliamentary taxation revealed but did not resolve the fundamental tension at the heart of American freedom.

DEFINING REPRESENTATION

Among the many responses to the colonial petitions opposing the Stamp Act, one pamphlet received outsized attention because the anonymous author was widely believed to be the British prime minister, George Grenville. After discussing at length the economic wisdom of the American Duties Act, the author (actually a top Grenville lieutenant, Thomas Whately) insisted that Americans were, in fact, represented in Parliament and therefore could fairly be taxed.

The colonists are represented just as much as their peers in the mother country, Whately insisted—or rather, just as little. No, Whately admitted, the colonists do not get to vote, but "neither are Nine Tenths of the People of *Britain* Electors."[43] There were regions, known as "rotten boroughs," that elected members of Parliament despite being nearly uninhabited, while the bustling industrial cities Leeds, Manchester, and Birmingham had no representation in Parliament at all. So, while there were no seats in the House of Commons for members from Virginia or Massachusetts, the colonists were far from the only British subjects unable to vote.

Whately's argument, one might think, proved exactly the opposite of what he intended. Rather than suppress a tax revolt in America, surely his argument would provoke a tax revolt in Britain.

But Whately saw no issue with admitting that most Britons could not vote because he was defending an entirely different idea of representation. All Britons, both those who could vote and the millions who could not, were represented "virtually." Members of Parliament were not agents of the specific people who elected them; rather, they were representatives of the commons as a whole and were expected to act independently to achieve the general good. Every member of Parliament was supposed to represent the rights and interests of all Great Britain, "however his own Borough may be affected." Voters had no special claim on the people they elected, and representatives owed their allegiance to the nation. "All British subjects" are in the same situation as the colonists, argued Whately; "none are actually, all are virtually represented."[44]

This idea of virtual representation is so distant from our contemporary perspective that it can be easy to assume that it was regarded even in its time as a flimsy justification cooked up to excuse a new tax on colonial documents. But it is an anachronism to think of virtual representation as an obviously flawed deviation from "one person, one vote." In eighteenth-century Britain, the anomalous idea was the assertion that representatives should act on behalf of their constituents. Virtual representation was the generally agreed-upon interpretation of what it meant to be represented in government in England.[45] As a member of Parliament in 1774, philosopher Edmund Burke would insist that Parliament was not and should not be "a congress of ambassadors from different and hostile interests." Instead, Parliament was "a deliberative assembly of one nation, with one interest . . . the general good." While he owed his electors in Bristol his attention, Burke believed that he was not and *should not be* their representative; he was, he said, a member of Parliament, not a "member of Bristol."[46]

The implications of virtual representation for voting rights are worth considering in detail. If one accepts the premise of virtual representation, who exactly can vote is not terribly important—or, at least, it is not important in the way that we see voting as important today. If representatives felt no compunction to defend the interests of their electors, but instead always did what was in the general interest of the country, the most important qualification of voters is that they be able to correctly identify those superior and disinterested souls capable of achieving the common good. If one could not personally vote, one would be at no disadvantage, because voters would not see specific, personal gains from their role as electors. There is little reason, under this logic, that representatives would need to be drawn from all constituencies, or that all people should be able to vote, much less that all constituencies be represented in proportion with their population.

Confronting the Stamp Act, American colonists discredited and abandoned the idea of virtual representation. Daniel Dulany wrote the definitive rebuttal in his 1765 anti–Stamp Act pamphlet. Because "not a single actual elector in England" would be affected by taxation in America, he wrote, oppressive taxes in the colonies, to the extent they reduced tax obligations at home, "might become popular in England." If the colonies and the mother country had divergent interests, what then was the common good? "Virtual representation of the colonies," Dulany concluded, "is a mere Cob-web, spread to catch the unwary, and intangle the weak."

The institutions that could legitimately apply taxes, the Stamp Act's opponents believed, were the colonial assemblies. While it is important not to overidealize these legislatures, about half of adult freemen in the American colonies owned enough property to vote for their local representative.[47] Colonial legislators were undoubtedly more attuned to local concerns than members of Parliament an ocean away, and they could, at least in principle, be held to account by the voters. What is more, colonial legislatures were also used to being told what to do. It was common for Americans to "instruct" their representatives, and those instructions were generally seen as binding.[48] Voters, therefore, had a specific power over their representatives that nonvoters lacked.

This peculiarly American articulation of what it meant to be represented "took place rapidly," according to historian Bernard Bailyn, and "for all practical purposes concluded in the two years of the Stamp Act controversy."[49] But it had ramifications far beyond the illegitimacy of the Stamp Act. Abandoning "virtual" representation drastically increases the significance of voting as a political right for free people. The opponents of parliamentary taxation insisted that the interests of those who cannot vote were, in fact, *not represented*. Unless one's interests are perfectly aligned with the interests of those who can vote, nonvoters are bound by laws and taxes to which they do not (and would not) consent. Being able to vote is therefore an essential aspect of one's political personhood and one's political freedom.

The rhetoric of "no taxation without representation" was rapidly adopted by those seeking to expand the franchise. We "apprehend ourselves to be aggrieved," wrote Paul Cuffe, a freeman of African and Wampanoag descent, in a 1780 petition to the Massachusetts legislature. Cuffe, along with six other nonwhite men, objected that "we are not allowed the privilege of freemen of the State, having no vote or influence in the election of those that tax us."[50] The patriot cause was no abstract matter for Cuffe; he had worked on a blockade runner during the war and had spent some months in a British prison. But now, he argued, the state of Massachusetts was treating him and other Black taxpayers in precisely the way Parliament had treated the colonies: They were taxed without representation. As Cuffe's petition put it, "Many of our colour (as is well known) have cheerfully entered the field of battle in the defence of the common cause," but had come home to experience "a similar exertion of power (in regard to taxation)."[51] Until his suffrage rights were respected, Cuffe insisted, he would pay no tax. For his tax strike, Cuffe was briefly imprisoned.[52]

TOWARD INDEPENDENCE

In the 1770s, questions about the legitimacy of parliamentary taxation rapidly gave way to far broader doubts about what role Parliament should have in legislating for the colonies, and eventually what right Britain had to meddle in American affairs. Rounds of colonial defiance and punitive parliamentary reaction eventually gave rise to a war for independence.

But if most of the war had little to do with taxes, the conflicts over parliamentary taxation nonetheless mattered a great deal—not only because it was a hot spark at the start of the great conflagration, but because it embedded in the independence of America the question of representation and the question of slavery. In abandoning the principle of virtual representation, the opponents of parliamentary taxation ensured that voting would become the standard of political representation. To this day, it is universally agreed among those who seek to expand the franchise and those who seek to shrink it that who should vote is the measure of who should matter. And by insisting that taxation without representation amounted to slavery—not just oppression, or vassalage, or injustice, but *slavery*—the rebellious American colonists opened themselves to charges of the basest hypocrisy at precisely the moment they sought a principled stand. It would be left to future generations to determine whether freedom in America meant freedom for some or freedom for all.

From the earliest confrontations with Britain, "radical possibilities, glimpsed but not wholly grasped," lay like seeds in the American foundation.[53] It is a soil that has only occasionally been conducive to growth.

SHAYS'S REBELLION AND THE ORIGINS OF THE CONSTITUTION

The Depredations which the Democratic
Spirit is Apt to Make on Property
—Alexander Hamilton

"Ignorant, wrestless desperadoes, without conscience or principals, have led a deluded multitude to follow their standard," wrote Abigail Adams in January 1787 to her friend Thomas Jefferson, who was then in Paris.[1] At great cost in blood and treasure, the United States had won its independence, but now the young nation was deeply indebted. Jefferson had written to inquire about the rural uprising in western Massachusetts, where, as John Adams described it, the "Assembly had, in its Zeal to get the better of their Debt, laid on a Tax, rather heavier than the People could bear."[2] Massachusetts farmers had responded to the heavy taxes intended to pay down the war debt by forming militias and forcing the closure of courthouses. Just a few days before Abigail penned her letter, the federal armory at Springfield had been attacked by several thousand men—including one regiment led by Daniel Shays, a struggling farmer and decorated war veteran who would later be misrepresented as the driving force of the rebellion.

Jefferson was inclined to see the tumult as a freedom-loving people's defense of its liberties: "I like a little rebellion now and then," he would reply.[3] But Abigail saw it differently. The farmers' grievances had no "existance but in their immaginations," she wrote tartly. She was sure she knew why, when the "lower order of the community were prest for taxes," they were "unable to answer the Demand." The problem was a spirit of licentiousness, a desire for "luxery and extravagance both in furniture and dress" that had pervaded the country. During the revolution, the people had been stalwart citizens, but in the years since, Abigail lamented, "vanity was becoming a more power-full principal than Patriotism." Abigail closed her letter with a request that Jefferson procure for her some expensive French lace.[4]

Adams had personal as well as patriotic interest in the nation's fiscal system. She was herself a canny trader in government debt. By law, all the family property belonged to her husband, but politics often took John away from home. As Abigail managed the household finances, she recognized the immense profits available from government bonds. Three years earlier, she had explained to her husband that "monied Men" were buying Massachusetts debt at one-third its face value, so the 6 percent interest on the notes yielded them an 18 percent rate of return. And the proceeds were, Abigail noted, "subject to no taxes."[5]

Abigail Adams apparently saw no problem with these enormous tax-free windfalls available to those with cash to spare, paid for with taxes that fell heavily on the state's poorest residents. But for others, the policies of the Massachusetts Assembly looked like a reprise of the oppressive taxation of the British. Yeoman farmers had not fought a revolution to have a new aristocracy built on their tax dollars. Instead, they wanted taxation for a republic: fiscal and monetary policies that would preserve the rough parity of wealth that ensured the political equality of citizens, and impositions that would fall equally on the rich and the poor. Most of all, they wanted paper money, so that taxes could be paid even when gold and silver coins were impossible to find.

The farmers' tax rebellions—known to participants as "Regulations"—led many among America's political elite, like Abigail Adams, to abandon their faith in the virtue and good sense of the American people, and to conclude that democracy in America had gone too far. In the wake of Shays's Rebellion, as the Massachusetts uprising became known, the nation's political leadership was moved to replace the weak and unwieldy Articles of Confederation and to ensure that the new Constitution was far less democratic than the state constitutions enacted during the revolution.

A strong government must be sheltered from public preferences, the framers believed, because they did not trust the people with the capacity to tax. And so they designed an intentionally unresponsive government with long terms in office, large districts, and ample opportunities to slow or prevent the people from enacting their will. The Constitution we live under today reflects the founders' disbelief in the fiscal probity of the public.

WAR'S DEBTS, WAR'S PROFITS

The road to the Constitution began with debt. The colonists went to war— war against a global superpower—with almost no central government to speak of, and no national taxing capacity at all. Under the Articles of Confederation, Congress did not have the power to tax. Instead, Congress had to go hat in hand to the states, making "requisitions" with which the states only partially complied. Inefficient tax collection was the norm across the colonies, and by the end of 1777, only half the states had passed any tax legislation. Almost all wars are fought on credit, but America's revolutionaries really racked up the IOUs.[6]

Tax revenues were low in part because many states were only capable of applying simple, regressive taxes. Taxes proportionate to wealth would have been both less burdensome and more productive, and many poorer Americans demanded such a system. When wealthy Pennsylvanians opted out of the militia by paying a fine, militiamen petitioned for each draft dodger's payment to be calculated "in proportion to his Estate."[7] But wealth-proportionate taxation was beyond early America's capacities— both because the wealthy did not want to pay and, relatedly, because many state governments, especially in the South, were simply not up to the job of assessing property.[8] Congress had originally intended to allocate its requisitions based on the states' land values but was obliged to fall back on a population-based system.[9]

Popular demands for more egalitarian taxation would come to define not only the politics of the postwar period but the framework of American government for the centuries to come. In the meantime, however, taxes could not even begin to meet the needs of the war. "The laying of Imposts unless from the last Necessity," said Robert Morris, the crafty Pennsylvania merchant who served as the war's superintendent of finance, "would have been Madness." So the Revolutionary War was paid for by issuing currency and taking on debt.[10]

About two-thirds of the cost of the war was funded through federal and state-issued "fiat money." This paper currency, not backed by gold or silver, had been used successfully in the colonies before, including to finance the American engagement in the Seven Years' War. The risk of this approach was inflation. Some amount of currency depreciation was not necessarily a problem; it could even work as a progressive, real-time "tax on money," as Benjamin Franklin argued. But the American governments usually printed far too much and taxed far too little. With such a glut on the market, the value of money plummeted. The value of the Continental dollar dropped by two-thirds in 1777 and then to nearly nothing. A barber in Philadelphia reputedly used the dollars as wallpaper.[11]

The rest of the cost of the war was financed by public debt. Millions were owed to foreign creditors, and tens of millions were owed domestically. This debt was held in numerous forms: government bonds and certificates, each with its own intricate repayment schemes; securities given to soldiers in lieu of pay; and IOUs to farmers, artisans, and merchants who had seen their goods requisitioned. Poorer people could rarely afford to hold on to their debt papers. Some soldiers sold their securities as soon as they were issued, just so they could afford to get home from the war.[12] But speculators were willing to invest, for pennies on the dollar, with the hope of spectacular gains should the government eventually honor the debts at face value.

And that was the key question: Could the postwar government impose enough taxes to pay off its debts? The market in government debt spiked and crashed with investors' confidence in the tax system. But if you had the capital to invest, the risks of buying were not as high as they might seem. Elites sometimes had inside information about which forms of debt were likely to get their interest paid. Even if a government scaled down its repayment, as sometimes occurred, there were profits to be made if the government paid more than the buyer had staked.[13]

As domestic debt consolidated in the hands of those with the money to speculate, the very richest people in America became the primary beneficiaries of debt repayment. Less than a decade after the Revolutionary War, nine in ten government securities were no longer in the hands of their original owners, and just 2 percent of Americans owned bonds. In Pennsylvania, 96 percent of all state war debt belonged to 434 people, with more than 40 percent held by just 28 men. In Rhode Island, more than a third of the $800,000-plus in federal bonds was owned by 9 people.[14]

Paying down this debt required taxation. The easiest source of revenue would have been tariffs, and Congress twice sought to enact a national 5 percent impost on foreign goods. But the Articles of Confederation required unanimous consent of the states for such a policy, and at least one state was always in opposition to each variation of the plan. So state governments had to "open the Purses of the People," as war financier Robert Morris was blunt enough to say.[15] And the people's purses were very near empty.

TAXATION FOR AN ARISTOCRACY, TAXATION FOR A REPUBLIC

At the time of the revolution, nine in ten white Americans were farmers, and two-thirds lived on land their household owned. There were relatively few paupers in colonial America, and the largest American fortunes were a small fraction of the grandest estates in Britain. But this "happy mediocrity," as Benjamin Franklin famously described it, was destabilized by the deep economic depression that followed independence. America's GDP is estimated to have dropped by as much as 30 percent. Economic stagnation hit rural and frontier areas especially hard and lingered there the longest. At the same time, property ownership became much more concentrated. From the 1780s to the 1790s, the percentage of Philadelphia's wealth owned by the bottom 90 percent of residents fell from 56 percent to only 18 percent. The countryside saw similar wealth consolidation. In some counties, over 60 percent of farmers faced foreclosure in the decade after the war.[16]

These were not simply economic losses; they threatened Americans' freedom. Falling into debt could put a person in prison. And even if a debtor retained his physical liberty, he often forfeited his civic rights with the foreclosure of his land. Almost all states had property standards for voting and officeholding. More broadly, poverty put men in a position of dependence, a violation of the ideals of republican citizenship. Becoming a tenant meant having a landlord. Becoming a wage earner meant having a boss. In these subordinated positions, Americans of this era believed, those who controlled your economic fate could also dominate your political will.[17]

For the revolutionary generation, therefore, equality and liberty were not in opposition; they required one another. Or in the words of patriot and lexicographer Noah Webster, a "general and tolerably equal distribution" of property was "the whole basis of national freedom" and "the very soul of a republic." For many among the country's farmers and artisans, the promise of the revolution had been that ordinary people—or rather, ordinary white men—could hold the reins of government. But to have fought a war against the British monarchy only to face losing your farm and with it your rights: What kind of republic was this?[18]

It was with this question in mind that rural Americans viewed the states' new tax policies. American taxes, still profoundly regressive, were three times higher than they had been under British rule. As much as 90 percent of that money was devoted to debt repayment. The tax system was therefore pushing regular citizens into dependency while also making the rich richer. To the early American yeomanry, a small class of well-connected elites that lived in comfort on the public dime sounded very much like an aristocracy.[19]

Rural Americans proposed a different system of taxation, one that conformed to their vision of republican government. They wanted to reduce the upward redistribution of public debt repayment, force wealthy people to pay a larger share of the tax burden, reduce taxes on those who had fallen on hard times, and make all taxes easier to pay.

To shrink the windfall going to war debt speculators, farmers proposed that the states buy back debt on the open market at reduced rates, pay interest based on the market rate rather than on the face value of debt certificates, or even require bondholders to exchange their bonds for paper money.

Many proposals called for treating original debt holders differently from those who had bought debt on the market.[20] "Our people," a York County, Pennsylvania, farmer asserted, "will never consent to pay such an enormous perpetual tax, purely to enrich a few men who have bought up the certificates for a mere song."[21]

Farmers also wanted taxes to be proportionate to wealth. In some states, land speculators had negotiated special tax breaks for their holdings and special protections against foreclosure for nonpayment.[22] Government securities, like those held by Abigail Adams, were commonly tax-free investments. Petitioners in North Carolina decried tax breaks that accrued to the "Wealthy part of the Community" and demanded that "the Citizen is assessed in exact proportion to His property."[23] To ensure that land speculators paid their share—and to encourage them to sell homesteads to those who would farm the land—rural petitioners demanded new taxes on undeveloped land held as an investment. To reach the largely untaxed riches of the merchant class, farmers called for new taxes on wealth held on paper, including debt paper. They also sought to lower court fees, which made it hard for those in debt to get back on their feet again. In one county in Pennsylvania, a quarter of all foreclosures were *exclusively* the result of unpaid court costs.[24]

Finally, farmers proposed making taxes and debts easier to pay through the emission of paper money. This was the most consistent demand of rural America in the postrevolutionary period. Money shortages had already spurred tax opposition during the Stamp Act crisis, and now there was perhaps a fifth as much *specie* (money in gold and silver coin) in America as there had been before the war. As usual, almost none of that money was in the countryside.[25] In daily life on the frontier, the lack of money was less troublesome than a modern person might expect. Much of what a farm family needed they produced themselves. Rural people sometimes had to settle a private debt with hard money, but they often had long-running account books with neighbors that did not require exchange of currency. They did, however, always need money come tax time—precisely the moment when everyone else in the neighborhood needed money too. In desperate moments, farmers petitioned tax collectors to delay the taxes due so they would have more time to find currency, or to accept farm produce as payment. But the far more common demand was for the state to print paper money, not limited by the supply of gold or silver, and for that money to be accepted for tax payments.

The farmers' proposals were intended to preserve the nation's rough economic equality. But while yeoman farmers saw their tax demands as essential to preserving their independence and therefore their liberty as citizens, others saw in their agenda a mortal threat to the new republic.

OPPOSITION TO THE FARMERS' AGENDA

Writing in 1777, British loyalist William Smith Jr. predicted with horror that the revolution would result in "Land Tax and no Room for an Aristocracy."[26] He would sail from New York with the British evacuation in 1783. During the war, Smith's republican friends had mocked his fears. But after independence, rural Americans demanded precisely what Smith had predicted—and many of the nation's leaders began to think that their faith in the people had been misplaced.

To be fair, there were good reasons to be nervous about the farmers' demands. As the experience of the Continental dollar demonstrated, paper money emissions sometimes lost value precipitously. The radically egalitarian pamphleteer Thomas Paine opposed paper money because inflation ate into the earnings of artisans.[27] There were also good reasons to want to protect the country's credit. Defaulting on debt would demonstrate a destabilizing weakness in America's experiment in self-governance. It would be hard to raise funds in emergencies—for example, if facing an invasion. Moreover, government debt could function as money, if its payouts were predictable; the debt would hold its value, lose its appeal to speculators, and serve as stable currency.

But a certain amount of elite resistance can be ascribed to self-interest, or at least to class interest. Legislators were generally wealthy people, and many were creditors and bondholders who wanted the debt they held paid with interest, or landlords who feared inflation eating into their incomes.[28] Even among the indebted elite, including James Madison and Robert Morris, some believed additional foreign investment would straighten out their affairs—but foreign investment would only be forthcoming if the government seemed adequately committed to enforcing debt repayment.[29] Thus, some of the opposition to the farmers' tax and monetary proposals came from those literally invested in the prompt and complete repayment of war debt.

Of course, people think about their economic self-interest within a larger mental edifice of social values and political commitments. Debt was seen as a moral failing and paying one's bills as a matter of honor. Abigail Adams was far from alone in imagining that the lower orders had become enamored of luxury. "Say not a word about taxes, judges, lawyers, [or] courts," one observer wrote to the farmers of Connecticut, "the fault is all your own."[30] William Livingston, the governor of New Jersey, imagined a "lazy, lounging, lubberly fellow sitting nights and days in a tippling house," squandering his earnings "in riot and debauch, and then complaining, when the collector calls for his tax, of the hardness of the times and the want of circulating medium." As for the farmer who "shakes his head at the name of taxes" and says he cannot pay, "Why, he is a man whose three daughters are under the discipline of a French dancing-master when they ought every one of them to be at the spinning wheel."[31]

Skepticism of the poor was accompanied by explicit arguments in favor of upward redistribution. The superintendent of finance, Robert Morris, was what you might call an extremely early convert to trickle-down economics.[32] As he saw things, society ought to distribute "property into those hands which could render it most productive"—that is, "the monied men" of "the mercantile Part of Society."[33] And many early American statesmen, including Morris and Alexander Hamilton, were influenced by the ideas of the Scottish philosopher David Hume, who saw poverty as the only thing that kept the naturally indolent lower orders working. Regressive taxation, therefore, was understood to stimulate the economy by forcing the poor to "encrease their industry" and "perform more work."[34] New taxes on paper wealth, according to this view, were precisely the opposite of what would bring prosperity to the country.

Unlike the late twentieth-century supply-siders, however, Morris and Hamilton were not seeking to shrink the state. On the contrary, they believed the fledgling government needed to be far stronger and more centralized. Great Britain's power rested on her commercial empire, her burgeoning industrialism, and above all her unparalleled ability to borrow for war-making. For America to follow the British model, the government must pay public debts reliably and concentrate wealth at the top. If the new government demonstrated itself a trustworthy friend of the monied elite, the nation's economic and political power would be bound together. For Hamilton, an ardent nationalist who had served as Washington's aide-de-camp during the war, the farmers' demands endangered the whole endeavor for which he had fought: to free America to become a great power.

THE REGULATORS' TAX RESISTANCE

Yeoman farmers, despite their numbers, did not have an easy time achieving their preferred tax and monetary policies in the states.[35] For one, all policy-making was impeded by the terrible economic circumstances of the postwar period and the utterly dysfunctional structure of the Articles of Confederation. In addition, the state legislatures tended to heavily overrepresent long-settled regions. Even in Pennsylvania, where an exceptionally democratic state constitution imposed no property requirement for male suffrage, it was enormously challenging to organize widely dispersed frontier people. Just getting to a polling place could take days in a large rural county, and holding legislators accountable once they went to the distant state capital was nearly impossible.

Where the legislative road proved impassable, there was a second route to political power in America's backcountry: the repertoire of protest tactics developed under British rule. The yeomen called this form of protest "regulation," the act of setting things right. The first prominent regulation in the American colonies occurred in North Carolina in 1768. Farmers were angry that colonial officials gave special tax exemptions to the rich and personally profited from tax collection. They responded by occupying the courthouse, destroying property, and abusing local officials. Their demands included paper currency to pay taxes, public oversight of tax lists and collections, limits on speculation, lower court fees, and taxes proportional to wealth.

After independence, regulations recurred whenever farmers came to believe that the actions of the new governments constituted, in the words of historian Terry Bouton, "a betrayal of the American Revolution."[36] Farmers refused en masse to pay taxes, closed courthouses, and blocked roads. They also threatened, abused, and sometimes killed tax collectors. Where resistance was most organized, farmers seized control of local tax institutions. Communities organized boycotts of the property auctions intended to sell off debtors' belongings, replaced the closed courts with arbitration systems of their own devising, and in at least one case, pooled their money and purchased the position of tax collector so that no one would have to pay.[37]

Regulations often extracted concessions from legislatures that had previously ignored the farmers' demands. These were usually haphazard measures of tax and debt relief, and occasionally measures that reduced public debt repayment, but not measures that raised taxes on the rich. The most famous of the 1780s regulations, Shays's Rebellion, in Massachusetts, would follow this pattern. But the ramifications of Shays's Rebellion went much further than a few tax breaks. It was with Shays's Rebellion in mind that the framers wrote the Constitution.

TURMOIL IN MASSACHUSETTS

In 1785, Congress attempted to requisition $3 million from the states. The majority of the requisition needed to be paid in hard currency, gold or silver specie, and the plurality of the revenue was earmarked for domestic bondholders—America's wealthiest people. Knowing that their constituents simply did not have the gold and silver to pay, some states said outright that they would not even try to collect the money.

But not Massachusetts. If the other states were willing to abandon their commitments for political expediency, Massachusetts would have to lead the way to sound finance—or so many state legislators believed. Massachusetts decided not only to pay their part of the federal bill but also to pay state debts with new direct taxes. Massachusetts had already committed to pay back its heavily depreciated debts at face value, and to start paying back the state debt three years early. The result was the heaviest direct specie tax that had ever been imposed in the state.[38] Though a great effort had been made to develop a new system of assessment of property, about a third of the revenue was still slated to come from highly regressive poll taxes.* And while the previous governor, John Hancock, had been content to let taxes fall into arrears and thereby give taxpayers more time to find currency, his replacement, James Bowdoin, was committed to full and immediate tax collection.[39]

The Massachusetts tax plan was not just a political miscalculation; it was economic malpractice. If the state legislature had succeeded in extracting that much money from the middle and poorer classes to line the pockets of the very rich, it would have induced a recession (even if the state's economy were not already stalled). But the state government had an exceptionally strong bias in favor of the wealthy East. The state constitutional convention had been held during the harsh winter of 1779–1780, when bad weather had closed the western roads and stranded western delegates at home. Some towns in rural Massachusetts had grown so disenchanted with the East's disproportionate power that they stopped even bothering to send representatives to the legislature.[40] So it was easy for the elite-dominated legislature to totally misread both the economic situation and the political mood of the western part of the state.

Confronted with the legislature's new tax plan, rural communities sent increasingly desperate and angry petitions. "Many of our good inhabitants are now confined in jail for debt and taxes," wrote citizens of Greenwich. The citizens of Dracut had previously answered the "repeted calls of Government for Men & Money," but no longer possessed any hard currency with which to pay, they explained. Perhaps, Dracut's petitioners suggested, the money might be found in the wealthier regions of the state, "in the

---

* Poll taxes are commonly remembered in the United States today for their role in disenfranchising Black voters in the Jim Crow South (as will be described in detail in Part Two of this book). However, poll taxes are not intrinsically linked to suffrage rights. "Poll" was once a common synonym for "head," and a "poll tax" was a tax that applied per head. One of the simplest forms of taxation, poll taxes have been used since antiquity and were common in early America. Poll taxes were often graded by age and gender to focus on those presumed able to earn money—for example, a fifty-cent tax applied to every man from eighteen to forty. Because a rich and a poor man would owe the same amount of tax, poll taxes are highly regressive.

secret Confines of those who have a greater love of their own Interest, then they have to that of their Neighbours." It was a transparent reference to the undertaxed mercantile elite of Boston, where thirty-five men held 40 percent of the state debt.[41]

When the legislature refused to back down, western towns set up committees of correspondence, organized meetings, and made proclamations. A December address by Daniel Gray, a farmer in the town of Pelham, lists among the local grievances that the "monies raised by impost and excise" were "being appropriated to discharge the interest of governmental securities" that were themselves "not subject to taxation." Rural militias surrounded and closed courthouses across the state. In the town of Great Barrington, a militia of a thousand men was raised to reopen the local courthouse; eight hundred of them voted to join the regulation instead. The governor was obliged to fundraise among the merchants of Boston to pay an army to march westward and put down the insurrection.[42]

As with previous farmers' revolts, the military aspects of Shays's Rebellion were anticlimactic. The rebels failed in their effort to seize the federal armory at Springfield. A few skirmishes occurred over the following weeks, and the rebellion soon petered out.

The real success of Shays's Rebellion was in shifting the political winds. Though the legislature finally agreed to postpone tax collections and property seizures, nearly three-quarters of the representatives lost their seats in the April elections, and Governor Bowdoin was defeated by a three-to-one margin. The new legislature instituted even more tax relief, and in fact levied no state taxes whatsoever in 1787. Speculators in paper debt panicked, and the price of state bonds collapsed as the hoped-for windfalls evaporated.[43]

Henry Knox, a Boston bookseller turned general in the Continental Army, wrote urgently to George Washington. While high taxes were the "ostensible cause" of the insurrection, Knox said, the reality was that "the insurgents have never paid any, or but very little taxes." What the regulators really wanted, Knox was sure, was for wealth to be "the common property of all." It was time for "every tried friend to the liberties of his country," Knox importuned his former commander, to "step forward."[44]

Washington concluded that he must attend the upcoming federal convention in Philadelphia that had been called to try to revise the Articles of Confederation. He had not wanted to go; he was busy on his plantation and, given the track record of previous conventions, the meeting was far from guaranteed to result in anything productive.

But Shays created a new urgency among the nation's elite for a fundamental reconsideration of the framework of the government. Massachusetts was not only unable to impose taxes effectively; it could barely manage to raise an army to put down an internal rebellion. In the wake of this lawlessness, the legislature had given in to the protestors' demands. And then the voters ousted them anyway! Many elites concluded that the governments put in place during the revolution were far too responsive to the recalcitrant and spoiled masses—that is, the state legislatures were far too democratic. Clearly, the nation needed a strong central government insulated from popular control.

It is ironic, of course, that while elites took rural unrest as evidence the states were too beholden to the multitude, small farmers engaged in uprisings because they felt their legislatures were unresponsive to their needs. At base, the Articles of Confederation were simply not working very well for anybody. A central government with the power to tax was clearly necessary. But it was with an antidemocratic diagnosis in mind that the framers gathered at Philadelphia. In mobilizing the country's leaders to finally address the inadequacies of the Articles of Confederation, the farmers of western Massachusetts played a critical role in the formation of a new government explicitly designed to resist their influence.

CHECKS AGAINST THE DEMOCRACY

"Our chief danger arises from the democratic parts of our constitutions," said Edmund Randolph of Virginia.[45] It was the third day of what would become known as the Constitutional Convention. In the same room where a decade earlier the Declaration of Independence had been signed, fifty-five delegates from twelve states were meeting, nominally to propose revisions to the Articles of Confederation. Instead, they would design an entirely new governing structure. The presence of George Washington, the beloved hero of the revolution, was of inestimable importance in legitimating this bold step. To allow for frank discussion, the convention was sworn to secrecy, took no official record of the proceedings, and even kept the windows shut.[46]

Randolph was introducing a set of fifteen propositions drafted by his fellow Virginian, James Madison, that would form the basis for a new government framework. Randolph began by summarizing the limitations of the Articles of Confederation. There was no shortage of defects. Most obviously, Congress lacked the power to tax, and so the central government relied on state requisitions that simply did not come. The US Board of Treasury, which needed millions to meet its obligations, had in five months received . . . $663 in specie. The requisition system was, in the words of George Washington, "a perfect nullity," "little better than a jest." And that was not all. Under the Articles' unwieldy structure, the government could not effectively negotiate treaties with other nations or even resolve the occasionally violent border disputes between the states.[47]

But for Randolph and many other critics of the Articles of Confederation, the most fundamental problem was not Vermont guerillas raiding across the New York border; it was the leveling instincts of the state legislatures. Though this would change in only a few years, the term "democracy" was in the 1780s an insult, implying something akin to "mob rule." To Randolph's mind, not even the most elite-dominated state legislatures provided "sufficient checks against the democracy." Maryland, for example, had a powerful senate, with strong property requirements, indirectly elected members, and five-year terms. But even this, Randolph complained, was not enough to prevent the "late distractions" in the state. The previous June, Maryland's Charles County courthouse had been forced to close by an angry mob. Of course, one could have taken this upheaval as evidence that Maryland had too *little* democracy. Maryland's Senate had consistently rejected efforts by the lower house to institute paper money, provoking outrage among the state's farmers.[48] But for Randolph, the solution to popular unrest was a government even less beholden to the people.

Others at the convention shared Randolph's diagnosis. When James Madison rose to speak, he expressed his belief that the "enlightened & respectable citizens" were too easily overwhelmed by the "unreflecting multitude."

Elbridge Gerry of Massachusetts admitted that he had "been too republican heretofore." Though still republican, he had "been taught by experience the danger of the levelling spirit." Gerry now agreed that "the evils we experience flow from the excess of democracy." In Massachusetts, he continued, "it has been fully confirmed by experience" that the people "are daily misled into the most baneful measures and opinions by the false reports circulated by designing men."

Unsurprisingly, the strictest limits on popular participation were put forward by those most committed to upward redistribution. Alexander Hamilton wanted senators and the president to serve for a lifetime. The seven-year appointments for senators then under consideration would not be nearly enough, considering the "amazing violence & turbulence of the democratic spirit," Hamilton insisted. That ordinary people could govern themselves was, in Hamilton's view, a myth: "All communities divide themselves into the few and the many. The first are the rich and well born, the other the mass of the people. The voice of the people has been said to be the voice of God; and however generally this maxim has been quoted and believed, it is not true in fact. The people are turbulent and changing; they seldom judge or determine right."

Hamilton would go on to praise the British government as "the best in the world"—a bit of a faux pas, even to the conservatives in the room.

Hamilton's elitism was extreme, but his critique of popular government was merely an amplification of the views of Randolph, Gerry, Madison, and others. The framers agreed that the wealthy few were a minority in need of greater protection from the people.[49] So they divested the states of their power to print money and to engage certain forms of debt relief, and devised a central government insulated by bicameralism, long terms in office, indirect election of the president and senate, and large districts. With these protections in place, the federal government could be assigned the power to tax. As Alexander Hamilton wrote pithily in his notes, the "impost begat convention": it was taxation that drove the Constitution's framers to design a new form of government.[50] The federal government's fiscal and monetary powers are enumerated before even its military authority and are described in greater detail. Article I, Section 8 gives Congress the power to impose taxes and pay debts, to borrow money, to coin money, to set bankruptcy laws, and to punish counterfeiting.[51] The point was to ensure that the nation's fiscal and monetary powers were held by a government sheltered from the demands of the masses.

On September 17, 1787, after months of deliberation, debate, and compromise, the Constitution was finally submitted to the delegates for signing.[52] Over the following year and a half, as Americans debated this government framework, Madison and Hamilton would become its greatest proponents. In *Federalist 10*, Madison's first contribution to the famous series of papers arguing for ratification, he singled out the "apportionment of taxes" as a primary danger of majority rule: There was "no legislative act in which greater opportunity and temptation are given to a predominant party to trample on the rules of justice." The new Constitution, Madison declared, had adequate checks on the fiscal instincts of the masses.

Hamilton was similarly sure that the Constitution was a solid protection for wealth. In his private notes labelled "Conjectures About the New Constitution," he listed the circumstances in favor of its ratification, including "the good will of the commercial interest," "the hopes of Creditors," and "the good will of most men of property" who seek protection from "the depredations which the democratic spirit is apt to make on property."[53]

Hamilton was largely right in his prediction that the wealthy would be more supportive of the Constitution than the poor. But the close-fought ratification battle did not break down exclusively along economic lines. Many elite anti-Federalists were nonetheless against paper money and against tax and debt-relief policies. They opposed the Constitution because they wanted to maintain state power—a view that, in the South, coincided with a fear that a powerful central government was a threat to slavery. Other opponents were primarily concerned about the lack of a Bill of Rights. The convention in Philadelphia had not written one; these protections for civil liberties were promised to win popular support for ratification. Some backcountry farmers worried that the Constitution would further empower the aristocracy of wealth, while others thought that a stronger national government would stabilize the economy and that national tariffs could replace the painful direct specie taxes.[54]

Nonetheless, the ratification of the Constitution represented a fundamental shift in the locus of fiscal and monetary power—not just to a central government but to one intended to resist the economic policy preferences of the majority. At the heart of America's constitutional framework is an emphatic denial that average Americans should determine how to tax themselves.

3

THE WHISKEY REBELLION

The Fight for Equal Taxation

Equal Taxation and No Excise

—Sign carried by the Whiskey Rebels

In rural western Pennsylvania in July 1794, an armed militia of more than five hundred men was headed to the luxurious plantation home of the local tax collector, John Neville, to force him to resign. Neville, a wealthy speculator in both land and government bonds, was responsible for enforcing the widely despised federal tax on whiskey and had, just two days earlier, accompanied a federal marshal serving writs on distillers delinquent on their taxes. Panicked farmers raced through the countryside to inform the local militia, recently called up to fight Native Americans in the Ohio Territory. On hearing the news, the militiamen held an emergency meeting and voted to fight a different battle.[1]

Now, marching in formation to the cadence of fife and drum, the militiamen carried a message insisting that Neville give up his commission. If he did, the militiamen promised, Neville "would be received as a good citizen, and restored to the confidence of the people" and, more ominously, "no harm should be done to his person or property." The threat was a serious one; some individuals associated with the whiskey tax had been assaulted, or worse. Only a few weeks earlier, a man was attacked by an armed mob, threatened with hanging, tarred and feathered, and left tied to a tree in the forest overnight, just because he had rented space to Neville for use as an excise office.[2]

During the four-mile march to Neville's plantation, a man named John Baldwin began having second thoughts. His problem was not the plan to threaten a government official. Instead, Baldwin worried that the group's written message might wrongly give the impression that the farmers were opposed to all forms of taxation. If so, the document should be revised.

Baldwin raised his concern with the elected leadership of the Mingo Creek Association, an umbrella group for the local militias that organized excise resistance. One might expect that an army on the march would afford little time to semantic quibbles. But for the revolutionary generation, militia service was part of republican citizenship, of a piece with voting and petitioning. The hundreds-strong armed militia stopped to deliberate on Baldwin's question, right there on the dusty road. Ultimately, the group accepted Baldwin's point and amended the paper they were to present to Neville, making explicit that "the people did not refuse to pay a proportional part of the revenue."[3] Frontier farmers believed in taxation, so long as it was based on a taxpayer's wealth.

There is a stereotype that the early American frontier was full of hard-drinking, violent people unwilling to pay taxes. On the contrary, frontiersmen were hard-drinking, violent advocates of more progressive taxation.

And they hated the whiskey excise. Under the guidance of Treasury Secretary Alexander Hamilton, Congress had passed a tax on spirits in 1791. The tax fell on the primary source of profit for Western farmers, and its revenue would pay interest to America's wealthy bondholders. Farmers had been resisting this kind of regressive scheme for a decade, with some success. But the new Constitution was designed to empower the federal government and shelter it from the economic demands of the masses. Western Pennsylvania was to be the proving ground, where the federal government would demonstrate it was finally strong enough to impose upward redistribution by force.

In the plans developed by Hamilton's opponents appear the outlines of a different political economy: still a strong government, but one in which the fiscal system was intended to preserve equality among the citizenry. Inspired by the French Revolution and the works of Thomas Paine, "democratic-republican" societies and newspapers proposed more progressive systems of taxation and even the beginnings of a tax-funded welfare state. The fate of those societies, and the political viability of their radical ideas, would be determined by the western Pennsylvania uprising that became known as the Whiskey Rebellion.

HAMILTONIAN FINANCE AND THE WHISKEY TAX

After the ratification of the Constitution and the election of President Washington, Alexander Hamilton became treasury secretary. With his almost unparalleled understanding of fiscal and monetary issues, Hamilton would rapidly straighten out America's disastrous public finances. A signal achievement, but his plans were even more ambitious. To make America a powerful,

Treasury Secretary Alexander Hamilton designed his whiskey excise to provoke resistance on the frontier. (Credit: Library of Congress)

industrialized state led by rich merchants and manufacturers, Hamilton was building an engine for upward redistribution.

The first step was to prove the government's creditworthiness. In 1790, Hamilton had brokered a plan for the federal government to assume the remaining $25 million in state war debt, which would raise the total federal debt to about $80 million. The plan paid creditors at face value and made no distinction between original holders of debt and those who had bought debt cheaply on the open market. The news of Hamilton's plan unleashed one final wave of speculation, as well-connected elites sent agents to the back-country in search of any rubes still holding on to their once-worthless paper and unaware of the government's new commitment to honor the debt. On the House floor, Virginian William Branch Giles decried the debt system as "the most powerful machine to stimulate this growing inequality in the distribution of wealth."[4]

Debt repayment required revenue, of course, but less than you might think. Taxes were to be allocated to allow for the payment of interest on the debt, but not the principal. Bonds coming due would be replaced with new bonds. Creditors would not mind this plan, modeled on British policy, because regular interest payments would make the value of the debt stable. If you needed your money back, you could just sell your certificate on the open market. The monied class would therefore be perpetually invested in the fiscal health of the new nation.[5] (Or, in the view of Hamilton's opponents, the new funding system created a class of aristocrats, living high on tax-free government funds.)

Debt financing made up more than half of government expenditure.[6] The other reason the United States needed revenue was for an army. Eastern elites generally preferred a fig leaf of diplomacy, but they had few scruples about coercing treaties from Native nations or using force when coercion failed. (George Washington himself was known in some Native communities as "the Town Destroyer."[7]) Federalists' primary concern was that land seizure and sale occur by an orderly process, ideally in large tracts to—as Hamilton predictably put it—"Monied individuals," companies, and associations.[8] Under the Articles of Confederation, "the finances of the United States" had been so poor that the nation was "utterly unable to maintain an

Indian war with any dignity or prospect of success," Secretary of War Henry Knox had admitted in 1787.[9] But with the new fiscal and military powers of the Constitution, the United States could engage in violence against the Native nations on a far greater scale.

The vast majority of federal revenue would come from the tariff. The United States was soon raising more money in a single year than it had in the entire duration of the Articles of Confederation. Though the tariff raised prices, its costs were borne more easily than direct taxation had been. Duties were mostly placed on luxury items and were applied at the ports, so they avoided exacerbating money shortages in the countryside. And because the federal government had assumed the states' debts, direct state taxes plummeted by three-quarters or more.[10]

From Hamilton's point of view, however, tariffs were not enough. Only successful internal taxation would prove the new government's authority over its citizens. In his first report on the public credit, Hamilton had proposed a tax on spirits, a policy he had thought through in such detail that he had, for the convenience of Congress, appended draft legislation to his report.[11] As Hamilton had anticipated, Congress was quicker to adopt the debt repayment and tariff proposals than an unpopular excise. But in March 1791, spurred by the financial demands of the debt plan they had adopted, Congress finally passed an excise on domestically distilled spirits.[12]

Hamilton and his allies in Congress defended the tax on whiskey as a tax on consumers. The tax was good for public health, they said; it even had the endorsement of the Philadelphia College of Physicians. Some in Congress objected heartily to this level of government intrusion into Americans' private lives. If things went on this way, Congress might "pass a law interdicting the use of ketchup," grumbled one legislator.[13] But focusing on alcohol consumption allowed the tax's proponents to paint their opposition as no more than angry drunks.

The consumer argument ignored—and indeed, disguised—that the tax also had serious implications for the entire frontier economy. It was only by converting bulky grain to alcohol that frontier farmers could profitably ship produce across the Allegheny Mountains. Opposition to the tax went well beyond whiskey distillers, moreover, because whiskey was often used in place of currency when money was scarce.[14] The drink was portable, non-perishable, divisible into increments, and generally held its value; it was not unusual for workers to be paid in whiskey, or for landlords to accept whiskey for rent.

Hamilton's tax was also designed to give big distillers an edge over smaller ones. Because the tax applied to the volume of whiskey, not its price, the tax fell more heavily on the frontier, where whiskey was cheap. In the upcountry, the tax doubled the price. There were also tax breaks built into the law for those who could run their stills at maximum production and for those who could pay their tax in cash up front—that is, the big distilling operations, not the mom-and-pop outfits. John Neville, the western Pennsylvania tax collector, was also a large producer of whiskey; successful enforcement of the tax would have the added bonus of driving his competitors out of business.[15]

Many federal legislators were probably unaware of the ins and outs of distilling in the hinterlands. But Hamilton knew what he was doing; his goal was "industry consolidation," as historian William Hogeland put it, via a tax that would concentrate "wealth in the hands of the few."[16] Hamilton also knew his whiskey tax would provoke rural resistance—in fact, he welcomed it. He wanted the chance for the new federal government to prove itself capable of putting down an insurrection. The Whiskey Rebellion, we will see, was Hamilton's brainchild almost as much as the tax that inspired it.

THE FIGHT FOR INDEPENDENCE ON THE AMERICAN FRONTIER

Frontier farmers responded to the whiskey excise with a regulation, employing the same techniques they had used since the colonial era to protest unfair taxation: blocking roads; hindering legal processes; and threatening, abusing, and occasionally killing officials. Taxes needed to be proportionate to wealth, the farmers believed—and this was no minor fiscal quibble. Hamilton's plans were, in the eyes of the frontiersmen, a danger to the new republic because they would enrich the bondholding aristocracy in the East and would further undermine widespread landownership on the frontier. Land was, for frontiersmen, the economic basis for equality and independence among the (white, male) citizenry—and land was increasingly hard to come by.

The first major anti-excise meeting in western Pennsylvania was held at the Green Tree Tavern in Pittsburgh in September 1791. Delegates from all four western counties drafted and signed a remonstrance to Congress. The Green Tree delegates objected that the excise would fall heavily "on the laborious and poorer class" and direct "a capital of nearly eighty millions of dollars in the hands of a few persons." This plan, the delegates wrote, was not just economically unfair but politically "subversive." It would impoverish the citizenry and empower an elite who might wish to "evade the Constitution." Similar themes would be sounded in later petitions, as whiskey tax opposition grew more widespread and more organized. The excise was a problem, a 1792 remonstrance explained, because it "operates in proportion to the number and not to the wealth of the people." In its place, petitioners in 1794 requested "a more equal and less odious tax," which would "be cheerfully paid by the people of these counties."[17]

The promise of cheerful payment was perhaps an exaggeration, but other taxes were indeed tolerable to Westerners. Rural populations had shown great fiscal patriotism during the Revolutionary War. In 1775, when many Philadelphia notables dared not whisper the word "independence," Cumberland County "took the unprecedented step of levying £27,000 in taxes on themselves to defray military expenses," historian Terry Bouton notes. And when it came to land taxes, taxpayers in the western counties were more reliable and timely than their eastern counterparts. It was not uncommon for frontier protestors to carry banners that simply read, "Land tax."[18]

The whiskey tax, however, was anathema to the frontiersmen, because it threatened to further exacerbate rising inequality. Many rural families had lost their farms during the depression of the 1780s, while prime farmland was "engrossed" (monopolized) by wealthy Eastern speculators. As a result, an increasing percentage of people in the country were now poor, and about 60 percent of the households in the older townships did not own land.[19] The whiskey tax's upwardly redistributive structure would push small farmers into tenancy and give large landowners even more money and power.

In the past, when land had become unaffordable, Americans had moved west. Southwestern Pennsylvania was part of the "New Purchase," acquired by England from the Six Nations of the Iroquois in 1768 in the Treaty of Fort Stanwix—a treaty to which the Shawnee and others who lived or hunted on those lands had not agreed.[20] The following decades saw attacks and reprisals of almost unimaginable cruelty. There were those who opposed violence, but most frontiersmen saw Indians as an enemy race that deserved to be "extirpated."[21] Native towns in Ohio became diverse communities that incorporated many people driven west by settler and militia atrocities.

In the early 1790s, an alliance of the Wyandot, Shawnee, Lenape, Miami, and other Native nations, known as the United Indian Nations or North-west Confederacy, was successfully fending off US military incursions into their territory across the Ohio River.[22] In 1790, under General Josiah Har-mar, and again in 1791, under General Arthur St. Clair, an American army invaded Native lands to destroy their crops and burn their villages—and was ambushed and utterly routed by the Native confederacy. Of St. Clair's 972 men, 671 were killed and 271 wounded, a casualty rate of 97 percent. The Native forces, led by Little Turtle of the Miami and Blue Jacket of the Shawnee, lost fewer than two dozen warriors. The battle remains the worst defeat in US military history. Only a few small beachheads of poor Ameri-can settlers dared to squat on land north of the river.[23]

Members of the Native confederacy were struck by these Americans' abject poverty. When, after the defeats of Harmar and St. Clair, US com-missioners offered the confederacy "a large sum, in money or goods, as was never given at any one time, for any quantity of Indian lands," the official reply of the United Indian Nations was categorical: "Money, to us, is of no value." No amount of bribery would persuade the nations to part with their land. But, the Native council continued, if the United States was indeed willing to spend great sums of money to buy peace, they had a suggestion.

"Brothers," they addressed the commissioners, "we know that these set-tlers are poor," or they would not keep venturing across the Ohio in search of a homestead. "Divide, therefore, this large sum of money, which you have offered to us" and "the great sums you must expend in raising and pay-ing armies, with a view to force us to yield you our country," among the poor Americans instead. The commissioners could indeed buy peace, the United Indian Nations were saying, but they needed to buy it *with their own people.* Give your own people the money to stay on American soil, and "we are persuaded, they would most readily accept of it."[24]

The US commissioners were not interested. "The negotiation," the Americans wrote in a terse missive the next morning, is "at an end." Under the command of the fierce Revolutionary War veteran General "Mad Anthony" Wayne, a new army, five thousand strong, was already training outside Pittsburgh to begin yet another invasion of the lands north of the Ohio.[25]

But in suggesting that the United States could pay its poor rather than fund an army, the United Indian Nations had correctly identified a fundamental dynamic in the history of the United States. "American society," in the words of historian Alan Taylor, "transformed class conflict into westward expansion."[26] The frontier farmers' reaction to the whiskey excise was one manifestation of this class conflict. But the frontiersmen were not the only ones resisting Hamiltonian finance, and the United Indian Nations were not the only ones suggesting America do more for its poor.

THE DEMOCRATIC-REPUBLICAN SOCIETIES

While the frontiersmen blocked roads and threatened excise collectors, other opponents of the Hamiltonian funding system coalesced in a network of dozens of newspapers and societies that came to be known as "democratic" or "democratic-republican." Inspired by the French Revolution and the writings of Thomas Paine, democrats—largely craftsmen, mechanics, laborers, and small farmers—advocated for policies that would encourage the rough economic equality they deemed necessary for a participatory republic.

Like the Western farmers, democrats called for taxes proportionate to wealth. As a writer in the Philadelphia *Independent Gazetteer* argued in 1789, property was a "creature of society" because it accumulated thanks to the "joint strength of society, in the execution of its laws." Citizens owed a debt to the nation that had made their success possible; that debt was to be paid with taxes, in proportion to the property they had accrued. It was unjust, argued a writer in the *New-York Journal*, that working people would "pay a tax on all they possess, eat, drink or wear, while the rich man pays no tax whatever" on the wealth he holds in "public funds or banks."[27] Regressive taxation was evidence of corrupt rule by the rich. For Alexander

Thomas Paine, author of *Common Sense* and *Rights of Man*, proposed a graduated tax on the income from wealth with a top marginal rate of 100 percent. (Credit: Library of Congress)

Smyth, a member of the Democratic Society of Wytheville, Virginia, the consequence of extreme economic inequality was that wealthy representatives would "favor themselves in modes of taxation, by adopting such as do not fall on the citizen in proportion to his property, but in proportion to his consumption of articles necessary to his support and comfort."[28]

If the would-be aristocrats wanted taxes to fall heavily on the poor, should democrats adopt the opposite system: taxes that were not just proportionate to wealth but progressive? That is, should a republican government not merely avoid exacerbating economic inequality, but take active steps to prevent or reverse the consolidation of wealth? Some democrats were beginning to consider the possibility.

In *Common Sense*, the revolutionary pamphleteer Thomas Paine had rallied Americans to cast off British rule and the very idea of monarchy. Fifteen years later, now living in Europe and supporting the revolutionary cause in France, Paine would propose an idea at least as radical as republicanism. In his second volume of *Rights of Man*, he proposed an innovative tax on the income from wealth. For one, the tax he proposed was graduated; much like the income tax today, each higher rate was applied only to the portion of one's income above the previous threshold. The idea of marginal tax rates was new enough that the French mathematician Condorcet, a friend of Paine's, would in the same year write an entire pamphlet explaining its operation, titled *On Progressive Taxation*.

But Paine did not merely devise a progressive income tax; he took progressivity to its natural limit. Starting with a rate of 1.25 percent, Paine's tax culminated with a marginal rate of . . . 100 percent. No matter how large one's estate grew, under Paine's proposal one could not realize an income of more than £12,370 annually. This was an extremely generous maximum income, the equivalent of about $27 million in annual income today. The top tax rate would have applied to no more than a handful of Britons at the time. But Paine believed that at some point, far above the income necessary to raise a family or achievable through personal effort, "there ought to be a limit to property." The limit on wealth was, for Paine, a protection for republican government. Extreme wealth led to an "overgrown influence" of the rich, "one of the principal sources of corruption at elections."[29]

Paine, as usual, struck a nerve with America's radicals. One hundred thousand copies of *Rights of Man* were published in the United States, a copy for one in twenty free adults at a time when pamphlets were regularly shared and loaned and read aloud. Much of the appeal of the text was not in its tax tables, of course. People read it for its stirring defense of the French Revolution and the republican cause. But Paine's argument for a legal property maximum was picked up in democratic newspapers, including the *National Gazette*, which argued in 1793 that "in every democratical government the laws ought to destroy, and prevent too great an inequality of condition among the citizens. Otherwise, an equality of constitutional rights will be a mere chimera." The New York *Time Piece* argued that in "such a republic as this, men should by every fair means be legally prevented from becoming exorbitantly rich."[30]

The assertion that government should actively prevent the accrual of wealth marked a departure from earlier egalitarian thinking about how government should ensure economic equality. Extremes of wealth inequality had commonly been seen as a consequence of unequal government. One only had to look to Europe to see how regressive taxes, government funds for the nobility, and aristocratic inheritance laws could ensure that wealth flowed upward and stayed there. Eliminate those policies and a rough parity between citizens should preserve itself, with only small differences in condition justified by differences of talent or effort.

Or so most thought at the time of American independence. The idea of active egalitarian governance of the economy had been only briefly contemplated by a few of the revolution's most radical leaders. In 1776, when Pennsylvania patriots had unseated the colony's old guard and were drafting a new state constitution, they had considered including the following clause in the state's declaration of rights: "That an enormous Proportion of Property vested in a few Individuals is dangerous to the Rights, and destructive of the Common Happiness, of Mankind; and therefore every free State hath a Right by its Laws to discourage the Possession of such Property."[31]

The clause may have been drafted by James Cannon, a mathematician and friend of Paine's, or, just possibly, by Benjamin Franklin.[32] The proposal persisted through several rounds of discussion but was eventually dropped; no record exists of the debate the proposal presumably engendered.[33] But notably—and just as Paine would later argue in *Rights of Man*—the Pennsylvania radicals considered the state's authority to limit the accrual of property *a part of the protection of individual rights.* The power of the government to limit the concentration of wealth was put alongside the right to a jury trial and freedom of assembly.[34] The rationale for limiting extreme wealth was to protect the liberty of the citizens.

By 1792, an increasing number of democrats were beginning to believe in the idea that had been too extreme even for the radical '76ers: that, to preserve liberty, a republican government must intervene to preserve some level of economic equality among the citizenry. As the historian Eric Foner observes, Paine outlined in *Rights of Man* not merely new egalitarian taxes but "an economic program as close to a welfare state as could be imagined in the eighteenth century," including a pension program for the elderly poor, payments to poor families for the care of children, and a fund to cover the funeral expenses of itinerant workers.[35]

Many lesser-known democratic republicans also proposed new government interventions to improve the economic lot of average citizens. William

Manning, a tavern keeper in Massachusetts, called for a government-funded national society for laborers that would allow them to educate themselves on civic and political matters.[36] Robert Coram, a librarian and schoolteacher in Delaware, proposed a national system of universal public education for all children, funded by a general tax on land. An education would enable young people to "support themselves when they come of age," so they could participate in and contribute to "that society of which they constitute a part."[37]

It was, and remains, an idea most radical: If a nation were truly to protect the liberty and rights of its citizens, it needed also to ensure that they had a livelihood. Freedom was the consequence of equality because one's rights as a citizen were guaranteed by one's economic independence. These ideals permeated the petitions of the Whiskey Rebels and galvanized democrats across the country. But the defeat of the Whiskey Rebellion would bring this radical egalitarian politics to an untimely end.

DEFEAT OF THE REBELLION

Alexander Hamilton was gunning for a fight with America's unruly backcountry. For Hamilton, policies intended to protect the interests of small farmers or reduce the consolidation of wealth were nothing more than nostalgic foolishness. If America was to be a great nation, these ideas would have to be defeated—militarily, if necessary. As early as 1792, he encouraged military action against the rural tax resisters, suggested that Washington personally lead an army westward, and identified the area around Pittsburgh as the most appropriate place for the government to assert its authority.[38] He sought criminal indictments against those holding meetings in opposition to the excise.[39] Attorney General Edmund Randolph was obliged to remind the Treasury secretary that, far from being actionable, petition and peaceable assembly were explicitly protected constitutional rights.[40] As treasury secretary, Hamilton certainly had cause to stand firm for the collection of taxes. But Hamilton's ferocity in support of the excise was in marked contrast to his reaction to the risk of customs evasion by Northeastern merchants. "The good will of the Merchants is very important," he told the federal tax collector in Providence, in a letter encouraging him to be "accommodating" and not "too punctilious."[41]

In the summer of 1794, Hamilton found a way to incite violent opposition by the frontiersmen on a scale that the federal government could no longer ignore. The government issued a handful of writs against western Pennsylvania distillers who had not been paying their taxes. The summonses, which obliged their recipients to defend themselves in the Philadelphia court three hundred miles away, would require weeks of travel at harvesttime.[42] It was a burden enough to ruin a poor farm family, and it meant judgment by strangers rather than sympathetic Westerners. If the writs had been delayed even a week, they would have come under a new law that allowed for local trials, but Hamilton did not want trials under local authority, and he did not want to wait.[43] He wanted a confrontation—and he got one.

After local tax collector John Neville accompanied the federal marshal as he attempted to deliver his ruinous summonses, a small group of militiamen responded by riding to Neville's plantation and firing on his house. But Neville was prepared; his house was well barricaded, and Neville himself well armed. After calling a warning to the militiamen, Neville fired on them, killing a sixteen-year-old boy. The following day, July 17, a much larger militia marched to his house to demand his resignation. It was on this march that the militiamen stopped and voted on an amendment to clarify their willingness to pay taxes. When they arrived, they discovered that Neville had fled, leaving his estate and family under the protection of eleven US Army troops.[44]

Under a flag of truce, the militia and the army exchanged messages. If Neville was unavailable, the militia wanted his official papers. But the soldiers and militia could come to no resolution, and after the women were allowed to leave the house, the shooting began. In the skirmish that followed, the militia leader and Revolutionary War veteran James McFarlane, reputedly tricked by the display of a white flag from Neville's house, came out into the open to renew the negotiation and was promptly shot dead. The militiamen then burned Neville's mansion to the ground.

Two weeks later, in August 1794, thousands of tax resisters mustered outside Pittsburgh at Braddock's Field, the site of a major defeat of the British forces during the French and Indian War, the Battle of the Monongahela. Among those on the losing side had been a young Colonel George

Washington. Among the French and Indian victors: Wyandot, Miami, Delaware, and Shawnee warriors.[45] Now, nearly forty years later, as the Whiskey Rebels took the field, members of those Native nations were again preparing for battle, this time 250 miles to the west against General Wayne's advancing army.[46]

The Whiskey Rebels were nominally led by a local lawyer named David Bradford, though Bradford quickly developed cold feet as the reality of armed rebellion became clear. He and other rebel leaders tried to abort a plan to seize guns and ammunition from Fort Lafayette, using an excuse intended to appeal to the self-interest of the militiamen: that the guns were intended to fight the Indians. But the militiamen would not be dissuaded from assembling. As many as eight thousand men, about half the able-bodied men of western Pennsylvania, hoisted liberty poles with slogans like "Equal Taxation and No Excise, No Asylum for Traitors and Cowards" and marched through the village of Pittsburgh. Flying their own six-striped flag, the rebels appeared to have superseded all governmental authority.[47]

President Washington was aghast. Now in his sixties, he would personally lead the military intervention, donning the uniform he had worn as the commander of the Continental Army. The Militia Act had been passed in the aftermath of St. Clair's defeat to give the federal government greater latitude in waging war against Native nations; now it would be used to fight American citizens. From the temporary capital at Philadelphia, Washington and Hamilton prepared to ride west at the head of a force nearly thirteen thousand strong, larger than the Continental Army had ever been.

The battle was over before it began. Long before the army's arrival in the western counties, the rebellion dissolved. Federal commissioners riding in advance of the army offered the rebels pardons in exchange for a promise to obey the law, and most of the cowed rebels took the deal and signed the oath. Nonetheless, when the federal army arrived, mass arrests began. Men, selected seemingly at random, were marched through the mountain snow to be prosecuted in Philadelphia. Few went to trial, and those who were convicted eventually received pardons. But the prisoners were held in terrible conditions for months, and some cases took years. Around two thousand of the Whiskey Rebels, including David Bradford, responded to the defeat as many American men of that era responded to failure: by moving west.[48]

"Our insurrection is most happily terminated," Hamilton wrote to his sister-in-law. "Government has gained by it reputation and strength, and our finances are in a most flourishing condition."[49] With the end of the insurrection, land values in the area skyrocketed; George Washington's own Western landholdings appreciated by about 50 percent.[50]

The administration used the failed rebellion to paint all its opponents as dangerous subversives. The uprising was equated with Robespierre's Reign of Terror in France. President Washington, in his November 1794 address on the rebellion, claimed that the "self-created" democratic-republican societies were to blame for inciting violence.[51] This was unfair. Though David Bradford was a member of the Washington County democratic society, the tiny group had barely ever held a meeting. The powerful Mingo Creek Association, the guiding force behind the excise resistance, stemmed not from the democratic-republican societies but from the revolutionary tradition of democratically organized militias and committees of correspondence.[52] And democratic societies elsewhere in the country denounced the violence in the western counties.[53] Nonetheless, the democratic-republican societies never recovered from the blow to their reputation, and the most radical aspects of their vision fell by the wayside.

WHITE MAN'S DEMOCRACY

Little Turtle and Blue Jacket disagreed about whether the United Indian Nations could defeat the Americans for a third time. Little Turtle believed the Americans had grown stronger, and that the British, who had in the past provided supplies to the Native nations in their battles against the United States, would not remain reliable allies. Little Turtle was overruled and so stepped down as leader of the confederacy forces; he would lead the Miami in the battles ahead.[54] But his presentiment was correct. On the day that representatives of the Whiskey Rebels met with the federal commissioners, US forces defeated the confederacy at the Battle of Fallen Timbers, and the British did not come to their Native allies' aid. The resulting treaty forced the Native nations to part with more than half of present-day Ohio.[55]

In 1794, the frontiersmen at Mingo Creek were called up to fight the Indians but chose instead to take up arms for fairer taxation. Yet in the decades that followed, any equality that existed among white men would be based not on the taxation of wealth but on a genocide.

What remained of the frontier's democratic impulse was channeled into Jeffersonianism. The frontiersmen had been subdued; now they would be appeased. Land grants became the prototypical American welfare program, and the organization of westward expansion became the federal government's primary purpose and source of strength. The Jefferson administration oversaw more than thirty treaties with Native nations, who ceded about two hundred thousand square miles of their homelands. But even among white men, the frontier's equalizing effects were brief at best. Within fifteen years, land was as unequally held in Ohio as it had been in western Pennsylvania when the Whiskey Rebel army paraded through Pittsburgh.[56]

Unlike equal taxation, the federal commitment to cheap land was no threat to the elite. Indeed, Easterners were as ready to speculate in land as Westerners were to settle it, and the slaveholders, whose lucrative cotton crops rapidly exhausted the soil, were the most land hungry of all. The Indian Removal Act of 1830, which forced the deportation of ninety thousand Native people across the Mississippi River, would not have passed without the inflated Southern representation achieved by the three-fifths clause, historian Claudio Saunt notes. Jefferson had suggested such a policy as early as 1803; when removal was implemented, as many as one-fifth of those sent west died on the march.[57]

Jeffersonian democracy was definitively less egalitarian than that of Thomas Paine, whose radicalism fell so completely from favor that, upon his return to the United States, he was publicly reviled and lived the rest of his life in obscurity. In the aftermath of the failed Whiskey Rebellion, farmers were reticent to speak their minds. Among some of the poorer yeomanry in the once-rebellious western counties, any criticism of the government was now feared to be treason.[58] The very word "democracy" was gentrified, stripped of its revolutionary implication of direct mass political engagement and participatory self-governance. In the new world of partisan electoral politics, Northern democratic-republican newspapers, which had previously decried the oppression of slavery, shed those commitments.[59] The more radical Paineite visions of a democratic economy found no home in the new political order.

Instead, the start of the nineteenth century saw Hamilton's strong fiscal state for the merchant class replaced with the Jeffersonian weak fiscal state dominated by the interests of slaveholders. Where Hamilton had envisioned a national bureaucracy of tax collectors strengthening the power of the national state, Jefferson would say with pride in his second inaugural address, "What farmer, what mechanic, what laborer, ever sees a tax-gatherer of the United States?"[60] As we will see in the following chapters, the defense of slavery undermined taxation in the United States. Instead of progressive taxation of the rich, the Jeffersonian era saw hardly any taxation at all.[61]

Part Two

Taxation for Black Liberation

THE EMANCIPATORY
POTENTIAL OF TAXATION

An Infallible Deathblow to Slavery

—Hinton Helper

The year 1857 saw the release of a treatise that one prominent historian has plausibly described as "the most important single book, in
terms of its political impact, that has ever been published in the United
States."[1] *The Impending Crisis of the South*, written by a previously obscure
North Carolinian named Hinton Helper, sold over one hundred thousand
copies.[2] On the floor of Congress, the book was called "foul," "infamous,"
"murderous," and "insurrectionary." The doctrine of "Helperism" was
decried as leading "to violence and bloodshed, to revolution and anarchy."
The author was burned in effigy and threatened with death. Those who
dared carry the book into the Southern states risked being lynched.[3]

What had Helper written to provoke such abomination? He proposed
to tax slavery out of existence. Taxes on slaves, Helper argued, should be
increased to whatever degree necessary to provide "an infallible deathblow to
slavery on or before the 4th of July, 1876."[4]

Helper was not as idealistic as a contemporary reader may imagine. He
was, in fact, a virulent racist. "In writing this book, it has been no part of my

Abolitionist author Hinton Helper called upon Southern nonslaveowners to vote for abolition by taxation. (Credit: A. H. Ritchie)

purpose," Helper was at pains to state in the book's preface, "to display any special friendliness or sympathy for the blacks." Moralistic attacks on slavery, Helper continued, were a fine subject for "Yankee wives"—a reference to the immensely popular novel *Uncle Tom's Cabin*, published by Northern abolitionist Harriet Beecher Stowe five years earlier—but "men should give the facts."[5]

Helper's book presented reams of statistics that compared the South unfavorably to the North in terms of agricultural productivity, land values, population growth, exports, manufacturing, railroads, canals, public schools, libraries, patents, life expectancy, and more.[6] Slavery "dwindled our commerce," Helper raged, "sunk a large majority of our people in galling poverty and ignorance," and "rendered a small minority conceited and tyrannical."[7] Helper denied what had become a core tenet of white Southern ideology: that slavery put all white men on an equal footing. To the contrary, Helper argued, nonslaveholding Southern whites were impoverished by the slave economy and oppressed by the slave oligarchy. When Helper imagined his taxes taking effect on Independence Day, it was the independence of Southern white men that he had in mind.

As such a man himself, writing to his brethren, Helper barely addressed Northerners at all; the South could end slavery on its own, he believed. After all, slaveholders were a minority of white men even in the South. "The total number of actual slave-owners, including their entire crew of cringing lickspittles against whom we have to contend," wrote Helper, "is but three hundred and forty-seven thousand five hundred and twenty-five."[8]

It was true. In a country with about five million adult white men, a total of 347,525 people were listed as slaveowners in the 1850 census.[9] Of course, slaveowners were usually the patriarchs of large families. About one-third of Southern whites were part of households that owned slaves. But even in the Deep South states, slightly less than half of white families were enslavers.[10] If nonslaveowning Southern whites awakened to their economic interests, Helper argued, they were numerous enough to implement abolition by taxation via the electoral process. "Give us fair-play, secure to us the right of discussion, the freedom of speech," he proclaimed, "and we will settle the difficulty at the ballot-box."[11] Perhaps the most radical aspect of his plan was, ironically, its assertion that abolition could be achieved within the existing political system. Helper insisted that revolutionary power—the power to vote and the power to tax—already rested in the hands of nonslaveholders. To the Southern slaveholding elite, this was sedition.

Seven decades earlier, proponents of slavery had done the same math as Helper, and his hope was their fear: Abolition could come via democratically determined taxation. Anticipating this, plantation owners limited the federal government's taxing power and hobbled their own states' political institutions. From Virginia to Florida, the planter class worked to keep suffrage restricted, the legislatures malapportioned, government bureaucracies ineffectual, and taxes strictly limited.

In the end, Helper was naïve to imagine that nonslaveholding white Southerners would heed his call for abolition by taxation. In Alabama and Mississippi, greater popular influence over government did result in higher taxes on property held in enslaved people, but not nearly at a level to endanger the profitability of the slave system. Just a few years after Helper's book was published, nonslaveowning Southern white men were not delivering a fiscal deathblow to slavery; they were taking up arms to defend it.[12]

FEDERAL TAXATION AS A THREAT TO SLAVEHOLDERS

Hinton Helper spoke to Southern nonslaveholders because he wanted the white South to free itself from the slave system. But there was a more practical reason to pin abolitionist hopes on state taxes: Federal emancipatory taxation was unconstitutional.

At the Constitutional Convention in 1787, Southern delegates had demanded and received, along with a system of representation heavily biased in their favor, strong limits on the forms of taxation that might touch slavery. The "three-fifths clause" increased Southern representation in Congress by counting three-fifths of the enslaved population in the apportionment of seats in the House of Representatives. It also precluded heavy taxation of slavery by requiring direct taxes to be apportioned among the states according to the same formula.[13] The apportionment requirement barred Congress from legislating a direct tax that fell heavily or exclusively on certain states, as a heavy tax on slaves would. The framers also capped taxes on the slave trade, the Constitution's only provision limiting federal tax levels. The tax on the "Importation of such Persons as any of the States now existing shall think proper to admit," as the framers euphemized it, could be no more than ten dollars a head.

None of this was enough to completely quell Southern fears. When Virginia held its state convention to consider whether to ratify the new Constitution, Patrick Henry and George Mason argued that the document would let the federal government use heavy taxes to abolish slavery. Henry imagined "a picture so horrid, so wretched, so dreadful" that he hated to "dwell upon it." If Virginia ratified the Constitution, he predicted, Congress would be able to impose a "grievous and enormous tax" on slaves and thereby "compel owners to emancipate their slaves rather than pay the tax." As the convention moved toward ratification, he became increasingly agitated. He shouted at his fellow representatives, "They'll free your niggers!"[14]

Patrick Henry was wrong; slavery was safely enshrined in the Constitution. Slaveholders never faced the slightest threat of emancipatory federal property taxes. So confident were slaveholders in their federal dominance that, on the few occasions that the United States imposed a federal property tax, Southerners sought to include slaves among the forms of property to

John C. Calhoun, slavery's most ardent defender in the US Senate, sought to keep the taxing power in the hands of the wealthy. (Credit: Library of Congress, Manuscript Division, Brady-Handy Collection)

be taxed. It allowed them to shift federal taxes off nonslaveholders in their states—and as we will see, using tax breaks to soothe class tensions was a common political strategy employed by elites in the slaveholding South.[15] Slaveholders were willing to pay most of the taxes when those taxes were low, the government's capacity to tax was safely constrained, and political power was firmly in their hands.

But if slaveholders no longer feared direct federal taxes, by the 1820s they objected to the portion of the federal government's taxing power unaffected by the apportionment clause: the tariff.

John C. Calhoun of South Carolina, slavery's greatest defender in Washington, was a steadfast opponent of democratic taxation. Called the "cast-iron man," Calhoun glowed with fury at the thought of rule by the "numerical majority." Democracy, in his view, meant nothing more than the absolute power of the "lowest and most worthless portions of the community," who would plunder the wealthy few if given the chance.[16] Historian Richard Hofstadter famously called him "Marx of the Master Class": Calhoun believed there was a class war, and he wanted the rich to win.[17]

Calhoun began his political life as a nationalist, confident that the protections the South had secured at the Constitutional Convention were adequate to protect Southern wealth held in slaves. But as the rapidly growing population of the North and West had begun to offset the Southern representational advantage provided by the three-fifths clause, Calhoun changed his mind. The rising tide of tariff protectionism, which benefited Northern industries at the cost of Southern agriculture and consumers, indicated the weakening of the slaveholder veto over national politics.[18] When Southerners were outmaneuvered in the negotiations of 1828, the resulting "Tariff of Abominations" provoked South Carolina, the state that enslaved more of its population than any other, to assert a powerful new limit on majority rule.

Writing on behalf of the South Carolina legislature—anonymously, because he was also serving as vice president of the United States—Calhoun made the case for what became known as "nullification."[19] A single state could declare any federal law unconstitutional and therefore inoperative within the state, Calhoun claimed.[20] Abiding by federal law, under this theory, was optional; the individual states were the real arbiters of the Constitution. Accordingly, a South Carolina convention moved to "nullify" the federal tariffs. In the port of Charleston, these revenues would not be collected.

President Andrew Jackson defused the constitutional crisis with a strategy both carrot and stick: working with Congress to reduce the tariff rates while also promising military action against South Carolina if the state did not enforce federal law. This approach ended the immediate crisis but resolved nothing of the underlying conflict. Calhoun would later wish for his epitaph to simply read "Nullification"; Jackson would publicly regret not having hanged Calhoun.[21]

From the Nullification Crisis until his death in 1850, Calhoun devoted himself to devising additional measures that would stymie democratic taxation, which he equated with the abolition of slavery. "While the tariff takes from us the proceeds of our labor, abolition strikes at the labor itself," he wrote in 1844.[22] His *Disquisition on Government*, written as he was slowly dying of tuberculosis and published posthumously in 1851, proposed a system of interlocking supermajority requirements that he believed would blunt the danger of taxation imposed by the masses. To the end of his life, Calhoun sought to further limit the power of the majority in American government—a power that, in his view, was always most dangerous when it came to taxation.

WHY SLAVERY WAS ESPECIALLY ENDANGERED BY DEMOCRATIC TAXATION

Like their hero Calhoun, the Southern planters were obsessively concerned about the power to tax. Of course, few rich Northerners wanted to see their wealth taxed away by the masses. But although Calhoun eloquently tried to convince Northern elites that they, too, were endangered by taxation under majority rule, he found little success. While Northerners fought over what to tax and how much, only Southerners treated the very existence of the state's fiscal power as a mortal threat.

Why was democratic taxation so much more dangerous to the economic elite of the South than to the North? One answer is prosaic: Taxing slavery was easy. Compared to taxing other forms of wealth, it took very little administration or expertise. The paper wealth of commerce can be disguised through clever bookkeeping. The valuation of farmland requires a consideration of location, soil, weather, and other factors affecting its productive capacity. Serious property assessment is difficult, technical work that requires a well-trained and competent bureaucracy to administer. People, by contrast, are simple to tax. Poll taxes have existed for thousands of years and served as a significant source of revenue in the early American states.

The relative ease of assessing people over assessing property was directly demonstrated in the early years of the republic. The United States, under the Articles of Confederation, tried to requisition revenue on the basis of the states' total real estate value; states were required to pay in proportion to that wealth. The principle was sound, but the system failed miserably in practice because the government had no capacity to calculate the value of land in the states. The federal government was obliged to revert to a more rudimentary system, apportioning requisitions based on state population.[23]

So slaveholders knew that it would take no great leap of governmental capacity to impose a new and much higher tax on enslaved people.[24] But the risk taxation posed to slavery was not merely a matter of bureaucratic ease. Slavery was particularly vulnerable to taxation because whether or not

whites recognized slavery as a moral crime, many thought it was an economic, political, and social blight.

Though supporters of slavery like Calhoun would come to declare slavery
a "positive good," the reality of the slave system could not be disguised. The
South's revered founding generation had recognized slavery to be wrong.
Thomas Jefferson, who over his lifetime enslaved six hundred people, called
slavery a "great political and moral evil."[25] As the decades wore on, the
eloquent testimonies of those who escaped bondage—including those of
Olaudah Equiano in 1789, Frederick Douglass in 1845 and 1855, Henry
Box Brown in 1849, Solomon Northrup in 1853, and Harriet Jacobs in
1861—revealed the cruel realities of the Southern system. And American
chattel slavery became an outlier internationally. Great Britain abolished
slavery in her colonies in the 1830s. In a country that so loudly proclaimed
itself a bastion of freedom, American slavery was a national embarrassment.

Even many unconvinced of slavery's evil could see its economic costs.
As the slave system turned plantation owners and Northern financiers into
millionaires, it undermined small farmers and local commerce. A third of
Southern wealth was held in enslaved people, and by 1860, 90 percent of
slaves were owned by just 10 percent of the adult white male population. Big
plantation owners, those enslaving more than one hundred people, made
up just 1.5 percent of Southern white households. Other forms of property were far more widely shared among freemen. At the same time, about
a third of Southern whites lived in conditions of such extreme poverty as
to shock visiting Northerners. Middling farmers had very little chance of
rising into the upper ranks of Southern society. In his unsuccessful campaign for governor of Kentucky in 1851, antislavery advocate Cassius Clay
appealed to working-class whites by decrying an economic system "diseased
with slavery."[26]

Wealth in the North, by contrast, was not commonly seen as a zero-sum
game. While Southerners sometimes asserted, against all evidence, that
Northern "wage slavery" was worse than actual slavery, most Northern
workers were self-employed, and Northerners generally saw wage earning
as a step to independent proprietorship.[27] Northern workers in the antebellum period did not possess the industrial class consciousness of the later

nineteenth century, in which labor and capital were seen as immutably opposed forces, with bosses and workers natural enemies.

But the slave system was widely seen as inimical to the prosperity of free labor. Abolition by taxation was therefore an even greater threat than direct emancipation, which most slave states' constitutions explicitly outlawed anyway.[28] There was, slaveholders perceived, an obvious incentive for nonslaveholders to tax slavery to the hilt—not just to shift tax obligations onto the rich, or to pay for public investments, but to resist an economic system that impoverished white citizens.

Slavery took an increasing toll on the civic fabric as well. Protections for the "peculiar institution" encroached, sometimes violently, on freedom of speech. Congress maintained a "gag rule" that automatically tabled antislavery petitions from 1836 to 1844. Southern states censored newspapers and the mail; those whose views could be construed as antislavery commonly risked imprisonment or assault.[29] When Massachusetts Senator Charles Sumner gave a fiery antislavery speech in 1856, a member of the House's South Carolina delegation beat him nearly to death on the Senate floor. For his outspoken opposition to slavery, Kentuckian Cassius Clay faced multiple assassination attempts. Far from ensuring the freedom of white people, as its proponents claimed, slavery was increasingly seen to threaten white liberties, and therefore the very foundations of republican government in America.[30]

Finally, the slave system was particularly endangered by property taxation because the process of tax assessment called into question the authority of the "master." Ad valorem taxation—that is, taxation based on a property's value—requires a system of government assessors passing judgment on the worth of a taxpayer's property. But a master's plantation was supposed to be a private dominion where he held complete power. It was utterly unacceptable that a local tax assessor, potentially someone of distinctly lower social rank, should be allowed to come into a master's home and insist he account for his property. There could be no oversight of the master's house, no implication that his power was anything less than absolute, and therefore no meaningful property assessment for tax purposes.[31]

Taxation of slavery was too easy, too popular, and too destabilizing to the master's authority. So slaveowners devoted themselves to limiting both the representativeness of the electoral system and the power of the government to levy taxes.

REPRESENTATION IN VIRGINIA

The "vital power of taxation," explained Benjamin Watkins Leigh of Richmond, Virginia, impelled "us of the East, to resist, to the bitter end, this transfer of power to the West."[32]

The year was 1829, and Leigh was speaking for a second day before Virginia's state constitutional convention—an event that, for Easterners like Leigh, was already a defeat.[33] Before the Civil War, Virginia stretched from the Atlantic coast to the Ohio River, including the mountainous area that is today West Virginia. For decades, the planter class had been staving off the political demands of the largely nonslaveholding small farmers from the western upcountry.

The planters' power was heavily reinforced by Virginia's 1776 constitution. The property requirement for suffrage disenfranchised about half of white males. If you were wealthy, on the other hand, you could vote in every district where you met the property requirement, a phenomenon known as "plural voting." Moreover, rather like the US Senate today, the apportionment of legislative seats was based on fixed geography, which gave a disproportionate number of seats to the planter class in the East at the expense of the increasingly populous western part of the state.[34]

But universal white male suffrage was becoming the norm, and western Virginia was getting restive. By 1829, assisted by support from Virginia's urban areas, western Virginians successfully called a new constitutional convention. Now, in the white-columned capitol building designed by Thomas Jefferson, the patrician Leigh was fighting a rearguard battle to preserve the status quo.

Sharing power with the growing population in Appalachia was objectionable to the aristocratic Easterners on purely snobbish grounds. To the consternation of his allies, Leigh could not restrain himself from calling Westerners the "peasantry." (His overt disdain provoked the citizens of one town to burn him in effigy.) But substantively, the issue was taxation. The "recurrent problem" in Virginia politics, in the words of historian William

Freehling, was the possibility that "a western nonslaveholder majority could emancipate slaves through 'soak-the-rich' taxation."[35]

This was precisely Benjamin Watkins Leigh's concern. Westerners might start out by raising taxes simply to fund schools, roads, or canals. But once the tax fever was upon them, Leigh was sure they would come to focus on "our slave property." And this taxation would lead inexorably to abolition. "When men's minds once take this direction," intoned the small, dark-eyed Leigh, "they pursue it as steadily as man pursues his course to the grave."[36]

To the horror of Leigh and his colleagues, the convention committee on the legislature—led by the venerable James Madison, by then seventy-eight years old—had suggested a white-male basis for the apportionment of the lower house. This would give Westerners the majority. To preserve slaveholders' disproportionate power, conservatives proposed that Virginia instead adopt either the federal system that counted three-fifths of the enslaved population, or preferably a "mixed" system of representation that took account of both the population and the taxes paid by each district. Both Leigh and the famed orator and self-described "aristocrat" John Randolph were particularly insistent that slave interests predominate in the lower house, where tax bills originated.[37]

The demand for extra representation, these slaveholders readily admitted, was motivated by a single issue: the threat of abolition by taxation. "Not that I have any fear, that when these gentlemen get the power, they will pass a general emancipation law," Richard Morris of Hanover assured the convention. "We have no danger to apprehend," agreed Abel Upshur of coastal Northampton County, "except from oppressive and unequal taxation; no other injustice can reasonably be feared." But for many Eastern conservatives, slave taxation and emancipation were both tantamount to unleashing a slave revolt. "I care not," continued Morris, whether abolition comes "by the passage of a law of emancipation, or a tax-law depriving the master of the power of holding his slave." In either case a "sword will be unsheathed, that will be red with the best blood of this country." Leigh, too, foresaw "rapine, anarchy, and bloodshed."[38]

Abel Upshur, a large and bellicose man, was perhaps less afraid of violence than the city lawyer Morris or the delicate patrician Leigh. As secretary of the navy to John Tyler, Upshur reportedly once ended a cabinet meeting dispute by breaking a chair over the head of the secretary of war.[39] But like Leigh and Morris, Upshur was convinced that slaveholders, more even than other rich people, could only be secure if they were the dominant political force. All "property is entitled to protection," Upshur explained on the convention floor, but "*our property* imperiously demands that kind of protection which flows from the possession of power."[40]

For others at the convention, including some Easterners, this went too far. William Henry Fitzhugh criticized his Eastern colleagues for demanding institutions that amounted to "throwing the whole power of legislation into the hands of a minority of the people." Given that the threat was simply that of "excessive taxation," Fitzhugh proposed that all property be taxed ad valorem at a single, uniform rate. In this way, Fitzhugh argued, taxes on slaves and taxes on land would always be balanced.[41]

The suggestion found little support among the slaveholding conservatives, and it may well have been beyond the state's capacities. Planter antipathy had undermined colonial Virginia's tax system from the beginning. While Massachusetts had been valuing property since the 1640s and Pennsylvania since the 1690s, colonial Virginia "never asked its tax officials to measure the value of anything," writes historian Robin Einhorn. Land, for example, was taxed based on a primitive system of categorization that was not updated to account for changing values.[42]

Without a functional tax system, Virginia languished in the early nineteenth century. Its roads were an embarrassment, with muddy, rocky, and uneven tracks that could bring carriage travel to an utter standstill in rainy periods. Nonetheless, the state legislature could not assemble a majority to raise revenue. Instead, the state fell back on public-private partnerships that achieved next to nothing. Most counties in Virginia would not set up a system of free schools until after the Civil War. The best Virginia could do was establish an insufficient "Literary Fund" with money from fines and other nontax revenue. Even this was too much for the aristocratic John Randolph, who thought free schools were evidence that poor people had adopted the "pernicious notion" that "all things must be done for them by the government, and that they are to do nothing for themselves."[43] White illiteracy rates in Virginia were more than three times higher than in New York and Massachusetts.

At the 1829–1830 Virginia Constitutional Convention, slaveholders' defensive maneuvers against democratic taxation were quite successful, largely because the apportionment of the convention itself was strongly biased in favor of the East. Though the property standard for suffrage was lowered, it continued to disenfranchise at least a third of white men.[44] Western representatives could only pass a reapportionment based on the already outdated 1820 census, and no matter how many people moved to the western part of the state in the future, there was no mechanism that would give them additional seats in the legislature. Representation in Virginia would be frozen in time.

The defining clashes of 1829–1830 were recapitulated at the next convention, in 1850. Westerners were obliged to accept a new and strict constitutional limit on the taxes applied to slaves. While all other property could be taxed ad valorem, slaves under age twelve were constitutionally excluded from taxation, and those over twelve were to be valued at a fixed amount, $300, even though an enslaved person could be sold for five times that figure.[45] After 1850, the state senate was apportioned on the "mixed basis" that Benjamin Watkins Leigh had proposed twenty years earlier, taking into account both population and wealth. Until the eve of the Civil War, Virginia's slaveholder aristocracy resisted the democratic taxation they saw as an existential threat to their way of life.

TAXATION OF SLAVERY IN THE WHITE MALE DEMOCRACIES

In the Carolinas, as in Virginia, slaveholders used overrepresentation and suffrage limits to protect themselves from democratic taxation.[46] The legislatures in the Southeast were much more malapportioned than those in the Northeast.[47] But even in the Southern states where "one white man, one vote" was the rule, the masses did not use high taxes to bring about emancipation.

As property standards for suffrage fell from favor nationally, states entered the Union with far more democratic constitutions. Mississippi and Alabama, for example, apportioned representation based on the free white population and had no property requirement to vote.[48] Just as the Virginia planters anticipated, nonslaveholding white men fought for property taxes to fall on slaves rather than land. Slaves made up a third or more of all wealth in Virginia, Alabama, and North Carolina—but only in Alabama, with its more equal franchise, did taxes on slaves account for a third or more of state revenue. In Virginia and North Carolina, taxes on slaves provided less than a fifth of the states' monies.[49] To this degree, the Easterners were correct that white male democracy would bring higher taxes on their slave property.

But this was emphatically not abolition by taxation. Slaveholders still received special tax dispensations in the Southwestern states; when Alabama and Mississippi instituted ad valorem taxation, they applied it only to land, not slaves.[50] And taxes were so low that their progressivity hardly mattered. As a fraction of total property, taxes in the South were less than half their level in the Northeast and Midwest.[51] In 1860, an Alabama slaveholder would pay a maximum of $1.10 in tax annually on an enslaved person they could sell for a thousand times that amount. As historian J. Mills Thornton has noted, even though the plantation elite paid most of the taxes, "any redistributive effect" of the tax system was "effectively nullified" by the low rates.[52]

There are several reasons why Virginia planters' fears of abolitionary taxation were not realized in these white male democracies. For one, a larger fraction of households held slaves in Alabama (35 percent) and Mississippi (49 percent) than in North Carolina (28 percent) or Virginia (26 percent). There were fewer men to whom "Helperism" might appeal. Moreover, though they lacked the electoral privileges their peers in the East had secured, Southwestern slaveholders were still heavily overrepresented in positions of power. More than two-thirds of legislators in Alabama and Mississippi owned slaves, and most of them enslaved at least twenty people.[53] What is more, the states simply did not do that much taxing in the early nineteenth century. Slaveholder wealth and dominance in the Southwest grew over time, reducing the political clout of nonslaveholders just as the demand for tax revenue was rising.[54] But most fundamentally, having a modicum of political power simply did not turn upcountry whites into tax-mad abolitionists. Small farmers were happy to tax slaveholders to off-set their own tax obligations but saw no need to go further.

Poor Southern whites were often unconvinced of the value of what taxes were intended to buy. In Richmond, Benjamin Watkins Leigh had imagined Westerners' desire for public infrastructure turning into a mania for eman-cipatory taxation. But in the Southwest, it was commercial planters who needed railroads and canals to get their cotton to market; upcountry farmers opposed taxes for these investments, which would do little to improve the lot of those growing food for their own subsistence.[55] Upcountry whites were also less motivated to pay for public schooling than one might expect—in part because what little funding existed for the Southern schools was com-monly redirected or outright stolen by the planter class.[56] Albert T. Morgan, a former Union Army officer serving as president of the board of supervisors in Yazoo County, Mississippi, after the Civil War, discovered that $50,000 from the prewar county school fund had instead been given as "loans" to local planters, without any pretense of seeking repayment. These same plant-ers were also paying themselves from the county poor fund.[57] If government spending would primarily benefit the elite, it was as well that revenues be as low as possible, many upcountry whites concluded.

Antitax attitudes among nonslaveholding whites were also encouraged by the Southern ideology of racial solidarity that encouraged all white men to see themselves as "masters" of their own little farms and families.[58] Georgia Governor Joseph E. Brown argued that there was only one "true aristocracy, the race of white men."[59] Whether he commanded a plantation of two hun-dred enslaved people, or simply his wife and children, the Southern "master" was jealous of any encroachment upon his private sovereignty. For the sub-sistence farmer and the plantation magnate, the invasion of one's dominion by a property tax assessor put this supposed mastery in doubt. Poorer whites largely accepted the credo encapsulated in the 1841 inaugural address of Alabama Governor Benjamin Fitzpatrick: The "essence of modern oppres-sion is taxation."[60]

An unbiased system of representation would have put greater pressure on slavery in Virginia and North Carolina than it did in Alabama and Missis-sippi. Slave ownership was less widespread in those states, and both states had a longer history of antislavery sentiment than the Deep South did. Hinton Helper was a North Carolinian, after all. Virginia's legislature had gone so far, in the aftermath of the 1831 slave revolt led by Nat Turner, as to publicly debate ending slavery. Had the Westerners won the apportionment fight the year before, perhaps that debate would have ended differently.[61]

But the cases of Alabama and Mississippi make clear that white male democracy did not intrinsically provoke taxation at a level that seriously threatened the slave system. Across the South, the only population that was in fact taxed at oppressive levels was free Black people.[62] In the Deep South, racism was one sop to the white masses and tax breaks were another. By and large, nonslaveholders could be bought cheap.

THE COMING OF THE WAR

When demographic shifts made inadequate their carefully crafted checks on national democracy, the Southern states chose war over losing an election. Alexander Stephens, vice president of the Confederacy, famously explained in his "Cornerstone" speech that slavery was the "immediate cause" for which the South had gone to war. Less well known is his explanation of why the North would accept war to maintain the Union. The North "has but one object," Stephens insisted, "and that is a collection of taxes." Similarly, in Georgia, the secessionist Governor Joseph E. Brown claimed that Northerners were planning to emancipate the slaves and tax poor Southern whites to compensate slaveholders for the loss of their property. To the end, the protection of slavery was understood by its most ardent defenders as resistance to taxation.[63]

Unsurprisingly, the Confederacy remained unwilling to levy substantial taxes on slaves for most of the war. While the North managed to raise one-fifth of its wartime revenue through taxation, the South collected only one-twentieth.[64] It was only when defeat seemed imminent that the South seriously attempted to apply substantial taxes on the system of property they had gone to war to protect.

The war also revealed that Hinton Helper was perhaps not so quixotic in believing that taxation was a political wedge between slaveholding and nonslaveholding whites. At the Richmond convention debating whether Virginia should secede from the Union, western delegates repeatedly demanded the repeal of the Virginia Constitution's tax protection for slavery. Secessionists responded with shock; that such an issue could be raised "at this crisis" was "ill-timed and ill-advised," read one proclamation.[65]

Westerners were unabashed. If their taxes could not be made fair, they would secede from the secession, Appalachian delegates threatened. And so, for weeks between Lincoln's inauguration and South Carolina's attack on Fort Sumter, the Virginia secession convention remained mired in a tax debate. Westerners eventually won an ordinance that rescinded Virginia's special property tax breaks for slaveholders. But these concessions proved inadequate. The tax debates at the secession convention had "awakened a spirit of independence in Western Virginia that did not previously exist," an Appalachian newspaper reported gleefully.[66] Just as many western delegates had predicted, their region seceded from the eastern portion of the state and joined the Union as West Virginia in 1863. "Every citizen shall be entitled to equal representation in the government," read the new West Virginia Constitution, and "all property, both real and personal, shall be taxed in proportion to its value."

RADICAL RECONSTRUCTION AND THE PROMISE OF TAXATION

> If there is any virtue in taxation, we will tax
> until we tax them out of their lands.
>
> —Texas State Senator Matthew Gaines

On a hot June day in 1871, hundreds of people gathered before the county courthouse in Brenham, Texas.[1] They were there to listen to the militant Black radical State Senator Matthew Gaines. Some thirty years earlier, Gaines had been born into slavery. As a child, he had secretly taught himself to read, hiding in a cornfield with a candle and contraband books. Twice Gaines tried to escape, and twice he had been caught; once, his enslaver had given him five hundred lashes on his back. But slavery was now outlawed, and Black men could vote. Not far from the plantation where he had been forced to work the fields, Gaines swept the 1869 election to represent Washington County, Texas.[2]

The crowd was undoubtedly expecting a barn burner. Though he was rail thin and barely five feet tall, Gaines spoke with the fire of a preacher, and his public addresses were widely known to be "spicy."[3] He did not disappoint. Over the course of his speech that day, Gaines gleefully insulted his political enemies, called out political corruption in his own Republican Party, and demanded racially integrated public schooling, a seat for a Black man in Texas's congressional delegation, and public investment to encourage immigration from Africa.[4]

But the main subject of Gaines's speech was a spirited defense of a new tax law. Responding to complaints from Democrats that the state had been "ruined with taxes," Gaines attempted to convince his audience that taxation was an essential part of the ongoing fight for Black freedom. For Gaines, like many emancipated people, freedom meant two things: schools and land. But if freedom meant schools and land, freedom also meant taxes.

Taxes, he argued, would free up land in two ways. First, they would pay for the new railroad, which would open new tracts in the West, where Black families could buy "homes at 10, 15, and 25 cents an acre, and build us school-houses and churches." He imagined the railroad line to California dotted with safe and welcoming communities for freedmen, where they would not fear to "throw the doors wide open." Second, the tax system would redistribute land from wealthy whites. As Gaines told his constituents, "Your old masters didn't give you any land or horses. The United States failed to confiscate them, and the [new Texas] constitution failed to. There is no way left but to tax and sell, so as to get cheap homes. If there is any virtue in taxation, we will tax until we tax them out of their lands."

Taxation, for Gaines, was a second-best solution. Even though he would have preferred direct confiscation and redistribution of land, high taxes on the planters would encourage them to sell their lands at prices that he hoped would make homes affordable to Black families. If "the Democrats say they are groaning under" their taxes, Senator Gaines was "Glad of it! Let them groan."

But Gaines did not just want to tax the rich. He also defended the new school tax that applied to all men from twenty-one to sixty. For people only a few years removed from slavery, the one-dollar tax was a serious expense, and Gaines knew his constituents were worried. To assuage their doubts, he distributed summaries of the new tax law and encouraged the crowd to "take them home with you and read them by the torchlight." As he passed out his pamphlets, Gaines described what taxes paid for, including a "system of free schools" and the "colored police" that were being organized

Enslaved before the war, Texas State Senator Matthew Gaines supported high property taxes to encourage land redistribution and poll taxes to fund the public schools. (Credit: DeGolyer Library, SMU)

to protect Black communities. "It is your interest to pay taxes," Gaines insisted.

"In 1856 I paid no taxes—old master did," Gaines said. "I made ten bales of cotton and got a pair of red shoes, a pair of white breeches, and a promise of a whipping Christmas to make me a good negro the next year." Now, though, Gaines was a proud property owner, and, he told his audience, "I like to pay taxes on it. It's my privilege." He put the choice to his constituents: Would they "rather live under this government and pay taxes" or "be tied up in slavery and pay no taxes"? Once his constituents had read the tax bill for themselves, he was sure they would "say there is not half taxes enough."

A REVOLUTIONARY PROJECT

Senator Gaines was one of at least fifteen hundred Black men who served in government during the brief period known as Radical Reconstruction. The era began in 1867, when Congress required Southern states to reconstitute themselves on the basis of universal male suffrage. Over the following years, the Southern states passed new constitutions, elected new legislatures, and engaged in a revolutionary project—what historian Eric Foner has described as the construction of "a democratic, interracial political order from the ashes of slavery."[5]

For the first time, Black men voted, ran for office, and won elections across the South. They were joined in the Republican Party by transplanted Northerners and a small fraction of Southern whites, mostly farmers from the poorer, hilly "upcountry" who despised the planter elite and had in some cases nursed Unionist sympathies during the war.[6]

Their revolutionary project did not last long. Georgia and Virginia, for all intents and purposes, never experienced a Radical Reconstruction. In Texas, Reconstruction did not survive the election of 1871. From the beginning, Republican governments faced a campaign of obstruction, sabotage, and terrorism from former Confederates, while support from the North waned rapidly. The last Reconstruction governments were overthrown in 1877. "We were eight years in power," lamented Thomas E. Miller, a legislator from Beaufort County, South Carolina.[7]

At the core of the Reconstruction agenda was tax policy. The Reconstructionists did not all agree with one another, especially when it came to how much economic transformation they thought the government should impose. The most radical few, like Senator Gaines, wished to redistribute wealth from the beneficiaries of slavery to its victims. But many believed that the end of slavery, the protection of civil rights and equality under the law, and the provision of public education would be enough to allow freedmen to prosper. For moderates and radicals alike, however, the hope for multiracial democracy rested upon the capacity of the new governments to tax their citizens. Social revolutions are expensive; the goals of Reconstruction required an influx of revenue.

Because Radical Reconstruction was so short-lived, and the backlash to it so immediate and so violent, the work of the Reconstruction governments has largely been overshadowed in American historical memory by the white supremacist movements that overthrew them. As Chapter 6 will show, taxes played a central role in Reconstruction's defeat. But the policies proposed and implemented by the Reconstructionists deserve thorough consideration, and so this chapter focuses on the Reconstruction tax agenda. During this period, America's political institutions aspired to racial equality in a way that would not be matched for nearly another hundred years. Americans should know what the Reconstruction legislators fought for, and what they achieved.

TAXES FOR SCHOOLS

As Frederick Douglass explained in his first autobiography, reading was the "pathway from slavery to freedom." In the antebellum South, to teach an enslaved person to read had been illegal, punishable by fines, imprisonment, and flogging; in some places, antiliteracy laws applied to free Blacks as well. Despite the dangers, some enslaved people taught themselves to read in secret, and 5 to 10 percent of Black people could read in 1860. Before the Civil War had even been won, Black Southerners organized hundreds of their own community schools. Their urgency amazed onlookers. "What other people on earth have ever shown," asked one visitor from the Freedmen's Bureau, "such a passion for education?"[8]

During Radical Reconstruction, Southern state governments attempted to provide universal public schooling for Black and white children. In Mississippi, for instance, the Republican state convention of 1867 resolved to "give free education to every child," a policy goal they listed even before universal suffrage.[9] The new schools at first often served people of all ages, so that adult freedmen could finally learn to read and write. The famed civil rights activist Ida B. Wells, born to enslaved parents in Mississippi in 1862, recalled in her autobiography that her mother attended school with Ida and her siblings "until she learned to read the Bible."[10]

Reconstruction also marked, in many parts of the South, the first time free public education was available to whites. Texas's first free public school opened its doors in September 1871; before Reconstruction, public money raised for schools had simply been divided among private schools that would accept some white students willing to enter as "paupers." In Mississippi, there were no public school buildings in the state outside a few in the larger towns. Overall, only 35 percent of Southern school-age whites were enrolled in school in 1860, compared to 72 percent elsewhere in America. During Reconstruction, legislators were obliged to raise enough revenue to build thousands of new schools for all children.[11]

One of the most important tasks was to develop, as rapidly as possible, a Southern teaching force. In 1870, the board of trustees of Shaw University, a recently opened private Black college in Holly Springs, Mississippi, offered to turn its teacher-training department into a public teaching college. The state legislature accepted the proposal, and Mississippi State Normal School for Colored Youth opened the following year, receiving around $4,000 a year from the state for salaries, materials, and student aid. State Normal, as it was known, was soon training over one hundred teachers a year. The principal, Margaret Hunter, a teacher from Illinois, reported in 1873 that the school had "a full supply of necessary text-books and maps" and that, thanks to donations, a "reference library has been begun." Frank Hazard Brown, who was born enslaved on the Mississippi-Louisiana border, earned his teaching certificate from State Normal. Over the following decades, Brown and his wife, Narcissa, another State Normal graduate, taught school in Mississippi and Arkansas, and organized a high school for Lawrence County. When Brown was seventy-five, his life story was recorded as part of the New Deal's Slave Narratives Project; his framed teaching certificate still hung on his wall.[12]

The progress in Black education came at enormous risk; from the end of the Civil War, Southern whites waged a terrorist campaign against Black schooling. Teachers were threatened, assaulted, and sometimes murdered. "Twice I have been shot at in my room," wrote Edmonia Highgate, a free Black woman from the North, who was teaching in 1866 in Lafayette Parish, Louisiana. "Some of my night-school scholars have been shot but none killed."[13] Schools were often destroyed. In March 1871, terrorists burned down every school building and every Black church that housed a school in Winston County, Mississippi.[14]

Reconstruction legislators did what they could to try to reduce Southern white hostility to Black schools. To accommodate the biases of white families, most states racially segregated their school systems, though separation opened the door to unequal facilities, and duplicative services made public education much more expensive. Only in South Carolina and Louisiana, where the state constitutional conventions had Black majorities, did the Reconstruction constitutions explicitly require integration. In other states, constitutions and school laws were vaguer in their wording, and in practice segregated schools were the norm.[15]

Another accommodation made to conservatives was the perpetuation of the poll tax. A poll tax, which levies a fixed sum on every individual, rich or poor, takes no account of a taxpayer's ability to pay. Many delegates to Reconstruction constitutional conventions proposed to ban this form of taxation. In Alabama, W. C. Garrison, a white Methodist preacher representing Blount County, and Arthur Bingham of Talladega, who would later serve as Alabama's first Republican treasurer, both introduced poll tax bans.[16] So did Matthew T. Newsom, a Black minister representing Claiborne County, Mississippi, who called the tax "grievous and oppressive."[17] Some legislators also worried—with reason, it would soon transpire—that the poll tax might be used as a tool of disenfranchisement, if voters were obligated to demonstrate that they had paid.[18]

But other delegates felt that a poll tax had advantages. A poll tax ensured that every man contributed to the new government, including the poorest Black and white families who would benefit most directly from free schooling. So poll taxes were reduced, capped, and earmarked for education. The Mississippi Constitution of 1868, for example, allowed that the "Legislature may levy a poll tax, not to exceed two dollars a head, in aid of the school fund, and for no other purpose." The Reconstruction poll tax was a compromise in the name of universal education.

TAXES FOR LAND

Only weeks after his "march to the sea" had debilitated the Confederacy, US General William Tecumseh Sherman met in Savannah with a delegation of Black religious leaders. Garrison Frazier was a sixty-seven-year-old Baptist minister who had purchased freedom for himself and his wife eight years earlier. "The way we can best take care of ourselves is to have land," he told the general, "and turn it and till it by our own labor."[19]

Without land, penniless freedmen would be forced to work for their former owners, who wanted to keep them in a state as close to slavery as they could achieve.[20] Could tax policy help Black families buy a homestead, and thereby achieve the economic independence that would secure their new political freedom? Many Reconstructionists hoped so.

In principle, land reform could have been accomplished by methods much more direct than state tax policy. The United States could have expropriated the insurrectionary planter class to reimburse the North for the costs of the war or as a penalty for treason. The federal government could then have redistributed plantation lands to freedmen, either as reparations for slavery, as a reward for loyalty to the Union, or through a favorable loan program of the sort made available to white settlers on the frontier. Indeed, only days after his meeting with Black ministers in Savannah, General Sherman decided to pursue this more direct path to land redistribution. Sherman's Special Field Order No. 15 reserved a four-hundred-thousand-acre swath of land between Charleston and Florida to be divided among freedmen in forty-acre plots.[21]

The federal government could also have achieved land reform through tax policy—in fact, it nearly did. Three years earlier, in the middle of the Civil War, Congress had passed a tax that applied to "insurrectionary districts" and was required to be paid in person. If you failed to pay your tax—for instance, because you were too busy leading a rebel army—your lands were seized. This legislation is why Arlington National Cemetery exists today. It was built upon Arlington, the Virginia plantation of Confederate General Robert E. Lee, whose lands were among those seized for tax debt under the 1862 law.[22]

The tax debt lands formed the basis for the first land redistribution to freedmen. Starting in the summer of 1863, Arlington was the site of a model community for the formerly enslaved, known as Freedman's Village, that came to encompass hundreds of homes, several stores, a school, a hospital, and two churches. That fall, President Lincoln issued orders to the Union tax commissioners for South Carolina to survey and sell lands held by Union forces that had been abandoned by owners abetting the rebellion. Lincoln specified that he wanted "heads of families of the African race" to be able to purchase small homesteads. In December, Lincoln added instructions that those already occupying and cultivating the land could choose and purchase up to "two tracts of twenty acres each." This order marks the first official reference to forty acres: the size of plot a family of freedmen could claim from the lands of the tax-defaulting planter rebels.[23]

Such promises were, however, ultimately forsaken. After Lincoln's assassination, President Andrew Johnson overturned the earlier land policies, returning confiscated lands to the former Confederate planters. Black people who had settled and built communities on abandoned lands were evicted. (Freedman's Village successfully resisted eviction for decades but was closed in 1900.) Despite the efforts of Republican House leader Thaddeus Stevens, who devoted his final years to the cause of land reform, the freedmen never received their "forty acres and a mule."[24]

At the state level, some Southern Republicans sought to achieve what the army and the federal government had not. In Texas and in South Carolina, radicals called for freedmen to receive back pay from the time of the Emancipation Proclamation, January 1, 1863, until the actual end of slavery, imposed by the Union Army in 1865. The legal premise here was unassailable: Because the Confederacy had never been legitimate, the law of the United States had always applied in the South, and so anyone enslaved in the insurrectionary South during or after 1863 was owed wages. Nevertheless, the idea of such immense redistribution was too subversive for the more moderate Republicans.[25]

Thus, while seizing Native land and redistributing it to white people was standard practice in America, seizing slaveholders' land to distribute to the formerly enslaved was beyond what could be achieved in even the most radical moments of the Civil War era. Confiscation was simply too revolutionary—even many Black legislators opposed the policy—and so the direct routes to land redistribution had been foreclosed by the time the Radical Reconstruction governments took office.[26] What remained was taxation.

Even here, the path was circuitous. In only one state, South Carolina, were taxes used to purchase plantations that were then divided into small plots and made available for purchase on easy terms.[27] In most states, taxes were expected to lead to redistribution by spurring private land sales.

Heavy taxes could make property hoarding less appealing, Reconstructionists believed—a hope that echoed that of frontier farmers and democrats in the early days of the republic. Most Southern farmland was undeveloped. The aristocratic planter held, in the words of South Carolina Governor Franklin Moses, "thousands of acres idle and unproductive merely to gratify his personal vanity." In Louisiana, a delegate suggested doubling the property tax for uncultivated land. Moreover, much of the cultivated

Southern land had fallen into disuse during and after the war. "Until this tax can be placed upon these lands it will be as in 1865," Thomas Bayne asserted at the Virginia Constitutional Convention in 1867, "and the same old dreary wilderness will remain."[28]

Bayne had escaped slavery twelve years earlier and prospered in his adopted home of New Bedford, Massachusetts, where he had been elected to the city council. But at the end of the war, Bayne returned to Virginia to lead the state's radicals.[29] He was one of the most outspoken proponents of a high property tax, decrying "that old slaveholding hell of touching the lands lightly." Lands were, indeed, extremely undertaxed across the South. In one county in Mississippi, land that was being rented for seven dollars an acre was valued for tax purposes at one dollar an acre.[30] Bayne wanted to eliminate these enormous tax subsidies of the antebellum era. "I ask this Convention to tax these lands and tax them heavy," Bayne told his colleagues.[31]

High taxes would make land available in two ways. Either planters would be obliged to sell their lands to pay their tax bills or, if they did not pay, the government could confiscate the land for tax debts. The landless poor, Black and white, might be able to acquire land in the resulting sales, if those lands were sold in small enough lots. There was some reason for hope in this strategy; freedmen had indeed managed to secure land from tax sales under President Lincoln's December 1863 order.[32]

In the absence of land reform, there was no direct way to provide compensation or economic independence to formerly enslaved people. But taxation might indirectly lead to the breakup of the great estates of the former slaveholders. Given how low land taxes had been before the war, it seemed plausible that regularizing the tax code might change patterns of landownership. William Beverly Nash, a South Carolina legislator who had opposed land confiscation, thought taxes were the right mechanism to make land available to freedmen like himself: "I want them taxed until they put these lands back where they belong, into the hands of those who worked for them."[33]

THE RADICAL PROPERTY TAX

A new and stronger property tax was a central component of the Reconstruction agenda, whether or not it encouraged land sales. This was a practical reality—after emancipation, most Southern wealth was in land—and also an ideological commitment. "If we do not tax the land," said Francis Moss, a freeborn Black man representing Buckingham County at the Virginia convention, "we might just as well not have come here to make a Constitution."[34] Making taxes proportionate to wealth would signal the government's new respect for labor and would comport with the broader goal of instituting equal treatment under the law. But it wasn't merely the distribution of taxation that was radical—the very act of property tax assessment was itself nothing less than revolutionary.

The right of a worker to his income was at the core of the antislavery argument, and this commitment carried over into Republican debates over taxation. As James Hunnicutt, a white Republican newspaper editor and minister, framed the issue, "Tax the property, but let the man go free." Property taxes were, in essence, wealth taxes, and it was only fair to make taxes proportionate to the taxpayer's resources. "I want the people, according to their ability, to pay the taxes," insisted Willis A. Hodges, a Virginia convention delegate who had been active in the Underground Railroad.[35]

Making taxes proportionate to wealth marked an enormous change in the Southern tax system. The prewar South had relied on a hodgepodge of professional licenses and specific taxes on luxury items like watches. By some accounts, merchants paid five or six times the amount of taxes paid by equivalently wealthy planters.[36] So the new general property tax was also a way of creating consistency and uniformity, eliminating the special tax breaks that typified the antebellum Southern fiscal system.

But applying a uniform property tax requires calculating what each piece of property is worth—and this process of assessment was among the most radical aspects of the Reconstruction tax agenda. Before the war, a petty bureaucrat valuing a slaveholder's property would have called into question his absolute patriarchal control over his estate. Slave states struggled to implement property taxes for precisely this reason—and when they did, they often avoided real assessment procedures. In Georgia, for example, property holders asserted the value of their estate and, by law, officials could not dispute the owner's estimate. A similar system existed in South Carolina. "The tax collector went around and received your own account of your property," one planter explained. "You were allowed to value your land at 50 cents or $10 an acre, just as you pleased."[37]

The Radical Reconstruction governments wanted to impose actual government assessments, both because this would prevent self-interested undervaluation and because it would make clear that the laws applied to everyone, including the planter class. Plantation owners, accustomed to the unquestioning acceptance of their own assessments, would undoubtedly have found the new system an adjustment under any circumstance—but real tax assessment was particularly galling during Reconstruction because the officials assessing and collecting the taxes were sometimes Black men.[38] Some tax assessors were former slaves, now tasked with evaluating the property of their former owners, a complete reversal of the social order that had existed under slavery.[39] And even when the tax assessors were white, they were still a very visible reminder that everyone was now accountable to a democratic government that included Black people.

Corruption-fighting South Carolina Treasurer Francis Cardozo was the highest-ranking Black man in the state's Reconstruction government. (Credit: Library of Congress)

Opposition to taxes under Reconstruction was exacerbated by the steep increase in tax rates. Taxes as a percentage of assessed value of property more than quadrupled in a decade. In part, rates had to go up because Southern wealth had gone down. The war had destroyed a substantial amount of Southern property, and land values had collapsed. But most of the "decline in property values" would be better understood as "emancipation." Nearly four million people who were once counted on slaveholders' property ledgers were now free. More than a third of antebellum Southern wealth had been held in slaves, and the abolition of slavery eliminated this part of the property tax base. Thus, tax rates would have gone up under any government, just to maintain even the paltry prewar tax revenues.[40]

Of course, Reconstruction governments were not simply trying to match the tax revenues of the prewar period; they were attempting to rebuild their states and put in place a public school system. An indication of the special commitment of Black officeholders to these goals, Reconstruction taxes increased more where Black political power was greater. Economist Trevon Logan estimates that each additional Black politician "increased per capita county tax revenue by $0.20, more than an hour's wage at the time."[41]

Despite these increases, Southern taxes only rose to levels comparable to those of the rest of the country. As a fraction of wealth, local taxes in Southern states remained at or below levels found in the Northwest and Midwest. The highest per capita tax rates in 1870 were found in Nevada, Massachusetts, California, Connecticut, and New York. The key fact about taxes under Reconstruction is not that they rose so high, but that they started so low.[42]

Although taxes went up, the idea of graduated rates was never seriously on the table. Though state property taxes did have exemptions for small amounts of property (for instance, a mechanic's tools or a small amount of livestock), property taxes were applied at a single rate. South Carolina legislator William Beverly Nash proposed that uncultivated land should be taxed at a 1 percent higher rate than cultivated land, which would have shifted the weight of taxation off small farmers—but his proposal was tabled. A graduated license tax on business proprietors and professionals was similarly criticized as unequal and unfair, and quickly repealed. Only in Virginia was there a surtax on high incomes. The kind of progressive taxation we are used to today, with higher rates on higher brackets, would only gain widespread currency in the United States many decades later.

Rapidly rising tax rates provided ammunition for charges of corruption and waste. Corruption was indeed an endemic problem among Democrats and Republicans, North and South, in the second half of the nineteenth century. According to historian Eric Foner, the most egregious cases of corruption in the South tended to be when the state provided loans to "finance grandiose dreams of railroad empire," which led to "a scramble for influence that produced bribery, insider dealing, and a get-rich-quick atmosphere." Ironically, one motivation for railroad investments was the hope that an economic boom would make Reconstruction more palatable for white conservatives.[43]

But opponents of Reconstruction were quick to attribute financial mismanagement to Republican governance and Black suffrage. In reality, Black legislators often spoke out against corporate-friendly investments, and the businessmen who were the instigators of bribes and beneficiaries of the resulting legislation were usually white Democrats.[44] However, the charge that tax money was being mishandled would serve as a fundamental claim of generations of racist historians who sought to malign the Reconstruction governments.[45] And, as we will see, accusations of wasted tax money would become a central argument of the planter elite in their bid to retake power.

VICTORIES AND DEFEATS

How effective were the Reconstruction tax reforms in providing funding for the schools and making land more available for freedmen? In a sense, we can never know, because the resistance of former Confederates to the fiscal policies of the Reconstruction governments was so strong. The economist Trevon Logan has found that for each additional dollar of per capita county taxes collected, the chances that a Black politician was physically attacked rose by more than 25 percent.[46] A powerful fiscal state in the hands of a multiracial majority was anathema to Reconstruction's opponents, and undermining the tax system was a key component of the effort to overthrow that democracy.

Almost as soon as new tax laws were passed, Reconstruction governments faced widespread tax evasion or, as W. E. B. Du Bois called it, "an organized and bitter boycott of property."[47] Evasion was abetted by a campaign of white supremacist terrorism against the representatives of the fiscal state. Tax assessors and collectors were regularly threatened with violence if they attempted to do their jobs. Those who persisted did so at risk of their lives. Across the South, tax officials were dragged from their homes at night, whipped, and beaten by masked Klansmen. Samuel Brown, a tax assessor in Alabama, reported to Congress that he was "unable in person to discharge my duty as an officer without protection." A white Southerner and former Confederate soldier, Brown nonetheless called for the federal military to intervene and restore order. In Jackson County, Florida, the Ku Klux Klan threatened Homer Bryan, a Black man serving as the local tax collector, when he sold lands owned by local whites who had not paid their taxes. Bryan escaped, but the Klan killed his assistant, a white Northerner. In Newberry County, South Carolina, Klansmen came in the night to the home of a Black county commissioner and shot and wounded him, his wife, and his child. Other tax officials avoided assault or murder by going into hiding, sometimes for weeks.[48]

Predictably, taxes went uncollected in regions where terrorist campaigns were underway. In Monroe County, Mississippi, a mob of 120 Klansmen threatened to lynch A. P. Huggins—a school superintendent responsible for estimating the county's tax revenue needs—if he did not abandon his job. When he refused, they beat him unconscious. Despite Huggins's personal bravery, the school tax was never collected; the local board of supervisors, who had also been threatened, refused to make assessments. Local tax boards and sheriffs ceased their work. Empty positions were left vacant.[49]

Violence also made it nearly impossible to assess taxes fairly. If tax assessors could not safely visit a property, they were of course less able to judge its value. Opponents of the Reconstruction governments regularly griped that assessments were inaccurate and that tax processes were occurring in secret, while winking at or participating in violence against any tax official daring to show his face. Moreover, though large amounts of land were nominally forfeited, whites colluded to prevent tax sales, or to return property to its original owners after the sale. Newspapers printed anonymous threats against those who might buy land being auctioned for tax debt; one such letter in the Charleston *Daily News* was signed "One hundred men who fought under Lee." In many places, tax sales were nothing more than a farce.[50]

Rampant tax evasion led to budget crises, as expected revenue did not appear on time, or at all. In 1870 in South Carolina, nearly a third of the total state levy was delinquent. Shortages of tax funds made higher tax rates necessary, encouraging yet more evasion. States were obliged to issue debt paper, which immediately lost value when tax collections seemed insecure, leading to even larger budget shortfalls.[51]

This is not, however, merely a story of defeat. Even in the face of a drastically smaller tax base and rampant tax resistance, Reconstruction governments did manage to raise funds. Much of that money went to the school system. Alabama, for instance, nearly doubled its school fund from its prewar level. By 1871, about nine hundred thousand young people were enrolled in public schools across the former Confederacy, amounting to nearly a third of young people in those states. South Carolina's Reconstruction government was particularly effective in increasing access to education. In 1857, only about nineteen thousand white students attended free public schools; by 1873, nearly eighty-six thousand students were enrolled, including thirty-seven thousand white students. Not only was public education being provided to tens of thousands of Black children, but almost twice as many white children were attending school as before the war. As late as 1871, a child in South Carolina was half as likely to be enrolled in school as a child in New York. By 1875, enrollment rates were *higher* in South Carolina than in New York. Mississippi, another Black-majority state with a comparatively long period of Radical Reconstruction, achieved nearly as much as South Carolina; enrollment rates in 1874 were only 2 percent below the comparable figure in New York.[52]

In both Mississippi and South Carolina, the end of Reconstruction coincided with a sharp decline in school enrollment. Nonetheless, Reconstruction-era investments had a lasting impact, particularly where more Black politicians had served. Literacy among Black males doubled in ten years, and Black women were for the first time more likely to be literate than Black men.[53]

But while the Reconstruction era saw measurable gains in Southern public education, tax policy did not result in widespread Black landownership. Some Black families did overcome the odds and acquire land, but the tax system did not do much to help them. High taxes led to farms being consolidated rather than being broken into smaller lots. South Carolina Representative William J. Whipper had anticipated this possibility as early as the constitutional convention of 1868. If lands were sold in large tracts, he observed, "nobody but a capitalist will be able to buy." Freedmen, only a few years removed from the destitution of slavery, only rarely had the resources necessary to purchase a farm. Leaders like North Carolina State Senator Abraham Galloway, who had escaped slavery in 1857 and served as a spy for the Union Army before running for office, believed that high property taxes would mean "we negroes can become land holders." But this hope remained unrealized.[54]

Taxation was at once too weak a reed and too blunt an instrument to achieve the great aspirations of Reconstruction. Too weak because without far more military support from the North, tax laws could not be effectively enforced. Too blunt because the new property tax laws could not target the planter class and therefore were no substitute for land reform.[55]

COUNTERREVOLUTION

Senator Matthew Gaines's agenda, as he outlined it in front of the Brenham courthouse in 1871, expressed a deeply radical version of what were widely shared goals among Reconstructionists: to use tax policy to provide schools and land. Taxes would pay for a new polity in which Black people could be free and equal participants.

We know what Senator Gaines said on that June day because Dan McGary, a vehement opponent of Radical Reconstruction, reported more than three thousand words of Gaines's speech in his newspaper, the Houston *Age*.[56] Democrats across Texas and as far away as Michigan and Indiana took Gaines's speech as evidence of the misrule and oppression of the Radical governments, reprinting the text under headlines like "Radicalism, as Expounded by a Leading Negro" and "A Misanthropic Darkie."[57]

Gaines's speech thumped any number of political hornets' nests, but if an intemperate speech might be overlooked, the tax law was not.[58] By August 1871, one of Texas's only reliable white Republican voting blocs, German Americans, were threatening to bolt the party over the taxes that Gaines had so eloquently defended only a few weeks earlier. Gaines tried to reach these voters through the papers, in a letter both cajoling and desperate:

> I am informed that you are going over to the Democratic party, so that you may help them to repeal the tax law; that you cannot stand the taxes you have to pay. So let me ask you one thing: Can you not stand the taxes you have to pay as well as you stood the Democratic storms of 1861, when you had to leave your wives and children and go to the war, risking your lives for the slaves, when you owned none? Now that peace has been restored, and you can stay at home, vote and hold office in peace, and pay your taxes as free men ought to do, are you ready to forsake the government to whom you are indebted for all these blessings, and turn it over to its and your own enemies? . . . If you are Republicans, stand fast to your principles, no matter what I have said or done—I am but one man and am liable to make mistakes as well as others. Do not depart from your first faith and order, pay your taxes and be free. . . . Let me hear from you through the papers.[59]

As Gaines feared, Unionist sentiment and lingering resentment over the war were not enough to keep German American voters solidly in the Republican column. The 1871 election brought an end to Radical Reconstruction in Texas. Gaines himself was re-elected, but a Democratic-led senate committee fraudulently declared him ineligible to serve; his opponent received his seat instead.[60]

In Texas and across the South, tax opposition was a powerful tool in the hands of Reconstruction's enemies. As we will see, taxes were essential to achieving the goals of Reconstruction and equally central to the destruction of those hopes.

6

REDEMPTION

Rise of the Taxpayer

For the holders of property and the payers of taxes, a voice
—South Carolina Tax-Payers' Convention

"My position here is peculiar, and, in many of its features, trying,"
said Daniel Chamberlain in a speech before the 1871 South
Carolina Tax-Payers' Convention.[1]

This was an understatement. An abolitionist from Massachusetts, Chamberlain had served as an officer in the Union Army and led a cavalry regiment of Black volunteers into battle. After the war, he entered politics as a delegate to the South Carolina Constitutional Convention that enfranchised Black men. Now, only a few years later, he was serving as vice president of a convention that was led by South Carolina's old guard, men who regretted nothing about the war other than the outcome. His fellow executive officers at the convention included W. D. Porter, who had described the new state constitution as an "enormity" and pledged that the white men of the country would "assert their common, natural and indefeasible right to be the rulers of the land"; Matthew C. Butler, a former Confederate general and first cousin to Preston Brooks, the South Carolina congressman who had beat Massachusetts Senator Charles Sumner nearly to death on the

Senate floor in 1856; and James Chesnut, the former Confederate general who, ten years after ordering the firing on Fort Sumter, declared himself utterly "unrepentant." One of the most active members of the Tax-Payers, the former Confederate General Martin W. Gary, had famously refused to surrender at Appomattox.[2]

No wonder Chamberlain felt ill at ease. But what on earth was he doing there? Chamberlain seems to have believed that by participating in the Tax-Payers' Convention, he could travel a middle ground between Reconstruction's radicals and its most ardent opponents, thus creating a space for comity and consensus. At the convention, he advanced a system of proportional voting to give whites greater say in the Black-majority state. Chamberlain also asked the convention to investigate "alleged" Ku Klux Klan violence, hoping that the terrorism might subside if the state's native white elite registered their objections.[3] Above all, Chamberlain believed that by addressing the fiscal concerns of the Tax-Payers, he could convince them to support the new government.

The Tax-Payers, meanwhile, were thrilled to count a Republican among their ranks, which they pointed to as evidence that their movement was not "political."[4] The Tax-Payers similarly referred to the four Black attendees, among the hundreds of convention-goers, to demonstrate that their concerns were not a matter of race.[5] And while the Tax-Payers insisted that they sought only "a voice and a representation in the councils of the State," their tepid response to Chamberlain's proposed system of proportional representation made clear that their goal was complete political control.[6] One participant, former Governor John L. Manning, complained, "We, by this cumulative voting, shall be confined to one-third the power to which we are entitled," while General Gary, chair of the committee on elections, described universal suffrage as a "monstrous political fallacy."[7]

Nonetheless, Chamberlain was apparently convinced of the sincerity of the Tax-Payers' fiscal concerns. Appealing to white taxpayers was a central part of his political strategy when he became the Republican governor of the state in 1874. Working closely with the Black state treasurer, Francis Cardozo, Chamberlain fought against government corruption. His administration lowered the property tax rate and revised the tax assessment process, cut appropriations for public schools by one-fourth, and instituted a system of convict leasing to reduce penitentiary costs.[8] The state university, which served almost exclusively Black students, was to be reconfigured, as Chamberlain put it, into a "good high school."[9]

For a time, Chamberlain basked in conservative praise, but his strategy of appeasement was ultimately unsuccessful. For many former Confederate leaders, the goal was never fiscal probity; it was unalloyed political power. Chamberlain should have expected as much. In Louisiana, Governor William Pitt Kellogg's personal honesty and tax cuts had not forestalled the rise of the terrorist White Leagues in 1874. After the governor condemned the 1876 Hamburg Massacre, in which his fellow Tax-Payer Matthew C. Butler had directed the murder of Black militia members, Democrats decisively broke with Chamberlain.[10]

Soon thereafter, Martin W. Gary, another of Chamberlain's erstwhile Tax-Payer colleagues, orchestrated a campaign of election violence in support of Chamberlain's opponent, the Democratic leader and former Confederate General Wade Hampton. Remarkably, the original draft of Gary's "Plan of the Campaign 1876," which was edited and sent to Democratic county leaders across South Carolina, has been preserved. "Democratic Military Clubs are to be armed with rifles and pistols," he wrote. "Every Democrat must

Martin Witherspoon Gary, a leader at the South Carolina Tax-Payers' Convention, orchestrated the 1876 campaign of election violence that overthrew multiracial democracy in the state. (Credit: Duke University Libraries Digital Collection)

feel honor bound to control the vote of at least one Negro, by intimidation, purchase, keeping him away or as each individual may determine, how he may best accomplish it."[11] Outside local Republican meetings, armed riders sang, "We'll hang Dan Chamberlain to a sour apple tree." The goal, as one participant would nostalgically recall many decades later, was "to hold up to the gaze and din into the ears of the negroes the picture and sound and menace of war against them."[12]

The terrorism of the "Red Shirts," as the Democratic paramilitaries were known, was effective. In Edgefield, where Gary resided, Democrats received two thousand more votes than the total white voting population. Fraudulent and coerced votes gave Democratic candidate Wade Hampton a narrow,

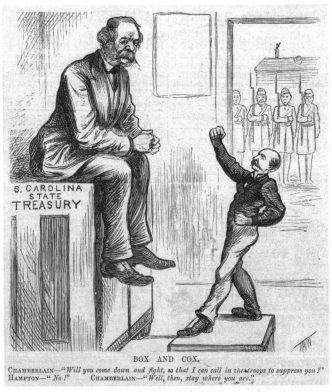

BOX AND COX.

CHAMBERLAIN—"*Will you come down and fight, so that I can call in the troops to suppress you?*"
HAMPTON—"*No!*"   CHAMBERLAIN—"*Well, then, stay where you are.*"

In 1877, Wade Hampton seized the South Carolina Treasury and promised President Hayes that if he was not recognized as governor, every Republican tax collector in the state would be "hanged within twenty-four hours." (Credit: Library of Congress)

thousand-vote lead in the gubernatorial race.[13] Citing voter intimidation and fraud, Chamberlain refused to concede the election.

For a brief period, South Carolina had two competing administrations. But Chamberlain's failed strategy of courting Democrats had weakened the Republican Party statewide, and within weeks, Hampton had consolidated control of key aspects of the state apparatus, including the Treasury. The only thing keeping Chamberlain in the state house was an armed guard of federal troops.

Hampton and Chamberlain were called to Washington to meet with the new president, Rutherford B. Hayes. Hayes had recently been declared the winner of the contested 1876 presidential election, despite losing the popular vote, because he had been awarded the disputed electoral votes for South Carolina, as well as Florida and Louisiana, where Democrats had similarly relied on violence and voter intimidation to challenge the state's Reconstruction governments.

Chamberlain was obliged to admit to the president that he could not stay in power without the support of the army. Hampton, by contrast, was pugnacious. President Hayes asked Hampton what would happen if he were not recognized as governor. Every "Republican tax collector in the state," Hampton told the president, would be "hanged within twenty-four hours."[14] One might think openly threatening to murder government officials, members of President Hayes's own party, would be a dangerous provocation. But by this time everyone knew that the North no longer had the stomach to protect democracy in the South. Hayes ended military protection for Chamberlain.

At first, Chamberlain wished to fight on. But State Treasurer Francis Cardozo, the highest-ranking Black man in the South Carolina state government, convinced him that the result would only be additional bloodshed.[15] In his address to the Republicans of South Carolina, upon withdrawing from office, Chamberlain wrote, "Today, April 10, 1877, by the order of the President whom your votes alone rescued from overwhelming defeat, the Government of the United States abandons you."[16]

General Wade Hampton, hero of the Confederacy, became the governor of South Carolina. Only a few months later, Matthew C. Butler was seated in the US Senate. Reconstruction was over.

TAXPAYER LEAGUES, TERRORISM, AND THE
REDEEMERS' APPEAL TO POORER WHITES

The South Carolina Tax-Payers are the best known of the many taxpayer associations that sprang up to help overthrow the Radical Republican governments. The associations were themselves only transient institutions, but their impact was substantial and long-lasting.[17] Across the South, opposition to taxation allowed former Confederates to successfully challenge the radical egalitarian promise of Reconstruction. As we saw in the previous chapter, the effort to undermine tax collection was a direct and effective attack on the functioning of a multiracial government. Taxes empowered Reconstruction governments, and tax resistance weakened them. And in defining themselves as taxpayers, opponents of Reconstruction, known as "Redeemers," also cemented two crucial groups as allies: poorer whites and Northern elites.

Organizing as "taxpayers" helped elites make common cause with whites of middling wealth, whose support they needed to retake political control. Small white farmers, some of whom had previously voted Republican, struggled to pay rising land taxes and actively resisted federal taxes on liquor. The category of "taxpayer" elided the vast economic gulf between a millionaire plantation owner and a small farmer, allowing complaints about taxes to cut across class lines and, as the historian Eric Foner has argued, to serve as "an effective rallying cry for opponents of Reconstruction."[18]

At the same time, by casting taxpayers as victims of a corrupt government, Southern elites disguised a violent movement to seize power as a respectable campaign for good governance. The Ku Klux Klan, the White League, the Red Shirts, and other paramilitary and terrorist groups intimidated, assaulted, and murdered voters and public officials—but Southern elites minimized the violence and insisted it was a localized and understandable reaction to the corruption and oppressive taxation of the Reconstruction governments. While supporters of Reconstruction often pointed out that the violence began with Black suffrage in 1868, before the Radical Reconstruction governments had even formed, much less collected any taxes, these protests had little effect on public perception. Complaints about burdensome taxes and government corruption appealed to moderate whites in both the North and South.

As "taxpayers," wealthy whites could directly attack the functioning of government, overcome divisions among Southern whites, and make their grievances appear reasonable to Northerners. By asserting that the taxpayers were those with a right to rule, they turned a critique of government corruption into a case for oligarchy.

A core concern of the planter elite was to stymie any kind of cross-racial working-class alliance. The Southern elite needed whites of middling wealth for their votes and for their paramilitary support. The taxpayer leagues helped achieve both ends.

The planter class had good reason to worry about the loyalty of the upcountry. Poorer whites had contested the political power of the planters in the antebellum period and, during the Civil War, had been the primary source of pro-Union sentiment in the white South. As the Confederate regime seized their crops and sent their sons to die in defense of slavery, communities in the South's more mountainous regions engaged in an active campaign of draft resistance.[19] The white South's class tensions were never far from the surface.

Early in the Radical Reconstruction period, upcountry voters shocked conservatives by voting Republican. "Let no foolish prejudice stand in the way" of an interracial alliance against the "rebels," argued one newspaper in North Carolina, where about a quarter of white voters endorsed a government based on universal suffrage. Of course, Southern whites willing to support Reconstruction shared the racist views of other whites of the era, but upcountry radicals were enthused about defeating the planter class. A Union League leader in Alabama wrote that his county was "in for a confiscation of the property of the secessionists." About half of registered whites in the poorer counties of the state voted with Black Southerners to hold a constitutional convention. A year later, when most whites were observing a statewide election boycott, about a quarter of whites in those counties (and a tenth of white voters statewide) voted to ratify that new constitution.[20]

Although upcountry radicals comprised only a minority of whites, their participation in the Reconstruction conventions and legislatures came as a shock to the genteel antebellum elite. They believed these "scalawags," as Southern white Reconstructionists would become known, were almost equally unfit to serve in office as their Black colleagues. As one conservative from Tennessee would say, white Republicans were those "paying no taxes, riding poor horses, wearing dirty shirts, and having no use for soap."[21] But the upcountry whites were nevertheless a vital bloc at the ballot box and in the legislatures. Conservative planters realized that they would have to muffle their aristocratic disdain for the white masses and work to bring them back to the Democratic Party.

With taxation, conservatives found a policy that would help them secure control of the upcountry.[22] Because land taxes in the prewar period had been very low, the tax increases imposed by Reconstruction governments hit small white farmers hard, particularly because these farmers generally did not have much in the way of cash income. A small number of Republican farmers saw the increases as simply a price worth paying. Edward E. Holman, a white farmer from Holly Springs, Mississippi, saw his taxes nearly double in a single year, yet remained a Republican stalwart: "I have said to people that I was perfectly willing to pay my taxes, as it was to educate the country; that education was what we wanted; that if we had had more of it before the war, we never would have had the war."[23]

For far more small white farmers, however, the tax increases undermined whatever faith they had in the Republican Party. The were convinced by Democratic arguments that white taxes were paying for Black extravagance. The "poor whites of the country are to be taxed—bled of all their little earnings," as one conservative paper put it, "in order to fatten the vagabondish negroes."[24] Tax opposition became the central plank of the Democratic platform because it so effectively convinced poorer whites that their interests were at odds with those of Black freedmen. The electoral consequences were unmistakable. John Lynch, a freedman who represented Mississippi in the US House of Representatives, believed that the increase in taxation, though unavoidable, was so "unpopular that it came near losing the Legislature" for the Republicans in 1871.[25]

Anger about taxation was mobilized in part through taxpayer associations, which appeared in some states as early as 1868 and across the South by 1871. Taxpayers' "conventions," "unions," and "leagues" were active in Alabama, Florida, Louisiana, Mississippi, South Carolina, Tennessee, and

Texas.[26] Though the level of activity varied among the associations, they commonly held meetings, wrote memorials and resolutions, met with state leaders, rallied voters, and sometimes took officials to court. They also were critical to coordinated campaigns of nonpayment. As we saw in the previous chapter, the tax boycott was itself an effective attack on the Reconstruction governments.[27]

These were the official activities of the taxpayers' leagues. But they were not the only activities. Their more ominous role is hinted at in the proceedings of the South Carolina Tax-Payers' Convention, where the Tax-Payers suggested that the local unions would exact "just punishment" of government officials they deemed "robbers of the people."[28] Taxpayer organizations, in South Carolina and elsewhere, were very active in the violence against Reconstruction.

On March 9, 1871, a manifesto printed in a South Carolina newspaper, the *Yorkville Enquirer*, and signed with the initials "K.K.K.," contained the following line: "We do intend that the intelligent, honest white people (the tax-payers) of this county shall rule it!"[29] The Klan was, in this era, as much a tactic as a formal organization: Masked night riders would surround the homes of Black people and white Republicans and then threaten, assault, and sometimes murder them. In that campaign of terrorism, it was not uncommon for the Klan and allied paramilitary groups to present themselves as defenders of the taxpayer. One popular slogan went, "Old men in the Tax Unions and young men in the Rifle Clubs."[30] Antitax leagues and paramilitary groups were two prongs of the same campaign, and often two faces of the same organization.[31]

Paramilitary groups used tax resistance to gain popularity in areas where there were substantial numbers of white Republicans. The Klan was able to find a foothold in Appalachia by preventing the collection of a federal tax on liquor, thereby taking advantage of the region's long-standing resistance to whiskey taxation. It became widely known for its attacks on revenue agents, killing twenty-five officials in less than two years. Federal tax collectors, typically pro-Union Republicans, were indeed intimidated; one revenue agent reported that "'he dare not attempt to collect any taxes,' for fear of being 'Ku-Kluxed.'"[32]

Some men who by day attended taxpayer conventions terrorized their neighbors after nightfall. During a Klan trial in Raleigh, North Carolina, for instance, a Klansman testified that his plans to summon men in preparation for a raid the following night were delayed because he had stopped to attend a local "tax-payer's convention." Conveniently, however, several of the other attendees were already preparing for the raid at the convention that evening.[33] The following night, as planned, the local Klan attacked a white Republican state representative, James M. Justice, who was dragged from his bed into the street, threatened with lynching, and beaten unconscious.

In 1874, a taxpayer association in Vicksburg, Mississippi, provoked one of the most infamous massacres of the Reconstruction period. A freedman and US Army veteran named Peter Crosby served as the local sheriff and was responsible for the collection of taxes. On the date that taxes were due, five hundred members of the Vicksburg taxpayers' league marched to the courthouse and demanded the resignation of all Black officeholders. Crosby, fearing for his life, stepped down, but rode that night to the governors' mansion for assistance. With the support of the Republican governor, a small militia of Black citizens assembled and attempted to reinstate Crosby at the courthouse. They were met on the edge of the city by a white militia, who started firing, killing between seventy-five and three hundred Black citizens in what became known as the Vicksburg Massacre. "Those that fell wounded were murdered," reported Blanche Ames, the governor's wife.[34]

In taxation, Southern elites found an issue that could build an alliance with poorer whites who had initially shown some tenuous support for Reconstruction. That alliance was both electoral and paramilitary. From the upcountry Klan attacks against federal revenue agents to the murderous taxpayer league in Vicksburg to Martin W. Gary's "Red Shirts" in South Carolina, the taxpayers' associations were inseparable from campaigns of white supremacist terror.

TAXATION AS AN EXCUSE FOR VIOLENCE

Despite their participation in political violence, the taxpayer leagues managed to maintain a certain respectability. Because they were not explicitly partisan, or explicitly whites-only, participants could claim (however implausibly) that they were merely citizens oppressed by high taxation, rather than unrepentant Confederates contesting the Civil War by new means. In a hearing regarding the Vicksburg Massacre, one member of the local taxpayers' league insisted that "there was nothing political in it; colored men, if tax payers, could join."[35]

However thin the pretense, the taxpayers' respectability was crucial, because the overthrow of Reconstruction governments required the tacit approval of Northerners. Reconstruction's more publicly decorous opponents often switched from partisan and race-specific language to the facially color-blind language of taxpaying. Tax-Payer W. D. Porter, for example, had in 1868 described South Carolina as divided into "the educated white class" and "the uneducated colored class."[36] By 1874, he was referring to the two great classes of the state as "the one property-holding and taxpaying, the other non-property-holding and non-taxpaying."[37] It was not that overt racism was suddenly unacceptable in America, far from it. But if former Confederates were too obvious in their efforts to return the old order to power—for example, by calling for the wholesale exclusion of Black Americans from the political process—that could look to watching Northerners like a failure to accept the consequences of the war, and therefore a resurgence of secessionist treason. But when Reconstruction's opponents attacked the fiscal basis of the Reconstruction regimes, they found they could distract from, minimize, and even justify atrocities to Northern eyes.

The hearings into Klan violence held by Congress in 1871 offered an early indication of the effectiveness of taxpayer rhetoric in the North. In response to the wave of "Ku Kluxism" in 1870 and 1871, Congress passed new legislation, known as the Enforcement Acts, which gave federal and military officials in the South new powers to protect civil rights. It was a major victory for the supporters of Reconstruction. Democrats had tried unsuccessfully to stymie the legislation via a time-honored Washington maneuver: They called for the formation of a committee. In the partisan wrangle, a Joint Special Committee was formed in April 1871 to investigate Klan-style violence. The Ku Klux hearings were held in Washington and in seven Southern states, resulting in twelve volumes of transcripts. The testimonies remain historians' best source of firsthand accounts of the Klan during this period.

But the hearings were not intended to inform historians; they were intended to sway the public. To downplay the violence and to discredit the Republican governments in the South, Democrats on the committee turned attention from terrorism to taxes.

The first evidence of Democrats' success was the decision, in May, to expand the committee's purview from political violence to the fiscal state of the South. The Democrats then called Southern conservatives to testify about the burden of taxation and portray the Klan's violence as merely the unfortunate but understandable reaction of impoverished taxpayers to government malfeasance. The Democrats thereby changed the debate. Republicans were obliged to respond with evidence to the contrary, pointing out that taxes, if high, were within reason, and were in any case only a pretext for the violence, not its root cause. Taxes are mentioned literally thousands of times in the Ku Klux hearings, an average of once every three pages.

The Tax-Payers' Convention featured prominently in the hearings on South Carolina. In addition to testimonies from two of the convention's leaders, James Chesnut and Matthew C. Butler, the entirety of the official proceedings is included in the Joint Special Committee record—with careful notice given to the handful of Republican and "colored" members of the convention as an indication of the convention's nonpartisan nature.

Having been identified as unbiased observers, the Tax-Payers took every opportunity to downplay the violence in their state. Some South Carolina counties had seen literally hundreds of Klan attacks, but Chesnut assured Congress that disorder was "local and limited," and that "politics" was "not the basis" of any violence that occurred.[38] He also read from the report on violence produced by the Tax-Payers' Convention, which asserted that "in by far the larger number of the counties of the State, not a single instance of such violence has been brought to their attention."[39] When they were not denying the violence, the former Confederates defended it on fiscal grounds. Chesnut and Butler insisted to the Joint Special Committee that the disorder in South Carolina was a consequence of the fiscal crisis in the state: People were justifiably angry, they claimed, at the excessive taxation and spending.

Similar dynamics played out in hearings held in other states. Some moments are beyond parody. Asked about the Klan, Alabama secessionist Edmund Pettus asserted, "I have never known of any such organization myself" before offering a lengthy diatribe on the evils of the tax on cotton. Pettus is today remembered primarily for the bridge named after him, the site of "Bloody Sunday," where Alabama state troopers assaulted Martin Luther King Jr.'s nonviolent marchers, nearly killing John Lewis. But in his time, Pettus was the Grand Dragon of the Alabama Klan.[40]

What is most startling about the hearings, however, is not that Southern opponents of Reconstruction would deny the political violence in their states and their own role in that violence. Nor is it that they would attempt to discredit the Reconstruction governments on tax policy; the states were indeed in dire fiscal straits. What stands out is how fully Northern conservatives on the committee accepted fiscal issues as a reasonable excuse and even a justification for terrorism and murder.

The leader of the committee's Democrats was Senator Francis Blair of Missouri. Though he was a former Union general who had participated in Sherman's famed March to the Sea, Blair was deeply sympathetic to Reconstruction's enemies. He regularly suggested in his questioning that the Klan violence should be seen as a natural consequence of frustration with fiscal mismanagement. In an exchange typical of his approach, Blair asked one witness whether he attributed "much of the dissatisfaction and discontent and the disturbances which have taken place in your section of the State to the fact that these excessive taxes are levied?" Blair also evinced what can only be described as an obsession with the idea that Black people did not pay taxes, asking question after leading question on this subject. Occasionally, the witness would correct him. "The entire tax is paid by the white people; is it not?" Blair asked Finis H. Little, a farmer and state senator representing Monroe County, Mississippi. "No sir," the witness replied.[41]

At the end of the investigation, Blair led the Democrats of the committee in issuing a report that complained of a "non-tax paying junta" controlling the Reconstruction states and insisted that poor white people, driven to desperation by confiscatory taxes, were "all, or nearly all, there is, or ever was, of Ku-Kluxism." Reconstruction tax policy was, Blair argued, nothing more than a mechanism of racial domination: "True, indeed, is it that the best way to bring the white man down to the level of the negro is to *tax him down*."[42]

Immediately after the war, Blair's level of racist vitriol had been out of step with most Northern opinion, and in at least one prominent campaign, race-baiting on taxes had failed to produce a political victory. In Pennsylvania in 1866, Hiester Clymer's campaign for the Pennsylvania governorship included campaign posters attacking his opponent's support for the Freedmen's Bureau, declaring it "an agency to keep the Negro in Idleness at the Expense of the white man." In 1864 and 1865, the campaign poster alleged, the Freedmen's Bureau had "cost the Tax-payers of the Nation at least Twenty Five Millions of Dollars." The picture juxtaposed a white man chopping wood, who must work to "pay his taxes," and a reclining freedman, whose features were as stereotyped as his accent: "Whar is de use for me to work as long as dey make dese appropriations," he wonders.[43]

A campaign poster from the 1866 Pennsylvania governor's race presaged the racist antitax rhetoric of Radical Reconstruction's opponents. (Credit: Library of Congress)

Clymer lost his campaign in 1866, but the idea of free Black people as a threat to "the taxpayer" would soon gain traction in the North. The 1871 South Carolina Tax-Payers' Convention received a great deal of strikingly positive coverage in the Northern press. The convention proceedings were picked up by the Associated Press and widely republished. So well known was the convention that one Pennsylvania congressman described the Tax-Payers' protest as "a matter of public notoriety." *The Nation* magazine, founded by abolitionists, declared the convention "a most respectable body" that "represented almost the whole of the taxpaying portion of the population," the very people who, "it is conceded on all hands[,] . . . must eventually purify Southern politics, if they can be purified."[44]

The Nation's newfound sympathy for the Southern elite was in evidence again the following year, when Senator Blair made his final report on the fiscal situation of Reconstruction states. "In the single county of Kershaw, possessing a population of only 11,000, there were 3,600 tax executions issued," the magazine reported.[45] This estimate of tax liens in the district came from Blair via testimony from Gabriel Cannon, yet another member of the South Carolina Tax-Payers. Cannon had, on further questioning, admitted that the tax sales had never occurred, having been suspended by the Republican governor—but Blair omitted that point in his report, and *The Nation* accepted his misleading version of the facts.[46] Still, the real victory was not in the fiscal details; it was that Northern papers were focusing on taxation rather than on the wave of violence that was undermining the democratically elected governments of the South.

Another prominent critic of Reconstruction who embraced and embroidered the propaganda of the South Carolina Tax-Payers was James Pike, a Maine abolitionist who had once been an ardent Radical. In articles for *The New-York Tribune* and in an influential book, *The Prostrate State*, Pike declared Reconstruction in South Carolina a fiscal failure and justified the political violence as the reasonable response of oppressed taxpayers. In a March 1872 article, Pike wrote, "The condition of things now existing in South Carolina would not be borne a month in any Northern State without a tax-payers' league being organized to resist the payment of all taxes imposed for fraudulent purposes and without the swift establishment of a court of lynch law."[47]

Of course, corruption was endemic in many Northeastern cities, but municipal officials did not face public execution by vigilantes, and if they did, no one would consider their murder justified by the tax rates.[48] It was only in the Southern governments, where Black Americans held positions of political authority, that fiscal impropriety was seen as warranting lynching. High taxes and excessive spending became a catchall excuse for conservatives wishing to ignore or justify antidemocratic violence against the multiracial governments of the South.

CORRUPTION, SUFFRAGE, AND REDEMPTION IN THE NORTH

In July 1876, after the Hamburg Massacre, led by Tax-Payer Matthew C. Butler, South Carolina Congressman Robert Smalls addressed the US House of Representatives. Smalls had famously emancipated himself and his family during the Civil War by commandeering a Confederate military transport in Charleston Harbor and sailing it to Union lines. He was now introducing an amendment to ensure that federal troops would stay in the state as long as necessary to prevent vigilante violence. In response, Democrat Samuel "Sunset" Cox of New York, seeking to derail Smalls's proposal, rose and cited Pike's book on state debts and land commission frauds; the "scoundrelism of the State government," Cox argued, was such that it did not deserve a federal defense.[49]

"Have you the book there of the city of New York?" Smalls responded, provoking laughter. New York was as much a byword for government corruption as South Carolina. As the "Tweed Ring" scandals had revealed, the city's political machine relied upon self-dealing, bribery, and embezzlement. Indeed, in their coverage of the South Carolina Tax-Payers, *The Nation*'s editors had emphasized the "resemblance" between the convention's report of corruption in South Carolina and those "financial exhibits which municipal reformers occasionally lay before the public in this city."[50]

Nonetheless, corruption in their cities did not encourage Northerners to adopt an air of humility in their judgment of the Reconstruction governments. Rather, Northerners adopted the Redeemers' diagnosis to explain the endemic corruption in governments of the South and North: Public malfeasance was a problem *because nontaxpayers had too much power.*

Former Confederates had been making this argument for years. In 1868, the South Carolina Democratic Party, led by Wade Hampton, had petitioned the United States Senate to reject the new state constitution that provided for universal male suffrage because, the party alleged, it had been written by *nontaxpayers*. Two-thirds of the convention delegates "pay no tax at all," the South Carolina Democrats asserted. The incoming government was devising "a monstrous plan of public spoliation," with spending "twenty times as great as before the war," it was alleged, though the new government had not yet levied a single dollar of taxes.[51]

In attempting to discredit freed people for failing to accrue taxable property while literally enslaved, the charges were reprehensible. They were also obviously untrue. Poll taxes applied to every man, and most delegates were property holders as well. The median amount of property owned by South Carolina's delegates was $1,500; even considering just the Black delegates,

Propaganda opposing the "radical" members of the South Carolina state legislature asserted that the legislators paid little or no taxes. (Credit: Collection of the Smithsonian National Museum of African American History and Culture)

the median was still north of $900.[52] But the truth of the numbers was never the point. The point was to declare in advance that the incoming government was irredeemably corrupt and illegitimate because it represented those too poor to be burdened by taxes.

Three years later, Wade Hampton would repeat these canards about South Carolina legislators before the committee investigating the Klan. By then, the participation of "nontaxpayers" in government had become the Redeemers' very definition of corruption. The "worst feature" of the state's Reconstruction government, convention president W. D. Porter claimed at the 1871 Tax-Payers' Convention, is that "they who lay the taxes do not pay them, and that they who are to pay them have no voice in the laying of them." Legislators who pay little in taxes have no personal concern about rising government expenses. The problem, therefore, was not particular legislators or lobbyists, but rather the very presence of poor people in positions of power. The "center of the corruption charge," as W. E. B. Du Bois put it, was "that poor men were ruling and taxing rich men"—a diagnosis that conveniently foreclosed any possibility of reform within a system that enfranchised the Black and the poor.[53]

With this analysis in place, all government spending could be deemed suspect. There was no need to specify which particular spending was objectionable, and Reconstruction's enemies were not inclined to engage in subtle, or even plausible, analyses. The South Carolina Tax-Payers, like other Southern taxpayer groups, consistently compared pre- and postwar expenses, ignoring the fact that emancipation had doubled the number of citizens in the state, while war had decimated its infrastructure and economy.

For many prominent Tax-Payers, the superficial nature of the investigation into corruption served another purpose: It ensured that their own illegal dealings remained hidden. Porter, for instance, had personally profited from the railroad frauds that the Tax-Payers' Convention criticized.[54] When resolutions were proposed calling for an investigation of profiteering in the sale of bonds to complete the Blue Ridge Railroad, one Tax-Payer, W. H. Trescott, demurred, calling such action the "first step to social anarchy." Trescott's opposition to the investigation was easily explicable; as another convention participant angrily noted, Trescott was trying to protect the "bonds of the Company he represents."[55]

Remarkably, Matthew C. Butler and Martin W. Gary used the Tax-Payers' Convention itself to engage in some self-dealing. They ensured that the convention would endorse the state's bonds only after arranging to profit personally from the bonds' expected rise in value.[56] Butler saw no harm in suborning a government he saw as illegitimate; as he admitted frankly to the committee investigating the Ku Klux outrages, if a state senator indicated he would accept a bribe, "I would buy him up as I would buy a mule."[57]

In the opportunism of their anticorruption fervor, the South Carolina Tax-Payers were not alone. In Texas, the expenses of railroad investments rose in counties controlled by white conservatives as much as or more than in those with Republican legislators. Nevertheless, Redeemers still treated the issue as a consequence of Black suffrage.[58]

Honest Republicans, like the corruption-fighting South Carolina State Treasurer Francis Cardozo, were left in a bind by the bad-faith critiques. While conservatives treated corruption as a boon to poor and Black citizens at the expense of taxpaying whites, profiteering was in fact of great concern to freedmen and their representatives. It was they, not the former slaveholder class, who were truly invested in the effectiveness of the government. Corruption siphoned funds away from essential goods like public education and undermined programs with the potential for real economic liberation.[59] But Republican attacks on corruption were used by conservatives as evidence that poor people, the purported nontaxpayers, did not belong in government. And so it became vastly harder for genuine reformers to address misconduct, as doing so risked empowering an opposition whose goal was to drive the Republican Party out of existence and to return Black Americans to political and economic subservience.

In redefining corruption as the participation of poor people in government, the Redeemers had hit upon an analysis that would resonate powerfully with wealthy Northerners. By the mid-1870s, many elites, including Republicans, were coming to question whether universal suffrage *even in the North* was too much of a danger to the poor beleaguered taxpayers.[60] Merely two months after its largely positive review of the South Carolina

Tax-Payers' Convention, *The Nation* would consider the "vast horde" of immigrants to New York and conclude that democratic city government was a "ridiculous anachronism."[61] In reaction to the specter of working-class political power, Eastern industrial elites came to see themselves as a victimized minority under attack, and the North took a sharply antidemocratic turn. Years before the Southern states codified their Jim Crow laws, wealthy Northerners tried to roll back universal male suffrage and put "the taxpayers" in charge.

The first victory for the Northern taxpayers was the repeal of the Civil War income tax. Early in the war, bombarded with petitions demanding higher taxation to support the war effort, Congress had instituted a new revenue act that taxed, as one Treasury official put it, "everything under the sun," from inheritances and dividends to telegrams and playing cards. The law also included, over the vehement opposition of many Northeastern manufacturers and financiers, a federal income tax that would eventually touch 10 percent of Northern households. A progressive tax that applied only to high earners, it had a top rate of 5 percent that was later raised to 10 percent. It was only right that millionaires like "Mr. W. B. Astor" and "Commodore Vanderbilt," wrote *The New York Herald*, "contribute a fair proportion of their wealth to the direct support of the national government."[62]

Once the war was won, however, patriotic fervor and wartime revenue demands subsided. An Anti Income Tax Association was founded in New York. Business groups sent petitions to Congress calling for an end to the income tax. Success came quickly. The Civil War–era income tax was repealed in 1872.[63]

On the heels of this federal victory, elites in New York moved to regain control of taxation in the cities. Samuel Tilden, a corporate lawyer who would later be tried for wartime tax evasion, was a vocal opponent of the war, of congressional Reconstruction, and of universal male suffrage. Tilden had carefully studied the reports of the South Carolina Tax-Payers' Convention and adopted some of their rhetoric in his own speeches. When he was elected governor of New York in 1874, he called for the formation of taxpayer associations in his state, and he cut state taxes in half.[64]

In 1875, Tilden organized a commission to address government corruption—but the commission's report would be delayed by the contested presidential election of 1876. Tilden's reputation as a reformer had won him the Democratic nomination, and he outpolled Rutherford B. Hayes in the national popular vote. During the few months that the election outcome was in dispute, Tilden and his allies found themselves in the uncomfortable position of preaching the virtue of democratic decision-making. But just four days after a congressional commission handed the election to Hayes, Tilden's commission finally released its plan for municipal reform.

The Tilden Commission concluded that "the choice of the local guardians and trustees of the financial concerns of cities should be lodged with the taxpayers," and proposed a state constitutional amendment that would require fiscal policies to be determined exclusively by people of adequate means.[65] It was a call for an end to universal suffrage, which had existed for white men in New York since 1821.

The proposed amendment would have made city borrowing unconstitutional in all but the most extreme circumstances, and would have put all decisions concerning municipal taxation, spending, and debt in the hands of a "Board of Finance," elected by those who either paid annual taxes on property assessed at $500 or more or paid a yearly rent of at least $250. The latter figure represented approximately half the annual salary of a skilled worker. The amendment would have disenfranchised between one-third and two-thirds of eligible voters. A "New York Taxpayers' Association" soon began organizing in support of the amendment. Its meetings were, as *The New York Times* put it, "a notable demonstration of the solid wealth and respectability of the Metropolis."[66]

It took a certain degree of audacity to argue that men of property were the proper custodians of government just as the term "robber baron" was entering the national lexicon. While Boss Tweed maintained his power in New York City through patronage to immigrant and poor voters, Wall Street financiers were manipulating the Treasury Department to corner the gold market. And yet Jay Gould, one of the capitalists at the center of the Gold Ring scandal, would argue that the danger to good government came from the "large masses of uneducated, ignorant people." As the Southern planter class had for generations, New York's wealthy came to see themselves as a separate class. One prominent lawyer, George Templeton Strong, wrote in his diary in 1874 that the South had a Black "niggerocracy" and New York City an Irish "Celtocracy."[67] No wonder the South Carolina Tax-Payers found such a receptive audience in New York newspapers.

The New York taxpayer-suffrage constitutional amendment failed, thanks to a concerted campaign by the state's workers to defend their voting rights. Though Black workers in the South had already started organizing by the late 1860s, Northern workers were more experienced in political participation, and their newspapers and associations were more firmly established. Northern elites could play upon ethnic divisions and anti-immigrant and anti-Catholic sentiment, but not the racial chasm that divided the working South. Most critically, there was in the North no equivalent wave of extra-legal violence to prevent workers from voting.

But the antitax, antidemocratic attitudes of New York's business leaders were shared by other Northern elites. Francis Parkman, the prominent Boston historian, wrote an article in 1878 titled "The Failure of Universal Suffrage." In the cities, the "dangerous" effect of "flinging the suffrage to the mob," Parkman argued, was that the "industrious are taxed to feed the idle." Rather than seeing cities as civic institutions beholden to the public, Parkman reimagined them as business entities, "great municipal corporations, *the property of those who hold stock in them.*" Taxpayers, in Parkman's view, owned the government just like stockholders own a company; the "theory of inalienable rights" is an "outrage to justice and common-sense."[68] Even the Fifteenth Amendment, ratified less than a decade earlier, was subject to new criticism. Two members of the House Judiciary Committee suggested "further amendments looking to educational or other qualifications for Federal suffrage."[69] Northern elites were finally heeding John C. Calhoun's warning: The power of taxation in the hands of the majority was as much a threat to the Northern industrialist as it was to the Southern plantation owner.

In both the North and South, as the historian Sven Beckert has argued, "taxes" became "a code word for concerns about the political power of the propertyless." Several other states seriously considered measures like the one in New York, and tax standards for suffrage actually passed in some Northern municipalities. Southern Republicans could see the writing on the wall. As David Russell, a leading white Republican in North Carolina, would note, "If Massachusetts and Rhode Island can disfranchise the poor and the humble citizens of foreign birth within their limits, then South Carolina and Mississippi may easily avoid what they regard as the danger of universal negro suffrage."[70]

•◆•

After the overthrow of his government in South Carolina, Daniel Chamberlain moved to New York and became a successful corporate lawyer. He did not, in later life, reconsider the wisdom of his failed attempt to woo white Democrats with tax and spending cuts. Instead, he came to adopt the racist, mainstream view of the late nineteenth century: that the failure of Reconstruction was the inevitable consequence of the incapacity of Black men for self-governance.

"A modicum of mental and moral character" was required for good government, Chamberlain wrote in *The Atlantic* in 1901, and that character could not be found in "the mass of 78,000 colored voters in South Carolina." Even "tolerable administration" could not be had "from such an aggregation of ignorance and inexperience and incapacity." A quarter century after Wade Hampton had overthrown the government Chamberlain led, Chamberlain lauded Hampton as a "natural leader" and judged the violence of his seizure of power an inevitable consequence of national Reconstruction policy.[71]

Chamberlain's former allies, the Black and white Republicans of South Carolina, were left to fend for themselves. In a bid to further tarnish the reputation of Reconstruction, and as a bargaining chip to secure the release of white men charged federally with Ku Klux violence, Governor Wade Hampton trumped up false corruption charges against leading Black Republicans, including State Treasurer Francis Cardozo and Congressman Robert Smalls. Cardozo would spend months in prison before being pardoned and released.[72]

Apart from show trials to punish and politically debilitate their enemies, the Redeemers quickly lost interest in serious investigations of corruption once white rule had been restored.[73] But for nearly a century thereafter, their fiscal critiques would warp the public memory of Reconstruction and its overthrow. Historians, most famously those associated with William Archibald Dunning at Columbia University, adopted the Redeemers' story about nontaxpaying Black legislators abusing the public trust and driving hardworking white taxpayers to ruin.[74]

As the historian Heather Cox Richardson explains, Reconstruction's opponents "laid out the argument that has dogged American politics ever since: that government activism means special help for Black people paid for by hardworking white taxpayers."[75] The success of this strategy helped undermine the most radically egalitarian experiment in government the United States had ever seen and provided a rhetorical road map that conservatives have followed for generations.

7

JIM CROW

Rule of the Taxpayer

We want that poll tax to pile up so high
that he will never be able to vote again.
—Oliver Roland Hood, delegate to the 1901
Alabama Constitutional Convention

"Public free schools are not a necessity," wrote Virginia Governor
Frederick W. M. Holliday in 1878. "They are a luxury . . . to be
paid for, like any other luxury, by the people who wish their benefits."[1]

For years, the Virginia government had been robbing the state's school
fund to pay debts incurred in sweetheart deals made with the railroads
before the Civil War. The legislature had passed a bill requiring the state to
follow its constitutional mandate to support the public schools, but no such
funds would be forthcoming on Holliday's watch. He vetoed the bill.

Even after pilfering its education monies, however, the state wasn't fully
paying its debts. The government could have reduced the shortfall by eliminating some egregious tax breaks favoring corporations and bondholders,
but the "funders"—as men like Governor Holliday were known—were

unwilling to do so. A year earlier, one of the funders had said he would burn the schools before he would renegotiate the debt. As a prediction, it was not far off. By 1879, half of the state's public schools had been forced to close, and most of the others started charging tuition.[2]

The debt debacle provoked the most successful interracial movement in the South between Reconstruction and the civil rights movement: the Virginia Readjusters. Named for its plan to "readjust" the state's debt repayment schedule, the movement could hardly have been led by a less plausible figure. William "Little Billy" Mahone, who weighed barely a hundred pounds and sported a beard that reached to his third shirt button, was a ferocious former Confederate general, a Democratic Party leader, and the president of three railway lines. But Mahone had also attended the Virginia Military Institute on a public scholarship. He was, as he put it in 1877, "a friend of the public school system" and a public proponent of the idea that "the large class of persons recently admitted to the privilege of citizenship should receive careful and ample instruction."[3] Mahone rapidly organized a remarkably effective political machine—one that was, from the beginning, open to Black Virginians.

One of those Black Readjusters was Thomas Bayne. Bayne, born into slavery, had escaped to Massachusetts via the Underground Railroad, where he prospered as a dentist and won election to the New Bedford City Council. After the war, he returned to Virginia, where he served as a vocal advocate of heavy property taxation at Virginia's 1867–1868 constitutional convention. When conservatives retook control of the state, Bayne struggled to reinvigorate Virginia's moribund Republican Party. With the rise of the Readjusters, he put his considerable oratorical skills to work for the coalition, pushed his fellow Republicans to align in support of a joint ticket, and was elected to represent Norfolk at an 1882 state convention. Dr. Bayne and General Mahone headlined a mass meeting together in Norfolk in 1883.[4]

Building an interracial party in the shadow of the Civil War was no easy task. White Readjusters were, at best, condescending to their Black colleagues, and they worried, correctly, that Democrats would use the biracialism of the party as a line of attack. Black Virginians, meanwhile, were loath to shift their allegiance from the party of Lincoln, and the national

Republican Party was conservative on debt issues. Black Readjusters were also, with good reason, deeply suspicious of the reliability of their white allies.

Against these obstacles, what encouraged interracial alliance was pragmatism: Only together could upcountry white farmers, Black voters in the plantation region, and urban workers break the conservative Democratic stranglehold on state government. After 1879, the Readjusters and Black Republicans together held a majority in the legislature. At a convention in Petersburg in 1881, many Black Republicans allied more formally with the Readjusters. The convention published a broadside reminding Virginians of the taxes they had paid for the schools, only to see the schools closed and the tax money diverted. They called for biracial cooperation against the funders, those "misguided citizens" who seemed to "believe that their rights and privileges can only be secured by a denial of the rights and privileges of others."[5]

The Readjusters won again in 1881 and 1882. They now branded themselves as "Liberals" to indicate that their platform went beyond the debt issue to defending fair elections, fighting corporate power, rebalancing the tax code, and funding the schools. Many—North and South, Black and white—saw Mahone's party as a beacon of hope for a new South.[6]

One of the Readjusters' most significant achievements involved repealing a state constitutional amendment, passed by conservatives in 1876, that required voters to have paid their poll taxes. After the Readjusters' repeal, voter turnout nearly doubled.[7] Pushed by Black leaders within the movement, the Readjusters also eliminated the use of the whipping post as punishment for crimes. This humiliating relic of the slavery era was also a tool of disfranchisement, since those receiving such a punishment lost their right to vote.

The Readjusters shifted taxes onto the economic elite. They put an end to the policy of letting corporations assess their own property values—a practice that, unsurprisingly, encouraged extremely low estimates. In a single year, assessments on railroads and canals went up by 150 percent, and revenue from corporate taxes doubled. Small farmers saw their taxes go down, both because their assessments were more accurate and because the state government cut their tax rate by 20 percent. Localities under Readjuster control took similar steps; the town of Petersburg even imposed a municipal capital gains tax.[8]

The Readjusters fulfilled their initial campaign promise to readjust the debt—and did so with such skill that the funders abandoned the issue. While Virginia had previously been spending more than half its state revenue on debt repayment, that figure dropped below 25 percent under the new regime.[9] Hundreds of thousands of tax dollars flowed into the school system. The schools reopened, and kids returned to the classrooms. Black schools saw gains in parity with white schools, and the Readjusters increased the hiring of Black teachers and ended racial discrimination in teacher pay. They also appointed Black men to school boards.[10]

Democrats, predictably, used the increasing visibility of Black people in positions of power and prominence to engage in racist fearmongering about "Negro domination" and "social equality." In Norfolk, Democratic newspapers attacked Mahone for his association with Thomas Bayne.[11] The presence of Black men on school boards was presented as a threat to the purity of white female teachers and students.[12]

The coup de grâce occurred in Danville, a Readjuster-led town on Virginia's southern border. Danville had served as the final capital of the Confederacy when President Jefferson Davis fled southward after the fall of Richmond. In 1883, the old South would once again make its stand in Danville, this time with far greater success.

In October, only a few weeks before the statewide elections, a pamphlet titled *Coalition Rule in Danville*—also known as the Danville Circular—purported to represent the views of the town's small-business men. The circular painted a lurid and inaccurate picture of a city beset by filth and street violence, and recounted with horror that Black citizens no longer stepped aside for whites on the sidewalk.[13] But the leading injustice "to which our white people have been subjected," according to the circular, was unfair taxation: the false but predictable claim that "the negroes of the town do not contribute one single dollar to the use of the town."[14] Democratic papers across the state reprinted the pamphlet in full, accompanied by editorial remarks like "WHITE MEN, CONSIDER!!! 'Danville's

Appeal' to you, before you cast your vote for this iniquitous Coalition party."[15]

With racial tensions running high, a street scuffle erupted in Danville only three days before the election. The skirmish, which ended with white men shooting unarmed Black men, was presented by Democrats as a "negro riot" and the natural consequence of coalition rule. In the climate of fear that followed, Thomas Bayne expected to see blood in the streets on election day.[16]

The Democrats' race-baiting, combined with lavish campaign funding from the railroad companies, led to substantial defections among the Readjusters' white base. Returned to power, Democrats put partisan election judges in charge of future vote counts. From then on, one party leader explained, they could "change the ballots to suit themselves" and "save those counties from Negro domination."[17] Democrats' control of Virginia would not be seriously contested for more than eighty years.

As the historian C. Vann Woodward observed, "Redemption governments, often describing themselves as the 'rule of the taxpayer,' frankly constituted themselves champions of the property owner against the propertyless and allegedly untaxed masses."[18] Between the fall of Reconstruction and turn of the twentieth century, conservatives instituted a fiscal program to rebuild and reinforce the South's racial and economic hierarchy, including large reductions in public spending, tax cuts that heavily favored the wealthy, supermajority requirements for tax increases, and a criminal justice system that used forced labor as a replacement for government revenue.

Under these regimes, racism could not always disguise the shared material interests of Blacks and poor whites. "They are in the ditch just like we are," remarked one white Texas organizer for the Populist Party.[19] The Readjusters were the most successful of these alliances, but they were far from the only effort to build a Southern interracial coalition that would legislate for poor and working people.

In response to this looming threat, conservatives continued to use the fiscal system to consolidate the power of their racial oligarchy. At the turn of the century, the Southern states adopted new constitutions that included poll taxes to disenfranchise Blacks and poor whites. Many white Populists convinced themselves that eliminating the Black vote would mean conservatives could no longer undermine economic egalitarianism by race-baiting or win elections by allocating coerced or falsified Black votes to conservative candidates.[20] They were wrong. Plutocratic one-party states would rule the South for more than half a century.

REDEEMERS' BUDGET CUTS AND TAX LIMITATIONS

The "government will be the most highly esteemed that gives the greatest protection to the individual and industrial enterprises at the least possible expense to the tax-payer," insisted Florida Governor George Franklin Drew in his inaugural message to the legislature.[21]

"Millionaire Drew," as the lumber industry magnate was known, came to power in the 1876 election that overthrew the state's Reconstruction government. Though overshadowed by the Red Shirts' campaign in South Carolina that year, voter intimidation in Florida was also widespread, and election subversion was similarly justified in terms of taxpaying.[22] Among other coercive tactics, the Democrats' executive committee in Jefferson County—the county with Florida's largest Black population—posted a circular at polling places promising to deny employment, land rental, and credit to "those who vote for high taxes."[23]

Once in office, Governor Drew made taxation his top issue, insisting on immense cuts to taxes and public services: "The pruning knife must be used with a fearless and impartial hand."[24] Over seven years, the property tax rate in Florida dropped to less than a third of its previous level.[25] Redeemer regimes made similar decisions across the South. Mississippi cut the state budget 50 percent over ten years.[26] Alabama closed its public hospitals. In several states, salaries for government officials were cut in half, a move that ensured that only the independently wealthy could afford to serve in public office.[27]

The public school system, the pride of Reconstruction, was decimated. Spending per pupil in the South dropped by 40 percent between 1870 and 1880. In 1881, public education spending in nearly all former Confederate states was less than $2 per school-age child. Every other state in the Union spent more than $4.50. School terms became 20 percent shorter on average.

Public education was so underfunded in Louisiana and Tennessee that illiteracy rates among whites actually rose. But while chronic underfunding slowed educational advances for Black Southerners, it could not stop them. At the start of the Civil War, some 95 percent of Black Southerners were illiterate. Within two generations, more than two-thirds of Black people in the South could read.[28]

The tax system was also used to allocate the South's meager school funds disproportionately to whites.[29] Some states tried to earmark white taxes for white schools and Black taxes for Black schools.[30] Other states implemented two separate levies on property, with a higher tax for the white schools and a lower one for Black schools. Another approach was fiscal gerrymandering: Districts were drawn to exclude Black homes and businesses so that no money would be raised for their schools, or Black neighborhoods were included in two districts so that Black families paid taxes for their own school *and* for the white school they could not attend. (Not every locality bothered with legal niceties; instead, officials simply redirected money for the Black school to the white school.)[31]

The tax reductions that accompanied the Redeemers' budget cuts offered little benefit to poorer people. Lower property tax rates were offset by biased assessments that favored the rich and increases in other taxes that fell heavily on the poor. The Redeemers protected tax breaks for large estates and winked at tax evasion by the wealthy, while reducing or even eliminating traditional property tax exemptions for the means of subsistence. "The small farmer's little home and the tenants' mules had as well be exempt from taxation as the millionaire's money invested in railroads," argued an agrarian newspaper in Mississippi in 1881. But the state government's "abominable" tax policy "relieves the money kings from bearing their share of the burdens of government while it exacts tithes from the hard earnings of the poorer classes."[32]

The other tax policy that shifted costs to the poor was tax localization. Conservatives prided themselves on their cuts to state taxes, but often they were just pushing the costs of government onto the counties instead. It was a strategy that worked out very nicely for the plantation elite. Rich counties could get by with low rates because they had a lot of property to tax, while poorer counties needed relatively high rates to raise adequate revenue. And because the plantation counties were home to most Black people, whites in these areas could then shift their local taxes to nearby Black communities. Rich whites in the Black Belt could thus cut their own taxes twice over, just by switching the domain of taxation from the state to the county.[33]

The net effect was very low taxes for rich whites, higher taxes for poor whites, and the highest taxes on Black people. In North Carolina, for example, whites in poor counties were paying 70 percent more in taxes per dollar of property than whites in rich counties. And while white families paid twenty-one cents in property and poll taxes for every hundred dollars of their wealth, Black families paid $1.33. In other words, North Carolina's taxes on Black wealth were six times higher than on white wealth.[34]

These stark figures still underestimate the level of inequity in taxation because Black property was systematically overassessed compared to white property. Throughout the Jim Crow period and thereafter, this overcharging combined with fraudulent and predatory tax delinquency processes to push Black families into tax debt and foreclosure.[35]

One of the Black property owners to lose his land to tax debt was Matthew Gaines, the formerly enslaved field hand who was elected to the Texas State Senate during Reconstruction. Driven from office and repeatedly arrested on trumped-up charges, Gaines eked out a living as a rural preacher, remembered by younger generations for his fiery Juneteenth sermons and inspiring Sunday school lessons. His land was sold at auction, in front of the very courthouse where he once spoke to his constituents about the schools their taxes would pay for and about his personal pride in property ownership and taxpaying.[36]

While Black families were being taxed out of their homes, the wealthiest whites were benefiting not just from preferential property tax assessments, but from very low corporate taxation. In 1882, manufacturers in Mississippi received ten-year exemptions from all state and local taxes on their new factories; Florida, Louisiana, and South Carolina soon followed suit.[37] In Georgia, nine-tenths of all railroad property went untaxed in 1890. Corporations also benefited from special legislative favors for industry—including from deals decried as corrupt during the Reconstruction era.[38] However much the Redeemers talked about purifying politics after the purported horrors of Reconstruction rule, "rule of the taxpayer" meant tax cuts for the rich, not a commitment to honest government.

Even by the standards of the Gilded Age, the Redeemers were astoundingly corrupt. In no fewer than six of the eleven former Confederate states— Virginia, Georgia, Tennessee, Alabama, Mississippi, and Louisiana—the Redeemer state treasurer was found to have misappropriated hundreds of thousands of dollars.[39] In several instances, the missing sums amounted to six months or more of state tax revenue. Some treasurers were impeached or convicted of embezzlement; others absconded with the loot. "So much for Democratic administrations in the South," concluded *The Weekly Pelican*, a Black New Orleans newspaper in 1889, after hundreds of thousands of dollars' worth of fraudulent state bonds were discovered in the white Redeemer treasurer's personal bank box. "Under eight years of Republican rule," when the state treasurer was a Black man, "no defalcation occurred in the State Treasurer's office," the *Pelican*'s editors noted caustically.[40]

The Redeemers' fiscal malfeasance also sparked anger among whites. "The people have been taxed and swindled, since the war," wrote a Democratic paper in Jefferson, Georgia, in 1875, and under Democratic rule, "the barter and sale in office seems still to go on" and "taxes are almost as onerous as ever." "We demand, in the name of the people, that there shall be complete justice . . . a bold, fearless and prompt cleaning of the Augean stables," wrote another Georgia editor, four years later. Populists were angry at corrupt officials and at the corporations that did much of the corrupting. The Alabama legislature, according to one newspaper, was "sandwiched through with railroad lawyers" who prevented tax legislation in favor of average people and forced through measures that would "shield the corporations."[41]

Widespread corruption and tax breaks for the wealthy were not popular policies. Elites thus faced an ever-present threat: What would happen if the unruly masses should regain political control? To address this worry, the Redeemers had an innovative solution. They wrote new state constitutions that imposed state and local limitations on property taxes. These provisions ensured that the wealthy could keep their taxes low even if a majority of voters wanted more progressive taxation.[42]

The first constitutional property tax cap was passed in Arkansas in 1874, only a few months after the collapse of the state's Reconstruction government. The tax limitation, which barred the General Assembly from levying taxes above 1 percent of the total assessed value of property in the state, was instituted over the objections of delegate William Thompson, an attorney from tiny Woodruff County, who argued, "We must leave something to the good sense of the legislature and the people."[43] But this was a faith most delegates did not share.

The next year, Alabama's tax limitation was the first item on the constitutional convention's agenda. The convention's president urged the passage of a tax limit as an alternative to explicitly restricting suffrage—at this early date, Northerners might still take umbrage at a more direct policy of disenfranchisement. The convention decided on a lower cap than Arkansas; instead of 1 percent, Alabama's legislature would be prevented from taxing property at more than 0.75 percent of total assessed value. Over the following years, Texas, Missouri, Georgia, and Louisiana would also adopt property tax limitations into their state constitutions. Texas's 1876 constitution capped property taxes at 0.5 percent of the valuation; Louisiana in 1879 adopted a 0.6 percent cap (while also providing manufacturers with a ten-year property tax exemption). Georgia's rule was particularly stringent: Passing a local tax increase required endorsement by a grand jury and the electoral support of two-thirds of registered voters. It was, in the words of one contemporary education reformer, "an ironclad protection against taxing property."[44]

But while property taxation was being cut, another revenue source was growing: government funds from a new form of slave labor known as "convict leasing."[45] In the words of historian Matthew Mancini, the new system was "morally shameful and fiscally brilliant."[46]

STATE REVENUE FROM FINES AND FORCED LABOR

In 1918, Moses Chambers, a Black man in Georgia, was looking for a job. He had come up to Cartersville from Atlanta to meet with a recruiter for Alcoa, the aluminum company with a new smelting plant over the border in Maryville, Tennessee. Alcoa recruiters had been sent across the Deep South to find cheap Black labor for the grueling work near the factory furnaces.

The meeting was a success: Chambers was not only hired but given a train ticket for the next morning, a promotional picture of Alcoa's new company town, a quarter to pay for his dinner, and a place to stay for the night.[47]

The next morning, he headed to the train station. Excited by the prospect of a wage of $2.50 a day, Chambers told two other Black men about his new job, showed them the picture he had been given, and suggested they could get jobs too. Chambers's enthusiasm was likely overheard by the two men's white employer, a man named Vaughan, who was also at the train station that morning, and who would not have taken kindly to his workers' hearing about a comparatively well-paid job. What is certain is that Moses Chambers was arrested for having failed to pay the tax on job recruiters. The law, first passed in 1877, required "emigration agents" to pay a fee of $500 in each Georgia county where they wanted to hire locals into out-of-state jobs. Chambers was convicted and sentenced to pay a $1,000 fine or spend six months on the chain gang.[48]

The purpose of such laws, which were adopted in several Southern states, was to trap workers like Chambers in the exploitative Jim Crow economy.[49] But taxing and criminalizing job recruitment was just one small component of a fiscal-carceral system that made Black forced labor profitable for business and for government. The most infamous part of this system was "convict lease," through which corporations contracted with states to use prisoner labor in their factories, plantations, and mines. A similar but more informal system existed on a local level, where governments hired out convicts to businesses and farms.[50] In addition, convicts were forced to work directly for the government, via prison chain gangs for road repair and other public works.

The Jim Crow carceral system had much in common with the tax policies regulating free Black people in the pre- and immediate postwar periods, but ironically it was the Radical Reconstruction governments that began the practice of leasing prisoners to labor for local industries. During the Civil War, many state penitentiaries had been destroyed, and afterward, state treasuries were so severely depleted that there was no funding to repair them; convict leasing was seen by Reconstructionists as a temporary coping measure. These first leases did not raise state funds. Instead, state governments paid private contractors for taking over the state's responsibilities to house and clothe felons, who were often put to work on infrastructure projects. But a much more expansive, profitable, and abusive system would emerge in the post-Reconstruction period.[51]

The convict labor system functioned as follows: First, a state or county official would convict someone, almost always a Black man, of a "crime." Some were crimes of poverty, such as vagrancy. Others were violations of the racist social code, such as "speaking loudly in the presence of white women." Crimes were invented to preserve local systems of economic exploitation; arrests were more common where the local Black community was more economically independent and employers would sometimes demand a quota of arrests from local officials to meet their labor needs.[52]

Next, the minor or purported crime would result in an extreme penalty. The Arkansas Larceny Act of 1875 made the theft of two dollars a felony punishable by one to five years in prison. "Pig laws" in Georgia and Mississippi made stealing a hog a felony. In North Carolina in the late 1870s, nonpayment of taxes was punished with forced labor. Sentences were generally accompanied by exorbitant fees and fines designed to be too expensive for a poor person to pay. Instead, the convict would be obliged to work off the debt, which significantly extended the length of their terms.[53]

Once convicted, instead of going to prison, leased inmates served their sentence working for employers who made deals with the state or county. Every former Confederate state except Virginia adopted convict leasing, often sending prisoners en masse to the owners of mines, brickmaking or turpentine factories, and similar enterprises.[54] In 1880 in Georgia, a Black man named Monday Haines received a twelve-year sentence for stealing four hogs, a term he served as a forced laborer for the Chattahoochee Brick Company.[55]

Difficult as it is to conceive, the conditions under which leased convicts labored were commonly described as worse than slavery. Malnutrition, overcrowding, and disease were rampant; prisoners worked all day at hard labor without adequate clothing or food, or access to sanitation or clean water to drink. Torture as punishment for failure to meet work requirements was standard practice. Women and children were sometimes housed with grown men and subject to the same treatment.[56]

A shocking percentage of leased convicts died in custody. In the early 1880s, the death rate for Black convicts in Mississippi was 11 percent a year; in Arkansas, it was 25 percent; and in Alabama, the annual mortality rate climbed to 45 percent. These numbers are in no way comparable to other criminal justice systems of the period; the annual death rate in Northern prisons hovered around 1 percent. At their highest, the Southern figures rival the annual death rates in the prisoner-of-war camps in Japan during World War II, or during the deadliest years of the Soviet gulags.[57]

The system was almost impossibly cruel. It was also extremely lucrative. In the words of Southern novelist and antisegregationist George Washington Cable, convict leasing sprang "primarily from the idea that the possession of a convict's person is an opportunity for the State to make money." To fail to seize this opportunity was to impose upon the "tax-paying public." Cable was a committed foe of the racist criminal justice system, but its supporters said much the same thing. South Carolina Congressman George Tillman saw the leasing of convicts as a way to avoid compelling "taxpayers to support them in idleness"; Florida Governor William D. Bloxham asserted that selling the labor of convicts, rather than paying for their upkeep in prison, was "much better for the tax-payers of the State."[58]

Convict lease poured hundreds of thousands of dollars into government treasuries in a period when total state budgets were but a few million dollars. In Tennessee, a lease would only be renewed if it would "guarantee $50,000 per year" in revenues. In 1881, the Texas governor gloated about the amount of "cash [that] goes into the treasury" as a result of leasing. In Alabama in 1915, revenues from the Convict Department made up one-sixth of the state government's total income, an amount comparable to that raised by poll taxes. A few years later, an Alabama prison inspector rejoiced that "our jails are money-making machines."[59]

Some politicians had a more personal reason to exult. Fees and fines were designed to go directly into the pockets of local officials. In 1884, a man named Henry Gale in Mississippi, who was sentenced to ninety days for being a "tramp," also owed $5 in fines and an additional $9.95 in fees to the jailer, officer, and mayor.[60] Some leading politicians were heavily invested in convict-lease industries. Joseph E. Brown, Georgia's Civil War governor, called for the abolition of the penitentiary in favor of convict leasing. Over the following years, Brown used hundreds of convict laborers in his coal mines, where prisoners, including women, were starved and tortured, a policy of which he expressly approved. In 1880 alone, Brown pocketed $98,000 in profits from his coal company.[61]

Against repeated reform efforts in the late nineteenth century, the convict lease persisted precisely because of its profitability to business and government alike. Alabama was the last state to abandon convict leasing, in 1927. By that time, between one hundred thousand and two hundred thousand workers had been caught in the convict-leasing system.[62] But even as convict lease waned—in part because corporate demand for heavy labor declined—Black forced labor continued to substitute for white tax revenue: Convicts were used to improve public roads.

The brutal chain gang system had much in common with convict lease, including prisoners' malnutrition and torture. Though it recapitulated the antebellum system of "public hands"—slaves owned by the state and used for infrastructure maintenance—the chain gang was promoted as a progressive reform. Convict leasing competed with free labor in mines, mills, and factories, and thus undermined free workers' capacity to negotiate with their employers. Public chain gangs, by contrast, kept forced labor confined outside the private labor market. In some states, moreover, penal labor on public roads also brought an end to the in-kind tax called the *corvée*, in which men were required to work a certain number of days of hard labor on country roads unless they could afford a steep cash fee. Because it avoided competition with free labor and because it could lift the *corvée* from the white poor, the states' reliance on the chain gang was seen by many whites as a populist step.[63]

The chain gang system also found support from other constituencies. With prisoners rather than free labor repairing the roads, less tax revenue was needed, as forced labor was estimated to cost half as much as that of free men. Southern campaigners in the national "good-roads movement" quickly discovered that reliance on convict labor at least partially assuaged wealthy fears that this infrastructure investment would raise their taxes. Business owners also benefited from improved roads, of course, in getting their products to market, and proponents pointed to the "increase in the taxable value of property" where roads were convict-built.[64]

The use of road-repair chain gangs quickly spread, particularly in counties with a large Black population. In Georgia, about five thousand convicts worked on public roads each year. Convicts also served in other publicly owned enterprises. In Tennessee, the end of the leasing system simply meant transferring convicts from private enterprises to Brushy Mountain, a state mine; convict labor continued to profit the state to the tune of $200,000 a year. In 1905, the Parchman prison farm in Mississippi netted $185,000 annually, a figure that increased to about $1 million by 1917. Road-repair chain gangs could still be seen in some parts of the South in the mid-twentieth century.[65]

POLL TAXES AND DISENFRANCHISEMENT

"ATTENTION WHITE MEN" read the advertisement in *The Wilmington Messenger* on November 9, 1898. The notice announced a mass meeting, to be held at the courthouse at eleven a.m. the following morning, at which "business in the furtherance of White Supremacy will be transacted."[66]

The day before—fifteen years after the defeat of Virginia's Readjusters—North Carolina's biracial governing coalition of Populists and Republicans had been ousted from power. Over the previous four years, this "Fusion" alliance had rolled back unfair election laws, raised taxes on corporations and railroads, and, despite an economic depression, increased school funding for all public schools, while bringing Black schools' funding closer to parity with that of white schools.[67]

But the Populist-Republican alliance had always been fragile, a local anomaly in the national partisan landscape, bedeviled by internal disputes and strategic missteps. The Democrats, by contrast, were united behind a white supremacist standard. Their campaign of racial hatred was, as white Populist Senator Marion Butler said presciently, the "one hope for the railroads to capture the next legislature." White supremacy in North Carolina rode back into office on a wave of corporate campaign contributions and Red Shirt–style voter intimidation.[68]

Wilmington, a majority-Black city, did not have local elections in 1898, so despite the statewide loss of the Populists and Republicans, it was still led by a biracial, majority-white, fusion government. But not for long. For months, white elites in the city had been planning what can only be described as a coup—the violent overthrow of a legitimately elected government.[69] Over the summer, the group had stockpiled weaponry and stoked white fears of Black violence. Then, on November 10, they set the final component of their plan in motion. Hundreds of men, a who's who of white Wilmington, attended the courthouse meeting. They signed a manifesto of white supremacy with seven proclamations, the first of which read, "That the time has passed for the intelligent citizens of this community owning 95 per cent. of the property and paying taxes in like proportion, to be ruled by negroes."[70]

The next day, white militias marauded through Black neighborhoods, shooting indiscriminately and burning the building that housed the local Black newspaper.[71] The elected leadership of the city was forced to resign, and prominent Black leaders and white Republicans were dragged through the streets, threatened with lynching, and banished from Wilmington. An estimated sixty people were killed, while hundreds of Black citizens fled and hid in the swamps outside the city. A leader of the coup was installed as mayor.

To forestall interracial populist politics in the future, Democrats decided they could no longer rely on a patchwork system of election fraud and intimidation. The new North Carolina government moved to amend the state constitution to disenfranchise Black men through a series of voting restrictions, including a poll tax.

By the turn of the century, the Southern states—confident that the federal government would not intervene to protect Black civil rights—formally removed Blacks and poor whites from political life. In the space of less than twenty years, disenfranchising state constitutions were adopted in Florida (1885), Mississippi (1890), South Carolina (1895), Louisiana (1898), Alabama (1901), and Virginia (1902). Arkansas and Texas, like North Carolina, amended their constitutions to achieve the same ends.

Among the most popular tools of disenfranchisement was the poll tax. Poll taxes were nothing new, of course, and tax requirements for voting had existed in many Northern states, often as an intermediary, liberalizing step between a property qualification to vote and universal male suffrage. Under conservative Southern rule, however, the poll tax was redesigned and almost inverted. Rather than impose a mandatory tax that was meant to be paid by every man, Southern states made the poll tax optional and even difficult to pay, with the intention of disfranchising unwanted voters.

Georgia pioneered this antidemocratic innovation. The state poll tax had been a prerequisite for voting even in the antebellum period. Suspended after the war, the tax was still used by election officials to illegally disenfranchise Georgia voters in 1870, and it was fully reinstituted the following year, when the Democrats returned to power. In 1877, Georgia made its poll tax cumulative, which meant that missing one year of payments could disenfranchise a voter for years to come. In 1878, a Georgia conservative could still complain that "capitalists and taxpayers of the country are at the mercy of a class of men whose only capital are their votes"—but by the 1880s, turnout in Georgia had fallen substantially below that of other Southern states.[72]

Virginia also experimented with a poll tax to vote, starting in 1876. Before the Readjusters repealed the measure, the voting-linked poll tax had reduced turnout by 10 percent and had cut the number of Black delegates in the General Assembly in half.[73] Not only was the poll tax a steep cost for poor and Black citizens, but government officials often literally refused to accept poll taxes from Black Americans in order to prevent them from voting. At the Richmond tax office in 1882, a cook named William Blair waited in vain for two full days, with a crowd of other Black would-be voters, to pay his poll tax. The white officials admitted Black citizens so rarely and processed their simple one-dollar tax payment so slowly that most were never able to pay. But when a white-passing Black man named John H. Gregory arrived at the crowd, he was quietly guided through a different office to a window where he paid his tax in not more than "two minutes."[74]

Depressed Black turnout in Georgia did not go unnoticed by white supremacists in other states, and between 1889 and 1902, every other former Confederate state adopted a constitutional suffrage-discouraging poll tax—including Virginia, which reimplemented a poll tax in the state's 1902 constitution.[75] Many states adopted Georgia's cumulative tax structure.[76] "We want that poll tax to pile up so high," Alabama convention delegate Oliver Roland Hood asserted, that undesirable voters "will never be able to vote again."[77] Some states also included provisions that explicitly forbade mandatory tax collection, which all but guaranteed the taxes would have a discriminatory impact. "No legal process, nor any fee or commission shall be allowed for the collection" of the poll tax, the 1901 Alabama Constitution specified. There was no tax collector knocking at your door for your poll tax payment. The only penalty for not paying was disenfranchisement, and the poll tax's due date was intentionally scheduled many months ahead of election day. The poll tax disqualified Black and poor white voters by untaxing them.

The implications of a nonmandatory poll tax were apparently too subtle for some. Proponents found they had to spell things out, both at the conventions and thereafter. "If you provide a compulsory way of collecting the poll tax," explained Alabama delegate Hood, you "destroy the objects and purposes" of the tax provision: disfranchisement of the "vicious voter."[78] Twenty years after the passage of the Mississippi Constitution, former delegate Marye Dabney was still obliged to connect the dots for some of his colleagues. The design of the poll tax, he said, "is intended to keep negroes from being forced to pay poll taxes, thus making voters of them." Calls to "raise revenue by collecting the poll tax from negroes" were nothing short of "suicidal," in Dabney's estimation. They would "destroy the whole work for which the Convention of 1890 was called": the formation of a government that was "completely in the control of the white people."[79]

The poll tax was far from the only suffrage limitation passed in the turn-of-the-century South. Literacy tests and other measures were also put in place to reduce the Black vote. Scholars still debate the relative effectiveness of the poll tax compared to these other disenfranchisement policies.[80] And, of course, all the legal restrictions on voting were backed by the threat of violence against those who would dare to try to exercise their rights.

But legislators expressed special confidence in the poll tax. "As a means of negro disenfranchisement," insisted a delegate to the Mississippi Constitutional Convention, the poll tax was "worth all the rest." In Louisiana, poll taxes were lauded not only for excluding Black voters but for getting "rid of many whites at the same time."[81]

As intended, the new constitutions drastically reduced Southern voter turnout and increased the political dominance of wealthy whites. In

Tennessee, the percentage of adult men who voted dropped from 78 percent to 50 percent in two years, and continued to fall thereafter. In Louisiana, the number of Black men on the voting rolls dropped by 90 percent in eight years. This loss of political power was accompanied by a steady increase in fiscal exploitation. Racial disparities in school funding grew even more stark. A study in 1909 demonstrated that, if (as racist populists had long demanded) Black taxes were assigned to Black schools and white taxes to white schools, Black schools in North Carolina, Virginia, and Georgia would be owed tens of thousands of dollars a year.[82]

As usual, opposition to Black voting went hand in hand with opposition to taxation of the rich. When, in 1899, the Democratic State Convention of Alabama called for a constitutional convention "to perpetuate the rule of the white man in Alabama," it resolved that questions of suffrage should be decided in the best interest of the "tax payers of Alabama," and that "there should be inserted in such a constitution a provision limiting the rate of taxation."[83] Alabama had already imposed a constitutional limit on the rate of taxation in 1875, but the 1901 Constitution made the tax cap even more stringent. Mississippi, on the other hand, had not passed a tax limitation in the Redemption era, but the state's 1890 Constitution instituted an exceptionally broad measure: a provision requiring three-fifths of the legislature to approve all state tax increases. Limitations to taxation and to majority rule were two solutions to the same threat. In Mississippi, they passed in tandem.

Many components of the Jim Crow fiscal system remain in place to this day. Mississippi still requires a supermajority to pass a state tax increase. Alabama's strict limits on state and local property taxes, first passed in 1875, are still in operation, as are the property tax limits in Texas, Arkansas, and Missouri.[84] The lease of prisoners to private corporations has seen a resurgence.[85] In fact, as we will see in Part Three of this book, the fiscal pathologies of the Southern Redeemers would spread to the nation as a whole, after Jim Crow disenfranchisement was finally overturned.

Taxation for the General Welfare

THE FEDERAL INCOME TAX

Highly graduated taxation realizes most
completely the supreme danger of democracy.

—Memorandum from J. D. Rockefeller's
lawyers to the New York State Assembly

In the summer of 1862, a man named George Boutwell arrived in Washington to take up a new post essential to the Union war effort: commissioner of internal revenue. Just two weeks earlier, President Lincoln had
signed into law the first federal income tax in American history.

Boutwell, an abolitionist and former governor of Massachusetts, was
a radical in his politics. He would go on to serve in Congress, lead the
impeachment of President Andrew Johnson, and help author the Fourteenth
and Fifteenth Amendments. A consistent defender of Black civil rights—
both earlier and later than many of his colleagues—Boutwell ended his
career a committed anti-imperialist, serving as an advocate for Haiti, the
kingdom of Hawaii, and an independent Philippines.

But Boutwell was also, by all accounts, a rather dry little man. His
speeches were famously boring, even his friends agreed.[1] His political career
rested not on any great charisma or oratory, but on an obvious integrity and
exceptional capacity for organization. He was, therefore, a superb choice

to manage the revenue service, an institution Boutwell was obliged to set up wholly from scratch. In 1862, the federal government hadn't applied domestic taxes in nearly fifty years. "I examined the records of the Excise Bureau during the War of 1812, but they furnished no aid whatever," Boutwell recalled in his memoirs. Unlike the costly wars taking place in nineteenth-century Europe, America's military endeavors, including its genocide of the Native nations, never pressed too heavily on the federal budget nor long interrupted the international trade upon which the tariff system was based.

But the Civil War was a different kind of war, one that placed entirely new demands on the nation. Within a year, the revenue service grew from Boutwell and three clerks to the largest department in the government, with nearly four thousand people on staff, and collected $39.1 million. By the end of the war, 30 percent of internal revenue came from the income tax. The

Abolitionist and Radical Republican George S. Boutwell was the first commissioner of the Bureau of Internal Revenue. (Credit: Library of Congress)

North's far superior tax capacity contributed to the Union's victory; as one Confederate later said, "We were whipped in the Treasury Department."[2]

Against Boutwell's advice, the income tax was allowed to lapse after the war.[3] The error of that choice was made apparent in 1894, when Congress attempted to reinstate the tax and a conservative Supreme Court unexpectedly reversed its earlier rulings and declared the income tax *unconstitutional*, a decision that, in the words of George Boutwell, impaired "the means by which alone the continuing existence of the national government is made secure."[4]

What followed was a decades-long campaign to rescue the income tax. At issue was not just the fiscal health of the nation, but the definition of democracy in an age of increasingly extreme economic inequality. The federal government had, since the ratification of the Constitution, been charged with promoting the nation's "general welfare." The Civil War had given the government new responsibilities—most obviously, to care for the nation's wounded, widows, and orphans. It had also imbued the government with new capacities, including a bureaucracy that could raise revenue. At this, Boutwell expressed some mild pride. Though the income tax had been outlawed, the "frame work" of the revenue service that he had designed, "including the system of bookkeeping with its checks and tests," remained in place in 1901, ready to help the nation meet the needs of the twentieth century.[5] How this new, more powerful government would serve the general welfare in a modern world of global war, grinding poverty, and unimaginable wealth has been the great question of American politics ever since.

THE GILDED AGE AND THE INCOME TAX

In November 1884, Omer Madison Kem, a Nebraska farmer, found himself in desperate financial straits. The crops had been good that year, but he was already indebted, and with wheat bringing less than fifty cents a bushel, the prices were too low "to tide us over another year," he explained in his memoirs. His wife having died of typhoid fever, Kem was obliged to board his children with family and spend a punishing winter herding sheep for twenty dollars a month. There were record blizzards that year; the lows reached negative thirty-eight degrees. In the spring, to pay for farm tools and a new sod house, Kem took out another loan, though he knew he'd have to repay 170 percent of what he'd received within only a few years. "The most unsophisticated can see at a glance what a tremendous graft this was," Kem wrote, "but what could I do? It was the last resort."[6]

While Kem was worrying about how he would repay his loans, Alva Vanderbilt was purchasing what was at the time the largest yacht in the world, costing half a million dollars, and naming it after herself. The previous year, the Vanderbilts had thrown a housewarming party, for which the family reputedly spent $65,000 on champagne ($2 million in today's dollars). One guest wore a dress embroidered with real rubies, emeralds, and sapphires; another, called "Puss" by her friends, appeared with a headdress made from a taxidermized cat.[7]

The second half of the nineteenth century was a disorienting time, and an unequal one. Americans born in log cabins lived to see the invention of the telegraph, the radio, the light bulb, the automobile, and the skyscraper. Chicago, a town of thirty thousand at midcentury, saw its population double nearly every decade, reaching 1.7 million by 1900. By the start of the twentieth century, American wealth was five times what it had been when the Civil War began.[8]

That vast new wealth was held in increasingly few hands. The biggest businesses, known as "trusts," came to dominate entire industries. John D. Rockefeller's Standard Oil controlled 90 percent of the oil market. U.S. Steel, which merged the interests of J. P. Morgan and Andrew Carnegie, held two-thirds of the steel market. Operating without competition was extremely lucrative, and the gains from the explosive economic growth concentrated in the hands of a tiny cohort of Northeastern industrialists: The richest 1 percent of households owned about a third of the nation's wealth in 1870 and 45 percent of wealth by 1910. (Today, the top 1 percent again own about a third of the national wealth.)[9]

Meanwhile, ordinary citizens were struggling. Workers striking for better wages and an eight-hour day saw their organizing violently suppressed by militias and federal troops. In the cities, poor families crowded into single tenement rooms. Children, who had previously worked on family farms, were increasingly consigned to dangerous jobs in mills and mines. Declining farm prices, the closing of the Western frontier, and the rise of commercial agriculture drove farmers into debt, foreclosure, and tenancy.[10]

In a society so marred by extreme inequality, the appeal of instituting an income tax was self-evident. Public anger was stoked by journalists' and scholars' exposés of the new poverty and the new wealth—and especially by the revelation that the owners of immense fortunes paid next to nothing in taxes.[11]

In fact, the federal tax system exacerbated the rapid concentration of money and power. In the late nineteenth century, more than half of federal revenue came from the tariff, the schedule of duties applied to foreign goods imported to the United States. Tariffs raised prices, which hurt poor consumers, especially farmers who paid for protected goods yet received little benefit for the products they grew. The tariff also insulated domestic industries against foreign competitors, enriching the owners of the big corporations that were clustered in a handful of Northeastern states. Modern analyses suggest that the tariff redistributed to its beneficiaries as much as 8 percent of the nation's gross domestic product. But even at the time, the impact of the tariff was widely recognized. Political economist and lawyer Thomas Shearman made headlines in 1889 when he calculated that wealth in the United States was more unequal than in aristocratic England—and cast the blame on the tax system. "In no other country," Shearman wrote, "has the burden of taxation been cast so exclusively upon the working class, or the machinery of public taxation been used so unscrupulously for private profit." As muckraking journalist Charles Edward Russell put it, "The root of the evil was the accursed tariff. Under its operation the wealth that should be for all was seized by the favored few." For its role in corporate consolidation, the tariff became known as "the mother of trusts."[12]

Republicans from the industrial Northeast recognized the tariff's political weaknesses and worked to shore up support for it. They argued that the benefits of the tariff trickled down to industrial workers—but in an era of vicious strikebreaking, the idea that big business was looking out for its workers was not terribly convincing. Republicans also added duties to some farm goods, like wool, to protect agriculture as well as industry. On many products, however, American farmers could compete without trade protections, so this did little to muster support for the tariff. Most significantly, Republicans spent the embarrassingly large sums raised by the tariff on military pensions for Union war veterans, providing a safety net to hundreds of thousands of Americans decades before the welfare programs of the New Deal.[13] But even this policy was not enough to make the tariff widely popular. Union pensions did nothing to increase tariff support in the former Confederate South, or among recent immigrants in Northern cities. And if Union veterans were committed to protecting federal revenue, many were happy for that money to come from a more progressive tax than the tariff.

In the campaign to reduce or eliminate the tariff, the income tax was not the only tax proposal that found popular favor as an alternative source of revenue. By the early twentieth century, more than thirty states and the federal government had experimented with a tax on inheritance. Another proposal involved taxing lands held by speculators—an idea that had been popular with agrarians since the country's founding.[14]

No tax proposal, however, encouraged fanaticism quite like Henry George's "single tax," a proposal to replace *all other taxes* with a tax on the unimproved value of land. George's 1879 book on the topic, *Progress and Poverty*, sold millions of copies, inspired the formation of hundreds of "Single Tax" clubs, and in 1886 pushed George to a solid second-place finish in the race for mayor of New York City (in which he outpolled the Republican, Theodore Roosevelt). Several utopian colonies were founded on the basis of the Georgist tax. The single tax was, in the words of historian Ajay Mehrotra, "a kind of flypaper for social movements."[15]

The single tax was a digression in the history of American taxation, but it was so popular that we should digress as well, and consider why a tax plan could provoke such fervor. There is nothing so terribly wrong with the variation on a property tax that was the sole demand of the Georgist movement; some localities impose a similar tax today. However, to balance one's *entire* fiscal edifice atop one narrow tax, particularly one applied to something as unstable as land values—that is where the Single Taxers tipped into crackpottery. But committed Georgists believed that the single tax was a panacea: a way to replace every other source of government revenue and single-handedly eliminate poverty.

What Georgism offered, other than the appeal of a silver bullet, was a tax that seemed to apply only to the portion of one's wealth that one did not "earn." All efforts to improve the land—with buildings or irrigation systems—went untaxed under George's plan. Taxes fell only on the value of the land, and no one could claim to have personally created that value. In rural America, the soil was a gift of nature (or a gift from God, to many religiously inclined citizens). More prosaically, the value of a plot of farmland had everything to do with its access to the railroads and the markets. In the cities, the value of land was even more obviously tied to the society and economy that surrounded it—the roads and sewers, the parks and schools, the stores and neighbors. The emotional appeal of Georgism lay in a fundamental truth of the industrial world: that wealth was increasingly a social product. This reality, as we will see, was central to the fight for the income tax.

The income tax never provoked monomaniacal zeal on the order of Georgism, but it had substantial advantages, including that it was far more closely tied to the taxpayer's ability to pay and it could raise vastly more money. From the 1870s onward, prominent economists were among the strongest proponents of an income tax.[16] The income tax had also already been proven successful. Other countries had taxed income for decades; some states had also experimented with income taxes.[17] A federal income tax was proposed as early as the War of 1812 and, of course, had served as an effective source of revenue during the Civil War.

Almost as soon as the Civil War–era income tax was repealed, a panoply of populist reform organizations called for it to be reinstated. The proposal for an income tax was regularly found alongside demands for railroad nationalization and an eight-hour day. Members of the rural association known as the Grange petitioned for an income tax in the 1870s. So did an early union, the Knights of Labor, in the 1880s. The Northern Farmers Alliance endorsed an income tax in 1889; the following year, the Southern Farmers Alliance did so as well. Graduated income taxes were proposed by the Greenback-Labor Party in 1878, the Anti-Monopoly Party in 1884, and the Union Labor Party in 1888. In Congress, Southern and Western legislators introduced income tax legislation dozens of times.[18] In 1892, when various strands of the populist movement converged in the People's Party, its platform included the simple statement "We demand a graduated income tax." (One of the Populists elected to Congress was Omer Madison Kem, the impoverished farmer who had years earlier been forced to risk his life herding sheep in a deadly Nebraska winter.)

By the 1890s, the income tax had become the primary tax demand of both those aiming to reverse the Gilded Age's extreme wealth consolidation and those seeking a replacement for the long-despised tariff. The fiscal tide was turning, it seemed.

THE ILL-STARRED INCOME TAX OF 1894

In the spring of 1893, C. H. Jones, the editor of *The St. Louis Republic*, wrote to the young Congressman William Jennings Bryan with a piece of advice: "I want to suggest to you that by far the most effective weapon for use against the Plutocratic policy is the graded income tax."[19] Bryan took the suggestion to heart and that autumn devoted himself to the cause.

The timing was certainly auspicious. In the election of 1892, populist fervor had helped give Democrats control of both houses of Congress and the White House for the first time since the Civil War. Democrats were not uniformly supportive of an income tax, but even the relatively conservative President Grover Cleveland had indicated his openness to a tax on income from corporate investments. When the GOP had been in the majority, Northeastern Republicans had been powerful enough to block an income tax, but now a bipartisan coalition of income tax proponents from the South and the West could make legislative headway.

William Jennings Bryan led the charge. He offered voluminous research into income taxes applied in other countries, but he also underscored the tax's moral appeal. Responding to a claim that the wealthy would leave the country rather than pay an income tax of 2 percent, Jennings thundered, "Of all the mean men I have ever known, I have never known one so mean that I would be willing to say of him that his patriotism was less than two per cent deep." In response to the assertion, on the part of an income tax opponent, that the tax would mean that poor people did not contribute to the government, Bryan pointed to the burden of the tariff. "If taxation is a badge of freedom, let me assure my friend that the poor people of this country are covered all over with the insignia of freemen."[20]

In the end, a small federal income tax was enacted as a part of the Wilson-Gorman Tariff Act: A 2 percent rate was to be applied to net corporate incomes and to individual incomes over $4,000. The legislation, set to go into effect the following year, closely approximated the Civil War income tax that had operated until 1872.

Conservatives in both parties were outraged. One Democrat was overheard saying, "The Democratic hen has hatched a Populist chicken at last."[21] Insisting that wealthy people would be put "at the mercy of the rapacious majority," the Republicans denounced the income tax as "communism pure and simple" and suggested that any political party foolish enough to impose one should prepare for its "funeral."[22]

Reports of the Democratic Party's death were premature—but so were the hopes for federal income tax revenue. The following year, in *Pollock v. Farmers' Loan & Trust Co.*, the Supreme Court rendered its shocking decision: The new income tax law was unconstitutional.

More precisely, the court decided that the income tax fell under the "direct tax" clause of the Constitution. An ill-considered vestige of the requisition system and the three-fifths compromise, the clause required that "direct" taxes, a phrase left undefined, be apportioned to the states by the same rule as House representation.[23] Under this apportionment system, the federal government would determine a total amount of revenue a tax was supposed to raise, and then assign each state a share of the tax responsibility based not on the amount of the taxable item in each state, but on the state's population.

Apportionment does not, frankly, make much sense. When the government wants to tax an item, it should simply set a rate that applies uniformly in all states. There is no earthly reason that tax rates should have anything to do with state population. One hundred years earlier, the Supreme Court had addressed the clause's nonsensical implications. The 1796 case concerned a tax on carriages, a luxury item much more common in the wealthier states. If the carriage tax were a direct tax, however, states would owe carriage taxes based on their population, whether or not their citizens owned many (or, indeed, any) carriages. In response, Justice William Paterson deemed the apportionment system "oppressive and pernicious," and Justice James Iredell, after asserting that the apportionment scheme was "too manifestly absurd to be supported," concluded that any tax that "cannot be apportioned" in a reasonable manner is therefore "not a direct tax in the sense of the Constitution."[24]

Few expected the direct tax clause to be applied to the 1894 income tax. The Civil War income tax had been unanimously approved by the Supreme Court as recently as 1881, and the new tax hewed closely to the previous version. But if the precedents had not changed, the ideological tenor of the court had. *Pollock* was an early entry in the long string of decisions that put government on the side of the powerful. Only a few months before, the court had sharply limited the scope of the Sherman Anti-Trust Act; a week after, the justices would sign off on the arrest of Eugene Debs for leading the Pullman strike. The following year, in *Plessy v. Ferguson*, the court would defend the standard of "separate but equal," offering constitutional protection to racial segregation.

It was this increasingly reactionary Supreme Court majority that reclassified the income tax as a direct tax that needed to be apportioned.[25] There was no practical way to do so without unleashing a smorgasbord of paradoxes and perverse outcomes. To pick just one example, apportionment would have required Nebraska to pay three times more in income taxes than the far wealthier state of Rhode Island, simply because Nebraska had three times more people.[26] To say that the income tax needed to be apportioned was, as former Internal Revenue Commissioner George Boutwell noted, "to declare, in effect, that it shall not be collected."[27]

The court's sudden and overwhelming concern for the sanctity of the ridiculous direct tax clause is easily explained: It wished to protect the wealthy minority against taxation determined by the masses. The attorney Joseph Choate, who argued the antitax position, had called upon the justices to protect the wealthy from the "passions" of sixty million Americans. James C. Carter, who spoke in defense of the income tax, argued that "American people can be trusted." Choate won the day. The majority's decision was a clear denial of the principle of democratic taxation. "Nothing can be clearer," Chief Justice Melville Fuller wrote for the majority, "than that what the Constitution intended to guard against was . . . an attack upon accumulated property by mere force of numbers." Fuller, a diminutive, amiable Mark Twain look-alike, stood in stark contrast to his colleague the sturdy and belligerent Justice Stephen Field, who had once been a gunslinger in Gold Rush California. But in their antipathy to the income tax, these men were in accord. The income tax law was an "assault upon capital," Field concurred, the first step in a bitter "war of the poor against the rich."[28]

The decision unleashed a furor. The Supreme Court was a "pitiful cat's paw of the plutocracy," their decision "a crime against the common people, a poisoned dirk driven into the very vitals of the American republic," said *The Louisiana Populist*. It was "the triumph of selfishness over patriotism," wrote the New York *World*. For its attack on human liberty, the ruling should rank on the same list as *Dred Scott*, insisted the Kansas *Advocate*. The Populist Party insisted that the decision was "a misinterpretation of the Constitution, and an invasion of the rightful powers of Congress." A Democratic congressman from Georgia described it as a "legal anomaly, a political anachronism, and an economic blunder."[29]

Strong words, but to little effect. As long as the Supreme Court's ruling held, the only route to an income tax was to amend the Constitution. This was a daunting task, to say the least. A constitutional amendment could be proposed by a two-thirds vote of both houses of Congress and ratified if it then received the support of three-fourths of the states. The first challenge, getting two-thirds of the House *and* two-thirds of the Senate to vote for something, was substantial. The tariff reform that contained the 1894 income tax had not met this threshold.[30] The second challenge, getting three-fourths of the states to agree, seemed almost insurmountable— surely the industrialists of the Northeastern states could exert enough control over their own legislatures to stymie ratification.

Ironically, the imposing height of the constitutional barrier was essential to the amendment's birth. In 1909, in the face of a budget deficit, a Republican-controlled Congress passed an income tax amendment as part of tariff reform. Conservative leaders, harried by progressive Republicans in the West, were unable to keep the income tax entirely off the agenda but were confident that the amendment would die in the states. After all, the Constitution had not been amended since Reconstruction, and only five times total since the Bill of Rights. So dire were the amendment's prospects that many progressives did not even see the legislation as a win.[31] The state-by-state campaign for the income tax soon revealed, however, that legislators in Washington had vastly underestimated the popularity of the income tax.

THE WESTERN CASE FOR BIG GOVERNMENT

From Midwestern farm country to the Pacific coast, the income tax was ratified so heartily that it was almost by acclamation. In Idaho, Montana, Nevada, California, Nebraska, South Dakota, and Arizona, the measure passed unanimously; in five other states, the number of legislators voting "no" was in the single digits. The Oregon House of Representatives endorsed the income tax amendment in "less than one-tenth of the time used in selecting an assistant sergeant-at-arms," reported the Portland *Oregonian*.[32]

The income tax made sense to Westerners. Farmers had been demanding "equal taxation"—that is, taxation proportionate to wealth—since the country's founding. And though the West had a proportionate share of people earning enough to pay the income tax, the region had very few people who were fantastically rich. Even counting the railroad barons of California and oil-rich Oklahomans, only twelve people in the entire western United States had incomes over $1 million a year.[33] Because incomes in the region were less extreme, Westerners would pay some income tax, but most of the revenue would come from the industrial Northeast.

But the appeal of the income tax was not simply about shifting fiscal responsibilities onto the very rich. It was about shifting economic power from private interests to the public. Western farmers, so commonly imagined as independent and local-minded aficionados of small government, for decades led a movement to vastly increase federal authority.[34] The Populist platform in 1892 declared, "We believe that the power of government—in other words, of the people—should be expanded (as in the case of the postal service) as rapidly and as far as the good sense of an intelligent people and the teachings of experience shall justify to the end that oppression, injustice and poverty shall eventually cease in the land."

The government is the people, the Populists believed, and the government's powers should be expanded to end oppression and poverty. As historian James Huston has observed, this was a "breathtaking" assertion, one "unmatched by any major party in American history in its call for government intervention in the economy."[35]

Confidence in the federal government was rooted in the Western experience. It is no coincidence that the Populist call for government expansion mentioned the post office. On the frontier, the federal government was basically the postal service and the army.[36] It delivered the mail and secured land for white settlers, who consequently held quite positive views of government. But Westerners chafed at the power of the big businesses—the mining companies, the railroads—that exploited their states, corrupted local government, and sent their profits back East. Farmers and other working people were by then operating in an entirely different kind of economy, one dominated by big businesses and global markets. In this context, democracy needed to scale up as well.[37] Government would be the counterweight to corporate control. For decades, the agrarian West stood for a democratic government strong enough to rein in big business.[38]

This is not to suggest that reformers thought the governing institutions of the United States were flawless—far from it. Proposals for secret ballots, the direct election of senators, and ballot initiatives were intended to rescue American democracy from the malign influence of wealth as it operated through the corrupt political parties.[39] But the campaigns to purify government were not accompanied by a desire to limit the state's purview. Instead, reformers agreed on the need for an immense increase in the authority of the federal government, which was seen as nothing less than an immense increase in the power of the American people. The income tax was essential to this mission of governmental expansion.

THE AMBIVALENT SOUTH

A towering, bearded figure in a long black coat, with a Texan's fondness for very large hats, the Populist orator James Harvey "Cyclone" Davis was every inch a white Southerner; his father had served in the Confederate Army and one of his eight brothers was named Jefferson Davis Davis.[40] But Cyclone

Texas Populist Cyclone Davis called for a top income tax rate of 100 percent and for corporate tax evaders to be treated as military deserters. (Credit: Library of Congress)

Davis wanted nothing more than to rein in the corporate elite, whom he called the "sweet-scented millionaire plutocrats," the "lordly luxuriant looters," the "gold-trimmed, diamond-bedecked masters of our country," and the "malevolent minions and myrmidons of Mammon." Davis helped write the People's Party's 1892 platform calling for a graduated income tax. But he was even more radical than his party, demanding a top income tax rate of 100 percent. "It is not right for any man or corporation to be allowed to have an income of over $1,000,000 a year," Davis insisted.[41]

In making his case for strong governmental interventions in the economy, Davis explicitly repudiated the "states' rights" doctrine, and instead located popular sovereignty in the federal government. It is "the duty of Congress *to act directly on the people and for the people*," Davis said, "not through the States, counties or any other subdivisions of government." And Davis evinced none of the antitax, antigovernment skepticism that had so long typified Southern white politics. The "government of the United States is not a separate thing from the people," Davis explained. "The government is the organized agency through which the people rule themselves."[42]

If Cyclone Davis were any indication, ratification of the federal income tax should have been a cakewalk in the South. The South, like the West, had been a hotbed of agrarian populism. Several Southern states had, in an effort to tamp down populist fervor, implemented or at least authorized state-level income taxes—though these taxes rarely raised much money.[43] Per capita Southern income was half the national average, and only about 1 percent of Southerners had incomes high enough that they might have to pay a federal income tax.[44] Replacing tariff revenue with an income tax would shift the cost of government onto the wealthy Northeasterners whose monopolistic businesses exploited Southern labor and Southern consumers. This argument alone should have been enough to win the day; what self-respecting Southerner could oppose a tax on the Yankees?

But as much as it was in the economic interest of the region to endorse the income tax, the Jim Crow South could not organize full-throated support for democratic taxation. For one, the disenfranchisement of Black people and poor whites massively reduced the political clout of the working class. The concomitant increase in the power of the economic elite privileged both wealthy native Southerners and the Northeasterners who owned vast amounts of Southern capital and regularly meddled in Southern politics when it suited their interests. The lack of political competition also led to inertia and dysfunction, turning governance into a morass of self-dealing and special interests. And, of course, no amount of Northern capitulation on racial justice was enough to entirely put to rest the old Southern antitax politics. Some white Southerners opposed a federal income tax because it would increase federal authority, commonly conceptualized as Black tax collectors employed in the South.[45]

By the time the Sixteenth Amendment came up for debate, however, most white Southerners were confident that Black civil rights were a dead letter. Since the defeat of the Federal Elections Bill in 1890, the federal government had shown no inclination to protect Black voters. The turn-of-the-century Jim Crow state constitutions had thoroughly stymied the possibility of an interracial working-class alliance. The solidification of the white supremacist regime thus allowed virulently racist Southern populists, like James K. Vardaman in Mississippi, to support the income tax.[46]

In the end, five Southern states (Alabama, Texas, North Carolina, Tennessee, and Missouri) passed the income tax amendment with no major opposition, while five states posed serious or insurmountable challenges. In Georgia, the amendment came within three votes of failure, and in Louisiana and Arkansas, it was initially defeated.[47] Two states, Virginia and Florida, failed to ratify at all. Southern acquiescence to the income tax was no overwhelming endorsement of a new strong-state democracy.

NORTHEASTERN INDUSTRIALISTS VERSUS THE INCOME TAX

It was one thing to ratify the income tax in the South or the West. But could the amendment win in the Northeast—that bastion of big-business conservative Republicanism, where legislative malapportionment kept the working class of the cities underrepresented and where newspapers regularly described the income tax as a communist plot?[48] The fight in the richest of those states, New York, was seen as a bellwether for the amendment's chances across the region.

Albany was deluged with opposition from prominent wealthy industrialists, including none other than John D. Rockefeller. The founder of the Standard Oil trust and the richest American who has ever lived, Rockefeller was very willing to direct his unparalleled wealth to political ends. In 1896, when William Jennings Bryan seemed a plausible contender for the presidency, Rockefeller and the other magnates of the big trusts each contributed hundreds of thousands of dollars to ensure that his opponent, William McKinley, had a campaign war chest ten times larger than Bryan's.[49]

Fifteen years later, Rockefeller mobilized longtime confidants from Standard Oil to draft an anti–income tax brief that was distributed to every legislator in Albany. Rockefeller's lawyers had a winning track record on this issue; the main author, Joseph Choate, had argued against the income tax in *Pollock v. Farmers'* in 1895. After some opening quibbles about the taxability of state bonds, the Choate memo turned into a manifesto against the principle of an income tax—and a wholesale repudiation of democratic fiscal authority. "Leading Lawyers in New York," blared *The New York Times*, "FEAR AN ABUSE OF POWER."[50]

If the majority is allowed to rule, Rockefeller's lawyers wrote, "Congress is certain to be led into waste and extravagance." Those who do not pay taxes "have no personal interest in governmental expenditures," they insisted. Politicians, competing for "the votes of very poor and very ignorant men," will spend hundreds of millions of dollars upon "irrigation, conservation, national highways, canals, and the innumerable schemes and fads which tempt and delude some sections of the country."[51]

Though troubled by the specter of government extravagance, Choate and his coauthors were mostly worried about taxation, not spending. Taxes were, they argued, "the easiest and most powerful instrument of oppression"—and those most endangered were not those with few resources, but those with many. The "few rich men," Rockefeller's lawyers wrote, always constitute the minority and are therefore threatened by the tax preferences of the majority. The power of the majority must be checked "for the very purpose of preventing abuse of the taxing power." The masses simply could not be trusted to determine fiscal policy, and the income tax was the clearest case against majority rule: "Highly graduated taxation realizes most completely the supreme danger of democracy."[52]

The arguments of Rockefeller's lawyers were widely repeated by foes of the Sixteenth Amendment.[53] It was not only the income tax's opponents, however, who saw taxation as fundamentally a question of democracy.

E. R. A. Seligman, the most prominent academic supporter of the income tax, argued that the modern economy necessitated not only the income tax but also a fundamental reconsideration of what it meant to be a citizen. Seligman, though he came from a wealthy banking family, was one of the nation's leading progressive economists. In his 1895 book, *Essays in Taxation*, he insisted, "It is now generally agreed that we pay taxes not because the state protects us, or because we get any benefits from the state, but simply because the state is a part of us."[54] From our current vantage point, dominated by the long post-Reagan backlash to so-called big government, it might be hard to imagine that it was ever "generally agreed" that "the state is a part of us." But Seligman's assertion is a common theme of Populist and Progressive thinking.[55] As the Texan Populist Cyclone Davis had written only the year before Seligman's essay, the "government of the United States is not a separate thing from the people."

Populists and Progressives also agreed that the modern economy required a vastly more powerful government.[56] While Davis, steeped in Jeffersonian nostalgia and enraged by corporate excess, saw the new economy as something to regret, Seligman took a more positive perspective: that industrialization had created a society in which people needed each other. Whatever a modern man's job, he was "dependent on the ceaseless cooperation of the society about him"—to grow his food, to build his house and tools, to ship his products, to buy his services. Long gone, if they had ever truly existed, were the yeoman farmers whose land had ensured their economic and political independence. Now, everyone's life and livelihood were dependent upon others. In this interconnected world, "the state is as necessary to the individual as the air he breathes," and wealth was a social and political product. "Individual labor," Seligman wrote, "has never by itself produced anything in civilized society." One's income was now inextricable from the social and political setting in which it was accrued.[57]

This new economic reality had three implications for taxation, in Seligman's estimation. First, since government was essential to wealth's production, government could fairly reclaim a portion of an individual's assets. Second, because one's income would not exist in the absence of government, tax levels could not be based on an individual accounting of government benefits. The benefits were incalculable. Thus, the only rational standard for taxation was the taxpayer's ability to pay—measured best, Seligman believed, by the taxpayer's income.

Rockefeller, as one might imagine, disagreed. The oil magnate explained his views on taxation in a rare public interview, conducted with a fawning reporter who trailed Rockefeller around his personal golf course at Forest Hill, the seven-hundred-acre estate that served as his summer home. Once a man had legally acquired wealth, Rockefeller insisted, "the people no longer have any right to share in the earnings resulting from the accumulation." Yes, Rockefeller agreed, "all men are bound together," but that shared interest did not alter a man's "right to undivided ownership." Wealth was not a social product, in Rockefeller's estimation; it belonged, free and clear, to the person who had managed to accrue it. The modern economy did not justify a new role for government. As his lawyers insisted in their memo to the Albany legislature, the tax limits inscribed in the preindustrial Constitution by "Hamilton and Washington and Jay and Madison" still applied—and were, in fact, "infinitely more necessary at the present time."[58]

For a while, it seemed the New York legislature would follow Rockefeller, not Seligman. In 1910, under a barrage of lobbying by Standard Oil, the income tax amendment failed three times.[59] But the issue could not be put to rest. In the spring of 1911, the measure was once again under consideration. The state senate ratified the amendment in April, so its fate was left to the lower house, the assembly, where it had been shot down the year before. Could the income tax's opponents stave off the amendment a fourth time? If so, it seemed they might be able to defeat it nationally. Twenty-nine state legislatures had so far voted to ratify, and though a handful of income-tax-friendly Western and Midwestern states had not voted yet, they were not enough by themselves to meet the threshold for ratification.[60]

On May 20, Seligman testified before the assembly's Judiciary Committee. The learned professor put on quite a show. He breezily dismissed concerns about the income tax undermining state bonds—an issue that had featured prominently in the opening of the Choate memo—insisting that he would "flunk without hesitation" a student who made such a claim. He concisely reviewed the history of the income tax in the United States and suggested that the *Pollock* decision had been wrongly decided. One unfortunate assemblyman attempted to impeach the professor's expertise by holding up a weighty book titled *The Income Tax* and asking whether Seligman had actually read the whole thing. Seligman had indeed read it—in fact, he had written it. Seligman was even asked directly about the taxes of John D. Rockefeller. "Well," the professor replied, "he doesn't smoke. If he drinks at all it is only a glass of beer." Since Rockefeller therefore paid little in tariffs, he "pays very little toward the National funds."[61]

Seligman's scholarly reputation likely helped drive up support for the amendment. But his erudition mattered far less than the indisputable popularity of the income tax. The previous November, voters angry about the rising cost of living had punished the conservative, protariff Republicans who had previously dominated the Northeast, putting progressive Republicans and Democrats in power.[62] Seligman—after calling himself "as good a Republican as any of those present"—ascribed the massive electoral defeat to intransigence on the income tax. "I believed the party would be snowed under at the polls if it refused to accept the amendment," he told the committee. "The Republican Party was snowed under, and one of the reasons was its failure to observe my warning."[63] Some politicians had come to the same conclusion. An opponent of the amendment in 1910, State Senator Howard Bayne of Staten Island, switched sides the following year, citing "the extreme disapproval of my constituents."[64] Crucially, the New York City Democrats of the "Tammany" machine—famously short on principles other than being re-elected—had also recognized the income tax as a political winner, appealing both to urban workers eager to tax the capitalists and to the middle class influenced by the mild progressive politics of experts like Seligman.

On July 12, 1911, the state assembly voted, ninety-one to forty-one, in favor of the senate resolution in support of the income tax amendment, and New York became the thirtieth state to ratify the federal income tax. "It is still to be hoped that the amendment will fail," sulked *The New York Times*, "but the betrayal of New York into the hands of the income taxers makes its failure less probable."[65]

The prediction proved sound. In the end, only six of the forty-eight states failed to ratify the income tax: Rhode Island, Connecticut, Pennsylvania, Utah, Virginia, and Florida. The striking success of the federal income tax amendment was a testament to the strength of the popular demand for a more powerful role for government in the economy.

THE INCOME TAX AND THE CONSCRIPTION OF WEALTH

On February 25, 1913, Secretary of State Philander Chase Knox officially certified that a new amendment had become part of the Constitution: "The Congress shall have power to lay and collect taxes on incomes, from whatever source derived, without apportionment among the several States, and without regard to any census or enumeration."

That fall, President Woodrow Wilson signed into law a tariff reform bill that contained a small income tax. For most Americans, the income tax was a nonevent; less than 4 percent of Americans earned enough to expect an income tax bill.[66] The collection process in March 1914 went smoothly, and in its first years, the income tax raised about 17 percent of federal revenue.[67] But if the income tax seemed at first a relatively minor source of revenue, it did not stay that way for long.

For Americans, the Great War only lasted nineteen months: from the declaration of war in April 1917 to the Armistice in November 1918. But the war was costly—immeasurably so to the families of the more than one hundred thousand Americans killed—and in economic as well as human terms. From 1916 to 1919, federal spending rose from $713 million, or less than 2 percent of the gross domestic product, to $18.5 billion, nearly a quarter of GDP.[68] The financial demands of war led to an explosive expansion of progressive taxation.

As tariff revenue dropped and military spending rose, progressives ensured that taxes on the rich increased. The income tax was applied to somewhat lower incomes, but mostly the rates got steeper. From 7 percent at the modern income tax's debut, the top rate rose to an astounding 67 percent by 1917 and 77 percent in 1918. The individual income tax, which had raised just $28 million in its first year, was now producing over $1 billion in annual revenue. Before the war, three-quarters of federal monies came from tariffs and excises; at the end of the war, that same fraction came from corporate taxes, estate taxes, and the income tax. To handle the workload, the Bureau of Internal Revenue more than tripled its workforce.[69]

War strengthened the case for the progressive income tax because it reinforced the basic assertions that underlay the tax in peacetime: that citizens owed a debt to one another and to the country, and that an individual's wealth was not merely a consequence of personal effort. As American soldiers prepared for service in the trenches, millionaires disputing their fiscal obligations could be painted not merely as selfish capitalists, but as unpatriotic profiteers. This did not, of course, prevent the representatives of business from trying to shift taxes off their industries, but it did muffle their public opposition to tax increases and gave proponents of progressive taxation a powerful argument in favor of their preferred policies.

The wartime fiscal obligation was called the "conscription of wealth." The phrase was almost unheard of prior to 1914, but by 1917 it appeared in hundreds of US newspaper articles. It was first used by war opponents, who believed heavy taxes would turn industrialists against military engagement. Representative Cyclone Davis of Texas, with his typical populist flair, took the idea of wealth conscription literally, repeatedly introducing legislation that would have applied a death penalty to corporate tax evaders, reckoning them guilty of the equivalent of military desertion.[70]

Some of Congress's strongest champions of progressive taxation, including Wisconsin Senator Robert "Fighting Bob" La Follette, were less influential on war finance than they might otherwise have been, because they had voted against the war. But the rhetoric of wealth conscription was readily adopted by proponents of American military engagement in Europe. Leading labor organizations, in a coordinated statement supporting the war, demanded "conscription of wealth as well as men" and "heavy taxes on incomes, excess profits, and land values."[71]

Members of the Wilson administration insisted on the moral imperative of wartime taxpaying by comparing it to military service. "I don't care how wealthy a man may be—if he gave half his fortune, if he gave it all—he couldn't give a tenth as much as that boy of yours that gives himself to his country," an assistant secretary of agriculture told farmers in Fargo, North Dakota.[72] Fifteen thousand volunteer public speakers, known as "Four-Minute Men," were mobilized to give short speeches at movie theaters and other public venues to encourage the buying of war bonds and to extol the virtues of the income tax. "Age may bar you from the trenches," read one suggested slogan, "but it does not block your progress to the collector's office with your income-tax return."[73] As the country's young men prepared to fight and die, the American public rallied behind the idea of equal sacrifice and demanded that the wealthy bear their share of war's burden.[74]

The case for high taxes was reinforced by the recognition that many industries were profiting from the war. Factory owners fulfilling military contracts could hardly describe their windfalls as the consequence of their own individual genius; the image of the industrialist as a self-made man rang hollow as public dollars poured into private coffers. To meet the demands of justice, a committee of American economists recommended that Congress drastically increase "the rates of the income tax, with a sharper progression in rates as incomes become larger" and a "tax which will take substantially all of special war profits." An "excess-profits" tax was implemented, intended to siphon away the very high profits that came from the war economy—and though many corporations still saw immense gains, this highly progressive tax provided more revenue than the individual and corporate income taxes during the war. War's call to shared sacrifice made the case for progressive taxation as nothing else could. In 1917, E. R. A. Seligman celebrated the nation's "appreciation of the democratic principles of fiscal justice."[75]

But if the old antitax forces were silenced by the demands of patriotism, they were not defeated. They were waiting.

THE COUNTERREVOLUTION BEGINS

"Pursuant to your request for a memorandum setting forth the various ways by which an individual may legally avoid tax," wrote the commissioner of internal revenue to Treasury Secretary Andrew Mellon in 1923, "I am pleased to submit the following, which has been prepared by a member of the Income Tax Unit of this Bureau." Mellon, financier and industrialist, became treasury secretary with the inauguration of the conservative Warren G. Harding in 1921, and held his post for twelve years, through the presidencies of Calvin Coolidge and Herbert Hoover. Throughout his term, Mellon dedicated himself to reversing the tide of progressive taxation. His antipathy to income taxes was personal as well as professional. With guidance directly from the federal tax service, Mellon managed to shelter two-thirds of his income from taxation; his income was $3.5 million annually, but Mellon paid taxes as if it were just over $1 million. He would eventually be charged with tax evasion.[76] In the meantime, Secretary Mellon pioneered a political strategy that would become a standard part of the twentieth-century antitax playbook: financing pseudopopulist campaigns to bring less-wealthy people to the antitax cause.

Mellon's first foray into popular politics was a book, *Taxation: The People's Business*, calling for a government run on "business principles" and asserting that high tax rates were blunting the "initiative" of the American people. Business interests mobilized to sell the Mellon plan to the public, including through a 1924 campaign, the National Tax Reduction Week, presented on vaudeville stages and in movie theaters.[77] Mellon also helped arrange the financing for a campaign targeting small-town bankers in Texas, who were angry about a tax exemption that benefited their competitors. The Texas bankers were persuaded to lobby for an income tax rate reduction, which would reduce their tax disadvantage—and it worked. Texas legislators who had previously opposed Mellon's tax cut plan now voted for it. The result was the Revenue Act of 1926, the biggest tax cut for the rich in American history.[78] Under Mellon's leadership, the excess-profits tax was eliminated, and five rounds of income tax cuts were enacted, reducing the top-bracket tax rate from 73 percent in 1920 to 24 percent in 1929.[79]

As far-reaching as Mellon's reforms were, he was skeptical of demands from his most conservative Republican colleagues to wholly eliminate the popular income tax. To do so might provoke even more radical attacks on wealth, for one.[80] Mellon was also a budget hawk, and wholesale repeal would risk deficits. So the new, flatter income tax continued to produce about half of federal revenue.[81] But progressive federal taxation mobilized the rich into politics as a far more unified constituency. Whereas the tariff divided finance, commerce, industry, and agriculture, the income tax gave all wealthy people a similar incentive to participate in politics and to oppose expensive public investments.[82] Conservative activists in the following decades would seek to complete the counterrevolution that Mellon had begun. If they could not prevent democratic control of taxation, they would adopt democracy's tools to subvert popular fiscal priorities. In the words of fiscal sociologist Isaac Martin, the income tax unleashed a "rich people's movement" that persists to this day—as we will see in the chapters to come.[83]

9

FDR TURNS AMERICANS
INTO TAXPAYERS

A legal, moral, and political right
—Franklin Delano Roosevelt

It was June 1941. Since the fall of France a year earlier, Great Britain had been fighting Nazi Germany nearly alone. President Franklin Delano Roosevelt, against the strong tide of American isolationism, was mobilizing the country for the war that he knew was coming. Civil rights leader A. Philip Randolph had promised a July 1 March on Washington a hundred thousand strong, unless Roosevelt signed an executive order banning discrimination in the defense industries. Then, on June 22, Germany invaded the Soviet Union; the three million German soldiers who had been assembled on the Eastern Front somehow took Stalin by surprise. By the end of the month, FDR had signed the antidiscrimination directive and an executive order authorizing an increase in the armed forces of nearly a million men.

In that same month, Luther Gulick, a bespectacled professor of public administration, had been appointed to a treasury committee tasked with assessing the coordination of federal, state, and local fiscal policies. One might expect that the president was too preoccupied to concern himself with

181

fiscal federalism. But taxes are always important, and never more so than in war. Gulick met with FDR to try to convince him to consider a national sales tax, which Gulick believed could raise immense sums for the federal government. New revenue was clearly necessary; Roosevelt had asked Congress to increase defense spending from $6 billion to nearly $11 billion. The unanswered question was, where would the money come from?

In talking up the sales tax to FDR, Gulick took the opportunity to suggest that this revenue could eventually replace the payroll taxes that funded the new Social Security system, signed into law only six years earlier. Gulick thought that payroll taxes, which applied to working people's wages, were a mistake, especially if another depression were to occur. Roosevelt demurred: "We put those payroll contributions there so as to give the contributors a legal, moral, and political right to collect their pensions and their unemployment benefits. With those taxes in there, no damn politician can ever scrap my social security program."[1]

FDR knew that taxation was politics as much as it was economics, and he knew that taxpaying could mobilize the American people, whether to defend their new system of social insurance or to win a war against Nazism. Roosevelt would offset the unprecedented costs of war not with the adoption of a sales tax, as Luther Gulick and others had recommended, but with the expansion of the income tax to middle- and working-class households.[2]

Though Americans have always contributed to the US Treasury indirectly, through the higher prices resulting from tariffs, it was FDR who turned the American people into direct federal taxpayers. First, during the Great Depression, the payroll tax was implemented to fund Social Security. Then, during World War II, the income tax was expanded from a tax on the rich to a tax on the masses. As Roosevelt himself anticipated in his defense of the Social Security payroll system, those taxes would rapidly be imbued with a political and even moral significance that continues to shape American politics to this day.

MASS TAXPAYING FOR PENSIONS

During the bleakest years of the Depression, Dr. Francis E. Townsend looked out his window and saw three elderly women digging through garbage cans to find food. The mild-mannered Townsend suddenly started shouting. "I swore and I ranted, and I let my voice bellow with wild hatred I had for things as they were." His wife rushed in, telling him he must stop before the neighbors heard. "I want all the neighbors to hear me!" Townsend roared. "I want God Almighty to hear me! I'm going to shout till the whole country hears!"[3]

His outrage led him to devise an ambitious pension system. With slogans like "Honor Your Father and Mother," the Townsend Plan promised to provide pensions of $200 per month to all Americans over sixty who promised to quit work and spend the money—requirements intended to reduce unemployment while encouraging an economic recovery. Benefits were not limited to the poor ("means-tested") and were not linked to contributions. Experts derided the lavishness of the proposed benefit—at the time, only about one in eight American households earned over $200 a month. But Townsend drew a devoted following. At its peak, the Townsend movement had millions of members organized in thousands of local clubs, and members of Congress were deluged with pro-Townsend petitions.[4]

The demand for a national pension system had been building for many years. A few decades earlier, federal pensions for nearly a million Civil War veterans and their dependents had made up as much as 40 percent of federal spending.[5] But later generations of the elderly had no such protection, even as the Depression pushed many into poverty. Townsend's unexpectedly vibrant movement only added to the pressure.[6] Even with all the competing needs during the Great Depression, old-age pensions were on the New Deal agenda.

The program that the New Dealers would eventually develop and adopt was, however, fundamentally different from the one proposed by advocates like Townsend, as well as those implemented in many European countries at the time. Roosevelt wanted to distinguish his social insurance programs from the myriad New Deal programs that were intended to provide for emergency needs during the Depression. And he believed that, with the right policy formulation and the right rhetoric, social insurance could avoid the stigma that left antipoverty programs small and politically vulnerable.

Roosevelt wanted to separate "social insurance" and "relief," a distinction that would be defined by the taxes that paid for the programs. Whereas relief programs were paid for by general government revenues, the insurance programs would be funded by "contributions" from future beneficiaries. Benefits would be earned via taxpaying. On June 8, 1934, when Roosevelt first informed Congress of his intention to design a system of old-age and unemployment insurance, he touted the contribution-based funding scheme.[7] He reiterated his commitment when he sent his proposed legislation to Congress seven months later. The first principle of his program was that old-age pensions be "self-sustaining in the sense that funds for the payment of insurance benefits should not come from the proceeds of general taxation."[8]

Roosevelt's advisors were not universally on board with his approach. One of FDR's most trusted confidantes, Harry Hopkins, argued passionately for relief and insurance to be a single program to which all people were entitled. Roosevelt responded that this was "the very thing he had been saying he was against for years—the dole." Roosevelt believed that long-term reliance on public relief encouraged "spiritual and moral disintegration" for the individual and the nation. Unlike the demeaning experience of relief, social insurance benefits would be an earned right. To ensure this distinction, the funding for the two programs had to be kept separate.[9]

One drawback to Roosevelt's plan was that payroll taxes were regressive, taxing income from work rather than income from wealth. What is more, there was (and remains) a cap on Social Security taxes. In 1937, the first $3,000 of one's earnings were taxed; any wage income above that went untaxed.[10] Putting a new tax on working people, particularly at a time when wages were still depressed, was a controversial choice. It took money out of people's pockets when many had little to spare, and it reinforced economic inequality.

When Roosevelt's Committee on Economic Security presented its final plan, it included the proposal that payroll tax contributions would eventually be supplemented by general revenues, as was the norm in other countries' old-age insurance systems. Roosevelt demanded that the report be rewritten, reiterating his concern that this approach would turn the program into "the same old dole under another name," and arguing that any reliance on general revenues would risk future cuts to the program. As he put it to Secretary of Labor Frances Perkins, "We can't sell the United States short in 1980 any more than in 1935."[11]

Congress accepted FDR's proposal, in part because pensions were seen as the least significant piece of the legislation. Lawmakers were more focused on immediate old-age poverty relief, aid to single mothers and their children, and aid to the blind. It was only at the president's insistence that Congress kept the old-age insurance component in the bill at all. Congress did, however, make one major change to the proposed insurance system: They excluded domestic and agricultural workers from coverage. Other countries' public pension schemes often initially excluded farm laborers and servants because it was difficult to administer the program for workers whose hours and wages were less regimented, and Treasury Secretary Henry Morgenthau had testified to this potential bureaucratic challenge in the United States (much to the irritation of Perkins, a strong proponent of universal coverage).[12]

The logistical considerations alone might well have been enough to motivate Congress to shrink the program's initial coverage. But there was an added political motivation at work, one that has frequently been decisive. The exclusion would render most Black Americans, predominantly employed in the domestic and agricultural sectors, ineligible for the program. As the general counsel for the NAACP testified, the new legislation was "a sieve with the holes just big enough for the majority of Negroes to fall through."[13] Of course, a bill that disappointed racial justice advocates necessarily pleased the immensely powerful Southern legislators, who were alert to the potential for tax-funded programs to undermine the racial hierarchy in their states.[14]

Despite the widespread demand for a national pension system, and the broad coalition in favor of Roosevelt's plan, the success of Social Security was in no way obvious or guaranteed at the time. In 1936, conservative business leaders saw the threat of a new payroll tax as an opportunity to make inroads into Roosevelt's support among working people. Two months before the election, Detroit factory owners devised a new campaign against FDR.

"YOU'RE SENTENCED TO A WEEKLY PAY REDUCTION FOR ALL YOUR WORKING LIFE," read messages posted on factory floors. "YOU'LL HAVE TO SERVE

THE SENTENCE UNLESS YOU HELP REVERSE IT NOVEMBER 3." On payday, workers found messages warning, "Effective January, 1937, we are compelled by a Roosevelt 'New Deal' law to make a 1 per cent deduction from your wages and turn it over to the government. . . . You might get this money back. . . . There is NO guarantee. Decide before November 3—election day—whether or not you wish to take these chances."[15]

Republicans were certain that fearmongering over taxes would aid their re-election chances. Property taxes had provoked protests and even strikes in the early years of the Depression—surely a new tax on working people would push voters away from FDR. But conservatives misjudged the country's mood. As one longtime Democrat put it, "Why didn't the boss put any political propaganda in your pay envelopes four years ago? Because there wasn't any pay envelopes."[16]

Roosevelt was livid at the bad-faith attack on Social Security. Corporate leaders were not really upset about social insurance. Indeed, a 1939 poll would find that merely 17 percent of businessmen wanted to repeal it. What really angered industrial elites were not the new taxes that fell on their workers—it was the new taxes they themselves were paying.[17]

SOAKING THE RICH

"We've been praying to the Almighty to send us a feast," proclaimed Louisiana Senator Huey Long in a December 1934 speech. At the time, millions of Americans were going hungry. "The Lord has answered the prayer! He has called the barbecue! Come to my feast, he said to 125 million American people." The United States had wealth enough for everyone, Long insisted. "But Morgan! and Rockefeller! and Mellon!" Long bellowed in his thick Louisiana drawl, his hands in fists and his arms pumping, "have walked up and took 85 percent of the victuals off the table. . . . Now how you gonna feed the balance of the people?" Long believed he had the answer:

> Give 'em a yacht! Give 'em a palace! Send 'em to Reno and give 'em a new wife when they want it, if that's what they want! But when they've got everything on the God's living earth that they can eat and they can wear and they

can live in . . . then we've got to call Mr. Morgan and Mr. Mellon and Mr. Rockefeller back and say, come back here, put that stuff back on the table here that you took away from here that you don't need. Leave something else for the American people to consume. And that's the program.

Huey Long's Share Our Wealth scheme promised a middle-class lifestyle for every American, to be paid for by taxes applied only to the very rich. By taxing away all income over about $1 million and all wealth over around $5 million, Long proposed to provide—among other things—every senior with a pension, every World War I veteran with an early payout of their promised bonus, and every family with enough money to buy a home, a car, and a radio.[18]

The details of Long's shifting proposal were hazy at best, and the figures upon which he based his economic calculations were often inaccurate. For one, rich people simply did not have enough money to lift all other Americans into the upper-middle class. But in the depths of the Depression, the populist spirit of the plan—and similar proposals from other would-be demagogues—resonated with many Americans. Millions joined Long's Share Our Wealth campaign. When the Democratic National Committee quietly polled the public in the spring of 1935, Long looked like a potential spoiler in the next presidential election. He might win three million or four million votes nationally, Roosevelt's campaign manager estimated, including hundreds of thousands in pivotal states. It was time, Roosevelt reportedly said among friends, to "steal Long's thunder."[19]

Some of the groundwork had already been laid for a new campaign to tax the rich. Congress had turned its attention to rich people's tax avoidance schemes in 1933, revealing that financier J. P. Morgan had paid no income taxes at all from 1930 to 1932. In March 1934, the Roosevelt administration brought charges of tax evasion against none other than former Treasury Secretary Andrew Mellon. The significance of tax fairness to the New Dealers was best summed up by Secretary Morgenthau, who declared, "I consider that Mr. Mellon is not on trial but Democracy and the privileged rich and I want to see who will win."[20]

But progressives were looking for more than closing loopholes and investigating tax cheats. "Mr. President, Begin to Tax!" cried a March 6 article in *The Nation*, demanding heavier income taxes.[21] In May, Wisconsin Senator Robert La Follette made a national radio address condemning the concentration of wealth and calling on the administration to take a "courageous position for heavily increased taxation" on incomes, estates, and inheritances.[22]

At the same time, Roosevelt was facing renewed pressure on the right. Business opposition to Roosevelt was increasing, despite the marked moderation, and even conservatism, of many of his economic policies.[23] For years, he had worked hard to placate and reassure conservatives, including those on the Supreme Court, to limited avail. Now he would tack to the left.

Less than six weeks after the DNC poll showing Long's electoral clout, FDR sent a message to Congress calling for new taxes on the rich. To reverse the tax code's "unfair advantage of the few" and the country's "unjust concentration of wealth and economic power," the United States needed new taxes on inheritances and gifts, new brackets to raise the income tax rates on the very highest earners, and new progressive rates in the corporate income tax.[24]

In contrast to Senator Long's bombast, the tone of Roosevelt's tax message was measured and conciliatory. By citing support for progressive taxation from the industrialist Andrew Carnegie and the Republican Theodore Roosevelt, FDR implied that his plan transcended partisanship and class. Rather than accusing wealthy individuals of stealing God's bounty, FDR gently punctured the enduring myth of the self-made man. "Wealth in the modern world does not come merely from individual effort," FDR explained. "The people in the mass have inevitably helped to make large fortunes possible," and the government itself contributes "the opportunities for advantage."

When Roosevelt turned to the consequences of extreme wealth, however, he abandoned his soft-spoken approach. Such inequality, he argued, resulted in a "great and undesirable concentration of control in a relatively few individuals over the employment and welfare of many, many others." When riches compounded over generations, it was a danger to democracy: "Such inherited economic power is as inconsistent with the ideals of this generation as inherited political power was inconsistent with the ideals of the generation which established our Government."

Roosevelt was picking a fight, and he knew it. When he read the tax message aloud to Secretary of the Interior Harold Ickes, he paused to smile and say, "That is for Hearst."[25] The newspaper tycoon William Randolph Hearst, a onetime supporter of the graduated income tax, had become an ardent opponent of progressive taxation, a policy he called "Soak the Thrifty" and, later, "Soak the Successful."

As usual, FDR's political instincts did not fail him. Upon learning of Roosevelt's tax message, Hearst wired the editors of his newspapers across the country, calling the tax plan "a bastard product of Communism and demagogic democracy," the brainchild of "Stalin Delano Roosevelt." From now on, he told his editors, the New Deal would be called the "Raw Deal" in Hearst's papers. He was joined in his tax-induced apoplexy by the major organizations representing big business. The government was "attempting to tax people who work, who create wealth and distribute wealth," the Philadelphia Board of Trade frothed, "to support the incompetents and the ne'er-do-wells."[26]

When Huey Long heard FDR's tax message, he "almost waltzed," *The New York Times* reported.[27] Long strutted around the Senate chamber, pointing at himself and saying, "Amen!"[28] He could not know he would not long survive the passage of the tax legislation for which his campaign had provided a political impetus. In September 1935, he was shot and killed by a political opponent in his home state of Louisiana.

Long's death did not change Roosevelt's political calculus. As the election grew nearer, FDR came to define his presidency in the terms he had used in his tax message: as a campaign against a new American aristocracy. This was the central theme of his speech in June 1936, when he accepted the nomination of the Democratic National Convention in Philadelphia and lambasted the "economic royalists." Just weeks before the election, at a campaign speech in Worcester, Massachusetts, Roosevelt again described the fight over taxation as a fight for democracy:

> Ever since 1776 that struggle has been between two forces. On the one hand, there has been the vast majority of our citizens who believed that the benefits of democracy should be extended and who were willing to pay their fair share

to extend them. On the other hand, there has been a small, but powerful group which has fought the extension of those benefits, because it did not want to pay a fair share of their cost. That was the line-up in 1776. That is the line-up in this campaign. And I am confident that once more—in 1936—democracy in taxation will win.[29]

The speech provoked a standing ovation from the crowd that ended only when the president, mindful of the radio audience listening at home, gestured for it to cease.[30]

If Roosevelt's tax message wrote the rhetorical playbook for his 1936 campaign, it was not nearly such a clear guide for actual policymaking. For the first years of the New Deal, Roosevelt had let Congress take the lead on taxation. As recently as that January, Roosevelt had told Congress that he did not think new taxes were advisable that year. The sudden and belated addition of progressive tax policy to the Roosevelt agenda left congressional leaders confused. (Roosevelt had gleefully predicted that the tax message would leave the chairman of the Senate Finance Committee "so surprised he'll have kittens on the spot.")[31]

Did FDR really expect Congress to rush together a complicated tax reform measure? Quietly, administration officials said no. There were those in FDR's Treasury Department ready with plans to tax the rich—and particularly, with plans intended to reverse the concentration of corporate power. But Treasury Secretary Morgenthau described FDR's tax message in his diary as "more or less of a campaign document" rather than a legislative proposal. Roosevelt himself sent mixed messages on what he was expecting, much to the irritation of his allies in Congress. His real role during the legislative process was to stoke public resentment about wealthy people escaping taxation without technically breaking the law—or, as the president explained, "you hire a $250,000-fee lawyer, and he changes the word 'evasion' into the word 'avoidance.'"[32]

It was progressives in Congress who pushed a tax bill forward that summer. The result was, as one congressman put it, "a hell raiser, not a revenue raiser." Corporate lobbyists had successfully weakened a number of Roosevelt's proposals and inserted substantial special breaks for their clients.

Overall, however, the law followed Roosevelt's lead. The Revenue Act of 1935 focused tightly on the largest businesses and the richest households. It raised income tax rates and estate taxes for the immensely wealthy and instituted a new graduated corporate income tax that applied higher levies to larger companies. Its passage planted a flag for taxation as a tool explicitly intended to reduce economic inequality and combat monopoly power.[33]

The law did not achieve what some progressives had demanded: an income tax that raised money from the plutocrats *and* from the merely well-to-do. The country should have the "guts to tax people," as one tax-increase proponent put it. Such a plan would have raised substantially more money. In taxing only the very rich, however, Roosevelt avoided enlisting new enemies among the upper-middle class. The top tax bracket applied to literally one taxpayer—John D. Rockefeller Jr.—who would now pay a 79 percent rate, rather than 63 percent, on the portion of his income over $10 million. Regressive excise taxes, on things like gasoline, cigarettes, and the recently relegalized alcohol, provided more federal revenue than income taxation. As the editors of *The Nation* wrote, while the president's tax message had been so "sweeping and courageous" that it had fired "the imagination of the country," the final bill was "little more than a travesty of the principles originally set forth."[34]

Whatever its substantive limitations, the so-called Wealth Tax marked a fundamental break between FDR and big business. By 1936, Harold Ickes would express wonder that "simply the fear of increased taxes" could make "such a bitter enemy out of practically everyone" among the industrial rich. But the other side of Roosevelt's political calculation—the popularity among the masses of taxing the very rich—also proved accurate. As Secretary Ickes put it in his diary, whatever the "clamor that will go up from Hearst and the big-moneyed groups," the tax plan would be a winner with the "average man and woman."[35] Despite the Republican bosses' campaign to frighten their employees about the coming payroll tax, workers stuck with Roosevelt. He rode his new economic populism to a resounding electoral victory in 1936, winning more than 60 percent of the vote and every state but Vermont and Maine.

Roosevelt's overwhelming victory boded well for further increases in taxes on the plutocratically wealthy. But the economic downturn of 1937 reinvigorated FDR's opponents, who stymied many of his progressive ambitions in the last years of the New Deal, including his tax plans. Still, making the rich pay remained a priority for Roosevelt. In what must have made for some awkward family dinners, his administration investigated the tax avoidance schemes of the wealthy du Pont family—just as FDR's son, Franklin Jr., was preparing to wed Ethel du Pont.[36]

If his administration had ended after two terms, Roosevelt's progressive tax legacy would be relatively modest: a recommitment to the tax-the-rich principles that Democrats had supported for decades, and renewed campaigns against tax evasion. The New Deal's fiscal innovation was not progressive taxation; it was the (regressive) payroll tax on working people to support social insurance. FDR had distinguished these two federal taxes in stark moral terms. One, the Social Security tax on wages, was an everyman's tax, sold as a positive contribution to one's own economic future. The other, the income tax, strictly limited to the nation's wealthiest households, was lauded as an exaction on a plutocratic class whose economic control hurt ordinary working people and whose political power endangered democracy.[37]

But federal taxation would change fundamentally in Roosevelt's third term. Once again, the fiscal system would be reforged in the heat of war.

TAXPAYING FOR WAR

A mere two months after the December 7, 1941, attack on Pearl Harbor, thirty-two million American moviegoers in over twelve thousand theaters viewed a new short film instructing them on how they could support the war effort. The cartoon, featuring Disney's Donald Duck, was titled *The New Spirit*.[38]

Marching to a patriotic song, his eyes aglow with American flags, Donald hears on the radio that "your whole country is mobilizing for total war." He speeds away, returning with a saucepan on his head and staggering under the weight of an ax, baseball bat, golf club, sword, shotgun, boxing gloves, and bear trap. "Okay! I'm ready," he quacks. "Are you a patriotic American?" the radio announcer asks. "Eager to do your part?" "Yes, sir!" Donald Duck shouts, presenting arms with the shotgun as the saucepan slides over his eyes. "There's something important you can do," the radio continues. "You won't get a medal for doing it . . . it may mean a sacrifice on your part . . . but it will be a vital help to your country in this hour of need." Donald Duck begs to know what it is, promising "I'll do anything! Anything!"

"Your income tax," the radio informs him. Donald collapses in shock and horror. "It's your privilege, not just your duty, but your privilege, to help your government by paying your tax and paying it promptly," the radio continues. "Your country needs taxes for guns, taxes for ships! Taxes for democracy! TAXES TO BEAT THE AXIS!"

"Let me at it!" Donald Duck cries, rushing away again, this time returning with a file drawer, a dictionary, a globe, two adding machines, a ruler, T square, pot of paste, compass, his piggy bank, and a bottle of aspirin. He is soon reassured that taxes are much easier than he expects, due to the new "streamlined!" 1040A form. As Donald races to deliver his taxes to Washington, cartoon planes emblazoned with swastikas explode, and "My Country 'Tis of Thee" swells in the background. "Taxes," the announcer concludes, "will keep democracy on the march!"

Protax propaganda was not entirely new in 1942. Many cities, facing unprecedented revenue shortfalls in the early years of the Depression, had launched "Pay Your Taxes" campaigns with slogans like "Don't Let Newark Down."[39] But the wartime effort was different, of course. Different in its justifications, and different in its scope. Between Pearl Harbor and V-J Day, the federal budget grew to twelve times its prewar size, and federal revenues reached nearly half the nation's GNP.[40] Funding the global conflict required taxing regular Americans at entirely new levels.

The Roosevelt administration had two major tax options in front of them. They could expand the income tax: raise rates so that people paid more, and lower exemptions so that more people paid. Alternatively, they could impose a general sales tax, a new form of taxation that had been adopted in nearly half the states over the previous decade. Before the war, Morgenthau's Treasury Department had developed plans for a sales tax and for a broad-based income tax, but neither had moved forward. Now, as war loomed, the decision could not be put off any longer.[41]

Roosevelt decided that a broader income tax was preferable, both for reasons of principle and as a matter of convenience. The Democratic Party had long been committed to income taxation because it was based on the ability to pay. A sales tax would add to the hardships of the poor by raising the cost of essential purchases. In addition, though getting millions more Americans to successfully file their income taxes would be challenging, it would have been an even bigger headache to design and implement a new federal sales tax system. Sticking with the income tax also avoided stepping on some toes. State governments did not like the idea of the feds dipping into their revenue sources, and some congressional leaders drew political power from their familiarity with the intricacies of the income tax and did not want a federal sales tax upending their legislative fiefdom.[42]

Americans also supported a broadened income tax. A new tax law in 1940 had already modestly reduced exemptions, increasing the income tax rolls by about two million people.[43] The following January—during the London Blitz but still nearly a year before Pearl Harbor—a Gallup poll showed that most Americans supported paying for new defense expenditures by extending the income tax to include all families not on public relief. The poll also showed much stronger support for an income tax than for a sales tax. In May, another Gallup poll reported that 70 percent of Americans wanted to pay for defense "chiefly by extra taxes," rather than borrowing, and 59 percent said they were personally willing to pay an additional "two weeks' salary."[44]

In the following years, the income tax went from a "class tax" on the rich to a "mass tax" on almost everyone. In 1936, the income tax applied only to about the top 6 percent of households. This was, in part, because exemptions were very high. Even until 1940, a married couple without dependents had an exemption of $2,500—at a time when the median income for a white man was $1,112. And those at the threshold of taxpaying (such as a successful dentist or engineer) would only pay the bottom rate, a mere 4 percent, on whatever they earned over their exempted income. During World War II, however, the vast majority of working Americans began to pay income taxes—and heavy taxes at that. It was a program that Treasury Secretary Morgenthau bluntly called "all out" taxation.[45]

This is not to say that FDR abandoned his commitment to progressivity—quite the opposite. The World War II income tax included top rates as high as 94 percent in 1944. Roosevelt wanted to push even further. He repeatedly, though unsuccessfully, called for setting a maximum income of $25,000, with "all excess income" going to the war effort. But the more significant change, both culturally and fiscally, was the expansion of the income tax system to the general public. Income tax receipts rose from $2.2 billion in 1939 to an astonishing $35.1 billion in 1944.[46] For the first time, a substantial amount of general federal revenue came directly from the paychecks of regular Americans.

From 1940 to 1942, exemptions were cut in half, bringing not just professionals but middle- and working-class people into the tax system. By 1944, the number of federal-income-tax payers increased sixfold. Tax rates in the lower brackets increased too. A single taxpayer with an income of $1,000—that of a telephone switchboard operator—owed taxes for the first time in 1941. Running her finger along the tables attached to the 1040A tax form, she would see that she owed $20. Consulting the same form for the following year, she would find a bill of $80. Her taxes had quadrupled in a year. On the tax tables for 1944, she would have found she owed $95, or more than a month's salary. (Tax withholding had begun in 1943, so with luck she had already paid much of what she owed.)[47]

Turning Americans into income-tax payers was an enormous challenge. Millions of Americans who had never seen a tax form needed to submit their returns accurately and on time. Less than a quarter of US adults had a high school diploma, and there was no such thing as a pocket calculator. In the first years of the war, before withholding, taxpayers had to pay months of taxes as a lump sum.[48]

What is more, the government needed Americans to pay taxes voluntarily. If even a substantial minority of Americans failed to file a return, faith in the system would collapse. So Americans had to not only know how to pay their taxes but also had to believe that it was their responsibility to do so. President Roosevelt had for years talked about the income tax as a cudgel against the undeserving wealthy. Now it had to become a shared rite of citizenship.

Patriotism made the transition to a mass income tax possible. Americans bore the cost of taxes the same way they bore the other, far more serious costs of war: wage and price controls, rationing, a military draft that would reach ten million men, and a growing toll of servicemembers wounded and killed. Taxes were, by comparison, hardly a sacrifice at all. "To those who complain that the tax is a heavy burden," gossip columnist Walter Winchell wrote in 1943, "remind them that a soldier's pack on his back weighs sixty pounds." Taxpayers envisioned their taxes purchasing vital equipment for the American boys serving on the front lines—an image strongly reinforced by Treasury propaganda. The government did everything in its power to stoke the citizenry's patriotism on the home front, including preparing Americans for their new income tax responsibilities. This included dry, informational Treasury documents about how to pay taxes, but also the enlistment of community leaders and popular media to create a "new culture of taxpaying," in the words of the legal scholar Carolyn C. Jones. Pamphlets, posters, radio spots, television skits, and movie shorts bombarded Americans with tax guidance and reminders.[49]

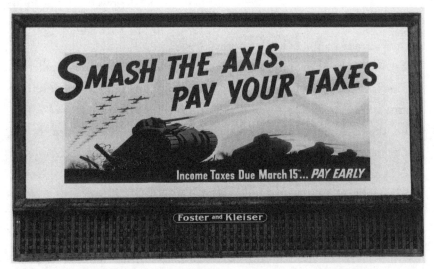

The extension of the income tax to middle-class Americans during World War II was supported by a national advertising campaign, including sixteen thousand billboards with this message, covering every major market in the country. (Credit: David M. Rubenstein Rare Book and Manuscript Library, Duke University)

The popular composer Irving Berlin, who had already contributed a ditty encouraging the purchase of war bonds, wrote a second song for the Treasury Department, "I Paid My Income Tax Today."[50] In the song, a low-income taxpayer addresses his "Uncle Sam":

> *I paid my income tax today*
> *I never felt so proud before*
> *To be right there with the millions more*
> *Who paid their income tax today*
> *I'm squared up with the U.S.A.*
> *See those bombers in the sky?*
> *Rockefeller helped to build 'em, so did I*
> *I paid my income tax today*

Though the singer is just "Mr. Small Fry" in the "lower brackets," he knows that his money is a valuable contribution to the war effort. "We must pay for this war somehow," the singer concludes. "Uncle Sam was worried, but he isn't now. I paid my income tax today!"

Recordings of Berlin's song, sung by *Hit Parade* star Barry Wood and by comedian Danny Kaye, were rushed from the Treasury Department to over eight hundred radio stations across the country in early 1942, with a request for frequent airtime ahead of the March 15 filing deadline.[51] At least one taxpayer appears to have taken the song literally. Among other voluntary contributions reported on Tax Day 1942, a local revenue office in New York City received a letter from a donor saying his income was too low to owe any income taxes, with a five-dollar check made out to "Uncle Sam."[52]

Even with the massive propaganda push, there were moments of panic in the Treasury Department. Each year during the war, the tax deadlines applied to millions more Americans. Would the expected returns come in? At four p.m. on March 9, 1943—six days before Tax Day—the pollster George Gallup placed an urgent call to Henry Morgenthau. "I didn't want to bother you," the survey analyst stammered as he spoke to the secretary of the Treasury. But "there is pretty desperate need to get to tell more people that they need to file returns next week."

"Oh really?" Morgenthau replied.

"We find quite a few people who apparently haven't yet been reached," the pollster continued, "and they—they have all kinds of confused ideas." People did not know they had to file, Gallup explained, or were confused about whether they had to pay if they had bought war bonds. "So it occurred to us that—that you might possibly want to fire all the 16-inch guns you've got down there between now and next Monday."[53]

Morgenthau leapt into action, releasing a new barrage of radio spots and enlisting everyone from senators to shop stewards to spread the word about the income tax.

In the end, it worked. As the political scientist Andrea Campbell has written, "The dawn of mass taxation came with surprising calm."[54] There was no crisis on Tax Day. The campaign to mobilize Americans into income-tax paying was a signal success. In fact, news reports regularly noted taxpayers waiving their deductions, paying earlier than required, or making entirely voluntary contributions.[55] About four in five Americans described their new income taxes as fair, a figure that did not vary by political party and that rose even higher in the later years of the war.[56] Most Americans were not simply compliant; they were persuaded.

Of course, not everyone was enthusiastic. Before, during, and after the war, there was a state-level movement to amend the Constitution to limit the top rate for federal income, gift, and estate taxes each to 25 percent. The campaign, the brainchild of oil baron Thomas Wharton Phillips Jr. and supported by wealthy notables including Andrew Mellon, never approached anything like the necessary levels of popular support, but it nevertheless provides a salutary reminder that even at the height of patriotic fervor, there remained serious elite opposition to progressive taxation.[57]

THE LONG POLITICAL LEGACY OF ROOSEVELT-ERA TAXATION

As in so many other economic arenas, Roosevelt-era tax policies redefined the contours of political contestation for generations thereafter.

In the postwar decades, the Social Security program blossomed into the program we know today. For decades, Congress passed tax and benefit increases on a bipartisan basis. In 1940, less than 1 percent of seniors received Social Security benefits; thirty years later, nearly 86 percent did. In 2022, Social Security lifted more than sixteen million elderly people out of poverty; without the program, nearly 40 percent of seniors would be poor. "No government bureau ever directly touched the lives of so many millions of Americans," wrote the historian Arthur Schlesinger in 1958—a description that remains accurate to this day. Social Security continues to enable seniors to live with dignity and to encourage their participation as citizens.[58]

Indisputably, the payroll tax funding mechanism helped protect Social Security when other social safety net programs were gutted.[59] It may also be the case, as Roosevelt believed, that even partial reliance on general revenues would have opened the door to cuts—though in point of fact, general revenues have supported Social Security through a number of backdoor channels.[60] Nevertheless, the widespread perception that Social Security benefits are solely the fruit of pensioners' own tax contributions has shielded the program against decades of conservative attack. The designers of Medicare followed the same blueprint: a payroll tax–based program with earmarked funds, a contributory program into which beneficiaries knew they had paid and of which taxpayers knew they would one day be beneficiaries.[61]

There was, of course, a cost to promoting the idea that Social Security was uniquely virtuous. If Social Security pensioners earned their benefits, the implication was that relief recipients did not. The danger of stigmatizing poverty relief was less obvious if one believed, as President Harry Truman did, that social insurance would "gradually reduce the need for public assistance."[62] But particularly once the federal government failed to commit to ensuring full employment, there was no possibility that social insurance could eliminate the need for other programs to lift Americans out of poverty. The dichotomy of welfare and earned benefits became, in the words of the sociologist Theda Skocpol, a "legacy of the New Deal."[63]

In turning the American people into taxpayers, FDR gave Republicans a new way to reach voters. With the end of the war, the patriotic rationale for the income tax was weakened, and the punitive rhetoric associated with taxing the rich could be co-opted by the right to encourage middle-income taxpayers to see themselves as put-upon. As the historian Molly Michelmore explains, voters could be convinced that their "economic security might be threatened, rather than enhanced, by new tax-and-transfer programs," an argument that helped undermine "popular support for the kind of cradle-to-grave welfare state liberal policymakers had hoped to build once the Depression and war emergencies had passed."[64]

As we will see in the next chapter, the Rooseveltian distinction between deserving and undeserving beneficiaries of government aid would be a powerful weapon in the hands of the New Deal's opponents, particularly once those benefits were made available to Black Americans.

10

TAXPAYERS, TAX "EATERS," AND THE RISE OF REAGAN

It would seem to violate all the rules of politics.

—*The New York Times*, July 17, 1978

"You say we are not taxpayers. What do you mean we are not taxpayers?" Alice Nixon asked the Senate Finance Committee.

It was the fall of 1967, and Nixon, a Black mother of three living in public housing in Pittsburgh, was a leader in the National Welfare Rights Organization (NWRO).[1] She and other women of the NWRO were testifying against legislation to cut benefits and impose work requirements for recipients of Aid to Families with Dependent Children (AFDC), a program established in the 1935 Social Security Act to provide money to support children in poor families. Earlier that year, President Lyndon Baines Johnson had proposed a small expansion to AFDC, along with a substantial increase to Social Security pensions. His staff thought the measure would be a good campaign plank in 1968, another step toward the "Great Society" in which "no child will go unfed." But Wilbur Mills, a Democrat from Arkansas and the powerful chair of the House Ways and Means Committee, had other ideas. The "taxpayers want us to be rough" with welfare mothers, Mills said.

Work requirements would help welfare recipients "become self-supporting taxpayers and not tax eaters."[2]

In her testimony, Alice Nixon denied this distinction. She and her NWRO colleagues demanded to be recognized as contributing citizens: taxpayers, consumers, voters, and mothers of boys who might be drafted for service in Vietnam. "Our Government any time they want to can change the image of the welfare recipients," Nixon insisted. Instead, Congress was grandstanding at the expense of America's poorest people. "We are tired of being used, black and poor white," Nixon exclaimed. "Will you please stop using us as a political football."[3]

After delivering their statements, the women, frustrated by the absence of many committee members during their hearing, conducted a "wait-in" to pressure legislators to listen to their testimonies. After nearly three hours, they were made to leave by the Capitol police.[4] When the hearing resumed the following morning, Russell Long, the chair of the Senate Finance Committee, railed against "those female broodmares who were here yesterday." The women of NWRO had talked about common experiences of welfare recipients: being trained for nonexistent jobs, being forced to put kids in daycare that cost more than their welfare check, their kids being stopped by police and questioned about where their parents were. But rather than engage with the testimonies of actual women who had appeared before his committee, Senator Long conjured up a fictive mother who sat at home drinking "Hi-Fi or Gypsy Gold wine all day," refusing to work, who "won't do anything except produce more children for the public to pay for at taxpayers' expense."[5]

When he was born, Senator Long had been named Huey—after his father, the populist Louisiana politician who had proposed confiscatory taxation of the rich. But much had changed since the elder Long had demanded that the nation's wealth be shared with every family. By 1967, a growing sentiment had emerged that it was not the Rockefellers and the Morgans and the Mellons who were taking an unfair and unearned share of the nation's bounty. It was families like Alice Nixon's.

The AFDC reforms that passed as part of the Social Security Amendments of 1967 were clearly directed at Long's imagined welfare mother.

The resulting legislation increased Social Security insurance benefits by 13 percent, but it froze spending for the children of single mothers and gave local welfare administrators more latitude in cutting benefits for those who failed to find work. No longer would support for the elderly and the poor rise in tandem. Within a few years, the average AFDC benefit began to decline, never to rise again.[6]

"That bitch of a war," President Johnson would later say, "killed the lady I really loved—the Great Society." There was some truth in this. Johnson had been forced to request a tax increase to offset the military expenses in Vietnam, leaving the leaders of the tax committees, Mills and Long, in an especially sour mood about expenditures. More broadly, a single year of spending on the war in Vietnam would have funded nearly the entire domestic agenda of Martin Luther King Jr.'s Poor People's Campaign.[7]

But the whole truth is more complicated. The reentry of Black Americans into political life, and particularly the demand not just for legal equality but for economic inclusion, provoked a decades-long backlash. As usual, contestation over the expansion of political power became a fight about taxes. Midcentury policies had encouraged the development of a homeowning suburban middle class, disproportionately white, sequestered from the increasingly poor cities, and highly sensitive to their property taxes. Geographic segregation was mirrored in the distinction of social insurance from poor relief. This twofold segregation trapped the urban Black poor in increasingly impoverished cities and consigned them to politically vulnerable spending programs. The taxes that paid for the great postwar expansion in domestic spending were, moreover, increasingly regressive. Taxes on the poor, working class, and middle class were going up while taxes on the rich were going down.

This was the fiscal landscape that confronted the leaders of the civil rights movement as they turned their attention from the South to the North and from political exclusion to economic exploitation. Poverty would prove even more resilient than the overt segregationist policies of the Jim Crow South. As the public came to associate antipoverty programs with aid to Black Americans, support for the programs collapsed. By the late 1960s, working- and middle-class whites looked out from their segregated enclaves at the poor and Black inner cities and felt themselves oppressed: hardworking taxpayers forced to support lazy beneficiaries of what was derisively termed "welfare." Although, as Alice Nixon insisted in her testimony before the Senate Finance Committee, poor people were taxpayers, that fiscal reality was no match for the juxtaposition of the symbolic "taxpayer" and the dog whistle of the "welfare queen."

THE REDEFINITION OF "WELFARE"

After World War II, Herb and Doris Kalisman were able to move from an attic in New York City into the new suburb of Levittown, with new kitchen appliances, a washer and dryer, and—thanks to federal subsidies for homeownership—a mortgage that cost only half that of a city apartment.

Eugene Burnett and his wife also looked at a house in Levittown. A veteran, Burnett intended to use his GI Bill benefits to buy a home. But when he asked the real estate agent for an application, he found that he could not buy a house in Levittown because he was Black. "It was as though it wasn't real," recalled his wife. "'Oh, man, look at this house! Can you imagine having this?' And then for them to tell me because of the color of my skin I can't be a part of it?"

The GI Bill is one of the most successful social welfare programs in American history; it helped millions of World War II veterans buy a home or go to college. But veterans like Eugene Burnett could only use their benefits within the racist confines of midcentury America. Of 67,000 GI Bill–backed mortgages in greater New York City, more than 66,900 went to white families. "I think we had the golden chance after World War II," the Levittown resident Herb Kalisman would later tell a documentary filmmaker. The GI Bill was supposed to be available to everybody, but "in a way they didn't make it available to everybody . . . and that was a golden opportunity in this country, and we missed it."[8]

As housing policy segregated the United States, the federal government poured money into the new white suburbs. The suburban South and West bloomed in the warmth of the military-industrial complex. Defense amounted to more than half of all federal spending in 1968 and was still a quarter of all federal spending in 1975. But though the people of Orange

County, California; Fort Worth, Texas; and other defense industry havens were living on government largesse, they were not seen (and certainly did not see themselves) in this light. No, it was people like Alice Nixon who were understood to be living on the government dime: poor Black Americans living in the cities—the very people who had been systematically excluded from the homeownership, higher education, and well-paying jobs that were the fruit of the mid-twentieth-century welfare state.[9]

The demonization of welfare has obscured the scope and successes of the postwar social safety net. As a share of the economy, federal nondefense spending nearly tripled between 1955 and 1975, rising to nearly 16 percent of GDP. By the mid-seventies, about one-fifth of federal money went to Social Security benefits; over three decades, the poverty rate among the elderly fell from one-third to one-tenth. The poverty rate of the Black elderly fell from over 60 percent to less than 25 percent. Food Stamps (launched in 1964), Medicare, and Medicaid (1965) reduced poverty, hunger, and disease. Black infant mortality dropped by 50 percent in seven years. States and localities also dramatically increased their spending on human welfare. As historian Ira Katznelson has written, the net effect of these programs was "a more equitable and less harsh society."[10]

But public views of welfare became increasingly negative and increasingly racialized—a shift that occurred with astounding rapidity. In 1963 and 1964, slightly less than a third of stories about poverty in the major newsmagazines were illustrated with pictures of poor Black people—a figure roughly in keeping with the fraction of poor people who were Black. Three years later, Black Americans made up more than two-thirds of newsmagazine pictures of the poor. Sympathetic or neutral stories were commonly illustrated with pictures of white people, while images of Black Americans more often accompanied stories about welfare fraud or about the purported moral failings of the poor.[11]

What happened from 1964 to 1967 to reverse media representations of poverty?[12] Following the passage of the Civil Rights Act and the Voting Rights Act, civil rights leaders turned their attention to poverty and discrimination in the North. Urban Blacks revolted against police violence and economic deprivation in the Watts neighborhood of Los Angeles and in other predominantly Black communities in dozens of other American cities.[13] It was in this context that the media came to strongly associate poverty, and especially welfare, with Blackness—a connection that undermined the always tenuous public support for antipoverty programs. In 1961, over 60 percent of Americans said the government should spend more on welfare, a figure that dropped to 20 percent by 1973.[14] "Welfare," once a positive word to describe a host of government investments in economic security and human well-being, became a racist epithet for wasteful and corrupt spending on an undeserving poor.[15]

Accusations of welfare fraud abounded and proved impervious to evidence. A 1966 investigation by the *Los Angeles Times* found fewer than two hundred cases of welfare abuse in a system that served forty-five thousand families. The program was too stringent, not too lax, the paper said; kids were going hungry.[16] The following year, the Kerner Commission, launched by President Johnson to investigate the causes of urban unrest, came to much the same conclusion: The welfare system excluded "large numbers of persons who are in great need" and provided "assistance well below the minimum necessary for a decent level of existence."[17]

But the facts didn't seem to matter. A former movie star by the name of Ronald Reagan promised to send "the welfare bums back to work" and won the governorship of California with particularly strong support from white neighborhoods near Black communities.[18] Reagan's welfare rhetoric had already been honed over years of public speaking. His national political debut was a 1964 speech in support of Barry Goldwater, in which Reagan described a young woman with six children, "pregnant with her seventh," who wanted a divorce from her husband because she would then be eligible for AFDC. "She got the idea from two women in her neighborhood who'd already done that very thing," Reagan concluded. In his inaugural address in 1967, Reagan promised to "stand between the taxpayer and the tax spender." (Ironically, though Reagan would push through a tightening of welfare rules in the state, he would also preside over what was at the time the largest tax increase in California history.)[19]

Reagan was not alone in taking advantage of the shift in media attention and public opinion. "We face a crisis in our social welfare system," intoned the Republican Coordinating Committee in 1967, a crisis that provoked "fear and alarm among taxpayers" and "ill feeling and disorder in smoldering urban ghettos."[20] No matter that most welfare recipients were white, or that poverty was endemic in many parts of rural America; "welfare" became a program for the "ghetto" paid for by the "taxpayers." And not just among Republicans. In their 1972 campaign for the Democratic presidential nomination, Hubert Humphrey and George McGovern fought over their respective antipoverty proposals in terms of their costs to "the taxpayer."[21]

One welfare reform proposal might have cut against the symbolic dichotomy of the taxpayer and the welfare recipient. President Richard Nixon's 1969 Family Assistance Plan (FAP), designed by his liberal advisor Daniel Patrick Moynihan, amounted to a negative income tax providing a small guaranteed minimum income for families with children, including both traditional welfare recipients and the working poor.[22] Though Nixon never strayed from the traditional rhetoric, scolding the poor to work and become taxpayers, the program itself held a different implication.[23] FAP lumped together all the poor in a single category, independent of work status.

FAP was stymied, ironically enough, by the joint efforts of Senator Russell Long and the women he had called "broodmares." The NWRO, after trying unsuccessfully to raise benefit levels, convinced the three most liberal members of the Senate Finance Committee to join conservatives in refusing to move FAP out of committee. Later, Senator Long moved to delete a liberalized FAP from legislation under consideration on the Senate floor. By then, Long was working on an alternative policy now known as the Earned Income Tax Credit (EITC). Unlike FAP, Long's policy would only be available for people with earned income, reinforcing the distinction between the worthy working taxpayers and the undeserving welfare poor. For this reason, and because the EITC could be slipped as a progressive carrot into otherwise regressive tax legislation, the credit was expanded in 1978, 1986, 1990, 1993, and thereafter.[24]

Nixon responded to the failure of his welfare reform program by taking a page from then-Governor Reagan. Quite literally, in fact. Early in 1971, Reagan—who vocally opposed FAP—gave an interview to *U.S. News and World Report* in which he described "one hearing where one of these women from the Welfare Rights Organization got fired up and screamed out: 'And don't talk to us about any of those menial jobs.'" Reagan was, to say the least, prone to invention on the subject of welfare recipients—but in this case, he seems to have been recalling the remarks of NWRO representative Ethel Camp, of Virginia, who told the senators, "We only want the kind of jobs that will pay $10,000 or $20,000. . . . We aren't going to do anybody's laundry or babysitting except for ourselves!" A few weeks later, Richard Nixon lifted Reagan's line for his own speech—a telling indication of the direction of the Republican Party.[25]

Whether FAP would have meaningfully blurred the line between "welfare recipients" and "taxpayers" in the American political imagination is debatable. But in the absence of an income-support program that united the working and nonworking poor, the taxpayer/tax-eater dichotomy survived—and grew stronger, as taxes on working families grew heavier and as tax policy intersected with racial segregation.

THE TAXPAYER RISES AGAIN

As the cost of government rose during the postwar years, taxes went up. But they didn't go up for everybody.

Taxes went down on the rich and on corporations. In the early 1950s, the federal government had received nearly as much revenue from taxes on corporate income as from taxes on individual income. By 1970, more than twice as much money came from individuals as from corporations.[26] High-income households also saw their taxes decline. Neither party saw taxation as a battlefield for class conflict; gone was Roosevelt's rhetoric about taxing the "economic royalists." The bipartisan Revenue Act of 1964 cut taxes for every bracket, but those cuts were smallest in the middle brackets and largest for the rich, with the top marginal income tax rate falling from 91 to 70 percent.[27] (Fifteen years later, President Ronald Reagan would point to the 1964 legislation as the inspiration for his own massive tax cut.)

Meanwhile, those in the middle of the income distribution were coping with "bracket creep." Unlike today, tax brackets were not automatically adjusted for inflation, so cost-of-living wage increases pushed working- and middle-class people from the wide, flat middle of the tax code into the narrower, steeper brackets originally intended to apply to the rich. After falling in the 1950s, the fraction of middle-class Americans reporting that their income taxes were too high rose in the 1960s and 1970s.[28]

The very rich also benefited from multiplying exemptions, deductions, and loopholes. In 1969, the Treasury Department reported on two hundred wealthy people who had managed to all but eliminate their income tax responsibilities. While the ensuing outrage spurred Congress to close some of the most egregious windfalls for the rich, many of their tax benefits persisted. Consider one provision for "capital gains," the income from selling an asset, like a stock, that has increased in value. Not only are long-term capital gains taxed at lower rates than income from work, but if you hold an asset until your death, your heir can sell the asset without ever paying income tax on the gains accrued over your lifetime. In 1977, the tax break for capital gains at death cost the government $7.3 billion, or about $1 billion more than the cost of AFDC. Two-thirds of the money went to those in the top 2 percent of households.[29]

Tax breaks also went to the middle and especially the upper-middle class to subsidize their housing, health care, and pensions—a system that amounts to, as political scientist Christopher Howard put it, a "hidden welfare state" in the tax code.[30] During the 1960s and 1970s, such private welfare tax expenditures amounted to about 2 percent of GDP, equal to about one-eighth of all federal nondefense spending at the time.[31] But—in stark contrast to the vastly smaller outlay on AFDC—these tax expenditures went largely undiscussed. As wealthier families increasingly got their social benefits via the tax code, they did not see themselves as government beneficiaries and had little incentive to support the development of more universal programs.[32]

While income taxation was getting less progressive, more regressive taxes were going up. Payroll taxes, which fall most heavily on working- and middle-class wage earners, rose dramatically to pay for Medicare and for bigger Social Security benefits. By 1970, payroll taxes were more than four times what they had been in the late 1940s. Increasing sales and excise taxes (like the gas tax) cost poor people almost 9 percent of their income by the mid-1970s. Rising property taxes also hit lower-income homeowners hard.

Families in the middle of the income distribution saw their total tax obliga-tions nearly double between 1953 and 1975. The poor and near-poor had it even rougher. The poverty rate in the 1960s was actually *higher* once benefits and taxes were taken into account; on balance, people were being taxed into poverty, not lifted out of it.[33]

Americans bore much of their increased tax responsibility with relative equanimity. Though by the 1970s economists and conservative think tanks regularly attacked the payroll tax system, public opinion remained support-ive of this method of funding social insurance. Then, as now, Americans consistently told pollsters that they preferred payroll tax increases to Social Security or Medicare benefit cuts.[34] Similarly, the sales tax was (and is) con-sistently listed as one of the fairest taxes.

Property taxes, however, were another story. A tax on homes has inherent problems. Home values do not necessarily reflect the income of the home-owner. Calculating the value of a home is tricky and can put unaccountable discretionary power in the hands of the tax assessor. But the real issue with the postwar property tax was the segregation and suburbanization of Amer-ica. Once lines of race and class formed geographic as well as social barriers, it became all the easier to see one's taxes going not just to someone else but to somewhere else, and to resist that perceived transfer.

In the decades after World War II, suburbs around major cities incor-porated themselves as separate towns. By the early 1970s, Detroit was sur-rounded by over 338 suburban governments and 116 school districts. Rich suburbs could invest heavily in their own public services at comparatively low cost, thanks to their strong property tax base, while avoiding having to contribute to nearby poorer communities. The fruit of those investments—like well-resourced public schools—would ensure that property values rose even further. Another incentive for suburbanization was the special tax deal, starting in 1954, for new commercial construction; the tax advantage encouraged the proliferation of shopping malls that freed suburbanites from needing to visit the commercial centers in the urban core. The year 1968 was the first in which a plurality of voters lived in the suburbs.[35]

The concentration of wealth in the suburbs meant a concentration of pov-erty in the cities. As property values declined, the tax base dwindled. As suburbs lured industry and wealthier residents with low tax rates, cities had to impose higher tax rates on their remaining residents, who were disproportionately poor and Black. It was a downward spiral: Declining property values demanded higher tax rates, while inadequate revenue reduced the quality of public services. High taxes and poor services encouraged more residents to leave, driving down property values even further.[36]

In some ways, working-class whites and Blacks were in the same fiscal boat: paying higher taxes while rich people absconded to exclusive suburbs and corporations received generous tax breaks. Many progressives tried to overcome the symbolic divide between the "working-class taxpayer" and the "welfare recipient" by redirecting anger about taxation upward. Ralph Nader investigated corporate tax avoidance. Jesse Jackson called for better welfare benefits and tax reform. The leader of the National Welfare Rights Organization, George Wiley, went on to found the Movement for Economic Justice, which he hoped would organize a "taxpayer's revolt that is shaped and directed not against welfare mothers" but against "the welfare of the corporations."[37]

But because the property tax was bound up with homeownership and therefore segregation, it divided rather than united the Black and white working class. Partly for fear of losing what remained of their middle class, city tax assessors systematically biased their assessments in favor of white areas (which also received far better public services). In the 1960s, homes in Boston's Roxbury, a Black neighborhood, were assessed at 150 percent of their value, while homeowners in middle-class white neighborhoods were assessed at less than half their value. Black homeowners were also preyed on by private companies that bought up tax liens from fiscally distressed cities and used red tape and bureaucratic maneuvers to force Black families from their homes.[38]

Though Black taxpayers were in fact subsidizing neighboring white communities, it was nonetheless as *taxpayers* that working-class whites came to resist desegregation once explicitly white supremacist rhetoric fell from favor. As bus lines, pools, and parks were desegregated, "taxpayer leagues" proliferated to resist spending on these public services. Recapitulating arguments made by the Redeemers one hundred years earlier, opponents of integration often argued that white people paid all or nearly all the taxes, conveniently ignoring the exploitation that kept Black Americans from forming greater wealth in the first place.[39] Working-class whites also relied on their status as taxpayers because segregation was for them a consequence of government action—far more than for wealthier whites, who could rely on high home prices to keep poor minorities out of their neighborhoods and who could afford to send their children to private schools. As the legal historian Camille Walsh has shown, the Supreme Court's pro-integration rulings provoked floods of angry letters in which self-described taxpayers insisted that by paying their taxes, they bought white neighborhoods and white schools.[40] Just as the "welfare recipient" was coded as Black, the "defense of the taxpayer" became a banner for white reactionaries.

Though taxes on working-class and lower-middle-class people went up, and taxes on corporations and the wealthy went down, George Wiley's dreams of a leftist, multiracial taxpayer revolt went unrealized. By building a welfare state on segregated lines and shunting Black families into tax-starved neighborhoods and stigmatized programs, by balancing the social safety net on an increasingly regressive tax system and reinforcing the idea that paying taxes was how one earned government benefits, and by ensuring wealthier families got their social benefits through tax-subsidized private intermediaries rather than through more direct and universal public services, midcentury liberals made the welfare state vulnerable to attack by antitax conservatives and their powerful new allies. The channeling of white racial resentment into the language of taxpaying stoked a conservative renaissance.

THE COUNTERREVOLUTION OF 1978

By the late 1960s, the resurgence of the antitax American right was already perceptible in the collapsing support for antipoverty programs, the failure of popular mobilization against corporate tax cuts, and the "taxpayer" resistance to desegregation. As early as 1969, Republican strategist Kevin Phillips could refer to "the emerging tax-revolt centers of middle-class suburbia."[41] But the inflection point between the politics of the mid-twentieth century and the politics of today—the moment when conservatives went from defense to offense—was 1978.

The year witnessed three major fights over taxation, and three major victories for the antitax right. The first was a tax limitation in California. The second was a top-heavy tax cut from a Democratic Congress. And the third was a reversal of an IRS policy attempting to prevent public funding of segregationist schools. After 1978, it was clear that constituencies as disparate as California suburbanites, Southern white evangelicals, and Wall Street financiers could be brought together behind a single banner: opposition to taxation.

By the spring of that year, a property tax crisis was coming to a head in California. Home values were rising at a rate more than twice the national average and more than four times what the state had experienced over the previous decade. Property taxes rose accordingly.[42]

The California legislature had the power to solve this problem. The state was sitting on a multibillion-dollar revenue surplus.[43] Many states had addressed rising property taxes by capping taxes for poorer homeowners. There was plenty of progressive firepower behind similar reforms in California. In Oakland, Bobby Seale, cofounder of the Black Panther Party, had promised during his 1973 run for mayor to keep property taxes from rising on low-income homeowners and to raise taxes on the wealthy and the corporations. In 1977, the Citizen's Action League, an organization that had grown out of the welfare rights movement, pushed hard for the Tax Justice Act, a measure that would have cut property taxes in half for working- and middle-class homeowners and raised income tax rates at the top. But the legislation fell a few votes short in the state senate.[44]

In the meantime, conservatives were also trying to organize for their version of property tax reform: a broad and strict tax limitation that would deliver enormous benefits to California's corporations and real estate moguls. The road seemed steep. California voters had voted down conservative proposals for fiscal limits in 1968, 1972, and 1973—the last time despite the vocal support of the popular governor, Ronald Reagan.[45]

In 1978, the antitax standard-bearer was not a former movie star; it was a man named Howard Jarvis. Jowly and ill-tempered, Jarvis was given to remarks about immigrants riding on "the taxpayers' gravy train" and diatribes about affirmative action and food stamp recipients.[46] Many conservatives were loath to work with him, as his previous forays into far-right politics had been both unsuccessful and distinctly shady. In 1964, Jarvis and two friends had launched an organization called Businessmen for Goldwater, kept 100 percent of the $115,000 raised to cover their own fees and expenses, and shut down after being sued by the actual Goldwater campaign.[47] In fall 1977, however, antitax activists put aside their differences to coordinate on a massive statewide petition drive to put another property tax limitation on the ballot.[48] Thanks to substantial assistance from representatives of the real estate industry, the conservative initiative qualified for the June primary ballot as Proposition 13.

Like Jarvis himself, Proposition 13 was blunt and conservative. It rolled back assessed property values to their 1975 levels and capped annual assessment increases at 2 percent a year (or the rate of inflation, whichever was lower). Any substantial increases in property wealth would therefore go untaxed. The measure also imposed new supermajority requirements for other tax increases. As Jarvis would later describe the measure, "We are telling the government, 'Screw you!'"[49]

Panicked, the legislature rushed forward an alternative, bipartisan measure, Proposition 8, which would have reduced property taxes by about half as much as the Jarvis initiative and focused the tax cut on homeowners, not business. The legislature's alternative was written so that it would only go into effect if it outpolled Prop 13, so voting for both measures was the safest strategy for voters seeking a tax cut.

By April, Proposition 8 was leading against 13. Then, unexpectedly, the Los Angeles tax assessor opted to publish the county's new assessments months early. Those who had been reassessed saw, on average, *a 50 percent tax increase.*[50] Within days, popular furor led the county to cancel the increases—but politicians had been caught completely flat-footed, and the damage was done. Voters were not going to vote for the establishment's tax cut; they were going to vote for the one that told the establishment, "Screw you."

On June 6, 1978—despite the opposition of elected officials, academics, and business and civic leaders—nearly two-thirds of the California voters supported Jarvis's massive tax cut. Proposition 8, the officially sanctioned alternative, failed to even achieve a majority. Surveys showed that Proposition 13 received its strongest support from whites, men, the middle-aged, homeowners, Republicans, conservatives, those cynical of government, and those harboring racial resentments—that is, those most like Howard Jarvis himself. In this, Proposition 13 mirrored other homeowner backlash measures that passed handily in California in the 1960s and 1970s to resist fair housing policies and school integration.[51] Revealingly, California voters told pollsters that if Proposition 13 resulted in deficits, the program they wanted to see cut was "welfare."[52]

Proposition 13 did indeed result in immediate and extreme deficits. It cut property tax revenue by nearly 60 percent, pushing every locality in the state into a fiscal crisis and obliging the state to use its surplus to shore up local budgets. Education funding in the state plummeted and now hovers unsteadily at or below the national average, while longtime owners of increasingly expensive property receive a very sizable tax-funded nest egg. Billionaire Warren Buffett once noted that if his California home were taxed like his home in Nebraska, he would pay an extra $100,000 a year in taxes.[53]

At least as important as the direct effects of Proposition 13, though, is how its passage was interpreted at the time. *Time* magazine said it was a "Pacific tidal wave" of antitax sentiment.[54] *Fortune* insisted that Californians were "voting for capitalism."[55]

These interpretations rested on a profoundly shaky foundation. Proposition 13 did not demonstrate that Americans had suddenly become ideological devotees of the so-called free market. Quite the opposite. Proposition 13 blunted the market's impact on property owners by decoupling property taxes from property values. It is, in essence, a welfare program distributed through the tax code, with its biggest benefits going to longtime property owners in areas with rising property values. What is more, Americans' attitudes about government showed no meaningful change during that period. On taxes, Americans remained focused on their long-standing grievance: that the wealthy and corporations should pay more. Three-quarters of those surveyed in the late 1970s believed this, and it remains Americans' number one concern about the tax system to this day.[56]

But because politicians *believed* that Proposition 13 demonstrated some deep antipathy to progressive taxation and an activist state, the tax revolt helped usher in an era of regressive finance and austerity. In this sense, conservatives were right to see in the success of Proposition 13 a new vista of possibility. Proposition 13 showed that real economic concerns could be channeled into a campaign for immense, regressive tax cuts. These cuts could be sold not as a mechanism for a larger policy agenda, but as a goal in themselves, without any serious consideration of what they meant for government budgets or services. In the post–civil rights era, dog whistles and xenophobia could pave the way for an attack on the very premise that government could help people.

Proposition 13 kicked off a brief wave of tax limit campaigns, which succeeded in more than a dozen states. Many of these measures were far less stringent than Proposition 13, and many of the most extreme ones failed.[57] Of those enacted, the strictest provisions have been found to slow the growth of public spending, make local government less responsive, exacerbate fiscal crises, and reduce the quality of education and other public services like fire prevention. And while California has gotten a large share of its post-13 revenue from its progressive income tax, other states have filled their budget gaps with far more regressive forms of revenue, including sales taxes and fees.[58]

Proposition 13 fever did not just infect the states, however. It spread rapidly to Washington, where liberals fell over themselves to demonstrate their fiscal conservative bona fides. "We ought not to come in here and panic under Proposition 13," said Massachusetts Republican Ed Brooke, the first Black senator elected since Reconstruction. "It's not some magic word." His colleagues were not so sure.[59]

By the late 1970s, a new, more powerful, and vastly more conservative business lobby was ready to convince nervous members of Congress that the only way to assuage the taxpayers was to pass an immense tax cut for business and the very rich. In just ten years, the number of businesses with registered lobbyists in Washington had increased fourteenfold. The US Chamber of Commerce doubled its membership and tripled its budget. Business groups organized mass lobbying campaigns, a striking novelty at the time; when President Kennedy had wanted a business association to help spur public support for his proposed tax cut in 1963, he had been obliged to help stand up a new organization. Business also grew far more ideological, as corporate leaders ceased splitting campaign contributions between parties or endorsing growth-oriented spending policies.[60]

The business lobby was able to rest its increasingly conservative demands on a new intellectual edifice. Donors launched conservative think tanks and university centers to develop and promote antiregulatory and antitax ideas.[61] One of the fashionable new notions was that tax cuts would "pay for themselves"—that is, reductions in tax rates would encourage so much economic growth that government revenues would rise, not fall. This claim, associated with an economist named Arthur Laffer, would spend the next several decades being repeatedly proven wrong, and yet surviving to be tested and debunked again.

While business was marshaling its power, labor unions were in decline. Nearly a third of private-sector jobs were unionized in the 1960s; that figure dropped by ten percentage points by 1978. Business political action committees, which had given less money than labor to congressional candidates in the early 1970s, matched labor contributions by mid-decade, and far outstripped labor's giving by 1980.[62]

This was the new landscape that greeted Jimmy Carter when he was elected president in 1976 with tax reform as a major piece of his campaign agenda, including a proposal for taxes on capital gains to be raised to the same rate as the tax on wage income. "The present tax structure is a disgrace to this country," Carter had said in a debate with President Gerald Ford. "It's just a welfare program for the rich." Once in office, however, Carter's advisors dithered about whether their tax proposals would encourage economic growth or worsen inflation. After a year, Carter delivered a tax package to Congress that abandoned serious reform and took a symbolic swipe at businessmen expensing their "three-martini lunches."[63]

As one Washingtonian famously described it, the lobbyists "were braced for an attack; when the attack never came, they decided to invade!" If Carter did not want to raise the capital gains rate, business would lobby to slash it instead. The counteroffensive was the brainchild of Charls Walker—a former lobbyist for the American Bankers Association later described as "the living, breathing, cigar-smoking embodiment of a three-martini lunch."[64]

Under Walker's leadership, "capital formation," a euphemism for the rich getting richer, became the key to unlocking economic growth. The basis for this analysis was laughably weak, but it found currency in the economic turbulence of the late 1970s. Conservative nostrums expanded to fill the vacuum of liberal self-doubt. One influential business-sponsored study asserted that cutting capital gains would create hundreds of thousands of jobs and increase the stock market by 40 percent in only five years, a figure so outlandish that Congress's own economists called it "fatuous" and "absurd." Wielding these implausible figures, Walker convinced not just conservatives but many liberals in Congress of the soundness of his economic analysis. In the Senate, Russell Long pushed a capital gains cut even larger than the one that passed the House.[65]

Worried that a veto would harm the Democrats running for re-election or provoke the passage of an even more extreme measure, Carter quietly signed the legislation on Election Day of 1978. The capital gains rate was cut nearly in half, but the promised economic boom failed to materialize. There was no rise in the stock market or any increase in government revenue. Even supporters had to admit the measure had not attracted new investment. "The only clear winners from the tax cut," reported *The New York Times* in 1979, were those who were "actually taking capital gains, and paying less in taxes." Four-fifths of those gains went to those in the top 1 percent of incomes.[66]

The other group of people who failed to benefit from the capital gains cut were the Democrats who supported it. As late as September 1978, Democrats were receiving, as in the last election cycle, about half the corporate campaign contributions. But then, just as the tax bill made its way to Carter's desk, corporate giving suddenly broke toward the Republicans. The GOP received more than two-thirds of corporate money in the weeks before the election. In the years to come, corporate campaign money would become more and more lopsided. By 1982, the US Chamber of Commerce was giving twenty-two times as much to Republicans as to Democrats.[67]

The success of the 1978 capital gains cut seemed "to violate all the rules of politics," wrote *The New York Times* in undisguised wonder.[68] How could a tax break so narrowly targeted to the richest Americans get such strong support in Congress? Today, of course, massive tax cuts for the rich are par for the course. But in 1978, it seemed bizarre. The most popular thing any politician could do on taxes, it was then believed, was *raise* rates on the rich. As an interpretation of public opinion, this was and remains true. But Carter's shocking defeat on capital gains demonstrated that public opinion on tax policy need not stand in the way of wealth consolidation.

By the fall of 1978, the antitax right had secured a permanent minority veto over tax increases in California and a massive federal tax cut for the nation's wealthiest people. The third victory, against the IRS, was twofold: It undercut government action against segregation and mobilized a new and vital conservative voting bloc.

For years, the IRS had been supposed to rescind the tax-exempt status of schools with racially discriminatory acceptance policies. Under the Civil Rights Act of 1964, the federal government could not financially support organizations that engaged in racial discrimination. In the early 1970s, the courts confirmed that this proviso included federal tax exemptions; if a private school discriminated based on race, it did not qualify as a tax-exempt charitable organization, and the donations it received were not tax deductible for the contributor. "Jim Crow With Your Own Dough," read one memorable protest sign demanding an end to tax breaks for racism.

The IRS was thus charged with a Herculean task: determining which among thousands of private schools were engaging in racial discrimination and therefore ineligible for a tax break. At first, the IRS intended to give all religious institutions a pass. But some religious schools, like famed televangelist Jerry Falwell's Lynchburg Christian Academy, were explicitly whites-only at their founding, and some of the whites-only "segregation academies" set up during the South's massive resistance to school desegregation described themselves as "Christian." The IRS tried requiring schools to assert they were open to all students, and then requiring schools to make public notifications of their nondiscrimination policy. A handful of schools—most infamously, Bob Jones University—were defiantly segregationist, and the IRS attempted to remove their exemptions. But most schools just chose to discriminate more quietly. In ten years, barely

3 percent of the segregation academies lost their tax-exempt status, according to the US Commission on Civil Rights.[69]

In August 1978, under pressure from the courts and civil rights supporters, the IRS tried again. The IRS commissioner, Jerome Kurtz, proposed a new rule requiring any private school with "an insignificant number of minority students" that was "formed or substantially expanded" while the local public schools were supposed to be desegregating would need to demonstrate that it was not racially discriminatory. It would need to either meet a racial diversity quota based on the local school-age population or engage in various activities to encourage more diversity in its faculty and student populations.[70]

This well-intentioned but somewhat ham-handed proposal—with its wide application, its presumption of racism, and its application of an apparently arbitrary quota for minority enrollment—was nothing short of a miracle for the conservative movement. Since the 1960s, conservatives had seen white Southerners, and especially white Southern evangelicals, as a political constituency ripe for the picking. But many evangelicals saw politics as too worldly an activity. Even abortion still divided evangelicals in the mid-1970s.[71]

But when the IRS came for their tax exemption, conservative Christians mobilized as never before. The IRS was swamped with 126,000 angry letters. Commissioner Kurtz received so many threats that the Secret Service stepped in to provide protection for him and his wife.[72]

Congressional hearings gave legislators a chance to grandstand—until they were interrupted by the mother of a boy from Pensacola Christian Academy. "My name is June Griffin, and I'm a taxpayer from Evansville, Tennessee," she began, before excoriating the listening senators and IRS officials. Despite her bold interruption of official Washington and her demand that her family's government benefits go unchallenged, Griffin was not derided as a "broodmare" or made to leave by the police. She was applauded and showcased on the evening news.[73]

The IRS rapidly released a revised policy that addressed schools on a case-by-case basis and put the burden of proof back on the government. Riding high on their victory over the IRS, Jerry Falwell and other conservative leaders launched a new organization: the Moral Majority. Years later, one of the organization's founders fondly remembered the IRS debacle as a turning point in conservative politics: "What galvanized the Christian community was not abortion, school prayer, or the ERA [Equal Rights Amendment]. I am living witness to that because I was trying to get those people interested in those issues and I utterly failed. What changed their mind was Jimmy Carter's intervention against the Christian schools, trying to deny them tax exempt status on the basis of so-called de facto segregation."

Or, in the words of another cofounder of the Moral Majority, Robert Billings, the IRS Commissioner "Jerome Kurtz has done more to bring Christians together than any man since the Apostle Paul." Though evangelicals had supported the born-again Jimmy Carter over Gerald Ford in 1976, they would four years later break decisively against the Democrats.[74]

•◆•

If there was a man who embodied the spirit of 1978, it was Ronald Reagan. The former California governor was hailed as a prophet after the passage of Proposition 13. Like Goldwater, Reagan had opposed the Civil Rights Act, and as president he would try to restore the tax exemption of even overtly discriminatory schools like Bob Jones University.[75] Following the fuzzy math strategy of the "capital formation" lobbying campaign, Reagan proposed an enormous tax cut that he claimed would result in a budget surplus. The trick, close observers noticed, was to assert that inflation was going to go both up and down.[76]

And it was Reagan who made the so-called welfare queen famous when he hit upon the story of Linda Taylor, a Chicago con artist who had defrauded Cook County of about $8,000 before being caught and tried in 1974. The story was a recurring feature of Reagan's stump speeches from 1976 onward—though Taylor's earnings grew in his telling to a "tax-free cash income" of "$150,000 a year" and even "a million dollars."[77]

In 1980, Reagan finally rode his antitax rhetoric to the White House. More than two-thirds of Reagan's voters thought government was doing too much to aid the economic advancement of Black Americans; more than nine-tenths of Carter's voters supported those initiatives.[78] Reagan strategist Lee Atwater believed the election hung on whether the public saw the "bad guy" as "some multimillionaire that has five Cadillacs and hasn't paid taxes since 1974," or the guy who buys "liquor using food stamps."[79] But Atwater is primarily remembered today for his more vulgar expression of the new Republican strategy:

> You start out in 1954 by saying "Nigger, nigger, nigger." By 1968 you can't say "nigger" . . . so you say stuff like forced busing, states' rights, and all that stuff and you're getting so abstract. Now, you're talking about cutting taxes and all these things you're talking about are totally economic things and a byproduct of them is blacks get hurt worse than whites. . . . "We want to cut this" is much more abstract than even the busing thing, and a hell of a lot more abstract than "Nigger nigger."[80]

Before serving as a strategist for Reagan in 1980, Atwater had worked for the segregationist Strom Thurmond; he would go on to lead George H. W. Bush's presidential campaign in 1988. The idea that Alice Nixon had so forcefully denied in 1967—that there were some worthy people and some unworthy—became the mobilizing core of the Republican Party.

11

THE TRIUMPH OF ANTITAX
POLITICS AND THE EROSION
OF AMERICAN DEMOCRACY

"There are 47 percent of the people" who will vote for President Barack Obama "no matter what." Speaking candidly to donors at a fundraiser held in the gold and marble dining room of a private equity manager, former Massachusetts governor and 2012 Republican presidential candidate Mitt Romney did not know that his comments were being recorded on a secret camera.

"There are 47 percent," Romney continued, "who are dependent upon government, who believe that they are victims, who believe that government has a responsibility to care for them, who believe that they are entitled to health care, to food, to housing, to you name it." The figure, Romney explained, was drawn from federal tax data. "These are people who pay no income tax. Forty-seven percent of Americans pay no income tax," Romney went on. "My job is not to worry about those people—I'll never convince them that they should take personal responsibility and care for their lives."[1]

Romney's remarks provoked widespread condemnation.[2] It was no scandal to describe poor people as lazy or to falsely assert that they do not pay taxes; that was and remains standard rhetoric in America. Nor was Romney castigated for failing to acknowledge that almost literally every American household depends on direct and indirect government subsidies.[3] Romney's mistake was simply that he had specified too large a fraction of the public—nearly half of US households—as part of the purported mooching class. As President Obama noted during his second debate with Romney, the 47 percent included millions of retirees, soldiers serving overseas, college students, and "people who are out there working hard every day."[4]

The breadth of Romney's attack was a misstep, but it was also the culmination of a long trend in Republican thinking. The political alchemy of taxation channeled working- and middle-class rage at imagined welfare chiselers into tax policies that directed billions of dollars to America's wealthiest people, transmogrifying racial resentment into upward redistribution. The federal program commonly known as "welfare"—Aid to Families with Dependent Children (AFDC)—had been eliminated under President Clinton in 1996, more than fifteen years before Romney's speech. But as AFDC withered and died, the meaning of "welfare" metastasized. Conservatives painted more and more of the government as a corrupt burden on an imagined self-sufficient taxpayer, and more and more Americans as undeserving freeloaders unworthy of representation in government.

The GOP's abandonment of the basic principle of democracy was a natural outgrowth of its increasingly strict antitax party line. That new attitude is often described as an antipathy to government, but this language is misleading; the Republican Party was not infiltrated by anarchists. The "big government" denounced by conservatives did not include the military or the police, the institutions that exercise the state's most extreme form of power: violence. Rather, Republicans came to oppose the portions of government that could limit the extreme accumulation of private wealth and private power. At the center of this agenda was an unalloyed opposition to taxation of the rich, both because taxes cost the wealthy money and because taxes fund public goods, the social safety net, and the regulatory agencies that limit corporate power.

In their rush to plutocracy, antitax conservatives came to see their opponents as illegitimate political actors and the functioning of democratic government as a roadblock to be overcome. Democrats' assessments of this political landscape were persistently a generation behind. They appealed to fiscal responsibility just as Republicans abandoned it. They sought compromise when their opponents had adopted a strategy of intentional dysfunction. They expected long-standing norms of governance to be upheld even as new and more radical actors came onto the scene.

The Constitution, which was designed to protect the wealthy minority against the will of the majority, already furnished plenty of tools to foster inertia. But Republicans also innovated, engaging in what scholars have called "institutional hardball" or even "gonzo constitutionalism."[5] Using filibusters, shutdowns, and manufactured crises, the GOP was increasingly willing to bring governance to a halt. Once Republicans became committed to minority rule whenever they could not win a majority, they no longer saw it as beyond the pale to stack the electoral deck, or to deny election results altogether. Some who were radical tax cutters in their youth were horrified to see the outcome of the politics they had espoused. They shouldn't have been surprised.

TAX CUTS ABOVE ALL

In 1981, President Reagan came into office with an agenda he had been espousing for decades, since back when his politics had put him on the far right. Within weeks of his inauguration, Reagan proposed an across-the-board cut to individual income tax rates, as well as reductions to estate taxes, capital gains taxes, and corporate taxes. In what would become their consistent and consistently unsuccessful reaction to Republican tax cut proposals, Democrats responded by offering a smaller tax cut of their own. Then, at the end of March, President Reagan survived an assassination attempt. His humor and confidence in the moment—telling his wife, "Honey, I forgot to duck," and asking the doctors who treated his bullet wound whether they were Republicans—drove up his approval ratings. One month later, Reagan delivered a rousing speech before a joint session of Congress in which he thanked Americans for their prayers and firmly turned the political conversation back to his tax cuts.[6]

It was an irresistible move—or at least one that the Democrats did not resist. Instead, in a last-ditch effort to recover the party's rapidly waning business support, congressional Democrats bedecked the tax cut measure with such an array of additional tax breaks that even corporate lobbyists were dazzled. The final bill, which received substantial Democratic support, reduced the top marginal tax rate from 70 to 50 percent and the capital gains rate from 28 to 20 percent. The fraction of federal revenue that came from the corporate income tax dropped by 40 percent.[7]

Drawing on the new theories of "supply-side" economics, Reagan insisted that his tax cut would "so stimulate our economy that we will actually increase government revenues."[8] It is not obvious whether Reagan or his economic team believed in supply-side magic even at the time; Reagan also promoted his tax cut on the grounds that it would reduce revenue and thereby create pressure for spending cuts. "We can lecture our children about extravagance until we run out of voice and breath," Reagan said. "Or we can cure their extravagance by simply reducing their allowance." Some in his administration would admit later that supply-side theories were a convenient Trojan horse, allowing them to pass a tax cut large enough that the resulting deficits would put a squeeze on government spending. Privately, when his economic advisors warned him about the coming deficits, Reagan said, "I don't care."[9]

Reagan did indeed cut spending. Telling his beloved welfare queen story long after the actual "woman in Chicago" had served her time, Reagan pushed through major reductions in programs for the poor. More than a million poor Americans no longer received food stamps, and hundreds of thousands of working mothers simultaneously lost AFDC and Medicaid. From the 1950s to the late 1970s, federal policy had succeeded in cutting poverty in America nearly in half. Under Reagan, that progress came to an end.[10]

But no matter how hard he squeezed antipoverty programs, Reagan could not balance his budget. The US simply did not spend that much on welfare. The big-ticket budget items were defense spending, which Reagan wanted to increase, and the federal safety net for the elderly, where cuts were too politically costly to pursue. Though Reagan had told America in his first inaugural address that "government is the problem," he quickly learned that Americans liked most of what government provided.

In the early 1980s there was still strong concern within the GOP about the economic effects of deficits, so Republicans felt obliged to backtrack.

In the Senate, the old guard of fiscal responsibility was represented by Bob Dole of Kansas. "Good news is, a bus full of supply-siders went over a cliff last night," Dole was known to joke. "Bad news is, there were three empty seats."[11] As chair of the Finance Committee, Dole pushed his fellow Republicans to roll back a substantial portion of the corporate giveaways of the previous year. Reagan brought his substantial clout to bear on House Republicans to secure their support for the tax increase package.

Thus Reagan did not fully adopt the recommendation, made by conservative commentator Irving Kristol in 1980, that Republicans act as a tax-cut Santa Claus, racking up deficits that they would leave to "be coped with by liberal interregnums." Nonetheless, Reagan's 1984 opponent, Walter Mondale, fell headlong into the trap of playing the fiscal Grinch. Pushed by his business-oriented economic advisors, Mondale announced that as president, he would both raise taxes and cut spending. This proposal was made even Grinchier when Mondale, after a barrage of phone calls from angry campaign donors, backed away from any reform to the loophole-ridden tax code. Loopholes for the rich and higher taxes for everyone else—not the most compelling of campaign messages, in retrospect. Those on the left wing of the party, desperate for something they could bring to the voters, like a jobs program, waited in vain. Ironically, Mondale's profoundly centrist campaign would be remembered by Democrats as proof that tax increases were a guaranteed political loser. But Mondale had not promised old-style liberal taxing and spending; he had promised austerity, which does indeed have no political constituency outside Wall Street. Mondale lost forty-nine states and received just over 40 percent of the popular vote.[12]

Reagan would sign additional tax increases in 1984, 1985, and 1987, reversing about half the revenue loss of the 1981 tax cut and implementing the largest peacetime tax increase in American history. Similarly, the loophole-closing, rate-lowering Tax Reform Act of 1986 more than doubled revenue from corporate taxes over the following ten years, temporarily reversing a decades-long decline. These tax increases did not undo the regressive effects of Reagan fiscal policy. The top individual income tax rate fell during Reagan's tenure from 70 percent to 28 percent. The working class saw its federal taxes *increase* in the 1980s, and households in the middle saw only minor changes. But while the mid-1980s GOP cut taxes for the rich, the Reagan-era party was still capable of supporting tax increases.[13]

Still, the Republican position on taxes continued to harden. A majority of Republicans in Congress opposed the last of the Reagan-era tax increases, but the real turning point came under Reagan's successor, the old-school fiscal conservative George H. W. Bush. In his acceptance speech for the Republican nomination in 1988, Bush included a line that he would soon regret: "My opponent won't rule out raising taxes, but I will, and the Congress will push me to raise taxes, and I'll say no, and they'll push, and I'll say no, and they'll push again, and I'll say to them, 'Read my lips: no new taxes.'" Intended to give Bush a bit of Clint Eastwood "Make My Day" machismo, the promise not to raise taxes would come to haunt the president. In 1990, as part of a deficit-cutting compromise with the Democratic Congress, President Bush agreed to some tax increases in return for spending cuts.[14]

The public paid no notice: the first Gulf War was brewing, and Bush's approval rating soon reached an astronomically high 89 percent.[15] But if Bush thought he could govern in the style of his predecessor, he seriously misjudged his party. A new generation of Republican activists and legislators were committed to enforcing a hard-line antitax position. Newt Gingrich, first elected to Congress from Georgia in the pivotal year of 1978, saw the first months of the Reagan administration as "a truly revolutionary period" and lamented the reversals that had followed.[16] He refused to sign on to the 1982 tax increases, even at Reagan's behest, and he dismissed Bob Dole as the "tax collector for the welfare state."[17] To seize power from the more moderate wing of the party, Gingrich set about recruiting and training a cadre of like-minded Republican legislators.

When President Bush accepted a tax increase in 1990, Gingrich saw a moment of political opportunity. After privately giving the administration the impression he would agree to the tax-raising compromise, Gingrich turned on Bush publicly, ostentatiously walking out of a meeting and rallying more than one hundred of his House Republican colleagues to vote against the budget deal. The immediate result was a more progressive budget, since Bush now needed to court more Democratic votes—but the revolt made clear that the Republican Party increasingly belonged to Gingrich.[18]

The other leader of the antitax wing of the Republican Party was Grover Norquist, who in 1985 founded Americans for Tax Reform. Norquist's antitax fervor was unparalleled. Norquist famously said he wanted to reduce the federal government so that it could be drowned in a bathtub. He also once compared the morality of the estate tax to that of the Holocaust. Norquist's absolutist "Taxpayer Protection" pledge obligated signing lawmakers to reject all increases in income tax rates and all reductions of tax deductions and credits that were not matched by rate decreases. Norquist told each lawmaker to take their oath on a Bible, and the signed document was stored in a safe.[19]

At first, not everyone was impressed by the pledge and its rigamarole. In his 1988 campaign for the presidency, Senator Dole refused to sign. But over the following years, hundreds of lawmakers swore the oath to never raise taxes under any circumstance.[20] It became increasingly difficult for prominent Republicans to refuse. Finally, the day before announcing his campaign for the 1996 Republican nomination, Dole, the man once derided as "the tax collector for the welfare state," signed the Taxpayer Protection pledge.[21]

The effectiveness of the antitax movement was not based in some popular groundswell of support. On the contrary, Norquist and Gingrich managed to make tax opposition a fundamental policy commitment of the Republican Party even though most Americans thought (and think) that the rich should pay more, not less, in taxes. And as they had in decades past and would for decades to come, Americans regularly reported that they liked government spending on health care, on roads, on schools, and on Social Security. For the most popular programs, bipartisan majorities not only called for increased spending, but said they would personally pay more in taxes to support it.[22]

But politics is not a public opinion poll. It is organized interests competing for power. A small, well-resourced, and highly motivated group stands a good chance of defeating a much larger, less resourced, and less motivated group. On taxes, most Americans support progressive taxes and many forms of social spending, but they are usually not especially motivated about these issues, much less organized into an effective political force, unless a very popular program, like Social Security, is under attack.

What changed in the 1980s was not Americans' basic attitudes and values when it comes to taxation; these have been strikingly stable over decades. Rather, political leadership and organization changed in ways that encouraged conservative maximalism and pushed Democrats to the center. The union movement continued to decline, while the political clout and rightward bent of business grew. Rising economic inequality, exacerbated by the decline in progressive taxes and combined with the collapse of campaign finance regulations, enhanced the political power of the wealthy, who have (no surprise) much more conservative attitudes about taxes than the public at large. Southern populism declined as the region became wealthier. White Southerners abandoned the Democratic Party as it became the party of civil rights, creating a conservative electoral bulwark in the Republican Party.[23]

These forces pushed the Republicans to the economic right and weakened the Democrats' economic left.[24] Already by 1990, the Democratic Leadership Council, an influential group formed after Mondale's defeat to push the Democrats to the political center, opposed *any* tax increases as part of deficit reduction—a position to the right of the plan eventually accepted by President Bush. On the conservative side, by contrast, legislators were watching the activists and donors on their right flank, groups that were willing to attack them for being inadequately committed to the new antitax dogma.[25] Accordingly, tax opposition became a pillar of the Republican message. Taxes were mentioned in just a quarter of Republican campaign ads in 1976. Twenty years later, in 1996, they were mentioned in more than half of ads—even though only 2 percent of Americans described taxes as the most important problem facing the nation.[26]

THE RISE OF AUSTERITY BY DYSFUNCTION

"The era of Big Government is over," President Bill Clinton promised. "But we cannot go back to the time when our citizens were left to fend for themselves." Triangulating between the increasingly radical Republicans and the ideologically diverse Democrats in Congress, Clinton adopted a strict fiscal conservatism and a rhetoric about the role of government that might best be described as "Republican lite." On the campaign trail, Clinton had promised to "end welfare as we know it," and soon after he was inaugurated, he put Vice President Al Gore in charge of a new initiative to root out government waste, fraud, and abuse.[27] In his first budget, Clinton made austerity a priority over social investments.[28] The Democrats' move rightward did not appease the Republicans, however. Not a single Republican voted for Clinton's 1993 tax increase, though it was smaller than the one Republicans had passed in 1982 and accompanied by substantial spending cuts.[29]

When Republicans gained control of Congress in 1995, Newt Gingrich, the newly elected Speaker of the House, believed he could finally put the Reagan Revolution back on track. The House passed a large tax cut, including a lower capital gains rate and new exemptions from the estate tax. To balance the budget, the House Republicans proposed to cut Medicare and abolish federal antipoverty programs, including Medicaid, AFDC, public housing, food stamps, and child nutrition. Under this plan, eligible Americans would no longer be entitled to these programs; instead, the federal government would provide states with a "block grant" of funds, at an amount lower than the programs' current costs.[30] When the money inevitably ran out before need did? Well, that was just too bad.

Gingrich's goal of block-granting aid to the poor would be partially achieved the following year, when President Clinton signed legislation that eliminated poor families' federal entitlement to welfare payments. But Gingrich's broader agenda ran into strong opposition because he had paired his large tax cuts with large cuts to popular programs. When the 1995 Republican budget bill reached the president, Clinton vetoed it with the pen that Lyndon Johnson had used to sign Medicare into law.[31]

"What you don't understand is that I've got a gun to your head and I'm going to use it," Gingrich told the president. "I'm going to shut the government down."[32] Under Gingrich, Reagan's antigovernment rhetoric became a strategic agenda of intentional government dysfunction.[33] The government shutdowns in late 1995 and early 1996 furloughed hundreds of thousands of American workers for several weeks. Eventually Gingrich backed down, but the episode marked the start of a new phase of the antitax movement. The GOP was shifting from opposing popular egalitarian economic policies to opposing the democratic institutions that made and defended those policies.

If Republicans could not redirect the government, they would disable it instead. Gingrich's "Contract with America" included a 60 percent threshold for tax increases, but not for tax cuts, adding an extra layer of insulation against majority preferences on public revenues. The move toward obstruction and minority rule was mirrored in the Senate, where Republicans began to routinely use the filibuster to hold up the basic functioning of government under Democratic presidents. The new Republican Party also sought to disable the Internal Revenue Service. The agency had been seriously underfunded for decades, which caused a steady decline in its capacity to collect the taxes that were legally owed. Nonetheless, in 1998, Republican-led hearings held by the Senate Finance Committee purported to uncover extreme abuses by the tax agency. One witness said that IRS agents pushed his son to the floor at gunpoint and made his daughter get dressed in front of male agents. Later investigations would debunk the lurid charges and laud the effectiveness and responsibility of IRS enforcement efforts, but the agency was cowed. The frequency of audits, which had already been declining for decades, fell sharply after the hearings.[34]

This destruction of government capacity was, notably, only directed at the portion of government that limited the power of the rich. Gingrich had no problem with audits of the poor; in fact, he pushed successfully for greater attention to potential "fraud" among taxpayers receiving the Earned Income Tax Credit, one of the only tax provisions targeted to benefit lower-income workers. By the 2010s, EITC recipients were being audited at nearly the same rate as the top 1 percent of earners, a policy that exacerbated the disproportionate audit rate borne by Black Americans. The focus on poorer taxpayers was reinforced by the agency's underfunding; only a well-resourced IRS could match wits with the tax accountants and lawyers of wealthy tax evaders.[35]

As Republicans grew more extreme, Democrats adopted conservative narratives that legitimated attacks on the state. After yet another tax-cutting and belt-tightening budget in 1997, Representative Charles Rangel of New York hoped his party had "shattered the myth that we Democrats are spending Democrats and taxing Democrats." But Democrats could never outflank Republicans on taxes; they could only give credence to the idea that the basic tasks of government—taxing and spending—were something to avoid. Democratic efforts to address accusations of fraud and mismanagement were similarly ineffective. The elimination of AFDC did little to change American attitudes about welfare. Perceptions of government waste were untethered from official efforts to improve government efficiency. Bad-faith critiques simply could not be disarmed by good-faith reforms; instead, these Democratic efforts reinforced the impression that "government is the problem."[36]

Adopting conservative framing also misled the public about how political economy works. President Clinton, for example, talked about his deficit reduction policies as though they created jobs. But the austerity that reduces deficits takes money out of the economy and thus, at least in the short run, increases unemployment. Of course, it made political sense for Clinton to present this economically unsound argument, since jobs are what the public cares about. But it also created a wildly inaccurate (indeed, entirely backward) vision of government spending as a drag on the economy.[37]

The rhetorical failure to convey the value of government was echoed in policymaking. Instead of creating prominent, direct government programs like the GI Bill or Medicare, new social policy was increasingly conducted through the tax code. The tax subsidies for homeownership, health insurance, and pensions expanded dramatically in the 1980s and 1990s. Today, we spend nearly four times as much on homeowner subsidies through the tax code as we spend on affordable housing for the poor. Two tax credits that reached working-class families, the Child Tax Credit and the Earned Income Tax Credit, also grew. But as political scientist Suzanne Mettler has explained, conducting government policy through private markets or tax subsidies makes it hard for the public to recognize when they are receiving a government benefit. Imperceptible government action is, Mettler notes, a danger to democracy. If ordinary citizens cannot see what government is doing, they cannot reward the politicians whose policies have improved their lives, nor can they hold accountable the politicians who are voting against their interests.[38]

By the mid-1990s, the antitax movement had solidified its hold on the Republican Party and adopted dysfunction as a political strategy. Democrats, in their rhetoric and policymaking, were poorly positioned to defend government against the assault. But the GOP continued to face the challenge of substantial popular opposition when their tax proposals were accompanied by cuts to most popular components of the social safety net. That constraint would soon be lifted, however, when the party finally abandoned fiscal conservatism.

REPUBLICANS LEARN TO STOP WORRYING AND LOVE DEFICITS

In the year 2000, the presidential election came down to a single state with serious election administration issues and a margin of a few hundred votes. In a surprise to many legal observers, the Supreme Court's conservative majority stepped in and stopped the vote count. "Although we may never know with complete certainty the identity of the winner of this year's Presidential election, the identity of the loser is perfectly clear," wrote Justice John Paul Stevens in his dissent. "It is the Nation's confidence in the judge as an impartial guardian of the rule of law."[39]

The court's unprecedented intervention handed the election to Republican George W. Bush, who moved rapidly to institute a massive tax cut. He would not make the same mistake as his father and focus on a balanced budget. Clinton left his successor an annual budget surplus of $230 billion. It was a tidy sum with which to be Santa Claus. Bush proposed not only slashing income tax rates, but also repealing America's most progressive tax, the estate tax. This tax applied only to the richest 2 percent of estates. The price tag for Bush's total tax package was estimated at $1.6 trillion.[40]

By the early 2000s, little remained of the old deficit-focused Republican Party. Bob Dole, champion of the GOP deficit hawks, had retired after 1996. The few Republicans who voiced concerns about the fiscal implications of the Bush tax cuts faced attack ads and primary threats from big-money conservative activist groups.[41] Moderate Democrats faced similar pressures. Nevertheless, with a Senate divided fifty-fifty between Democrats and Republicans, the Bush tax cut still had to navigate a relatively narrow pathway to passage.[42]

One potential challenge was that a big tax cut was not a popular priority. As administration officials noted in an internal memo, "The public prefers spending on things like health care and education over cutting taxes."

There was, of course, even less demand for tax cuts so heavily tilted to the rich. In the early 2000s, about two-thirds of Americans thought upper-income people pay too little in taxes. This was (and remains) Americans' top concern about the tax system. Americans were also increasingly concerned about economic inequality, and for good reason. At the end of the Clinton era, the top 0.1 percent of Americans received four times the share of the national income they had when Nixon was president.[43]

Selling the Bush tax cuts therefore required careful marketing. Yet some of the most prominent stories told about that campaign are wrong. For instance, describing the "estate tax" as a "death tax" did not significantly increase support for repeal; the estate tax has been called a death tax for a century, and surveys using one phrase or the other differed only by a few percentage points. People also did not support the Bush tax cut because they foolishly expected that they would one day become enormously wealthy. Overwhelming majorities of Americans did not expect to benefit much from the tax cuts.[44] The Bush-era tax cuts cannot be ascribed to the public's susceptibility to magic words or its misplaced faith in the American dream.

What did matter was the strategic decision by the Bush administration to entirely abandon fiscal conservatism.[45] Americans will object to tax cuts that result in spending cuts for popular programs, but will support tax cuts that have no apparent consequences. If you are promised the same goods and services, who doesn't prefer a lower cost to a higher one? In fact, thanks to the unique position of our currency in the global economy, the US federal government has been able to run very large and very long-term deficits—a reality that has been, for the Republican Party, extremely freeing.

Thus, when George W. Bush promoted his tax cuts, he never suggested any budgetary offsets at all. "It's crucial that you make clear that there are no trade-offs here," an internal memo counseled Bush's treasury secretary. The revenue directed to the Bush cuts could have shored up the entire projected shortfall in Social Security twice over, but because the tax cut legislation was not paired with explicit budget cuts, its costs remained abstract. There was no public outcry, as there would be only a few years later when President Bush tried to privatize Social Security. And Democrats did not make the debate a question of tax cuts or public investments; instead, they once again proposed a tax cut of their own. The dispute devolved into eye-glazing budget figures that were hard for the public to grasp—particularly as the Bush administration adopted accounting tricks that were exceptionally misleading, even by the usual Washington standards.[46]

Though most Americans had the general impression that the Bush tax cuts favored the rich, the full implications of the policy were not well understood. Half the public wrongly believed that the estate tax applied to most or all Americans, and these misinformed people were much more likely to endorse its repeal. When a survey informed poor Republicans that the estate tax was primarily paid by the extremely wealthy, their probability of supporting the estate tax went from less than a quarter to more than half. But most Americans did not absorb those facts during the tax debates of the early 2000s, in part because media coverage tended not to emphasize how much wealth was being redistributed upward. When the first Bush tax cut passed in May 2001, one-third of the cut went to the richest 1 percent of American households.[47]

A startling indicator of the supremacy of the antitax dogma within the Republican Party is that it survived the crucible of war. The total cost of the "War on Terror" that followed the terrorist attacks of September 11, 2001, has recently been estimated at $8 trillion.[48] In the midst of that war, a second round of Bush tax cuts reduced the rates for capital gains and dividend income, and also gave businesses tax breaks that brought corporate taxation back down to 1983 levels.[49] There was no echo of the rhetoric of shared sacrifice that had accompanied every American war from the revolution to Vietnam. "Nothing is more important in the face of a war than cutting taxes," said House Majority Leader Tom DeLay.[50]

In 2002, Bush gave Irving Kristol the Presidential Medal of Freedom for his role in enlarging the "conservative vision." That vision included the fiscal strategy Kristol had articulated two decades earlier, which Bush implemented as president: big tax cuts, deficits be damned.

OBAMA AND THE RESURGENT TAXPAYER POLITICS

"This is America!" shouted CNBC commentator Rick Santelli from the floor of the Chicago Mercantile Exchange. "How many of you people want to pay for your neighbor's mortgage that has an extra bathroom and can't pay their bills? Raise their hand."[51]

It was only one month into the Obama presidency and about six months into a global financial crisis. Obama was pushing forward a series of policies intended to prevent a second Great Depression. Though this recovery plan was estimated to cost nearly $800 billion, it was still substantially smaller than progressive economists believed was necessary to jump-start the economy. (These worries would prove prescient, as unemployment would not return to prerecession levels until 2015). More than a third of the bill was tax cuts.

Nonetheless, conservatives like Santelli were incensed. As the traders around him booed Obama, Santelli helped spark a movement. "We're thinking of having a Chicago Tea Party in July," he said. "All you capitalists that want to show up to Lake Michigan, I'm gonna start organizing." Santelli's rant, as it became known, was replayed endlessly on talk radio and on Fox News.

Spurred by conservative media, the grassroots conservatives adrift at the end of the Bush era began to reorganize themselves under the new "Tea Party" banner. Eye-catching protestors, some dressed in Revolutionary War costumes or with tea bags dangling from their hats, rallied in cities across the country and vowed to "take our country back." Credulous journalists reported on the movement as though it represented middle America speaking out in favor of fiscal conservatism.[52] In reality, Tea Party activists were older, white, conservative Republicans who evinced exceptionally high levels of racial resentment, and who were strongly motivated by their opposition to immigration. Above all, Tea Party activists objected to Barack Obama, the first Black president, elected by a country that was younger, more diverse, and more progressive than they were.[53]

Like Clinton before him, Obama hewed to a fiscally conservative agenda. "Families across the country are tightening their belts and making tough decisions," he said in his first State of the Union Address. "The federal government should do the same." He proposed to freeze federal spending for three years. But his moderation did nothing to reduce Tea Party rage. Their anger about taxation was based in symbolism, not policy. Tea

Party activists identified themselves as "taxpayers" in the same way that Reagan had used the term: hardworking and exploited citizens, defined in opposition to the undeserving poor and their liberal supporters. They ardently opposed Obama's signature legislative achievement, the Affordable Care Act, which provided health insurance to millions of Americans. In Reagan's time, the unworthy welfare cheats were typically imagined to be among the Black poor, but now the category also included millions of unauthorized immigrants (or, for those on the farther right, nonwhite immigrants in general).

As the "welfare" stigma extended to more and more government activity, the "taxpayer" became an increasingly narrow category. Fewer households paid net federal income taxes, mostly because of the expanded Earned Income Tax Credit and Child Tax Credit, and conservatives began to imagine that there were a substantial number of nontaxpayers.[54] Households that paid no federal income tax did pay other taxes, of course; the poorest people in America pay, on average, more than 11 percent of their income in state and local taxes.[55] But the conservative antitax movement wouldn't let facts get in the way of a good story; *The Wall Street Journal*, for instance, wrote in 2002 about the "lucky duckies" in the "non-taxpaying class."

Conservative ire about supposed nontaxpayers grew sharply when, in 2009, data showed that about 47 percent of US households did not owe net federal income taxes.[56] But vanishingly few Republican legislators wanted to address this issue by increasing the number of people who paid taxes.[57] Instead, they dismissed those they deemed nontaxpayers as illegitimate participants in public life. When people are "getting money out of the Treasury for nothing," Republican Rick Santorum said on Fox News, "then there's no end to the amount of government that people want."[58] This sentiment, shared by an increasing portion of Republican politicians, derided nearly half of Americans as motivated by insatiable personal avarice and described all of government as tantamount to a free bank account. This was welfare moocher rhetoric on a new scale.

As Grover Norquist put it, "All reductions in federal government spending weaken the left in America. Defunding government is defunding the left."[59] Norquist's claim was facially untrue—the Defense Department would presumably be quite surprised to discover its place in the leftist conspiracy—but it accurately conveyed the sentiment, by then widely held on the right, that government itself was politically suspect because of its capacity to respond to the economic preferences of nonconservatives. By treating social spending as the moral equivalent of bribery, the antitax movement could ignore the demands of purported nontaxpayers as if they were the tantrum howls of greedy children. As Mark Steyn wrote in *National Review*, the non-taxpayers want to "vote themselves more government lollipops."[60]

Rank-and-file conservatives were also coming to see so-called nontaxpaying Americans as unworthy of political representation. A survey in 2014 found that half of all Republicans agreed that only taxpayers should have the right to vote. An electoral map, circulated through social media after the 2012 election, claimed to show a landslide victory for Romney, if "only taxpayers voted." Tellingly, the doctored map was actually based on the Electoral College result if suffrage were limited to white people. Like the Americana adopted by the Tea Party activists to signal their sense that they were the "real" Americans, the statistics about net income tax liabilities resonated because they carried racial implications under a race-neutral cover.

The conservative attack on representation was not merely rhetorical. Starting in 2010, closely contested states with Republican governors and legislatures began passing a spate of new laws that purged voters from the registration lists, made it harder to vote, and reconfigured their electoral maps for partisan advantage—a strategy bolstered by the Supreme Court's decision in 2013 to overturn portions of the Voting Rights Act. Grassroots Tea Party organizations stoked fears of a (nonexistent) wave of voter fraud and challenged voters' eligibility in ways that disproportionately targeted Black voters.

AUSTERITY BY DYSFUNCTION, ROUND TWO

After the 2010 midterm election, a new generation of Republican radicals came into office, and Republican obstructionism reached new heights. Tea Party activists saw any compromise with Democrats as treasonous, and Republicans in Congress were happy to give them the gridlock they demanded.

Opposition was, by this point, the Republicans' safe space. In the majority, they found it hard to govern, since the priorities of the Republican base and the Republican elite were not the same. Elite Tea Party–aligned groups, like FreedomWorks and Americans for Prosperity, were backed by the libertarian billionaire Koch brothers and corporate lobbyists. But grassroots Tea Partiers were not radical free-marketeers. They were strongly supportive of the major portions of the welfare state of which they, as older Americans, were beneficiaries, and which they believed they had earned through their tax payments. Nonetheless, Tea Party grassroots activism in the lead-up to the 2010 elections helped deliver a House majority to the Republicans, whose proposals included turning Medicare into a voucher program. The massive disconnect between the motivations of the Republican base and the priorities of the Republican leadership remained theoretical, however, with Obama in the White House.

A clear-cut illustration of the governance problem for Republicans came from Kansas. In 2012, Republican Governor Sam Brownback—a long-time beneficiary of Koch Industries' campaign largesse—instituted massive tax cuts that, when the promised economic growth failed to materialize, resulted in huge cuts to public education, road construction, and other popular programs. Rating agencies downgraded Kansas's bonds, schools closed early, and Brownback's approval rating fell to 18 percent. Within five years, a bipartisan majority of Kansas lawmakers voted to overturn the tax cuts— and a Democrat won the governorship.[61]

Nationally, however, Republicans could focus on obstructing the agenda of President Obama and the Democrats. What little governing occurred was achieved through a series of self-imposed fiscal crises that centered on the expiration of the Bush tax cuts, the funding of the government, and the raising of the debt ceiling. In each case, Obama's negotiating position was critically weakened by the fact that many Republicans in the House were ideologically committed to the failure of government and therefore actively courting economic disaster. It was like playing chicken with someone who *wanted* to crash their car. Obama extracted some substantive concessions, including a partial rollback of the Bush tax cuts for the wealthy and protections for Social Security and Medicare. But he also persistently reinforced the conservative narrative that government spending was the reason for the lingering economic malaise, and by responding to obstruction with compromise, encouraged ever-more-extreme brinksmanship.

TAXATION, BLACK LIVES, AND THE RISE OF DONALD TRUMP

During the Tea Party era, Republican elites successfully channeled their base's antipathy toward President Obama into obstruction and austerity. They continued to activate conservatives' racial resentment primarily through dog-whistle concern for "the taxpayers." Starting in 2016, however, the leadership of the Republican Party would abruptly abandon its post-civil-rights-era politesse. A critical trigger of the change was a renewed Black activism—a political movement sparked by the police violence that accompanies fiscal predation.

On August 9, 2014, an unarmed Black teenager, Michael Brown, was shot and killed by a police officer in Ferguson, Missouri. The protests that followed saw violent reprisals from militarized local police forces and drew national attention to biased policing. A Department of Justice investigation found that the racism of the Ferguson Police Department was incentivized and exacerbated by the city's heavy reliance on fees and fines.

Ferguson received nearly a fifth of its general revenue from the criminal justice system, more than was raised from the property tax. The city had a population of just twenty thousand and was feeling the pressure of race-to-the-bottom tax competition with other small suburbs in greater St. Louis. When in 2010 Ferguson's finance director sent a worried email about "a substantial sales tax shortfall," the chief of police responded with a promise to "increase traffic enforcement." For years, city officials urged the police department to "fill the revenue pipeline," "PRODUCE traffic tickets," and "turn citations into cash." Emails from police officials reporting the rapid rise in ticketing and long lines at the court received gleeful congratulations.[62]

Officials were celebrating an increasingly Kafkaesque criminal justice system that extorted Ferguson's Black community. The city imposed unusually high fines for minor infractions, like poorly kept lawns or improper parking. Additional levies were imposed if a ticketed citizen did not appear in person at the municipal court, which was only open for a few hours, a few

242 | THE PRICE OF DEMOCRACY

times a month. Police officers regularly illegally detained citizens without reasonable suspicion, the DOJ noted, because of "an officer's desire to check whether the subject had a municipal arrest warrant pending"; these arrests were profitable for the city and therefore strongly encouraged. A sixty-seven-year-old woman living on a fixed income did not know that she had received a trash-removal citation until she was arrested for failure to pay. Another woman, so poor that she was intermittently homeless, had over the years paid $550 and spent six days in jail for the compounding costs of a single parking violation. She still owed $541.

The story of Ferguson's racist and predatory policing echoed in localities across the country. Nationally, Black Americans are disproportionately likely to be stopped by the police; between 2008 and 2019, nearly every state increased court fees; and local reliance on criminal justice revenue correlates with the fraction of a city's population that is Black. These extractions are an enormous economic burden on the poor, but the system has civic costs as well. Even comparatively minor interactions with the police—traffic stops or being detained but not arrested—make it less likely for citizens to vote. Fees and fines are also used to directly curtail suffrage. After a 2018 referendum in Florida restored voting rights to more than a million people with felony records, the state passed a law limiting eligibility to vote to those who have paid their outstanding court fees and fines, and prosecuted people for mistakenly voting while still owing court fees. This modern-day poll tax continues to disenfranchise hundreds of thousands of Florida citizens.[63]

The resurgence of Black civil rights activism saw an almost immediate backlash on the right that pushed the Republican Party to embrace a far more overt racial conservatism. One candidate was especially willing to abandon the norms of the post–civil rights era in favor of placating the base. In the early months of the 2016 campaign, when Black Lives Matter activists interrupted Donald Trump rallies, the candidate openly encouraged his supporters to assault the peaceful protestors.[64] Trump had already won a following among Tea Party activists for his commitment to the "birther" myth that President Obama was not a native-born American. He gave the Republican base what other contenders would not; he put down the dog whistle and pulled out the bullhorn. "When Mexico sends its people, they're not sending their best," Trump told his audience at his campaign launch. "They're bringing drugs. They're bringing crime. They're rapists."[65]

The explicitness of Trump's ethnonationalism freed him to discard the long-standing euphemism of the taxpayer. "Maybe he doesn't want the American people, all of you watching tonight, to know that he's paid nothing in federal taxes," said Hillary Clinton in the first 2016 debate.[66] As Clinton sought to lambaste Trump for failing to contribute to federal coffers, Trump interrupted: "That makes me smart." Trump's interjection broke with tradition; the last Republican candidate, Mitt Romney, had sworn that he had always paid at least 13 percent in federal income taxes.[67] But Trump did not need to describe himself as a taxpayer—both because much of his appeal to his supporters was in his gleeful subversion of the standards of civility and, more significantly, because he pandered directly to the racial resentment and white identity politics that had given taxpaying so much of its symbolic appeal on the right.

Trump's rhetorical shift did not signal any change in the fiscal policy commitments of the GOP. The primary legislative achievement of the Republican Congress that accompanied Trump to Washington in 2016 was the Tax Cuts and Jobs Act, a massive tax cut for the rich. The legislation was exceptional for its unpopularity, with only 32 percent of Americans supporting the legislation in the lead-up to its passage. This marked an important change in public attitudes about a tax cut. While reducing taxes had not been a priority for voters when Bush cut them in the early 2000s, and the cuts were promptly forgotten once they were passed, the legislation had been viewed favorably while it had been under consideration. Nearly forty years after the Reagan Revolution, however, it seemed that the Republican Party had ridden the tax issue as far as it could go with the public.[68]

But the GOP by this point had largely ceased to be concerned with what most Americans wanted, if those views did not align with the party's priorities. In 2020, it took the next logical step: ceasing to respect the will of the voters. Then-President Trump, knowing that he had failed to win re-election, refused to concede and instead sought to subvert vote counting and certification. Grassroots Trump supporters, including many leaders of Tea Party–era "voter fraud" activism, pushed the falsehood that the election had been stolen from Trump.[69] On January 6, 2021, President Trump urged his supporters to storm the US Capitol, part of what the House Select Committee that investigated the attack described as "a multi-part conspiracy to overturn the lawful results of the 2020 Presidential election."[70]

.◆.

From a naïve perspective, the antitax movement has racked up an extraordinary number of failures. The tax cuts have never produced the economic boom promised by their proponents, much less the increase in government revenue touted by the most adamant supply-siders. Tax cuts have also failed to reduce government spending. Federal outlays as a fraction of GDP have bobbled around 20 percent for several decades, with no conclusive trend line. Major portions of the social safety net, particularly the payroll-tax-funded programs for the elderly, have proven resistant to repeated efforts at retrenchment. Other programs, like the Medicaid health insurance program for the poor, are larger today than they were when Reagan took office. Tax cuts did not starve the beast or eliminate the welfare state.[71]

Amazingly, the antitax movement did not even lower most Americans' taxes. In 1970, the richest households paid more than 50 percent of their income in taxes, while the bottom 90 percent of Americans paid 22 percent. By the 2010s, the richest were paying only 33 percent, while the bottom 90 percent were paying 26 percent.[72] *Taxes went down only for the rich; everyone else's taxes went up.*

But if the goal of the antitax movement was to create an oligarchy, it has been a great success. Inequality, which had fallen from the mid-twentieth century until the late 1970s, rose steadily thereafter. Since 1980, the portion of the US national income received by the top 1 percent of earners has doubled—rising from 10 percent to 20 percent—while the income earned by the bottom half has been cut nearly in half, dropping from 20 percent to 12 percent. Looking at wealth rather than income, we find a similar pattern. The richest 1 percent of households have seen their wealth double since the late 1970s, increasing from 20 percent of the country's wealth to almost 40 percent, while the bottom 90 percent of households saw their wealth drop from 40 percent to a quarter.[73] Corporate income taxes, which equaled about 4 percent of GDP in the late 1960s, fell to less than 2 percent. Upward redistribution has been the signal achievement of the post-Reagan Republican Party.

In its fealty to an antitax agenda, the Republican Party ceased to operate within the bounds of democratic politics, first abjuring compromise and finally elections. This was no coincidence. The Republican tax position, at its extreme, was opposed to democratic practice, both strategically and ideologically. In seeking to slash taxes for the rich and benefits for everyone else, the party chose an agenda that was at odds with public preferences. Devoted to selling something that most Americans weren't buying, the GOP became increasingly committed to minority rule, to denying the legitimacy of its political opponents, and to stoking racial resentment through the coded language of taxpaying. In the end, the party was left ripe for the picking by a racist would-be autocrat.

The political story of the last forty years is, to a significant degree, the story of the Republican Party's descent into authoritarian politics. It is a story about taxes.

Conclusion

Within the limited record that reaches us from the past, a historian has a certain kind of floating omniscience: seeing all sides, weighing the evidence, and, above all, knowing what comes next. Shaken from the high perch of hindsight, I have landed in my own time. Now I am grounded, wondering—as so many of the figures on the previous pages did—how to interpret the political tremors I feel, and whether they portend a greater earthquake to come.

There is some comfort in the admission that the future is unforeseeable, particularly since I happen to be writing this in the days immediately after the 2024 election. Tax history, I remind myself, has its share of accidents and unintended consequences. When, at the Constitutional Convention, a delegate asked for the definition of a "direct" tax, no one answered; one hundred years later, that omission eased the way for the Supreme Court to declare an income tax unconstitutional. When Congress finally passed an income tax amendment, it was because conservative legislators were confident it would die in the states. Only four years after that, the amendment was ratified.

So I cannot know exactly where we are going. But here is what I believe will be useful to remember about where we have been.

The authoritarianism of the contemporary Republican Party is part of a long tradition of American politics. *Elites' fear of taxation is a fear of democracy itself.* It is not a complicated calculus: Oligarchs want democracy to be poor and weak so that they can be richer and more powerful. The possibility that people of moderate means would have a say over the tax system has persistently led wealthy people to undermine governments' democratic practices and fiscal capacity.

Elites' antipathy to democratic taxation—their fear that it would result in abolition, or "leveling," or "communism"—has been hysterical to the point of paranoia. Time and again, reactionaries have overreacted. There is nothing so consistent in American history as the moderation of the fiscal demands of the masses. When poorer people have proposed more progressive systems of taxation, they have insisted they would still pay their share. Even the most radical tax proposals have sought to narrow the inequality of wealth, not eliminate it. History has not "yet recorded an instance in which governments have been destroyed by attempts of the many to lay undue burdens of taxation on the few," as one of the lawyers defending the federal income tax told the Supreme Court in 1895. "The teachings of history have all been in the other direction."[1]

It's true. Throughout American history, the real threats to liberty, the violation of rights, and even the violent destruction of elected governments have come from the elites opposed to democratic taxation. Fear of the fiscal preferences of the majority led the framers of the Constitution to design a government with many checks on majority rule. To forestall the possibility of abolition by taxation, slaveholders undermined America's democratic institutions and their capacity to tax. It was as "taxpayers" that Southern whites overthrew multiracial democracy, and under the banner of white supremacy that those states put property taxation out of the hands of the majority. To defeat the income tax, the Gilded Age Supreme Court abandoned precedent and overruled Congress, usurping the lawmaking power that is supposed to be held by elected legislators. And in the long reaction to the civil rights movement, a radical antitax faction pushed the Republican Party to such an extreme that it abandoned first its commitment to governance and then its commitment to electoral democracy.

We are today continuing our reprise of the racist, antitax, antidemocratic politics of the Redeemer era, with the untaxing of the wealthy, the cuts to public investments and state capacity, the shifting of the costs of government onto the poor, the threat of election violence, and the subversion of voting rights. The decline of color-blind rhetoric in favor of a full-throated eth-nonationalism is consistent with the trajectory of that earlier antidemo-cratic movement. There is every reason to expect the other aspects of the post-Reconstruction regimes as well: destruction of state capacity, corrup-tion in government, corporate profiteering, and an increasingly predatory legal system that inflicts violence and terror on ethnic minorities.

Racism has been the single greatest ally of the antitax, antidemocratic elite. It is no coincidence that the federal income tax amendment succeeded—and the American social safety net grew—under conditions of strict racial apartheid. Antitax conservatives' scaremongering about the poor was less effective when it was whites who were receiving benefits or having a say over the tax rates.

When elites have succeeded in rolling back democracy and undermin-ing the tax system, they have found allies among poorer whites and have replaced taxation with predatory extractions from marginalized nonwhite people. Settlers in Pennsylvania, having unsuccessfully sought fairer prop-erty taxation, accepted instead low taxes and cheap land seized from the Native nations. Promises of lower taxes lured poor upcountry farmers back to the white supremacist Democrats, bringing an end to the Radical Recon-struction. After the civil rights era, suburban homeowners' anger about property taxes led to a spate of tax limitations that left state and local gov-ernments more reliant on fees and fines, which fall disproportionately on poor and minority Americans. The promise of lower taxes has repeatedly served as an effective bribe to entice middling white people away from the possibility of racial solidarity.

The deep question is whether racism will always undermine solidarity among the nonrich. "If you can convince the lowest white man he's better than the best colored man," President Lyndon Baines Johnson once said, "he won't notice you're picking his pocket. Hell, give him somebody to look down on, and he'll empty his pockets for you."[2] The politicians' paeans to "the taxpayer" have always been the dog-whistle prelude to Americans' pock-ets being picked. More often than not, those campaigns have succeeded.

This is not a peculiarly American problem. In the United States and abroad, places with higher levels of ethnic diversity offer fewer protections for the poor and impose less income taxation.[3] But in an important sense, that association is tautological. Ethnicity and race are not immutable biological categories; they are shifting social ones.[4] Cultural difference becomes significant when it carries implications about wealth and power.[5] So racism and poverty are not necessarily intractable. They are merely inseparable. We will have both, or we will have neither.

Taxation, as I noted at the start of this book, makes democracy consequential because it gives the government the capacity to act. A robust democratic government can impose egalitarian policies, such as progressive taxation or social spending, but it also has its own innate strength: It defines the space where public life and political contestation occur, a space that is supposed to ensure equal treatment and exclude private forms of power. The coming years will require not only a defense of electoral democracy, but a defense of the democratic state. *If there is one thing recent decades have made clear, it is that we cannot afford an impoverished democracy.*

When it comes to defending government, the American left has not yet rediscovered its voice. Democrats have, in recent years, readopted some of the ideas of the Populist and Progressive era, particularly in their attacks on corporate power and occasionally in references to the social origins of wealth.[6] But the defense of the public sphere—the words of Cyclone Davis ("the government of the United States is not a separate thing from the people") or E. R. A. Seligman ("the state is a part of us")—remains the rhetoric of a distant and more hopeful past. We have forgotten, too, the principle of Thomas Paine and other early democrats that equality and liberty are mutually reinforcing, and that the best argument for egalitarian economic policy is its role in protecting republican government. The state can impose policies to discourage the consolidation of wealth, radical Philadelphia patriots argued, because extreme economic inequality was "dangerous to the Rights" of a free people.

An essential aspect of the defense of government is the defense of taxes—including, I would argue, the taxes that fall on everyday people. Perpetually promising to raise taxes only on the rich is a capitulation to the conservative position that taxes are a punishment, rather than a responsibility. It forecloses the possibility of new egalitarian investments on the order of Social

Security or Medicare.[7] And it misunderstands the attitudes of the public; sales and payroll taxes, which working people know fall heavily upon them, are consistently the most popular taxes Americans pay.[8]

Having rid ourselves of the misperception that average Americans always oppose taxes, we can more carefully consider when and why taxation has, in fact, provoked mass opposition. This is a vital question because when taxes have caused real economic hardship, the resulting popular frustration has often been channeled into terribly reactionary policy.

The most obvious lesson is that taxes need to be easy to pay. That does not mean they need to be low; the manner of taxation is at least as important as the total revenue. Currency shortages made the Stamp Act and later specie taxes unbearable to early Americans; a tariff could raise the necessary revenue without demanding frontier farmers part with gold and silver coins that they did not have to give. In more recent instances of tax revolt, property taxes have been a common tripwire, and these taxes also often fail to meet the "easy to pay" standard. The value of one's homestead does not necessarily reflect the level of one's income. For low-income property owners, rising taxes during Reconstruction were genuinely onerous, as were the tax increases seen in California in the lead-up to Proposition 13.

But the property tax has also been a flashpoint because of the disparities of property ownership between Black and white Americans. The policies that created a segregated and disproportionately white homeowning middle class set the ground for opponents of integration to organize as "taxpayers." And this is a second lesson when we think about how to design tax policy: We should consider what allies a tax creates as it is raised and spent. The payroll-tax-funded Social Security system, for example, puts all wage earners from the working poor to the upper-middle class in the same program, creating a cross-class constituency. But that alliance has been whittled away, quite intentionally, by other tax policies to encourage private pensions.[9] Like Franklin Roosevelt, we need to think about taxation in political terms. There is, I believe our history would suggest, no other way to think about it.

•◆•

The ongoing contestation over American taxation and American democracy will almost undoubtedly occur in a series of crises. There are limits to growth, limits to deficit finance, and—infinitely more serious—limits on the carrying capacity of the planet. We have pushed beyond prudence, and the consequences are coming, one way or another. Somewhere, a bell is tolling.

The politics of scarcity could look very ugly indeed. Even in times of plenty, the right declares people unworthy of assistance and inclusion; there is no doubt what they will say in times of shortage. But politics in the absence of trade-offs has not worked out so well, either. The Republican Party benefited for decades from its gamble that deficits could be left to Democrats to clean up, or simply left to accrue. It created a blank check for the tax cuts that have made our economy vastly more unequal.[10]

It is possible, then, that the shocks of the coming years will inspire a more egalitarian politics. We do not have a historical model for our contemporary ecological disasters; humans have never lived in the climatic conditions that we have now unleashed. But the best available parallel is perhaps the case of mass warfare. As many historians have noted, it is in times of total war that we have seen sharp increases in state capacity and progressive taxation, and those gains have long outlasted the wars themselves.[11] America's greatest strides toward equality came after defeating the Confederates and the Nazis. If the examples of the Civil War and World War II are any indication, Americans are capable of mobilizing for shared sacrifice and demanding a more equal society in recompense. Perhaps we can do so again.

We do not get to choose our time, any more than Thomas Paine, or Matthew Gaines, or William Mahone, or Alice Nixon did. Perhaps we who believe in democratic taxation are like the abolitionists in 1857, having borne decades of defeat but only a few years from victory. Perhaps we have much further to go. What I do know is that many Americans have fought for a democracy with the power to tax, and they have passed the baton forward in conditions vastly harder and with far less reason to hope. Now it is in our hands.

Acknowledgments

This book has benefited from the thoughtful assistance of many people.

My agent, Lisa Adams, guided me expertly through the publishing process and provided some of the most attentive edits on the manuscript. My editor at Basic Books, Brandon Proia, championed this book and substantially improved its structure. James Brandt provided invaluable editing throughout the book's development. Lyra Fuchs provided sharp-eyed fact-checking on an early version of the introduction.

The Brookings Institution and the Urban-Brookings Tax Policy Center have supported me in innumerable ways as I conducted this research. I am grateful for the work of research assistants Ellis Chen, Naomi Maehr, and Jackson Gode, and interns Sarah Miller, Itai Grofman, and Zach Benzaoui. Special thanks are due to the Brookings library staff, especially Laura Mooney and Sarah Chilton.

Many brilliant people read drafts of this work, provided insightful feedback, and encouraged me along the way, and I am profoundly grateful to them. Thank you to Jeremy Bearer-Friend, Eric Bernstein, Laura Blessing, Len Burman, Andrea Campbell, Robin Einhorn, Bill Gale, Michael Graetz, Jordan Haedtler, Amy Hanauer, Alex Hertel-Fernandez, Chye-Ching Huang, Andrew Kahrl, Michael Kazin, Isaac Martin, Ajay Mehrotra, Suzanne Mettler, Molly Michelmore, Michael Mitchell, Beth Pearson, Steve Rosenthal, Mark Schlegel, Danny Schlozman, Theda Skocpol, Molly Sugrue, Kris-Stella Trump, and Camille Walsh.

Portions of this work were presented at the 2021 and 2022 Social Science History Association conference, the January 2024 NCAPSA conference, and the September 2024 Yale American Political Economy Exchange Tax Policy Workshop; thank you to all the participants for their comments. Some of this book's ideas appeared in Brookings and Tax Policy Center articles and in *Dissent* magazine, where Tim Shenk, Nick Serpe, and Lyra Fuchs provided excellent edits and suggestions. The research staff at the Heinz History Center, the Pittsburgh City Archives, and the Myaamia Center at Miami University provided vital materials and information. Thank you to Ken Regal, at Just Harvest, for sharing his recollections of Alice Nixon.

Nothing would be possible without the support of my family. To my parents, Liz and Arthur Williamson; my husband, Brad; and my sons, Storry and Daniel, my gratitude and love beyond measure.

Illustration Credits

Alexander Hamilton. Reproduction of a painting by John Trumbull. A. W. Elson, 1896. Library of Congress, Prints and Photographs Division, LC-DIG-ppmsca-46507.

Box and Cox. New York: *Frank Leslie's Illustrated Newspaper*, January 6, 1877, 304. Library of Congress, Prints and Photographs Division, LC-DIG-ds-15070.

F. L. Cardozo Sr. Between circa 1870 and circa 1880. Wearn and Hix, artists, Columbia, SC. Library of Congress, Prints and Photographs Division, LC-USZ62-126157.

The Freedman's Bureau! An agency to keep the Negro in idleness at the expense of the white man. 1866. Printed Ephemera Collection, Library of Congress, Rare Book and Special Collections Division, LC-USZ62-40764.

Hinton Rowan Helper. Frontispiece portrait from the 1860 edition of *The Impending Crisis in the South: How to Meet It*, held in the North Carolina Collection of the University of North Carolina at Chapel Hill Library. Digital copy via NCpedia and Wikimedia Commons.

Hon. George S. Boutwell of Massachusetts. Between 1870 and 1880. Brady-Handy photograph collection, Library of Congress, Prints and Photographs Division, LC-DIG-cwpbh-03788.

J. N. (Cyclone) Davis. December 30, 1914. George Grantham Bain Collection, Library of Congress, Prints and Photographs Division, LC-DIG-ggbain-18027.

John C. Calhoun. Date unknown. Brady-Handy photograph collection, Library of Congress, Prints and Photographs Division, LC-DIG-cwpbh-02605.

Martin Witherspoon Gary. 1860s. William Emerson Strong Photograph Album, Duke University Libraries.

Matthew Gaines (attributed), African American Activist and Texas State Senator. Circa 1870. Lawrence T. Johns III Texas Photographs Collection, DeGolyer Library, Southern Methodist University.

Radical Members of the South Carolina Legislature. Date unknown. Collection of the Smithsonian National Museum of African American History and Culture, 2016.49.4.

Smash the Axis, Pay Your Taxes. 1885–2019 and undated. Outdoor Advertising Association of America Archives, John W. Hartman Center for Sales, Advertising and Marketing History, Duke University Libraries.

Thomas Paine. Photographic reproduction of a circa 1876 painting by Auguste Millière, after an engraving by William Sharp, after a 1792 painting by George Romney. Library of Congress, Prints and Photographs Division, LC-USZ62-20180.

A View of the Year 1765. Line engraving by Paul Revere, adapted from an English print. P. Revere, 1765. Collection of the Massachusetts Historical Society.

Notes

Online Collections

Avalon Project
Chronicling America
Colorado Historic Newspapers Collection
Founders Online, National Archives
Franklin D. Roosevelt Presidential Library & Museum
Georgia Historic Newspapers
HathiTrust
HeinOnline
Internet Archive
JSTOR
Library of Congress Digital Collections
Mississippi State University Libraries
NewspaperArchive
Newspapers.com
The Portal to Texas History
ProQuest
Teaching American History
University of Florida Digital Collections
University of Michigan Library Digital Collections
Utah Digital Newspapers
Virginia Chronicle

Abbreviations

APP   American Presidency Project
ASP   American State Papers
FO   Founders Online, National Archives
JCC   Journals of the Continental Congress, 1774–1789
JSC   *Report of the Joint Select Committee to Inquire into the Condition of Affairs in the Late Insurrectionary States*, United States Congress, Government Printing Office, 1872
PA   John B. Linn and William H. Egle, eds., *Pennsylvania Archives: Second Series*, Harrisburg, 1896

Introduction

1. Alfred F. Young, *The Shoemaker and the Tea Party: Memory and the American Revolution*, Beacon Press, 1999; James Hawkes, *A Retrospect of the Boston Tea-Party*, New York, 1834; Benjamin Bussey Thatcher, *Traits of the Tea Party*, Harper and Brothers, 1835; Francis Samuel Drake, *Tea Leaves*, A. O. Crane, 1884; Benjamin L. Carp, *Defiance of the Patriots: The Boston Tea Party and the Making of America*, Yale University Press, 2010, 117–40.

2. See, e.g., Grover G. Norquist, "Tea, Taxes, and the Revolution," *Foreign Policy*, July 3, 2012.

3. Woody Holton, *Liberty Is Sweet: The Hidden History of the American Revolution*, Simon and Schuster, 2021, 124; Edmund S. Morgan, *The Birth of the Republic, 1763–89*, 3rd ed., University of Chicago Press, 1992, 58; Arthur Meier Schlesinger Sr., *The Colonial Merchants and the American Revolution, 1763–1776*, Longmans, Green, 1918, 263, 270–71; Joseph J. Thorndike, "Tax History: Four Things You Should Know About the Boston Tea Party," *Tax Notes*, April 12, 2010; Ray Raphael, "Tea Party Myths," *American History*, June 2010, 62.

4. "To Benjamin Franklin from the Massachusetts House of Representatives Committee of Correspondence, 21 December 1773," FO. Both George Washington and Benjamin Franklin thought the destruction of the tea was too radical. "From George Washington to George William Fairfax, 10–15 June 1774," and "From Benjamin Franklin to Thomas Cushing, 22 March 1774," FO.

5. Edmund S. Morgan and Helen M. Morgan, *The Stamp Act Crisis: Prologue to Revolution*, University of North Carolina Press, 1953, 95. By 1774, colonists were not just doubting the right of Britain to impose taxes; they were openly asserting that Parliament had no right to legislate for the colonies on any subject. Morgan, *Birth of the Republic*, 62. If the American Revolution were evidence of inborn antagonism to taxation, it would equally demonstrate that Americans are congenitally opposed to law.

6. Timothy H. Breen, *American Insurgents, American Patriots: The Revolution of the People*, Farrar, Straus and Giroux, 2010, 83; Mary Beth Norton, *1774: The Long Year of Revolution*, Alfred A. Knopf, 2020, 217–18, 258, 334; Timothy H. Breen, "Whose Revolution Is This?," opinion, *Washington Post*, March 30, 2010.

7. See, e.g., Richard W. Rahn, "American Income Tax Tyranny," Cato Institute, April 9, 2012.

8. See Chapter 1. On why this occurred in Europe and not elsewhere, see David Stasavage, "Representation and Consent: Why They Arose in Europe and Not Elsewhere," *Annual Review of Political Science* 19 (May 2016): 145–62.

9. Marina Nord, Martin Lundstedt, David Altman, et al., *Democracy Report 2024: Democracy Winning and Losing at the Ballot*, V-Dem Institute, March 2024; "Government Revenue, Percent of GDP," Database: Public Finances in Modern History, International Monetary Fund, December 2022.

10. Margaret Levi, *Of Rule and Revenue*, University of California Press, 1988; Margaret Levi, *Consent, Dissent, and Patriotism*, Cambridge University Press, 1997; Marcelo Bergman and Sven H. Steinmo, "Taxation and Consent: Implications for Developing Nations," in *The Leap of Faith: The Fiscal Foundations of Successful*

Government in Europe and America, ed. Sven H. Steinmo, Oxford University Press, 2018, 273–92.

11. Jeffrey D. Sachs and Andrew M. Warner, "The Curse of Natural Resources," *European Economic Review* 45, nos. 4–6 (May 2001): 827–38; Lisa Anderson, "The State in the Middle East and North Africa," *Comparative Politics* 20, no. 1 (1987): 1–18; Hazem Beblawi, "The Rentier State in the Arab World," *Arab Studies Quarterly* 9, no. 4 (Fall 1987): 383–98; Michael L. Ross, "Does Taxation Lead to Representation?," *British Journal of Political Science* 34, no. 2 (April 2004): 229–49; Wilson Prichard, Paola Salardi, and Paul Segal, "Taxation, Non-Tax Revenue and Democracy: New Evidence Using New Cross-Country Data," *World Development* 109 (September 2018): 295–312; Junko Kato and Seiki Tanaka, "Does Taxation Lose Its Role in Contemporary Democratisation? State Revenue Production Revisited in the Third Wave of Democratisation," *European Journal of Political Research* 58, no. 1 (February 2019): 184–208; Jonathan L. Weigel, "The Participation Dividend of Taxation: How Citizens in Congo Engage More with the State When It Tries to Tax Them," *Quarterly Journal of Economics* 135, no. 4 (November 2020): 1849–1903; James Tan, *Power and Public Finance at Rome, 264–49 BCE*, Oxford University Press, 2017, xxix.

12. Deborah Brautigam, "Taxation and State-Building in Developing Countries," in *Taxation and State-Building in Developing Countries: Capacity and Consent*, ed. Deborah Brautigam, Odd-Helge Fjeldstad, and Mick Moore, Cambridge University Press, 2008, 8.

13. When systems of representation precede effective taxation, as they have in many postcolonial countries, democracy can prove frail or unstable: Some elected leaders who prefer to be unaccountable to their citizens have avoided applying taxes so they do not have to respond to public demands. Lucy E. S. Martin, *Strategic Taxation: Fiscal Capacity and Accountability in African States*, Oxford University Press, 2023.

14. "John Adams to Abigail Adams, 14 April 1776," FO.

15. It was antislavery advocates who lifted the Declaration of Independence from obscurity, insisting at once on its place as a hallowed founding document and as a clarion call for human freedom. Eric Slauter, "Life, Liberty, and the Pursuit of Happiness," *Boston Globe*, July 3, 2011. Those fighting for equality in America did not need the Declaration of Independence to recognize their own oppression and were under no illusion that the United States was a country founded on universal freedom. But in seizing the most radical interpretation of the revolutionary tradition, they put their opponents on the defensive. See Chapter 1.

16. Timothy H. Breen, "Ideology and Nationalism on the Eve of the American Revolution: Revisions Once More in Need of Revising," *Journal of American History* 84, no. 1 (June 1997): 35–37.

17. Kelsey Davis Betz, "'Why Didn't They Vote for Us?,'" *Mississippi Today*, September 16, 2019.

18. Andrea Louise Campbell, "What Americans Think of Taxes," in *The New Fiscal Sociology: Taxation in Comparative and Historical Perspective*, ed. Isaac William Martin, Ajay K. Mehrotra, and Monica Prasad, Cambridge University Press,

2009; Molly C. Michelmore, *Tax and Spend: The Welfare State, Tax Politics, and the Limits of American Liberalism*, University of Pennsylvania Press, 2012, 1.

19. Martin Daunton, *Just Taxes: The Politics of Taxation in Britain, 1914–1979*, Cambridge University Press, 2002, xiii.

20. Michael Kwass, *Privilege and the Politics of Taxation in Eighteenth-Century France: Liberté, Egalité, Fiscalité*, Cambridge University Press, 2006.

21. Rudolf Goldscheid, "A Sociological Approach to Problems of Public Finance," in *Classics in the Theory of Public Finance*, ed. Richard A. Musgrave and Alan T. Peacock, Palgrave Macmillan, 1958, 202–13, 205.

22. Andrew Roberts, *Salisbury: Victorian Titan*, Faber and Faber, 2012, 21; John Walsh, "Practical Results of the Reform Act of 1832," *London Quarterly Review* 107, no. 214 (April 1860): 267–87, 286, cited in Daniel Ziblatt, *Conservative Parties and the Birth of Democracy*, Cambridge University Press, 2017, 28.

23. Particularly in recent decades, as the Democratic Party has grown more attuned to the preferences of the upper-middle class. Ilyana Kuziemko, Nicolas Longuet Marx, and Suresh Naidu, "'Compensate the Losers?' Economic Policy and Partisan Realignment in the US," working paper, National Bureau of Economic Research, November 2024.

24. Thomas Piketty and Emmanuel Saez, "Income Inequality in the United States, 1913–1998," *Quarterly Journal of Economics* 118, no. 1 (February 2003): 1–41; David Hope and Julian Limberg, "The Economic Consequences of Major Tax Cuts for the Rich," *Socio-Economic Review* 20, no. 2 (April 2022): 539–59.

25. Thomas Blanchet, Emmanuel Saez, and Gabriel Zucman, "Who Benefits from Income and Wealth Growth in the United States?," dataset for 1976–2023, Realtime Inequality, accessed October 2024.

26. Elise Gould, "Child Tax Credit Expansions Were Instrumental in Reducing Poverty Rates to Historic Lows in 2021," *Working Economics Blog*, Economic Policy Institute, September 22, 2022; Matt Bruenig, "The Myths of the Earned Income Tax Credit," People's Policy Project, May 18, 2020; Paul Kiel, "It's Getting Worse: The IRS Now Audits Poor Americans at About the Same Rate as the Top 1%," *ProPublica*, May 30, 2019; Courtney Subramanian, "You're Not Getting Child Tax Credit Checks Anymore. Here's Why," *Los Angeles Times*, January 3, 2023.

27. The federal government manifestly does not "pay for" spending with taxes; it has run a deficit for all but five of the last fifty years. Proponents of modern monetary theory (MMT) argue that, for governments like the US federal government that issue fiat currency and only borrow money in that currency, taxes do not fund the state in the sense of providing necessary dollars in a one-to-one ratio with spending. Rather, taxes are a partial offset for government spending that keeps the money supply in line with the real productive limits of the economy. An assessment of MMT is beyond the scope of this book, but for our purposes the principle of taxation holds in both MMT and non-MMT frameworks; taxes either fund or offset government spending, and taxes are always how governments require citizens to support the state. Stephanie Kelton, *The Deficit Myth: Modern Monetary Theory and the Birth of the People's Economy*, Hachette UK, 2020, 26.

28. Walter J. Blum and Harry Kalven Jr., "The Uneasy Case for Progressive Taxation," *University of Chicago Law Review* 19, no. 3 (Spring 1952): 517.

29. N. Gregory Mankiw, *Principles of Economics*, 2nd ed., Harcourt College Publishers, 2001, 175.

30. A real-life version of this underestimation occurred during the government shutdown of 2018–2019. Chuck Jones, "Shutdown's Economic Impact More Than Double the White House's Original Estimate," *Forbes*, January 16, 2019, updated January 21, 2019.

31. "Government Primary Expenditure, Percent of GDP," Database: Public Finances in Modern History, International Monetary Fund, December 2022. The US military budget, however, comprises more than a third of the total military spending in the world.

32. Dorothy A. Brown, *The Whiteness of Wealth: How the Tax System Impoverishes Black Americans—and How We Can Fix It*, Crown, 2022; Christopher Faricy, "How the U.S. Tax System Disadvantages Racial Minorities," *Washington Post*, April 18, 2016; Christopher Howard, *The Hidden Welfare State: Tax Expenditures and Social Policy in the United States*, Princeton University Press, 1999; Suzanne Mettler, *The Submerged State: How Invisible Government Policies Undermine American Democracy*, University of Chicago Press, 2011; Cathie Jo Martin, "Labour Market Coordination and the Evolution of Tax Regimes," *Socio-Economic Review* 13, no. 1 (January 2015): 50; Monica Prasad, *The Land of Too Much: American Abundance and the Paradox of Poverty*, Harvard University Press, 2012, 21–22.

33. Benjamin Veghte, "Social Security's Past, Present and Future," National Academy of Social Insurance, August 13, 2015; Kathleen Romig, "Social Security Lifts More People Above the Poverty Line Than Any Other Program," Center on Budget and Policy Priorities, updated January 31, 2024; Gary Engelhardt and Jonathan Gruber, "Social Security and the Evolution of Elderly Poverty," working paper, National Bureau of Economic Research, May 2004.

34. Mike Konczal, *Freedom from the Market: America's Fight to Liberate Itself from the Grip of the Invisible Hand*, New Press, 2021.

35. Andrea Louise Campbell, *How Policies Make Citizens: Senior Political Activism and the American Welfare State*, Princeton University Press, 2011.

36. Junko Kato, *Regressive Taxation and the Welfare State*, Cambridge University Press, 2003.

37. See, e.g., Leslie Carbone and Jay Richards, *The Economy Hits Home: What Makes the Economy Grow?*, Heritage Foundation, July 1, 2009.

38. Gabriel Ardant, "Financial Policy and Economic Infrastructure of Modern States and Nations," in *The Formation of National States in Western Europe*, ed. Charles Tilly, Princeton University Press, 1975, 164–242. Barter is not common among people unfamiliar with money. David Graeber, *Debt: The First 5,000 Years*, Melville House, 2011, 21–41. An underappreciated purpose of taxation is to maintain the social construct that money is valuable. Money itself is a "material proxy for the tax obligation." Christine Desan, *Making Money: Coin, Currency, and the Coming of Capitalism*, Oxford University Press, 2014, 58.

39. Quoted in Sheldon D. Pollack, *War, Revenue, and State Building: Financing the Development of the American State*, Cornell University Press, 2009, 1.

40. Political observers tend to have very strong presumptions about which taxes provoke protest and why. The data paint a far more complicated picture. Isaac William Martin and Nadav Gabay, "Tax Policy and Tax Protest in 20 Rich Democracies, 1980–2010," *British Journal of Sociology* 69, no. 3 (September 2018): 647–69.

41. Thomas Piketty, Emmanuel Saez, and Stefanie Stantcheva, "Optimal Taxation of Top Labor Incomes: A Tale of Three Elasticities," *American Economic Journal: Economic Policy* 6, no. 1 (February 2014): 230–71.

42. Liam Murphy and Thomas Nagel, *The Myth of Ownership: Taxes and Justice*, Oxford University Press, 2002.

43. Franklin Delano Roosevelt, "Address at Worcester, Massachusetts," October 21, 1936, APP.

Chapter 1. The Stamp Act: Taxation, Slavery, and Representation

1. Michael Mann, "State and Society, 1130–1815: An Analysis of English State Finances," in *Political Power and Social Theory*, ed. Maurice Zeitlin, JAI Press, 1980, 165–208; Deborah Boucoyannis, "No Taxation of Elites, No Representation: State Capacity and the Origins of Representation," *Politics and Society* 43, no. 3 (September 2015): 303–32.

2. A scutage was a tax paid by a vassal to his lord to avoid military service. An aid was a duty customarily imposed on vassals by a lord "to ransom his person, to make his eldest son a knight, and (once) to marry his eldest daughter." Magna Carta, 1215, cl. 12.

3. Magna Carta, 1215, cl. 14.

4. Clause 60 of Magna Carta also extends the protections the barons received to their own vassals and "all the men of our kingdom." The king was certainly not the only one prone to imposing upon his inferiors.

5. Nicholas Vincent, *Magna Carta: A Very Short Introduction*, Oxford University Press, 2012, 84.

6. Edmund S. Morgan and Helen M. Morgan, *The Stamp Act Crisis: Prologue to Revolution*, University of North Carolina Press, 1953, 75–91. Magna Carta was not well remembered until the seventeenth century. Jill Lepore, *These Truths: A History of the United States*, W. W. Norton, 2018, 40–43.

7. Timothy H. Breen, "Ideology and Nationalism on the Eve of the American Revolution: Revisions Once More in Need of Revising," *Journal of American History* 84, no. 1 (June 1997): 16; Timothy Besley and Torsten Persson, "The Origins of State Capacity: Property Rights, Taxation, and Politics," *American Economic Review* 99, no. 4 (September 2009): 2n1; Patrick K. O'Brien, "Fiscal and Financial Preconditions for the Rise of British Naval Hegemony 1485–1815," working paper no. 91/05, Department of Economic History, London School of Economics, 2005; John Brewer, *The Sinews of Power: War, Money and the English State 1688–1783*, Harvard University Press, 1990; Edgar Kiser and April Linton, "Determinants of the Growth of the State: War and Taxation in Early Modern France and England," *Social Forces* 80, no. 2 (December 2001): 411–48.

8. Boucoyannis, "No Taxation of Elites, No Representation." This interpretation differs from the literature asserting that it is the weakness of the ruler that leads to representation, e.g., Margaret Levi, *Of Rule and Revenue*, University of California Press, 1988, 113.

9. Philip T. Hoffman and Kathryn Norberg, *Fiscal Crises, Liberty, and Representative Government 1450–1789*, Stanford University Press, 2002, 310; Levi, *Of Rule and Revenue*, 120; Gabriel Ardant, "Financial Policy and Economic Infrastructure of Modern States and Nations," in *The Formation of National States in Western Europe*, ed. Charles Tilly, Princeton University Press, 1975, 231.

10. Lepore, *These Truths*, 48, 66.

11. Though some, including James Otis, proposed adding seats in Parliament for the colonies.

12. As Robin Einhorn has noted in "Age of Slavery," unpublished manuscript, July 2022, 22.

13. Woody Holton, *Liberty Is Sweet: The Hidden History of the American Revolution*, Simon and Schuster, 2021, 14–15; Terry Bouton, *Taming Democracy: "The People," the Founders, and the Troubled Ending of the American Revolution*, Oxford University Press, 2007, 16–30; Justin du Rivage and Claire Priest, "The Stamp Act and the Political Origins of American Legal and Economic Institutions," *Southern California Law Review* 88, no. 4 (May 2015): 875.

14. Justin du Rivage, *Revolution Against Empire: Taxes, Politics, and the Origins of American Independence*, Yale University Press, 2017; Breen, "Ideology and Nationalism"; Nick Bunker, *An Empire on the Edge: How Britain Came to Fight America*, Alfred A. Knopf, 2014; Steven Pincus, "Confederal Union and Empire: Placing the Albany Plan in Imperial Context," in *Scotland and the Wider World: Essays in Honour of Allan I. Macinnes*, ed. Neil McIntyre and Alison Cathcart, Boydell Press, 2022; James M. Vaughn, *The Politics of Empire at the Accession of George III: The East India Company and the Crisis and Transformation of Britain's Imperial State*, Yale University Press, 2019.

15. Edmund S. Morgan, *Prologue to Revolution: Sources and Documents on the Stamp Act Crisis, 1764–1766*, University of North Carolina Press, 1959, 4. The Morgans' claim that the colonists consistently thought both internal and external taxation required representation "elicited a certain amount of controversy." Morgan and Morgan, *The Stamp Act Crisis*, vii. For a recent critique, see William Hogeland, "Against the Consensus Approach to History," *New Republic*, January 25, 2021.

16. On the origins of the slogan, see J. L. Bell, "'No Taxation Without Representation' (Part 2)," *Journal of the American Revolution*, May 22, 2013.

17. James Otis, *The Rights of the British Colonies Asserted and Proved*, Edes and Gill, 1764.

18. Morgan, *Prologue to Revolution*, 10.

19. du Rivage, *Revolution Against Empire*, 12; Lepore, *These Truths*, 82.

20. Grenville had no interest in such a maneuver. Within only a few years, Britain would rue this decision, but by then it was too late. Holton, *Liberty Is Sweet*, 53, 191, 353; Morgan and Morgan, *The Stamp Act Crisis*, 22, 63.

21. Morgan, *Prologue to Revolution*, 15.

22. Andrew David Edwards, "Grenville's Silver Hammer: The Problem of Money in the Stamp Act Crisis," *Journal of American History* 104, no. 2 (September 2017): 347–48; du Rivage, *Revolution Against Empire*, 113, 121; Claire Priest, *Credit Nation: Property Laws and Institutions in Early America*, Princeton University Press, 2021, 115–27.

23. Morgan and Morgan, *The Stamp Act Crisis*, 54, 57.

24. du Rivage, *Revolution Against Empire*, 112; Edwards, "Grenville's Silver Hammer," 342.

25. Parliament had been misled on this point by Benjamin Franklin, who, living in London during the Stamp Act debacle, had testified before Parliament that "I have never heard any objection to the right of laying duties to regulate commerce; but a right to lay internal taxes was never supposed to be in Parliament, as we are not represented there." Bernard Bailyn, *The Ideological Origins of the American Revolution*, Belknap Press, 1967, 211–15; Morgan and Morgan, *The Stamp Act Crisis*, 282–87.

When colonial intransigence again brought Parliament to reverse its colonial taxes, they kept the tariff on tea as a symbol that Parliament maintained its authority to tax the colonies. The reduction of this tariff in 1773 provoked the Boston Tea Party.

26. Emma Rothschild, "A (New) Economic History of the American Revolution?," *New England Quarterly* 91, no. 1 (March 2018): 111.

27. John Dickinson, *The Writings of John Dickinson*, vol. 1, *Political Writings*, ed. Paul Leicester Ford, Philadelphia, 1895, 421–32, 357, 372.

28. Morgan, *Prologue to Revolution*, 83, 116; Holton, *Liberty Is Sweet*, 63.

29. Orlando Patterson, "The Unholy Trinity: Freedom, Slavery, and the American Constitution," *Social Research* 54, no. 3 (1987): 544.

30. du Rivage, *Revolution Against Empire,* 118; Morgan and Morgan, *The Stamp Act Crisis*, 88.

31. James L. Huston, *Securing the Fruits of Labor: The American Concept of Wealth Distribution, 1765–1900*, Louisiana State University Press, 2015, 37–38.

32. Patterson, "The Unholy Trinity."

33. Morgan, *Prologue to Revolution*, 15, 48; Breen, "Ideology and Nationalism," 33.

34. Morgan, *Prologue to Revolution*, 103. The term "American" took root in Britain before it did in America. Breen, "Ideology and Nationalism," 29–33.

35. Morgan, *Prologue to Revolution*, 86. Adams's "Humphrey Ploughjogger" letters were a painful effort at satire, written in the character of an uneducated farmer. "Humphrey Ploughjogger to the Boston Gazette, 14 October 1765," FO. Breen, "Ideology and Nationalism," 28–33; F. Nwabueze Okoye, "Chattel Slavery as the Nightmare of the American Revolutionaries," *William and Mary Quarterly* 37, no. 1 (1980): 28; Toni Morrison, *Playing in the Dark*, Harvard University Press, 1992, especially 38–51; Peter A. Dorsey, "To 'Corroborate Our Own Claims': Public Positioning and the Slavery Metaphor in Revolutionary America," *American Quarterly* 55, no. 3 (2003): 353–86; Edmund S. Morgan, *American Slavery, American Freedom*, W. W. Norton, 1975.

36. Breen, "Ideology and Nationalism," 37.

37. Massachusetts Anti-Slavery and Anti-Segregation Petitions, 1777, Massachusetts Archives Collection, v.212–Revolution Resolves, SC1/series 45X, Massachusetts Archives, Boston.

38. Dorsey, "To 'Corroborate Our Own Claims,'" 366, 370.

39. Gary B. Nash, *The Unknown American Revolution: The Unruly Birth of Democracy and the Struggle to Create America*, Penguin Books, 2005, 114–28, 210–12.

40. David Brion Davis, *The Problem of Slavery in the Age of Revolution, 1770–1823*, Cornell University Press, 1975, 283.

41. Douglas R. Egerton, *Death or Liberty: African Americans and Revolutionary America*, Oxford University Press, 2009, 56–57; Manisha Sinha, *The Slave's Cause: A History of Abolition*, Yale University Press, 2016, 41.

42. Nash, *The Unknown American Revolution*, 248.

43. Morgan, *Prologue to Revolution*, 21. Whately overstates the fraction of the British public that could vote: It was 5 percent, not 10. Gregory Claeys, *Thomas Paine: Social and Political Thought*, Unwin Hyman, 1989, 7; Holton, *Liberty Is Sweet*, 120.

44. Morgan, *Prologue to Revolution*, 21.

45. Morgan and Morgan, *The Stamp Act Crisis*, 83.

46. Among the important positions Burke held against the monetary interests of his constituents was an opposition to the slave trade. Burke was not re-elected.

47. Alexander Keyssar, *The Right to Vote: The Contested History of Democracy in the United States*, Basic Books, 2009, 5–20.

48. Bailyn, *Ideological Origins*, 170–71; Morgan and Morgan, *The Stamp Act Crisis*, 83.

49. Bailyn, *Ideological Origins*, 162.

50. The 1780 Constitution of Massachusetts implicitly extended suffrage to propertied Black men. James O. Horton and Lois E. Horton, *In Hope of Liberty: Culture, Community and Protest Among Northern Free Blacks, 1700–1860*, Oxford University Press, 1998, 70–71.

51. William C. Nell, *The Colored Patriots of the American Revolution, with Sketches of Several Distinguished Colored Persons: To Which Is Added a Brief Survey of the Condition and Prospects of Colored Americans*, Robert. F. Wallcut, 1855, 87–88.

52. Horton and Horton, *In Hope of Liberty*; Holton, *Liberty Is Sweet*, 420–21, 552–53.

53. Bailyn, *Ideological Origins*, 174.

Chapter 2. Shays's Rebellion and the Origins of the Constitution

1. "Abigail Adams to Thomas Jefferson, 29 January 1787," FO.

2. "To Thomas Jefferson from John Adams, 30 November 1786," FO.

3. "From Thomas Jefferson to Abigail Adams, 22 February 1787," FO.

4. "Abigail Adams to Thomas Jefferson, 29 January 1787," FO.

5. Woody Holton, "Abigail Adams, Bond Speculator," *William and Mary Quarterly* 64, no. 4 (2007): 821–38; "Abigail Adams to John Adams, 3 January 1784," FO.

6. Edwin J. Perkins, *American Public Finance and Financial Services, 1700–1815*, Ohio State University Press, 1994, 87. By the end of the war, Congress was considering military action against noncompliant states to force them to produce the funds needed for the Continental Army. Ben Baack, "Forging a Nation State: The Continental Congress and the Financing of the War of American Independence," *Economic History Review* 54, no. 4 (2001): 642, 649; Max M. Edling and Mark D. Kaplanoff, "Alexander Hamilton's Fiscal Reform: Transforming the Structure of Taxation in the Early Republic," *William and Mary Quarterly* 61, no. 4 (2004): 719.

7. Woody Holton, *Liberty Is Sweet: The Hidden History of the American Revolution*, Simon and Schuster, 2021, 386, 425–26; Michael A. McDonnell, "'The Spirit of Levelling': James Cleveland, Edward Wright, and the Militiamen's Struggle for Equality in Revolutionary Virginia," in *Revolutionary Founders: Rebels, Radicals, and Reformers in the Making of the Nation*, ed. Alfred F. Young, Ray Raphael, and Gary Nash, Knopf Doubleday, 2011, 146; Robert A. Becker, *Revolution, Reform and the Politics of American Taxation, 1763–1783*, Louisiana State University Press, 1980, 185.

8. Eric Foner, *Tom Paine and Revolutionary America*, Oxford University Press, 1976, 150; Robin L. Einhorn, *American Taxation, American Slavery*, University of Chicago Press, 2006; Becker, *Revolution, Reform*.

9. The requisition system used, for the first time, the three-fifths ratio to count enslaved people, which would be preserved in the Constitution to bias representation in favor of the slaveholder South.

10. Baack, "Forging a Nation State," 641; Gordon Wood, *The Radicalism of the American Revolution*, Alfred A. Knopf, 1991, 248.

11. Perkins, *American Public Finance*, 39, 99; Max M. Edling, *A Revolution in Favor of Government: Origins of the U.S. Constitution and the Making of the American State*, Oxford University Press, 2003, 150–51; Woody Holton, *Unruly Americans and the Origins of the Constitution*, Hill and Wang, 2008, 113; Benjamin Franklin, "Of the Paper Money of America, [1780?]," FO; Edling and Kaplanoff, "Alexander Hamilton's Fiscal Reform," 727; Michael J. Klarman, *The Framers' Coup: The Making of the United States Constitution*, Oxford University Press, 2016, 17; Perkins, *American Public Finance*, 96–97; Donald Stabile, *The Origins of American Public Finance: Debates over Money, Debt, and Taxes in the Constitutional Era, 1776–1836*, Bloomsbury Academic, 1998, 27; John Fiske, *The American Revolution: In Two Volumes* (illustrated ed.), vol. 2, Houghton Mifflin, 1896, 201. Eventually, "a continental" became synonymous with something of no value, as in "not worth a continental." Like "Boston Tea Party," the phrase does not appear to date to the revolutionary period.

12. Perkins, *American Public Finance*, 99, 101; Holton, *Liberty Is Sweet*, 496–97, 501; Roger H. Brown, *Redeeming the Republic: Federalists, Taxation, and the Origins of the Constitution*, Johns Hopkins University Press, 1993, 19; William Hogeland, *The Whiskey Rebellion: George Washington, Alexander Hamilton, and the Frontier Rebels Who Challenged America's Newfound Sovereignty*, Simon and Schuster, 2006, 40–47; Holton, *Unruly Americans*, 68–70.

13. Hogeland, *Whiskey Rebellion*, 38–39; William Hogeland, *The Hamilton Scheme: An Epic Tale of Money and Power in the American Founding*, Farrar, Straus and Giroux, 2024, 58; Holton, *Unruly Americans*, 79.

14. Holton, "Abigail Adams, Bond Speculator," 37; Klarman, *Framers' Coup*, 82; Terry Bouton, *Taming Democracy: "The People," the Founders, and the Troubled Ending of the American Revolution*, Oxford University Press, 2007, 85; Woody Holton, "'From the Labours of Others': The War Bonds Controversy and the Origins of the Constitution in New England," *William and Mary Quarterly* 61, no. 2 (2004): 289; Elmer James Ferguson, *The Power of the Purse: A History of American Public Finance, 1776–1790*, University of North Carolina Press, 1961, 280.

15. Perkins, *American Public Finance*, 111–13; Robert Morris, "Observations on the State of Affairs," January 13, 1783, quoted in Bouton, *Taming Democracy*, 61.

16. James L. Huston, *Securing the Fruits of Labor: The American Concept of Wealth Distribution, 1765–1900*, Louisiana State University Press, 2015, 89; Wood, *Radicalism of the American Revolution*, 112, 122–23; Clement Fatovic, *America's Founding and the Struggle over Economic Inequality*, University Press of Kansas, 2015, 10–11, 24; Peter H. Lindert and Jeffrey G. Williamson, "American Incomes 1774–1860," working paper, National Bureau of Economic Research, September 2012, 23; Hogeland, *Whiskey Rebellion*, 52; Frank W. Garmon Jr., "Mapping Distress: Taxation and Insolvency in Virginia, 1782–1790," *Journal of the Early Republic* 40, no. 2 (2020): 231–65; Bouton, *Taming Democracy*, 92, 101.

17. Including, at one time, war financier Robert Morris. Many imprisoned for debt were held in comparatively good conditions and for only a few days: Jonathan M. Chu, "Debt Litigation and Shays's Rebellion," in *Debt to Shays: The Bicentennial of an Agrarian Rebellion*, ed. Robert A. Gross, University of Virginia Press, 1993, 85. But there are also petitions from debt prisoners that include complaints of starvation: Michael Mann, "State and Society, 1130–1815: An Analysis of English State Finances," in *Political Power and Social Theory*, ed. Maurice Zeitlin, JAI Press, 1980, 2; Huston, *Securing the Fruits of Labor*, 26; Ruth Bogin, "Petitioning and the New Moral Economy of Post-Revolutionary America," *William and Mary Quarterly* 45, no. 3 (1988): 407. On the long history of debt-relief agitation in America, see Emily Zackin and Chloe N. Thurston, *The Political Development of American Debt Relief*, University of Chicago Press, 2024.

18. Huston, *Securing the Fruits of Labor*, 3; Fatovic, *America's Founding*, xix; Foner, *Tom Paine and Revolutionary America*, 124; Bernard Bailyn, *The Ideological Origins of the American Revolution*, Belknap Press, 1967, 373; Noah Webster, *An Examination into the Leading Principles of the Federal Constitution*, Prichard and Hall, 1787.

19. Holton, "'From the Labours of Others,'" 275–76; Holton, *Liberty Is Sweet*, 519; Holton, *Unruly Americans*, 31–32; Edling and Kaplanoff, "Alexander Hamilton's Fiscal Reform," 734; Edling, *A Revolution in Favor of Government*, 158; Huston, *Securing the Fruits of Labor*, xiv.

20. Holton, *Unruly Americans*, 55; Holton, "'From the Labours of Others,'" 278, 285–86; Woody Holton, "An 'Excess of Democracy'—or a Shortage?: The Federalists' Earliest Adversaries," *Journal of the Early Republic* 25, no. 3 (2005): 360–62.

21. Quoted in Bouton, *Taming Democracy*, 115.

22. Terry Bouton, "William Findley, David Bradford, and the Pennsylvania Regulation of 1794," in Young et al., *Revolutionary Founders*, 222, 238.

23. Bogin, "Petitioning and the New Moral Economy," 413.

24. Bouton, *Taming Democracy*, 89, 93–94; Klarman, *Framers' Coup*, 76; Chu, "Debt Litigation and Shays's Rebellion."

25. Klarman, *Framers' Coup*, 75; Perkins, *American Public Finance*, 28; Christian Parenti, *Radical Hamilton: Economic Lessons from a Misunderstood Founder*, Verso Books, 2020, 85; Bouton, "William Findley," 237; Mary M. Schweitzer, "State-Issued Currency and the Ratification of the U.S. Constitution," *Journal of Economic History* 49, no. 2 (1989): 319.

26. Quoted in Gordon S. Wood, *The Creation of the American Republic, 1776–1787*, University of North Carolina Press, 1998, 72.

27. Foner, *Tom Paine and Revolutionary America*, 190–91.

28. Wood, *Creation of the American Republic*, 251.

29. Bouton, *Taming Democracy*, 173; Holton, *Unruly Americans*, 230–31; Holton, *Liberty Is Sweet*, 520.

30. Quoted in Holton, "'From the Labours of Others,'" 282.

31. As "Primitive Whig," *New Jersey-Gazette*, January 9, 1786. Partially quoted in Klarman, *Framers' Coup*, 83.

32. Holton, *Unruly Americans*, 98–99; Woody Holton, "Did Democracy Cause the Recession That Led to the Constitution?," *Journal of American History* 92, no. 2 (2005): 455–56; Terry Bouton, "A Road Closed: Rural Insurgency in Post-Independence Pennsylvania," *Journal of American History* 87, no. 3 (2000): 864; Holton, *Liberty Is Sweet*, 488–89.

33. JCC, vol. 22, ed. Gaillard Hunt, Government Printing Office, 1914, 486. Quoted in Bouton, *Taming Democracy*, 71, 83.

34. David Hume, "Of Taxes," in *Writings on Economics*, ed. Eugene Rotwein, University of Wisconsin Press, 1955, 83.

35. Some state legislatures, including those in New York and North Carolina, avoided adopting heavy taxes. Edling, *A Revolution in Favor of Government*, 156; Perkins, *American Public Finance*, 172.

36. Bouton, "A Road Closed," 857.

37. David P. Szatmary, *Shays' Rebellion: The Making of an Agrarian Insurrection*, University of Massachusetts Press, 1980, 124–25; Bouton, "A Road Closed," 158; Wood, *Creation of the American Republic*, 407; Holton, *Unruly Americans*, 147.

38. Richard Buel Jr., "The Public Creditor Interest in Massachusetts Politics," in Gross, *Debt to Shays*, 54; Holton, *Unruly Americans*, 74–75; Robert A. Gross, "The Uninvited Guest: Daniel Shays and the Constitution," in Gross, *Debt to Shays*, 8.

39. Leonard L. Richards, *Shays's Rebellion: The American Revolution's Final Battle*, University of Pennsylvania Press, 2014, 83, 85–87.

40. Perkins, *American Public Finance*, 8, 179–80; Richards, *Shays's Rebellion*, 5, 72, 75; Buel, "Public Creditor Interest," 49, 51; Fatovic, *America's Founding*, 52; Holton, *Unruly Americans*, 131–32.

41. Bogin, "Petitioning and the New Moral Economy," 417; "Petition to the General Court from the Town of Dracut," September 25, 1786, Shays' Rebellion & the Making of a Nation (website), Documents and Artifacts, Springfield Technical Community College, Springfield, MA; Richards, *Shays's Rebellion*, 75; Szatmary, *Shays' Rebellion*, 32; Van Beck Hall, *Politics Without Parties: Massachusetts, 1780–1791*, University of Pittsburgh Press, 1972.

42. "An Address to the People by Daniel Gray of Pelham," December 27, 1786, Shays' Rebellion & the Making of a Nation; Richards, *Shays's Rebellion*, 12; Parenti, *Radical Hamilton*, 120, 123.

43. Thereafter, direct taxes were about one-tenth of the previous level. Richards, *Shays's Rebellion*, 38–39, 119; Holton, *Unruly Americans*, 76; Holton, "'From the Labours of Others,'" 296.

44. "To George Washington from Henry Knox, 23 October 1786," FO.

45. This and all following quotes from the Constitutional Convention are drawn from Max Farrand, ed., *The Records of the Federal Convention of 1787*, vol. 1, Yale University Press, 1911.

46. Our records of the proceedings come primarily from the copious notes of James Madison, which were published, after the death of the convention participants, in 1840.

47. Brown, *Redeeming the Republic*, 26; Klarman, *Framers' Coup*, 19; Parenti, *Radical Hamilton*, 95–105.

48. Dan T. Coenen, "A Rhetoric for Ratification: The Argument of the Federalist and Its Impact on Constitutional Interpretation," *Duke Law Journal* 56, no. 2 (November 2006): 485n76; Holton, *Unruly Americans*, 174.

49. Foner, *Tom Paine and Revolutionary America*, 89, 122; Wood, *Creation of the American Republic*, 218–22.

50. "New York Ratifying Convention. Notes for Second Speech of July 17, [17 July 1788]," FO.

51. As we will see in Chapter 4, Southerners demanded and received constitutional limitations on taxation where it might threaten slavery. These protections would later be used by a Gilded Age Supreme Court to declare an income tax unconstitutional (Chapter 8).

52. Several attendees, including Gerry and Randolph, would refuse to sign, worried the government they had helped to design would be too powerful.

53. "Conjectures about the New Constitution, [17–30 September 1787]," FO.

54. Saul Cornell, "Aristocracy Assailed: The Ideology of Backcountry Anti-Federalism," *Journal of American History* 76, no. 4 (1990): 1148–72; Hogeland, *Whiskey Rebellion*, 91.

Chapter 3. The Whiskey Rebellion: The Fight for Equal Taxation

1. William Hogeland, *The Whiskey Rebellion: George Washington, Alexander Hamilton, and the Frontier Rebels Who Challenged America's Newfound Sovereignty*, Simon and Schuster, 2006, 152; Thomas P. Slaughter, *The Whiskey Rebellion: Frontier Epilogue to the American Revolution*, Oxford University Press, 1986, 179; PA, 60; William Findley, *History of the Insurrection in the Four Western Counties of*

Pennsylvania, Philadelphia, 1796, 84–87; Dorothy E. Fennell, *From Rebelliousness to Insurrection: A Social History of the Whiskey Rebellion, 1765–1802*, University of Pittsburgh Press, 1981, 66; Terry Bouton, *Taming Democracy: "The People," the Founders, and the Troubled Ending of the American Revolution*, Oxford University Press, 2007, 232; testimony of James Therr in Hugh H. Brackenridge, *Incidents of the Insurrection in the Western Parts of Pennsylvania in the Year 1794*, M'Culloch, 1795.

2. Bouton, *Taming Democracy*, 234; Slaughter, *The Whiskey Rebellion*, 158, 179; James McAllister's testimony in Brackenridge, *Incidents*; John Baldwin's testimony in *United States v. Robert Porter*, 1795, MFF 2739, Library and Archives Division, Senator John Heinz History Center, Historical Society of Western Pennsylvania, Pittsburgh.

3. Bouton, *Taming Democracy*, 233; Terry Bouton, "William Findley, David Bradford, and the Pennsylvania Regulation of 1794," in *Revolutionary Founders: Rebels, Radicals, and Reformers in the Making of the Nation*, ed. Alfred F. Young, Ray Raphael, and Gary Nash, Knopf Doubleday, 2011; Brackenridge, *Incidents*, 6; Baldwin's testimony in *United States v. Robert Porter*.

4. Quoted in Woody Holton, "An 'Excess of Democracy'—or a Shortage?: The Federalists' Earliest Adversaries," *Journal of the Early Republic* 25, no. 3 (2005): 379.

5. Max M. Edling, "The Origin, Structure, and Development of the American Fiscal Regime, 1789–1837," in *Taxation, State, and Civil Society in Germany and the United States from the 18th to the 20th Century*, ed. Alexander Nützenadel and Christoph Strupp, Nomos, 2007, 28.

6. Max M. Edling, *A Revolution in Favor of Government: Origins of the U.S. Constitution and the Making of the American State*, Oxford University Press, 2003, 209.

7. Colin G. Calloway, *The Indian World of George Washington: The First President, the First Americans, and the Birth of the Nation*, Oxford University Press, 2018, 7.

8. "Report on Vacant Lands, 20 July 1790," FO.

9. JCC, vol. 33, ed. Roscoe R. Hill, Government Printing Office, 1936, 388. Similarly, "From George Washington to James Duane, 7 September 1783" and "To George Washington from Henry Knox, 4 January 1790," FO.

10. "An Act for Laying a Duty on Goods, Wares, and Merchandizes, Imported into the United States . . . May 16, 1789," Portfolio 211, Folder 6, Rare Book and Special Collections Division, Printed Ephemera Collection, Library of Congress; Clement Fatovic, *America's Founding and the Struggle over Economic Inequality*, University Press of Kansas, 2015, 139–41; Hogeland, *The Whiskey Rebellion*, 141; Max M. Edling and Mark D. Kaplanoff, "Alexander Hamilton's Fiscal Reform: Transforming the Structure of Taxation in the Early Republic," *William and Mary Quarterly* 61, no. 4 (2004): 732–33; Edling, *Revolution in Favor of Government*, 209, 212.

11. Bouton, *Taming Democracy*, 220; Donald Stabile, *The Origins of American Public Finance: Debates over Money, Debt, and Taxes in the Constitutional Era, 1776–1836*, Bloomsbury Academic, 1998, 143–44, 149.

12. Elmer James Ferguson, *The Power of the Purse: A History of American Public Finance, 1776–1790*, University of North Carolina Press, 1961, 149.

13. Slaughter, *The Whiskey Rebellion*, 100–101.

14. PA, 4; Daniel Marder, "Introduction," in *Incidents of the Insurrection*, ed. Daniel Marder, College and University Press, 1972, 11; Findley, *History of the Insurrection*, 41; Bouton, "William Findley," 238; Fennell, *From Rebelliousness to Insurrection*, 3.

15. Stabile, *Origins of American Public Finance*, 106; Eugene P. Link, *Democratic-Republican Societies, 1790–1800*, Columbia Studies in American Culture, no. 9, Columbia University Press, 1942, 67; Hogeland, *The Whiskey Rebellion*, 66–67; Fennell, *From Rebelliousness to Insurrection*, 235–48. Some of these provisions were later revised: Hamilton's report to President Washington, August 5, 1794, PA, 76; William Hogeland, *The Hamilton Scheme: An Epic Tale of Money and Power in the American Founding*, Farrar, Straus and Giroux, 2024, 259.

16. Hogeland, *The Whiskey Rebellion*, 28, 68.

17. PA, 17–18, 25, 135. The opposition to the whiskey tax and the demand for more progressive taxation was a feature of both more moderate meetings, led by frontier gentility, and more radical meetings, led by rank-and-file militiamen. Hogeland, *Hamilton Scheme*, 274–75.

18. Bouton, *Taming Democracy*, 51, 120–21, 222–23; Leland D. Baldwin, *Whiskey Rebels: The Story of a Frontier Uprising*, University of Pittsburgh Press, 2010, 15; PA, 42; Slaughter, *The Whiskey Rebellion*, 72; Stephen Aron, *How the West Was Lost*, Johns Hopkins University Press, 1996, 87.

19. Fennell, *From Rebelliousness to Insurrection*, 38.

20. William Hogeland, *Autumn of the Black Snake*, Farrar, Straus and Giroux, 2017, 61–62; Richard White, *The Middle Ground: Indians, Empires, and Republics in the Great Lakes Region, 1650–1815*, Cambridge University Press, 1991, 344–47, 351–54, 440; Gary B. Nash, *The Unknown American Revolution: The Unruly Birth of Democracy and the Struggle to Create America*, Penguin Books, 2005, 129; Randolph C. Downes, *Council Fires on the Upper Ohio*, University of Pittsburgh Press, 1968, 310–38.

21. White, *Middle Ground*; Alfred F. Young, *Liberty Tree: Ordinary People and the American Revolution*, New York University Press, 2006, 242. Participants in the Whiskey Rebellion included Herman Husband, a radical millenarian preacher who sought peace and fair dealing with the Native nations, and David Williamson, a colonel in the Whiskey Rebel army who a decade earlier led the Gnadenhutten massacre. James P. Whittenburg, "'The Common Farmer (Number 2)': Herman Husband's Plan for Peace Between the United States and the Indians, 1792," *William and Mary Quarterly* 34, no. 4 (1977): 647–50; White, *Middle Ground*, 389–91; Richard Taylor Wiley, *The Whisky Insurrection: A General View*, Herald Printing House, 1912, 14.

22. The name "Ohio" comes from the Iroquois word for the Ohio River. It is unclear what names were used for this region among the diasporic Indigenous population living in Ohio in the 1790s. "Myaamionki" is a word used by the Miami Nation today to describe their historical and contemporary homelands.

23. Hogeland, *Autumn of the Black Snake*, 113–15. Harvey L. Carter, *The Life and Times of Little Turtle: First Sagamore of the Wabash*, University of Illinois Press, 1987, 92–96; John Sugden, *Blue Jacket: Warrior of the Shawnees*, University of Nebraska Press, 2000; Stewart Rafert, "Little Turtle (Mishikinakwa)," in *Encyclopedia of North American Indians*, ed. Frederick E. Hoxie, Diane Publishing Company, 1999, 343; Alan Taylor, "Land and Liberty on the Post-Revolutionary Frontier," in *Devising Liberty: Preserving and Creating Freedom in the New American Republic*, ed. David Thomas Konig, Stanford University Press, 1995, 98. On western Pennsylvanians' participation in these campaigns, Colin G. Calloway, *The Victory with No Name: The Native American Defeat of the First American Army*, Oxford University Press, 2014, 138–39.

24. Message to the Commissioners of the United States from the Wyandots, Seven Nations of Canada, Delawares, Shawanese, Miamies, Ottawas, Chippewas, Senecas of the Glaize, Pattawatamies, Connoys, Munsees, Nantekokies, Mohicans, Messasagoes, Creeks, and Cherokees, August 13, 1793, ASP, 2, *Indian Affairs* 1:356.

25. Jeffrey Ostler, *Surviving Genocide: Native Nations and the United States from the American Revolution to Bleeding Kansas*, Yale University Press, 2019, 98, 106; David Andrew Nichols, *Red Gentlemen and White Savages: Indians, Federalists, and the Search for Order on the American Frontier*, University of Virginia Press, 2008, 164; Hogeland, *The Whiskey Rebellion*, 101; William H. Bergmann, *The American National State and the Early West*, Cambridge University Press, 2012, 67; Andrew R. L. Cayton, "'Separate Interests' and the Nation-State: The Washington Administration and the Origins of Regionalism in the Trans-Appalachian West," *Journal of American History* 79, no. 1 (1992): 53–54; Fennell, *From Rebelliousness to Insurrection*, 65, 90–92, 249–50; Hogeland, *Hamilton Scheme*, 299.

26. Taylor, "Land and Liberty on the Post-Revolutionary Frontier," 104.

27. Seth Cotlar, *Tom Paine's America: The Rise and Fall of Transatlantic Radicalism in the Early Republic*, University of Virginia Press, 2011, 124–25, 134, 155.

28. Link, *Democratic-Republican Societies*, 118.

29. Thomas Paine, *The Life and Major Writings of Thomas Paine*, ed. Philip S. Foner, *Citadel Press*, 1961, 433–37; Jeremy Bearer-Friend and Vanessa Williamson, "The Common Sense of a Wealth Tax: Thomas Paine and Taxation as Freedom from Aristocracy," *Florida Tax Review* 26, no. 1 (2022): 326–68.

30. "Extracts from Late French Papers," *National Gazette* (Philadelphia), September 18, 1793; Cotlar, *Tom Paine's America*, 39, 154, 130.

31. "Revisions of the Pennsylvania Declaration of Rights [between 29 July 1776 and 15 August 1776]," FO.

32. Eric Foner, *Tom Paine and Revolutionary America*, Oxford University Press, 1976, 133; Walter Isaacson, *Benjamin Franklin: An American Life*, Simon and Schuster, 2004, 315. Even if Franklin did not write the clause, he approved of it. "Revisions of the Pennsylvania Declaration of Rights, [between 29 July 1776 and 15 August 1776]." See also Woody Holton, *Liberty Is Sweet: The Hidden History of the American Revolution*, Simon and Schuster, 2021, 276.

33. Paul Leicester Ford, "The Adoption of the Pennsylvania Constitution of 1776," *Political Science Quarterly* 10, no. 3 (1895): 453; Gordon S. Wood, *The*

Creation of the American Republic, 1776–1787, University of North Carolina Press, 1998, 89.

34. Similarly, the Vermont Constitution of 1777 includes in its declaration of rights "that private property ought to be subservient to public uses, when necessity requires it."

35. Foner, *Tom Paine and Revolutionary America*, 218.

36. William Manning, *The Key of Liberty: The Life and Democratic Writings of William Manning, "a Laborer," 1747–1814*, ed. Michael Merrill and Sean Wilentz, Harvard University Press, 1993, 63.

37. Robert Coram, *Political Inquiries: To Which Is Added, a Plan for the General Establishment of Schools Throughout the United States*, Wilmington, 1791, vi–vii, 100–101. For more on Coram, see Cotlar, *Tom Paine's America*, chap. 4.

38. "From Alexander Hamilton to George Washington, 1 September 1792"; "From Alexander Hamilton to John Jay, 3 September 1792"; "From Alexander Hamilton to George Washington, 9 September 1792," FO.

39. "To George Washington from Alexander Hamilton, 5 August 1794," FO.

40. Findley, *History of the Insurrection*, 44; Hogeland, *The Whiskey Rebellion*, 125.

41. "From Alexander Hamilton to Jeremiah Olney, 2 April 1793," FO.

42. PA 8, 12.

43. Hogeland, *The Whiskey Rebellion*, 143.

44. Robert W. Coakley, *The Role of Federal Military Forces in Domestic Disorders, 1789–1878*, Center of Military History, US Army, 1988, 34.

45. David L. Preston, *Braddock's Defeat: The Battle of the Monongahela and the Road to Revolution*, Oxford University Press, 2015, 337–38.

46. Fennell, *From Rebelliousness to Insurrection*, 90.

47. Holton, *Liberty Is Sweet*, 558; Bouton, *Taming Democracy*, 235; Fennell, *From Rebelliousness to Insurrection*, 69, 181–82; Brackenridge, *Incidents*, 137.

48. Fennell, *From Rebelliousness to Insurrection*.

49. "From Alexander Hamilton to Angelica Church, 8 December 1794," FO.

50. Slaughter, *The Whiskey Rebellion*, 224. Washington held about forty thousand acres of Western land. Holton, *Liberty Is Sweet*, 508.

51. "From George Washington to the U.S. Senate and House of Representatives, 19 November 1794," FO.

52. Link, *Democratic-Republican Societies*, 146–47; Hogeland, *The Whiskey Rebellion*, 117–24.

53. Philip S. Foner, ed., *The Democratic-Republican Societies, 1790–1800: A Documentary Sourcebook of Constitutions, Declarations, Addresses, Resolutions, and Toasts*, Bloomsbury Academic, 1976, 29. Some democrats insisted that their preferred policies were needed to prevent events like the Whiskey Rebellion. In justifying the public cost of his educational society, Manning notes that this expense "would not cost much more than the pitsburge Insurrection did, which would never bin if such a Sosiety had bin formed." Manning, *Key of Liberty*, 63.

54. Hogeland, *Autumn of the Black Snake*, 260–64, 313–18, 336–37; Sugden, *Blue Jacket*, 175–76; Carter, *Little Turtle*, 134; Daryl Baldwin and George Ironstrack, "Mihšihkinaahkwa (Little Turtle)," in *Indiana's 200: The People Who Shaped*

the Hoosier State, ed. Linda C. Gugin and James E. St. Clair, Indiana Historical Society, 2016, 234.

55. Ostler, *Surviving Genocide*, 110.

56. Bouton, *Taming Democracy*, 250; Andrew Shankman, *Crucible of American Democracy: The Struggle to Fuse Egalitarianism and Capitalism in Jeffersonian Pennsylvania*, University Press of Kansas, 2004, 67; Laura Jensen, *Patriots, Settlers, and the Origins of American Social Policy*, Cambridge University Press, 2003; Joseph P. Ferrie, "Migration to the Frontier in Mid-Nineteenth Century America: A Re-Examination of Turner's 'Safety Valve,'" unpublished manuscript, 1997, 1–2; Paul Frymer, *Building an American Empire: The Era of Territorial and Political Expansion*, Princeton University Press, 2017, 57–58; Paul Frymer, "'A Rush and a Push and the Land Is Ours': Territorial Expansion, Land Policy, and U.S. State Formation," *Perspectives on Politics* 12, no. 1 (March 2014): 119–44; Ostler, *Surviving Genocide*, 135; Taylor, "Land and Liberty on the Post-Revolutionary Frontier," 108; Nichols, *Red Gentlemen and White Savages*, 59. In the slaveholding South, there was not even a temporary equalizing effect. Peter H. Lindert and Jeffrey G. Williamson, "American Incomes 1774–1860," working paper, National Bureau of Economic Research, September 2012.

57. Ostler, *Surviving Genocide*, 97, 307, 361. The Southern society, built upon racial hierarchy, was also uniquely threatened by the existence of free nations of color—both conceptually and because those nations could serve as a haven for people escaping slavery. On Southern versus Northern attitudes, see David A. Nichols, "Land, Republicanism, and Indians: Power and Policy in Early National Georgia, 1780–1825," *Georgia Historical Quarterly* 85, no. 2 (2001): 224; Leonard A. Carlson and Mark A. Roberts, "Indian Lands, 'Squatterism,' and Slavery: Economic Interests and the Passage of the Indian Removal Act of 1830," *Explorations in Economic History* 43, no. 3 (July 2006): 487; Claudio Saunt, *Unworthy Republic: The Dispossession of Native Americans and the Road to Indian Territory*, W. W. Norton, 2020, 77, 244–47; "From Thomas Jefferson to William Henry Harrison, 27 February 1803" and "From Thomas Jefferson to Indian Nations, 10 January 1809," FO.

58. Brackenridge, *Incidents*, 153.

59. Cotlar, *Tom Paine's America*, 10, 55; Link, *Democratic-Republican Societies*, 186.

60. "Continental Congress Remarks on the Collection of Funds by Officers of the United States [28 January 1783]," FO; Nicholas R. Parrillo, "A Critical Assessment of the Originalist Case Against Administrative Regulatory Power: New Evidence from the Federal Tax on Private Real Estate in the 1790s," *Yale Law Journal*, 130, no. 6 (April 2021): 1288–1457.

61. On direct taxation and the War of 1812, see Stabile, *Origins of American Public Finance*, chaps. 8 and 9; Christian Parenti, *Radical Hamilton: Economic Lessons from a Misunderstood Founder*, Verso Books, 2020, 207–13.

Chapter 4. The Emancipatory Potential of Taxation

1. George M. Frederickson, quoted in David Brown, *Southern Outcast: Hinton Rowan Helper and the Impending Crisis of the South*, Louisiana State University

Press, 2. Originally in George M. Fredrickson, *The Arrogance of Race: Historical Perspectives on Slavery, Racism, and Social Inequality*, Wesleyan University Press, 1988, 28.

2. Brown, *Southern Outcast*, 1.

3. Cong. Globe Appendix, 36th Cong., 1st sess., 34, 36, 49, 83, 88 (1860); Keri L. Merritt, *Masterless Men: Poor Whites and Slavery in the Antebellum South*, Cambridge University Press, 2017, 1–2.

4. Hinton Rowan Helper, *The Impending Crisis of the South: How to Meet It*, New York, 1860, 178.

5. Helper, *Impending Crisis*, v–vi.

6. The sectional comparison was a common one, e.g., Alexis de Tocqueville, *Democracy in America: The Complete and Unabridged Volumes I and II*, trans. Henry Reeve, Bantam Dell, 2004, 420; Laurence Shore, *Southern Capitalists: The Ideological Leadership of an Elite, 1832–1885*, University of North Carolina Press, 2018, 62.

7. Helper, *Impending Crisis*, 25.

8. Helper, *Impending Crisis*, 149.

9. Not literally all slaveowners were white men; a very small number of free Black men and single or widowed white women owned slaves.

10. William S. Rossiter, *A Century of Population Growth*, Johnson Reprint, 1966, originally published in 1909 by the Government Printing Office, 135–38, table 68; Otto H. Olsen, "Historians and the Extent of Slave Ownership in the Southern United States," *Civil War History* 18, no. 2 (1972): 101–16.

11. Helper, *Impending Crisis*, 149.

12. On the limited popularity of secession, however, see Merritt, *Masterless Men*, 35, 311; Roger Lowenstein, *Ways and Means: Lincoln and His Cabinet and the Financing of the Civil War*, Penguin, 2022, 25; Mario L. Chacón and Jeffrey L. Jensen, "The Political and Economic Geography of Southern Secession," *Journal of Economic History* 80, no. 2 (June 2020): 386–416.

13. The delegates at the Constitutional Convention did not fully consider the implications of the direct tax clause. Gouverneur Morris, who introduced the direct tax provision, saw it as a temporary expedient to bridge "a certain gulph" between the North and South. Max Farrand, ed., *The Records of the Federal Convention of 1787*, vol. 2, Yale University Press, 1911, 106. Adding taxes to the clause got Northerners on board with the South's inflated representation, because it seemed to mean that Southerners would pay for their disproportionate representation. Calvin C. Jillson, *Constitution Making: Conflict and Consensus in the Federal Convention of 1787*, Agathon Press, 1988, 98; Robin L. Einhorn, *American Taxation, American Slavery*, University of Chicago Press, 2006, 175–78; Michael J. Klarman, *The Framers' Coup: The Making of the United States Constitution*, Oxford University Press, 2016, 274–76. By the 1790s, however, the clause was widely understood to be a defense of slavery. *Hylton v. United States*, 3 US 171 (Supreme Court 1796), 177; E. R. A. Seligman, *The Income Tax: A Study of the History, Theory, and Practice of Income Taxation at Home and Abroad*, Macmillan, 1914, 555.

14. Robin Einhorn, "Patrick Henry's Case Against the Constitution: The Structural Problem with Slavery," *Journal of the Early Republic* 22, no. 4 (2002): 554,

559; Einhorn, *American Taxation, American Slavery*, 179, 181. Henry wished to further restrict the federal government's tax power in the Bill of Rights. Klarman, *Framers' Coup*, 578.

15. Donald Stabile, *The Origins of American Public Finance: Debates over Money, Debt, and Taxes in the Constitutional Era, 1776–1836*, Bloomsbury Academic, 1998, 129; Robin L. Einhorn, "Slavery and the Politics of Taxation in the Early United States," *Studies in American Political Development* 14, no. 2 (October 2000): 156–83.

16. John C. Calhoun, *The Works of John C. Calhoun*, vol. 1, ed. Richard K. Cralle, D. Appleton, 1854, 29–30, 41–42.

17. Richard Hofstadter, *The American Political Tradition and the Men Who Made It*, Alfred A. Knopf, 1973.

18. South Carolinians tended to overstate the effect of the tariff, seeing it as the primary cause of their state's economic and social stagnation. Merrill D. Peterson, *The Great Triumvirate: Webster, Clay, and Calhoun*, Oxford University Press, 1987, 191; William W. Freehling, *Secessionists at Bay, 1776–1854*, vol. 1 of *The Road to Disunion*, Oxford University Press, 1991, 255–57.

19. The *South Carolina Exposition and Protest* of 1828 was widely understood to be Calhoun's handiwork; Calhoun would publicly support nullification in his 1831 Fort Hill Address.

20. Freehling, *Secessionists at Bay*, 257–59. It would take three-quarters of the other states to overturn the decision of a single state, and that state would then have the right to secede from the Union.

21. Peterson, *Great Triumvirate*, 233.

22. Quoted in Hofstadter, *American Political Tradition*, 100.

23. This revision, in 1783, marked the first usage of the three-fifths ratio for counting the enslaved population. Einhorn, *American Taxation, American Slavery*; Stabile, *Origins of American Public Finance*, 58.

24. See, e.g., *Proceedings and Debates of the Virginia State Convention of 1829–1830*, Samuel Shepherd, 1830, 108–16.

25. Thomas Jefferson, *Notes on the State of Virginia*, Wells and Lilly, 1829, 93.

26. Ta-Nehisi Coates, "What Cotton Hath Wrought," *The Atlantic*, July 30, 2010; Edward E. Baptist, *The Half Has Never Been Told: Slavery and the Making of American Capitalism*, Basic Books, 2016; Sven Beckert, *Empire of Cotton: A Global History*, Alfred A. Knopf, 2014; Eric Foner, *Free Soil, Free Labor, Free Men: The Ideology of the Republican Party Before the Civil War*, Oxford University Press, 1995, 43–44; Sacha Dray, Camille Landais, and Stefanie Stantcheva, "Wealth and Property Taxation in the United States," working paper, National Bureau of Economic Research, March 2023; Chacón and Jensen, "Political and Economic Geography of Southern Secession," 149fn16; Lee Soltow, *Men and Wealth in the United States, 1850–1870*, Yale University Press, 1975; Merritt, *Masterless Men*, 70–71; Cassius M. Clay, "Speech of Cassius M. Clay, at Lexington, Ky.," *National Era*, November 13, 1851. Southerners pretended otherwise. "You meet more beggars in one day, in any single street of the city of New York, than you would meet in a lifetime in the whole South," swore South Carolina Representative James Henry Hammond in 1858.

27. Foner, *Free Soil, Free Labor, Free Men*, xiv, xvi.

28. The state constitution of Arkansas, for example, insisted that the "General Assembly shall have no power to pass laws for the emancipation of Slaves, without the consent of the owners." Similar clauses appear in the constitutions of Georgia (1798), Mississippi (1817), Alabama (1819), Missouri (1820), Mississippi (1832), Tennessee (1834), Florida (1838), and Texas (1845).

29. Eaton Clement, *The Freedom-of-Thought Struggle in the Old South*, Harper and Row, 1964.

30. Manisha Sinha, "The Caning of Charles Sumner: Slavery, Race, and Ideology in the Age of the Civil War," *Journal of the Early Republic* 23, no. 2 (2003): 233–62.

31. Einhorn, *American Taxation, American Slavery*, 51. In Georgia in 1852, when ad valorem taxation was finally instituted, taxpayers were allowed to simply declare the value of their own property—a declaration that by law could not be questioned. J. Mills Thornton III, "Fiscal Policy and the Failure of Radical Reconstruction," in *Region, Race, and Reconstruction: Essays in Honor of C. Vann Woodward*, ed. J. Morgan Kousser and James M. McPherson, Oxford University Press, 1 982, 358.

32. *Proceedings and Debates of the Virginia State Convention of 1829–1830*, 172.

33. Alison Goodyear Freehling, *Drift Toward Dissolution: The Virginia Slavery Debate of 1831–1832*, Louisiana State University Press, 1982, 45.

34. Freehling, *Secessionists at Bay*, 169. Ratcliffe estimates a slightly higher percentage enfranchised; Donald Ratcliffe, "The Right to Vote and the Rise of Democracy, 1787–1828," *Journal of the Early Republic* 33, no. 2 (2013): 219–54. Richard J. Ellis, "Legitimating Slavery in the Old South: The Effect of Political Institutions on Ideology," *Studies in American Political Development* 5, no. 2 (October 1991): 347; Douglas Keith and Eric Petry, *Apportionment of State Legislatures, 1776–1920*, Brennan Center for Justice, 2015, 72–73.

35. Freehling, *Drift Toward Dissolution*, 58; *Richmond Enquirer*, November 24, 1829, 3; Freehling, *Secessionists at Bay*, 512.

36. *Proceedings and Debates of the Virginia State Convention of 1829–1830*, 172.

37. Freehling, *Drift Toward Dissolution*, 57, 64.

38. *Proceedings and Debates of the Virginia State Convention of 1829–1830*, 75, 116; Robin L. Einhorn, "Species of Property: The American Property-Tax Uniformity Clauses Reconsidered," *Journal of Economic History* 61, no. 4 (2001): 996; Freehling, *Drift Toward Dissolution*, 51.

39. Claude Hampton Hall, *Abel Parker Upshur, Conservative Virginian, 1790–1844*, State Historical Society of Wisconsin, 1964, 170–71.

40. *Proceedings and Debates of the Virginia State Convention of 1829–1830*, 76.

41. *Proceedings and Debates of the Virginia State Convention of 1829–1830*, 220. Fitzhugh's suggestion of a uniformity clause to protect slavery from taxation was eventually applied in Florida and a number of other Southern states. Einhorn, *American Taxation, American Slavery*, 201–5.

42. Einhorn, *American Taxation, American Slavery*, 29, 78, 88–89; Edgar Sydenstricker, *A Brief History of Taxation in Virginia*, Davis Bottom, 1915, 62.

43. Susan Dunn, *Dominion of Memories: Jefferson, Madison, and the Decline of Virginia*, Basic Books, 2007, 72–73, 77, 102–3.

44. Freehling, *Secessionists at Bay*, 170, 177; Freehling, *Drift Toward Dissolution*, 49, 76.

45. William W. Freehling and Craig M. Simpson, eds., *Showdown in Virginia: The 1861 Convention and the Fate of the Union*, University of Virginia Press, 2010, 134. Dray, Landais, and Stantcheva, "Wealth and Property Taxation in the United States."

46. The fights over taxation and democracy in Virginia were most closely replicated in North Carolina, the home state of Hinton Helper. Slaveholders secured biased apportionment to inflate their representation and tax limitations to prevent tax-based emancipation. Western North Carolinians unsuccessfully demanded fairer apportionment and ad valorem taxation, which conservatives insisted would "sound the death knell of slavery." Paul D. Escott, *Many Excellent People: Power and Privilege in North Carolina, 1850–1900*, University of North Carolina Press, 1985, 15; Donald C. Butts, "The 'Irrepressible Conflict': Slave Taxation and North Carolina's Gubernatorial Election of 1860," *North Carolina Historical Review* 58, no. 1 (1981): 44–66, 59; Marc W. Kruman, *Parties and Politics in North Carolina, 1836–1865*, Louisiana State University Press, 1983, 189; George Ruble Woolfolk, "Taxes and Slavery in the Ante Bellum South," *Journal of Southern History* 26, no. 2 (1960): 198–99.

In South Carolina, where elites had since the colonial era used tax breaks to buy the support of nonslaveholders, representation in the upper *and* lower houses was based on a formula combining population with taxes paid. South Carolina's slaveholders held most of the state's wealth, paid a proportionate share of the very meager taxes, and had an unshakable majority in the legislature. Slaveholders bought their power at a very low price. By "all rules of commerce," wrote W. E. B. Du Bois, Charleston "should have been one of the great ports of the United States," but "the planters would not submit to public taxation" to pay for the necessary infrastructure. Einhorn, *American Taxation, American Slavery*, 93, 97; Jerome J. Nadelhaft, *The Disorders of War: The Revolution in South Carolina*, University of Maine at Orono Press, 1981, 126–27; Woolfolk, "Taxes and Slavery in the Ante Bellum South," 184; Peter Wallenstein, "Rich Man's War, Rich Man's Fight: Civil War and the Transformation of Public Finance in Georgia," *Journal of Southern History* 50, no. 1 (February 1984): 15–42. W. E. B. Du Bois, *Black Reconstruction in America, 1860–1880*, Atheneum, 1972, 407. John C. Calhoun was enamored of his home state's system, which he argued "guards effectually against the abuse of the taxing power." Calhoun, *Works of John C. Calhoun*, 1:404. Benjamin Watkins Leigh proposed this system for Virginia in 1830.

47. Chacón and Jensen, "Political and Economic Geography of Southern Secession," 150.

48. Alexander Keyssar, *The Right to Vote: The Contested History of Democracy in the United States*, Basic Books, 2009, 34–52; Freehling, *Secessionists at Bay*, 164. Two other Southeastern states, Georgia and Florida, had three-fifths clauses for their legislatures. In addition, Georgia's poll tax disenfranchised a substantial

percentage of poor whites. For Georgia's unsuccessful efforts to reduce or abolish the poll tax, see Merritt, *Masterless Men*, 170.

49. JSC, Majority Report, Report of Mr. Stevenson of Ohio, 102, 103, 106; Horace Mann Bond, "Social and Economic Forces in Alabama Reconstruction," *Journal of Negro History* 23, no. 3 (1938): 312; Kruman, *Parties and Politics in North Carolina*, 190; J. Mills Thornton, *Politics and Power in a Slave Society: Alabama, 1800–1860*, Louisiana State University Press, 1978, 102–3.

50. In Florida, the only Deep South state to assess and tax slaves according to value, slaveholders were protected by a clause requiring all forms of property to be taxed at the same rate. Thornton, "Fiscal Policy," 358.

51. US Census Office, *Ninth Census*, vol. 3, *The Statistics of Wealth and Industry of the United States*, compiled by Francis A. Walker, Government Printing Office, 1872. Author's calculations.

52. Dray, Landais, and Stantcheva, "Wealth and Property Taxation in the United States"; Thornton, "Fiscal Policy," 354.

53. Ralph A. Wooster, *The People in Power: Courthouse and Statehouse in the Lower South, 1850–1860*, University of Tennessee Press, 1969, 36–41; Ralph A. Wooster, *Politicians, Planters, and Plain Folk: Courthouse and Statehouse in the Upper South, 1850–1860*, University of Tennessee Press, 1975, 39–42.

54. John J. Wallis, "A History of the Property Tax in America," in *Property Taxation and Local Government Finance*, ed. Wallace E. Oates, Lincoln Institute of Land Policy, 2001, 138. The rise in slaveholder power led to a decline in slave taxation. Thornton, "Fiscal Policy." Another indication of the growing power of the planter class is the transition in Louisiana's 1852 constitution from apportionment based on qualified electors to apportionment based on total population, which inflated representation of planter regions by five-fifths, not merely three-fifths, of the enslaved population.

55. Peter Wallenstein, "'More Unequally Taxed than Any People in the Civilized World': The Origins of Georgia's Ad Valorem Tax System," *Georgia Historical Quarterly* 69, no. 4 (Winter 1985): 459–87; Peter Wallenstein, *From Slave South to New South: Public Policy in Nineteenth-Century Georgia*, University of North Carolina Press, 1987; Chad Morgan, "Progressive Slaveholders: Planters, Intellectuals, and Georgia's Antebellum Economic Development," *Georgia Historical Quarterly* 86, no. 3 (2002): 398–422; Steven Hahn, *The Roots of Southern Populism: Yeoman Farmers and the Transformation of the Georgia Upcountry, 1850–1890*, Oxford University Press, 2006.

56. Merritt, *Masterless Men*, 31, 154; William J. Collins and Robert A. Margo, "Historical Perspectives on Racial Differences in Schooling in the United States," working paper, National Bureau of Economic Research, June 2003; Douglas R. Egerton, *The Wars of Reconstruction: The Brief, Violent History of America's Most Progressive Era*, Bloomsbury USA, 2014, 145. On school attendance, see James C. Cobb, *Away Down South: A History of Southern Identity*, Oxford University Press, 2005, 51. Of the states that would join the Confederacy, only Louisiana and Texas provided substantial funding to schools via state taxation—and Louisiana's funding remained inadequate because localities failed to raise their share of

the taxes. Other states provided revenue for education when it could be provided without taxation. Georgia, for example, quintupled its spending on schools in 1860, when it had railroad dividends to spend. Alabama also began dedicating relatively large sums of nontax revenue to education in the mid-1850s, over the objections of representatives from the wealthy plantation counties. In Mississippi, an effort to raise a county tax for schools was undermined by a provision requiring a majority of householders in each county to provide written consent to the tax. Sarah L. Hyde, *Schooling in the Antebellum South: The Rise of Public and Private Education in Louisiana, Mississippi, and Alabama*, Louisiana State University Press, 2016, 124, 107–8; Wallenstein, *From Slave South to New South*, 68; Thornton, "Fiscal Policy," 378–80; Thornton, *Politics and Power in a Slave Society*, 293; Bond, "Social and Economic Forces in Alabama Reconstruction," 312; James B. Gerber, "Southern White Schooling, 1880–1940," PhD diss., University of California, Davis, 1986, 5; Clay, "Speech of Cassius M. Clay, at Lexington, Ky."

57. Stephen Budiansky, *The Bloody Shirt: Terror After Appomattox*, Viking, 2008, 183.

58. Stephanie McCurry, *Masters of Small Worlds: Yeoman Households, Gender Relations, and the Political Culture of the Antebellum South Carolina Low Country*, Oxford University Press, 1995; Edmund S. Morgan, *American Slavery, American Freedom*, W. W. Norton, 1975; Merritt, *Masterless Men*.

59. Joseph E. Brown, *Special Message of Gov. Joseph E. Brown, to the Legislature of Georgia, on Our Federal Relations, Retaliatory State Legislation, the Right of Secession, &c.*, Boughton, Nisbet and Barnes, state printers, 1860.

60. Thornton, "Fiscal Policy," 352.

61. Freehling, *Drift Toward Dissolution*, 123–24.

62. Southern whites' antipathy to taxation dissipated entirely when the tax code could be used to maintain the racial hierarchy. The poll taxes applied to free Black people were two to *twenty* times higher than those for white men. Wallenstein, *From Slave South to New South*, 93. Free Black people could be temporarily reenslaved if they could not pay. Theodore Brantner Wilson, *The Black Codes of the South*, University of Alabama Press, 1965, 39–40; JSC, vol. 1, 261. For the taxation of Black Americans in the North and West, see Christopher J. Bryant, "Without Representation, No Taxation: Free Blacks, Taxes, and Tax Exemptions Between the Revolutionary and Civil Wars," *Michigan Journal of Race and Law* 21, no. 1 (2015): 91–123.

63. Henry Cleveland, *Alexander H. Stephens in Public and Private*, National Publishing Company, 1866, 727; Brown, *Special Message of Gov. Joseph E. Brown*.

64. Romain D. Huret, *American Tax Resisters*, Harvard University Press, 2014, 32.

65. *Journal of the Acts and Proceedings of a General Convention of the State of Virginia, Assembled at Richmond, on Wednesday, the Thirteenth Day of February, Eighteen Hundred and Sixty-One*, Wyatt M. Elliott, printer, 1861, 99.

66. Freehling and Simpson, *Showdown in Virginia*, 133; William A. Link, "'This Bastard New Virginia': Slavery, West Virginia Exceptionalism, and the Secession Crisis," *West Virginia History* 3, no. 1 (2009): 37–56. North Carolina would

also institute ad valorem taxation during the war. Bill Cecil-Fronsman, *Common Whites: Class and Culture in Antebellum North Carolina*, University Press of Kentucky, 2015, 59.

Chapter 5. Radical Reconstruction and the Promise of Taxation

1. John P. Carrier, "A Political History of Texas During the Reconstruction, 1865–1874," PhD diss., Vanderbilt University, 1971, 478; *Houston Telegraph*, June 29, 1871; *The Representative* (Galveston, TX), July 1, 1871, 2.

2. Ann Patton Malone, "Matt Gaines: Reconstruction Politician," in *Black Leaders: Texans for Their Times*, ed. Alwyn Barr and Robert A. Calvert, Texas State Historical Association, 1981. An enslaved person teaching themself to read could be punished by amputation. Janet Cornelius, "'We Slipped and Learned to Read': Slave Accounts of the Literacy Process, 1830–1865," *Phylon* 44, no. 3 (1983): 171–86. Gaines may have escaped a third time; certainly he was not returned to his enslaver after his escape in 1863. Carl H. Moneyhon, "Gaines, Matthew," *Dickson-Gaye*, vol. 4 of *African American National Biography*, ed. Henry Louis Gates Jr. and Evelyn Brooks Higginbotham, 2nd ed., Oxford University Press, 2013, 426. But cf. Merline Pitre, *Through Many Dangers, Toils, and Snares: Black Leadership in Texas, 1868–1898*, Texas A&M University Press, 2016, 22.

3. "Spicy Speech by Matt Gains [*sic*]," *Jasper News-Boy* (Jasper, TX), August 10, 1871, 2.

4. The text of Gaines's speech was reported in the Houston *Telegraph*, June 29, 1871, 1, reprinting an article that first ran in the Houston *Age*. I have corrected the spelling and typographical errors of the *Telegraph*.

5. Eric Foner, *Reconstruction: America's Unfinished Revolution, 1863–1877*, HarperCollins, 2002, xix.

6. Southern conservatives provided these groups with enduring nicknames: "scalawags" for the Southern whites, and "carpetbaggers" for the new arrivals from the North. Michael Fitzgerald notes that "twenty to fifty thousand Northerners relocated after the war" and that "some 17 percent" of participants in the Southern constitutional conventions were "recent arrivals," generally representing heavily Black districts. Fitzgerald, *Splendid Failure: Postwar Reconstruction in the American South*, Ivan R. Dee, 2007, 78.

7. Pitre, *Through Many Dangers*, 37; J. Mills Thornton III, "Fiscal Policy and the Failure of Radical Reconstruction," in *Region, Race, and Reconstruction: Essays in Honor of C. Vann Woodward*, ed. J. Morgan Kousser and James M. McPherson, Oxford University Press, 1982, 388; Fitzgerald, *Splendid Failure*, 123.

8. Keri L. Merritt, *Masterless Men: Poor Whites and Slavery in the Antebellum South*, Cambridge University Press, 2017, 15; James D. Anderson, *The Education of Blacks in the South, 1860–1935*, University of North Carolina Press, 1988, 31; Richard M. Valelly, *The Two Reconstructions: The Struggle for Black Enfranchisement*, University of Chicago Press, 2004, 36; John Hope Franklin, *Reconstruction After the Civil War*, University of Chicago Press, 1961, 108; John W. Alvord of the Freedmen's Bureau, cited in Ronald E. Butchart, *Schooling the Freed People: Teaching, Learning, and the Struggle for Black Freedom, 1861–1876*, University of North

Carolina Press, 2010, 2. When the Freedmen's Bureau closed Black schools in 1866 in order to cut costs, the Black citizens of Louisiana petitioned the military to levy an extra tax on them to support a school fund. One petition, according to Alvord, was over thirty feet long, signed by ten thousand Black citizens. "It was affecting to examine it," Alvord noted in a report, "and note the names and marks (x) of such a long list of parents, ignorant themselves, but begging that their children might be educated, promising that from beneath their present burdens, and out of their extreme poverty, they would pay for it." Quoted in Anderson, *The Education of Blacks in the South*, 9–10.

9. "Radical State Convention," *Weekly Democrat* (Natchez, MS), September 21, 1867.

10. Ida B. Wells, *Crusade for Justice: The Autobiography of Ida B. Wells*, University of Chicago Press, 2020, 9.

11. JSC, vol. 1, 210–11; John R. Lynch, *The Facts of Reconstruction*, Neale Publishing Company, 1913, 33; Merritt, *Masterless Men*, 154. Even in Virginia, the Southern state with the strongest tradition of public education, less than half of poor white children attended school, and those who did attended less than three months a year. W. E. B. Du Bois, *Black Reconstruction in America, 1860–1880*, Atheneum, 1972, 639.

12. Edward Mayes, *History of Education in Mississippi*, no. 24 of Contributions to American Educational History, ed. Herbert B. Adams, Government Printing Office, 1899, 266–67; Wells, *Crusade for Justice*, 9; Stuart Grayson Noble, *Forty Years of the Public Schools in Mississippi: With Special Reference to the Education of the Negro*, no. 94 of Contributions to Education, Teachers College, Columbia University, 1918, 266; John W. Cook and James V. McHugh, *A History of the Illinois State Normal University*, Pantagraph Printing and Binding, 1882; Federal Writers' Project, *Slave Narratives*, vol. 2, *Arkansas Narratives: Part 1*, Works Progress Administration, 1941, 275–80.

13. Letter from Highgate to M. E. Strieby, December 17, 1866, *Reconstruction: The Second Civil War*, American Experience, PBS, originally aired January 12, 2004.

14. Noble, *Forty Years of the Public Schools in Mississippi*, 37. The Mississippi State Normal School survived the Reconstruction era but closed after Governor James K. Vardaman vetoed its state appropriation in 1904, saying that "the expenditures of fabulous sums" for the education of a Black man succeeded only in "making a criminal out of him." Ted Ownby, "Mississippi State Normal School for Colored Youth," *Mississippi Encyclopedia*, Center for Study of Southern Culture, last updated April 14, 2018.

15. James M. Smallwood, *Time of Hope, Time of Despair: Black Texans During Reconstruction*, Kennikat Press, 1981, 91; Carl H. Moneyhon, "Public Education and Texas Reconstruction Politics, 1871–1874," *Southwestern Historical Quarterly* 92, no. 3 (January 1989): 407; Richard L. Hume and Jerry B. Gough, *Blacks, Carpetbaggers, and Scalawags: The Constitutional Conventions of Radical Reconstruction*, Louisiana State University Press, 2008, 23, table 2.2; 1868 South Carolina Constitution, Article X, Section 10; 1868 Louisiana Constitution, Title VII, Article 135; Franklin, *Reconstruction*, 110–12; Fitzgerald, *Splendid Failure*, 85. State legislatures

tried to forestall unequal provision by mandating spending be allocated based on the number of children a school or district served. Mississippi's 1868 constitution required that "all school funds shall be divided pro rata among the children of school ages." North Carolina created a general statewide property tax that required equal amounts to be spent on each child throughout the state. J. Morgan Kousser, "Progressivism for Middle-Class Whites Only: North Carolina Education, 1880–1910," *Journal of Southern History* 46, no. 2 (1980): 173. Texas moved toward explicit segregation only in their second school bill. Pitre, *Through Many Dangers*, 31; Valelly, *Two Reconstructions*, 80–81.

    16. *Official Journal of the Constitutional Convention of the State of Alabama, Held in the City of Montgomery, Commencing on Tuesday, November 5th, A. D. 1867*, Barrett and Brown, 1868, 16, 56; Michael W. Fitzgerald, *Reconstruction in Alabama: From Civil War to Redemption in the Cotton South*, Louisiana State University Press, 2017, 147.

    17. *Journal of the Proceedings in the Constitutional Convention of the State of Mississippi, 1868*, E. Stafford, printer, 1871, 52; Foner, *Reconstruction*, 60. See also *The Debates and Proceedings of the Constitutional Convention of the State of Virginia, 1867*, vol. 1, Richmond, VA, 1868, 198.

    18. *Proceedings of the Constitutional Convention of South Carolina, Held at Charleston, S.C., beginning January 14th and ending March 17th, 1868*, Denny and Perry, 1868, 711–37; Alrutheus Ambush Taylor, *The Negro in South Carolina During the Reconstruction*, Association for the Study of Negro Life and History, 1924, 136–37, 159; Thomas Holt, *Black over White: Negro Political Leadership in South Carolina During Reconstruction*, University of Illinois Press, 1979, 131–32. Black education advocate John W. Cromwell felt so strongly that the capitation tax needed to be enforced that he argued in favor of making it a condition of suffrage.

    19. A transcript of the meeting, as reported by Henry Ward Beecher, was reprinted in full in the *New-York Daily Tribune*, February 13, 1865, 5.

    20. Theodore Brantner Wilson, *The Black Codes of the South*, University of Alabama Press, 1965; *The Debates and Proceedings of the Constitutional Convention of the State of Virginia, 1867*, vol. 1, 61.

    21. Douglas R. Egerton, *The Wars of Reconstruction: The Brief, Violent History of America's Most Progressive Era*, Bloomsbury USA, 2014, 100.

    22. Robert M. Poole, "How Arlington National Cemetery Came to Be," *Smithsonian Magazine*, November 2009.

    23. Egerton, *Wars of Reconstruction*, 98–99; Francis Butler Simkins and Robert Hilliard Woody, *South Carolina During Reconstruction*, University of North Carolina Press, 1932, 31, 227; "To the Hon. Abraham D. Smith, Hon. William E. Wording, and Hon. William Henry Brisbane, Tax Commissioners for the District of South Carolina," September 16, 1863, and "Additional Instructions to Direct Tax Commissioners," December 31, 1863, *Collected Works of Abraham Lincoln*, vol. 6, December 13, 1862–November 3, 1863, University of Michigan Library Digital Collections.

    24. Egerton, *Wars of Reconstruction*, 127; Dorothy Sterling, ed., *The Trouble They Seen: Black People Tell the Story of Reconstruction*, Doubleday, 1976, 44–45; Thaddeus Stevens, *Speech of Hon. T. Stevens, of Pennsylvania, Delivered in the House of*

Representatives, March 19, 1867, on the Bill (H. R. No. 20) Relative to Damages to Loyal Men, and for Other Purposes.

25. Lawrence D. Rice, *The Negro in Texas, 1874–1900*, Louisiana State University Press, 1971, 12; Du Bois, *Black Reconstruction*, 399. The back wages proposal was described as "infamous" in the Austin *Republican*. Charles William Ramsdell, *Reconstruction in Texas*, Columbia University, 1910, 179; Carrier, "A Political History of Texas During the Reconstruction," 215–16, reports this proposal as coming from the "Corresponding Committee" of the Travis County (Austin) chapter of the Union Loyal League.

26. Jack B. Scroggs, "Carpetbagger Constitutional Reform in the South Atlantic States, 1867–1868," *Journal of Southern History* 27, no. 4 (1961): 475–93; Alrutheus Ambush Taylor, *The Negro in the Reconstruction of Virginia*, Association for the Study of Negro Life and History, 1926, 210–11; Du Bois, *Black Reconstruction*, 393.

27. Fitzgerald, *Splendid Failure*, 156–57; John Hope Franklin, "Public Welfare in the South During the Reconstruction Era, 1865–80," *Social Service Review* 44, no. 4 (December 1970): 379–92.

28. Trevon D. Logan, "Do Black Politicians Matter?," working paper, National Bureau of Economic Research, January 2018, 8; *Journal of the House of Representatives of the State of South Carolina, Special Session, Commencing Tuesday, October 21, 1873*, Republican Printing Company, state printers, 1873, 42; Kenneth M. Stampp, *The Era of Reconstruction: 1865–1877*, Alfred A. Knopf, 1965, 170; *The Debates and Proceedings of the Constitutional Convention of the State of Virginia, 1867*, vol. 1, 695.

29. Eric Foner, *Freedom's Lawmakers: A Directory of Black Officeholders During Reconstruction*, Louisiana State University Press, 1996, 14.

30. Stephen Budiansky, *The Bloody Shirt: Terror After Appomattox*, Viking, 2008, 183.

31. *The Debates and Proceedings of the Constitutional Convention of the State of Virginia, 1867*, vol. 1, 695; Foner, *Freedom's Lawmakers*, 14. Thomas Bayne was nominated for state commissioner of the revenue for the City of Norfolk in 1877. Harrison W. Burton, *The History of Norfolk, Virginia*, Norfolk, 1877, 134.

32. Sterling, *The Trouble They Seen*, 44; Joel Williamson, *After Slavery: The Negro in South Carolina During Reconstruction, 1861–1877*, University of North Carolina Press, 1965, 55–58; Egerton, *Wars of Reconstruction*, 98–99, 108.

33. Heather Cox Richardson, *The Death of Reconstruction: Race, Labor, and Politics in the Post–Civil War North, 1865–1901*, Harvard University Press, 2009, 107. Richardson notes that this quote is secondhand, a white man's report of the Black senator's campaign speech.

34. *The Debates and Proceedings of the Constitutional Convention of the State of Virginia, 1867*, 713; Foner, *Freedom's Lawmakers*, 155.

35. *The Debates and Proceedings of the Constitutional Convention of the State of Virginia, 1867*, 686–87, 722; Foner, *Freedom's Lawmakers*, 106.

36. Eric Foner, *Nothing but Freedom: Emancipation and Its Legacy*, Louisiana State University Press, 2007, 67; Carrier, "A Political History of Texas During the Reconstruction," 143–44; Du Bois, *Black Reconstruction*, 405; Simkins and Woody, *South Carolina During Reconstruction*, 177.

37. Robin L. Einhorn, *American Taxation, American Slavery*, University of Chicago Press, 2006; Stephanie McCurry, *Masters of Small Worlds: Yeoman Households,*

Gender Relations, and the Political Culture of the Antebellum South Carolina Low Country, Oxford University Press, 1995; Thornton, "Fiscal Policy," 358; testimony of Edwin W. Seibels, JSC, vol. 3, 132.

38. Black men held a wide array of positions related to tax assessment and collection, including at least thirty-two state assessors, ten US assessors, three US treasury agents, thirty-five tax collectors, forty-one sheriffs, and twenty-five deputy sheriffs. Foner, *Freedom's Lawmakers*, 271–85.

39. Eric Foner, *Forever Free: The Story of Emancipation and Reconstruction*, Vintage Books, 2006, 159.

40. Author's calculation based on census data. See also estimates in Du Bois, *Black Reconstruction*, 384; Fitzgerald, *Splendid Failure*, 58; Sacha Dray, Camille Landais, and Stefanie Stantcheva, "Wealth and Property Taxation in the United States," working paper, National Bureau of Economic Research, March 2023; Michael R. Hyman, "Taxation, Public Policy, and Political Dissent: Yeoman Disaffection in the Post-Reconstruction Lower South," *Journal of Southern History* 55, no. 1 (1989): 49–76; Lynch, *Facts of Reconstruction*, 86.

41. Logan, "Do Black Politicians Matter?"

42. Moneyhon, "Public Education and Texas Reconstruction Politics," 406–7; JSC, vol. 1, 229; A. A. Taylor, "The Reconstructionists and Their Measures," *Journal of Negro History* 9, no. 4 (1924): 439; US Census Office, *Ninth Census*, vol. 3, *The Statistics of Wealth and Industry of the United States*, comp. Francis A. Walker, Government Printing Office, 1872. Author's calculations.

43. Foner, *Reconstruction*, 386–87; Foner, *Forever Free*, 166; Du Bois, *Black Reconstruction*, 425; Taylor, "Reconstructionists and Their Measures"; Paul D. Escott, *Many Excellent People: Power and Privilege in North Carolina, 1850–1900*, University of North Carolina Press, 1985, 160–61; Fitzgerald, *Reconstruction in Alabama*, 205; Valelly, *Two Reconstructions*, 86.

44. Eric Foner, *Politics and Ideology in the Age of the Civil War*, Oxford University Press, 1980, 117; Pitre, *Through Many Dangers*, 45; Sterling, *The Trouble They Seen*, 411–14; Fitzgerald, *Splendid Failure*, 114.

45. See, e.g., William A. Dunning, *Reconstruction, Political and Economic, 1865–1877*, vol. 22 of *The American Nation: A History*, ed. Albert Bushnell Hart, Harper and Brothers, 1907.

46. Trevon D. Logan, "Whitelashing: Black Politicians, Taxes, and Violence," working paper, National Bureau of Economic Research, June 2019. At least 153 of the 1,510 known Black Reconstruction officials were the victims of violence. Foner, *Freedom's Lawmakers*.

47. Du Bois, *Black Reconstruction*, 406.

48. Testimony of Samuel Brown, tax assessor, JSC, vol. 9, 1215; Foner, *Freedom's Lawmakers*, 30; testimony of James Orr, former governor, JSC, vol. 3, 3; testimony of Charles Dennis O'Keefe of Fort Mills, York County, SC, JSC, vol. 3, 37.

49. JSC, vol. 1, 75; JSC, vol. 11, 265, 268, 284–85; Moneyhon, "Public Education and Texas Reconstruction Politics," 411; E. T. Miller, "The State Finances of Texas During the Reconstruction," *Quarterly of the Texas State Historical Association* 14, no. 2 (1910): 94; JSC, vol. 10, 1428–33.

50. Testimony of E. W. Siebels, JSC, vol. 1, 408; testimony of Richard B. Carpenter, JSC, vol. 3, 241; Williamson, *After Slavery*, 153; Simkins and Woody, *South Carolina During Reconstruction*, 178–81; Thornton, "Fiscal Policy," 371; Foner, *Reconstruction*, 588; JSC, vol. 1, 112–13.

51. Simkins and Woody, *South Carolina During Reconstruction*, 180; Franklin, *Reconstruction*, 142–43.

52. US Bureau of Education, *Report of the Commissioner of Education for the Year 1872*, 5; JSC, vol. 1, 230; US Bureau of Education, *Report of the Commissioner of Education*, 1870–1878. See also *Reply to the Memorial of the Tax-Payers' Convention, Addressed to the Honorable Senate and House of Representatives of the United States*, Republican Party State Central Executive Committee, Republican Printing Company, 1874.

53. Noble, *Forty Years of the Public Schools in Mississippi*, 51–52; Logan, "Do Black Politicians Matter?"; Fitzgerald, *Splendid Failure*, 151–52.

54. W. E. B. Du Bois, "The Freedman's Bureau," in *The Sociological Souls of Black Folk: Essays by W. E. B. Du Bois*, ed. Robert A. Wortham, Lexington Books, 2013, 35; Taylor, *Negro in the Reconstruction of Virginia*, 130–34; Thomas W. Mitchell, "From Reconstruction to Deconstruction: Undermining Black Landownership, Political Independence, and Community Through Partition Sales of Tenancies in Common," *Northwestern University Law Review* 95, no. 2 (2001): 507; Logan, "Do Black Politicians Matter?," 29; Roger L. Ransom and Richard Sutch, *One Kind of Freedom: The Economic Consequences of Emancipation*, 2nd ed., Cambridge University Press, 2001, 78; Du Bois, *Black Reconstruction*, 395; Foner, *Reconstruction*, 376.

55. Foner, *Reconstruction*, 109; Jay R. Mandle, *Not Slave, Not Free: The African American Economic Experience Since the Civil War*, Duke University Press, 1992.

56. Thomas W. Cutrer, "McGary, Dan H.," Texas State Historical Association, Handbook of Texas Online, last updated May 17, 2017. It is worth asking, given that the speech was printed in a highly unsympathetic newspaper, whether the transcript is accurate. There is every reason to believe it was fair. Gaines made similar speeches in other contexts. Moreover, Gaines responded to the backlash with a letter that made no indication that the transcript had misrepresented his words. *Indianola Weekly Bulletin*, August 15, 1871. Foner includes an excerpt from the speech in his biographical entry for Gaines in *Freedom's Lawmakers*, 80–81.

57. *The Standard* (Clarksville, TX), August 26, 1871, 2; *Weekly Democratic Statesman* (Austin, TX), August 24, 1871, 1; *Cannelton Reporter*, July 22, 1871, 1; *Tri-Weekly State Gazette* (Austin, TX), August 30, 1871, 1.

58. Political hornets' nests: including Gaines's suggestion that Texas "send to Africa for better men than the Dutch" (a common corruption of the word "Deutsch," meaning German). This offended local German immigrants, one of the only groups of Texas whites that voted Republican. *Flake's Semi-Weekly Bulletin* (Galveston, TX), September 9, 1871, 6; *Indianola Weekly Bulletin*, August 15, 1871, 3. Only a few days later, Richard Nelson, a Black political leader and one of Gaines's closest allies, felt obliged to distance himself from Gaines's inflammatory remarks. John M. Brewer, *Negro Legislators of Texas and Their Descendants: A History of the Negro in Texas Politics from Reconstruction to Disfranchisement*, Mathis Publishing, 1935, 59; *The Representative* (Galveston, TX), July 1, 1871, 2.

59. *Indianola Weekly Bulletin*, August 15, 1871, 3.

60. Moneyhon, "Public Education and Texas Reconstruction Politics," 410, 413; Malone, "Matt Gaines," 69.

Chapter 6. Redemption: Rise of the Taxpayer

1. *Proceedings of the Tax-Payers' Convention of South Carolina, Held at Columbia, Beginning May 9th, and Ending May 12th, 1871*, Edward Perry, 1871, 61.

2. Attendees of the convention included "four Ex-Governors, two Ex-Lieutenant Governors, three Ex-United States Senators, five Ex-Congressmen, one Ex-Secretary Confederate Treasury, forty-three Ex-Members of the House of Representatives and five bankers." *Orangeburg News*, May 13, 1871; *Proceedings of the Tax-Payers' Convention of South Carolina, 1871*, 34, 38, 59; W. D. Porter, "Negro Supremacy in South Carolina," *New York Times*, April 19, 1868, 11; JSC, vol. 3, 472.

3. *Proceedings of the Tax-Payers' Convention of South Carolina, 1871*, 62; Chamberlain's testimony in JSC, vol. 3, 52.

4. JSC, vol. 3, 454.

5. A wealthy Black businessman, George Shrewsbury, attended in 1871; he would run for Congress as a Democrat, unsuccessfully, in 1872. Eric Foner, *Freedom's Lawmakers: A Directory of Black Officeholders During Reconstruction*, Louisiana State University Press, 1996, 194. In 1874, Samuel Lark and David Strother are listed among the delegates with "(colored)" after their names. Strother is reported as a county commissioner in Darlington "until his death in 1882." George Brown Tindall, *South Carolina Negroes, 1877–1900*, University of South Carolina Press, 2003, 66. In 1874, delegate J. M. Penceel of Colleton is not designated as "(colored)" in the proceedings but is so described in local newspaper coverage. *Anderson Intelligencer* (Anderson, SC), February 26, 1874. J. M. Penceel was likely related to William Penceel, a free Black slaveowner involved in the betrayal of Denmark Vesey's 1822 slave revolt. Philip F. Rubio, "'Though He Had a White Face, He Was a Negro in Heart': Examining the White Men Convicted of Supporting the 1822 Denmark Vesey Slave Insurrection Conspiracy," *South Carolina Historical Magazine* 113, no. 1 (January 2012): 50–67. For more on Black conservatives during Reconstruction, see the "Conservative Colored Men's Clubs" in A. A. Taylor, *The Negro in the Reconstruction of Virginia*, Association for the Study of Negro Life and History, 1926, 222.

The Tax-Payers struggled to maintain even a thin veneer of nonpartisanship and color-blindness. Speakers described Black men as childlike and incapable of reasoned judgment. General Gary's original plan to encourage white immigration is stricken from the convention proceedings and returned to the committee to "erase from the Report all allusion to political motive or purpose." *Proceedings of the Tax-Payers' Convention of South Carolina, 1871*, 37, 99, 42.

6. This system was expected to give "the taxpayers" approximately 40 percent of the legislative seats. *Proceedings of the Tax-Payers' Convention of South Carolina, 1871*, 17; A. A. Taylor, *The Negro in South Carolina During the Reconstruction*, Association for the Study of Negro Life and History, 1924, 227.

7. Gary also said he would accept cumulative voting "in the same spirit that I would receive a half loaf as being better than no bread at all." *Proceedings of the Tax-Payers' Convention of South Carolina, 1871*, 58.

8. Francis Butler Simkins and Robert Hilliard Woody, *South Carolina During Reconstruction*, University of North Carolina Press, 1932, 474–80; Taylor, *Negro in South Carolina*, 218–19.

9. Thomas Holt, *Black over White: Negro Political Leadership in South Carolina During Reconstruction*, University of Illinois Press, 1979, 181.

10. Michael W. Fitzgerald, *Splendid Failure: Postwar Reconstruction in the American South*, Ivan R. Dee, 2007, 197–98, 203; Joel Williamson, *After Slavery: The Negro in South Carolina During Reconstruction, 1861–1877*, University of North Carolina Press, 1965, 400–7; Holt, *Black over White*, 200. Butler also threatened to kill Harrison H. Bouey, a local probate judge, and other local Black officeholders. 6 Cong. Rec. 759 (1877).

11. In his "Plan of Campaign of 1876," Gary decided to omit the section on rifle clubs from the final printed version. Also marked for omission was this item: "Never threaten a man individually if he deserves to be threatened, the necessities of the times require that he should die." Simkins and Woody, *South Carolina During Reconstruction*, 564–69.

12. W. W. Ball, *A Boy's Recollections of the Red Shirt Campaign of 1876 in South Carolina*, The State Co., 1911, 9.

13. Holt, *Black over White*, 174.

14. Alfred B. Williams, *Hampton and His Redshirts: The Story of South Carolina's Deliverance in 1876*, Confederate Reprint, 2015, 446. Quoted in Simkins and Woody, *South Carolina During Reconstruction*, 541.

15. W. Lewis Burke, "Reconstruction Corruption and the Redeemers' Prosecution of Francis Lewis Cardozo," *American Nineteenth Century History* 2, no. 3 (2001): 72.

16. "The Withdrawal of Chamberlain," *Amherst Free Press*, April 14, 1877; Dorothy Sterling, ed., *The Trouble They Seen: Black People Tell the Story of Reconstruction*, Doubleday, 1976, 475.

17. Simkins and Woody, *South Carolina During Reconstruction*, 182; Heather Cox Richardson, *The Death of Reconstruction: Race, Labor, and Politics in the Post–Civil War North, 1865–1901*, Harvard University Press, 2009, 95.

18. Eric Foner, *Reconstruction: America's Unfinished Revolution, 1863–1877*, HarperCollins, 2002, 415.

19. Michael W. Fitzgerald, "Radical Republicanism and the White Yeomanry During Alabama Reconstruction, 1865–1868," *Journal of Southern History* 54, no. 4 (November 1988): 565–96.

20. Bruce E. Stewart, "Attacking 'Red-Legged Grasshoppers': Moonshiners, Violence, and the Politics of Federal Liquor Taxation in Western North Carolina, 1865–1876," *Appalachian Journal* 32, no. 1 (2004): 34; Eric Foner, *Forever Free: The Story of Emancipation and Reconstruction*, Vintage Books, 2006, 140; Fitzgerald, "Radical Republicanism," 579, 585, 592–93; Fitzgerald, *Splendid Failure*, 90.

21. Carl N. Degler, *The Other South: Southern Dissenters in the Nineteenth Century*, Northeastern University Press, 1982, 210.

22. Fitzgerald, *Splendid Failure*, 9.

23. JSC, MS 11, 352.

24. Richardson, *Death of Reconstruction*, 68; Horace Mann Bond, "Social and Economic Forces in Alabama Reconstruction," *Journal of Negro History* 23, no. 3 (1938): 313; Foner, *Reconstruction*, 415.

25. John R. Lynch, *The Facts of Reconstruction*, Neale Publishing Company, 1913, 49.

26. *Anderson Intelligencer*, June 4, 1874; Linda Upham-Bornstein, "The Taxpayer as Reformer: 'Pocketbook Politics' and the Law, 1860–1940," PhD diss., University of New Hampshire, 2009, 16–17; Michael W. Fitzgerald, *Reconstruction in Alabama: From Civil War to Redemption in the Cotton South*, Louisiana State University Press, 2017, 296; JSC, vol. 13, 208–15; "State Tax-Payers' Convention," *Weekly Floridian* (Tallahassee, FL), September 12, 1871, 2; John Hope Franklin, *Reconstruction After the Civil War*, University of Chicago Press, 1961, 145; Nicholas Lemann, *Redemption: The Last Battle of the Civil War*, Farrar, Straus and Giroux, 2006, 82; Mitchell Snay, *Fenians, Freedmen, and Southern Whites: Race and Nationality in the Era of Reconstruction*, Louisiana State University Press, 2010, 168; Simkins and Woody, *South Carolina During Reconstruction*, 183–84; James M. Smallwood, *Time of Hope, Time of Despair: Black Texans During Reconstruction*, Kennikat Press, 1981, 91; Alfred John Brown, *History of Newton County, Mississippi, from 1834 to 1894*, Clarion-Ledger, 1894, 182–83; Trevon D. Logan, "Whitelashing: Black Politicians, Taxes, and Violence," working paper, National Bureau of Economic Research, June 2019, 6.

27. Carl H. Moneyhon, "Tax-Payers' Convention," 1952, Texas State Historical Association, Handbook of Texas Online, accessed September 16, 2024.

28. *Proceedings of the Tax-Payers' Convention of South Carolina, 1874*, 19, 44.

29. JSC, vol. 5, 1348.

30. *Orangeburg News*, August 15, 1874, cited in Simkins and Woody, *South Carolina During Reconstruction*, 183–84.

31. Farmers' organizations played a similar role in providing an outwardly respectable front for paramilitary organizing. Charles Postel, *Equality: An American Dilemma, 1866–1896*, Farrar, Straus and Giroux, 2019, 105; Charles Postel, *The Populist Vision*, Oxford University Press, 2007, 74, 99, 103; Stephen Kantrowitz, *Ben Tillman and the Reconstruction of White Supremacy*, University of North Carolina Press, 2000, 53; Lemann, *Redemption*, 82.

32. Romain D. Huret, *American Tax Resisters*, Harvard University Press, 2014, 40, 51. One man, applying to be a tax agent, noted that he had been driven from town before the war for circulating Hinton Helper's abolition-by-taxation plan, *The Impending Crisis in the South*. Bruce E. Stewart, "'When Darkness Reigns Then Is the Hour to Strike': Moonshining, Federal Liquor Taxation, and Klan Violence in Western North Carolina, 1868–1872," *North Carolina Historical Review* 80, no. 4 (2003): 465–66, 472.

33. Testimony of M. M. Jolly in JSC, vol. 2, 428.

34. Lemann, *Redemption*, 88.

35. "The Vicksburg Massacre: The Street Fight and the Taxpayers' League," *New York Times*, January 3, 1875, 1.

36. "Negro Supremacy in South Carolina," *New York Times*, April 19, 1868.

37. *Proceedings of the Tax-Payers' Convention of South Carolina, Held at Columbia, Beginning February 17, and Ending February 20, 1874*, News and Courier Job Presses, 1874, 14.

38. JSC, vol. 4, 919–22; JSC, vol. 3, 447.

39. *Proceedings of the Tax-Payers' Convention of South Carolina, 1871*, 62.

40. JSC, vol. 8, 375, 383; Sydney Trent, "John Lewis Nearly Died on the Edmund Pettus Bridge. Now It May Be Renamed for Him," *Washington Post*, July 26, 2020.

41. JSC, vol. 9, 965; JSC, vol. 11, 372. See also testimony of Edward E. Holman, JSC, vol. 11, 352–53.

42. JSC, vol. 1, 378, 527–30.

43. Douglas R. Egerton, *The Wars of Reconstruction: The Brief, Violent History of America's Most Progressive Era*, Bloomsbury USA, 2014, 124.

44. Dorothy Sterling, ed., *The Trouble They Seen: Black People Tell the Story of Reconstruction*, Doubleday, 1976, 426; Richardson, *Death of Reconstruction*, 111; "A Southern View of the Southern Problem," *The Nation*, July 6, 1871.

45. "The State of the South," *The Nation*, March 28, 1872.

46. JSC, vol. 4, 771.

47. James Pike, "A State in Ruins," *New-York Tribune*, March 5, 1872, 2, quoted in Robert Franklin Durden, *James Shepherd Pike: Republicanism and the American Negro, 1850–1882*, Duke University Press, 1957, 187.

48. Taxpayer rhetoric was also used to legitimize racist violence outside the South. A double lynching of two Hispanic men in Santa Cruz, California, in May 1877 was defended in the local paper as the action of "property owners and tax payers." Michael A. Bellesiles, *1877: America's Year of Living Violently*, New Press, 2010, 199.

49. 4 Cong. Rec. 4707 (1876).

50. "A Southern View of the Southern Problem."

51. Democratic Party State Central Executive Committee, *An Appeal to the Honorable Senate of the United States*, Phoenix Book and Job Power Press, 1868.

52. Richard L. Hume and Jerry B. Gough, *Blacks, Carpetbaggers, and Scalawags: The Constitutional Conventions of Radical Reconstruction*, Louisiana State University Press, 2008, 27 (table 2.9). Wade Hampton is questioned regarding his assertions that the South Carolina convention participants were not taxpayers in JSC, vol. 4, 1219–25. See also Holt, *Black over White*, 36–37; Simkins and Woody, *South Carolina During Reconstruction*, 121; and Bond, "Social and Economic Forces in Alabama Reconstruction," 295.

53. JSC, vol. 4, 1219–25; *Proceedings of the Tax-Payers' Convention of South Carolina, 1871*, 17; W. E. B. Du Bois, *Black Reconstruction in America, 1860–1880*, Atheneum, 1972, 419.

54. Burke, "Reconstruction Corruption," 75.

55. *Proceedings of the Tax-Payers' Convention of South Carolina, 1871*, 89, 97.

56. Foner, *Reconstruction*, 388; W. Scott Poole, *Never Surrender: Confederate Memory and Conservatism in the South Carolina Upcountry*, University of Georgia Press, 2004, 78n51.

57. JSC, vol. 4, 1207. For another South Carolina Democrat with a similar view of bribery, see JSC, vol. 4, 729. R. M. Smith: "When it is understood that a man is for sale, like a sheep, or anything else, any man has a right to buy him." Smith is described as a "democratic member of the legislature" in Stevenson's report to the Joint Select Committee, where the mule comment is wrongly attributed to him. JSC, vol. 1, 123.

58. Smallwood, *Time of Hope, Time of Despair*, 91.

59. Sterling, *The Trouble They Seen*, 253–55.

60. David Quigley, *Second Founding: New York City, Reconstruction, and the Making of American Democracy*, Hill and Wang, 2015, 120–21.

61. Sven Beckert, "Democracy and Its Discontents: Contesting Suffrage Rights in Gilded Age New York," *Past and Present* 174, no. 1 (February 2002): 116–57.

62. Sidney Ratner, *Taxation and Democracy in America*, John Wiley and Sons, 1967, 67, 69; Roger Lowenstein, *Ways and Means: Lincoln and His Cabinet and the Financing of the Civil War*, Penguin, 2022, 126; Sheldon D. Pollack, "The First National Income Tax, 1861–1872," *Tax Lawyer* 67, no. 2 (2014): 8, 15; W. Elliot Brownlee, *Federal Taxation in America: A History*, 3rd ed., Cambridge University Press, 2016, 139–41; Steven R. Weisman, *The Great Tax Wars: Lincoln—Teddy Roosevelt—Wilson: How the Income Tax Transformed America*, Simon and Schuster, 2004, 86–87. An income tax was also included in the provisional Revenue Act of 1861, but this law was never implemented, being superseded by the 1862 law. On war spurring progressivity, see Kenneth Scheve and David Stasavage, *Taxing the Rich: A History of Fiscal Fairness in the United States and Europe*, Princeton University Press, 2016. On war and tax compliance, Naomi Feldman and Joel Slemrod, "War and Taxation: When Does Patriotism Overcome the Free-Rider Impulse?," in *The New Fiscal Sociology: Taxation in Comparative and Historical Perspective*, ed. Isaac William Martin, Ajay K. Mehrotra, and Monica Prasad, Cambridge University Press, 2009, 29–47.

63. Huret, *American Tax Resisters*, 40–42, 60–62; Sidney Ratner, *American Taxation: Its History as a Social Force in Democracy*, W. W. Norton, 1942, 111–35; Joseph J. Thorndike, "An Army of Officials: The Civil War Bureau of Internal Revenue," *Tax Notes*, December 27, 2001.

64. Beckert, "Democracy and Its Discontents," 131; Huret, *American Tax Resisters*, 45, 56; Quigley, *Second Founding*, 201n16, 123.

65. "Report of the Commission to Devise a Plan for the Government of Cities in the State of New York, Presented to the Legislature, March 6th, 1877," Evening Post Steam Presses, 1877.

66. Quigley, *Second Founding*, 147; Beckert, "Democracy and Its Discontents," 126; "The Government of Cities: A Reform Measure Sustained," *New York Times*, April 8, 1877.

67. Huret, *American Tax Resisters*, 57; Beckert, "Democracy and Its Discontents," 133, 149.

68. Alexander Keyssar, *The Right to Vote: The Contested History of Democracy in the United States*, Basic Books, 2000, 122; Francis Parkman, "The Failure of Universal Suffrage," *North American Review* 127, no. 263 (July–August 1878): 20.

69. US House of Representatives, *Alleged Misgovernment in South Carolina: Views of a Minority*, Government Printing Office, 1874, 2.

70. Beckert, "Democracy and Its Discontents," 148; Keyssar, *Right to Vote*, 133–35; Jeffrey J. Crow and Robert F. Durden, *Maverick Republican in the Old North State: A Political Biography of Daniel L. Russell*, Louisiana State University Press, 1977, 39.

71. Daniel Chamberlain, "Reconstruction in South Carolina," *The Atlantic*, April 1901, 477, 480.

72. Though W. D. Porter served as legal defense for Cardozo when the legislature attempted to oust him based on a spurious corruption charge in 1875, his firm would represent the state in the 1877 case. W. Lewis Burke, "Post-Reconstruction Justice: The Prosecution and Trial of Francis Lewis Cardozo," *South Carolina Law Review* 53, no. 2 (2002), 377; Fitzgerald, *Splendid Failure*, 199. *Birth of a Nation*, the 1915 film celebrating the Ku Klux Klan, features a character called Silas Lynch, a mixed-race man who becomes lieutenant governor of South Carolina and attempts to force himself upon the film's white heroine. She is then rescued by the Klan. Cardozo had died in 1903 and so did not live to see this defamation. Neil Kinghan, *A Brief Moment in the Sun: Francis Cardozo and Reconstruction in South Carolina*, Louisiana State University Press, 2023.

73. Foner, *Reconstruction*, 388; Du Bois, *Black Reconstruction*, 622.

74. See, e.g., Walter L. Fleming, "Taxation and the Public Debt," in *Civil War and Reconstruction in Alabama*, Columbia University Press, 1905.

75. Heather Cox Richardson, "Killing Reconstruction," *Jacobin*, August 19, 2015.

Chapter 7. Jim Crow: Rule of the Taxpayer

1. *Journal of the House of Delegates of the State of Virginia for the Session of 1877–8*, R. F. Walker, 1877, 428.

2. Jane Dailey, *Before Jim Crow: The Politics of Race in Postemancipation Virginia*, University of North Carolina Press, 2009, 28, 29–30, 185fn116; Brent Tarter, *A Saga of the New South: Race, Law, and Public Debt in Virginia*, University of Virginia Press, 2016, 59. Corporate taxes averaged less than 3 percent of state revenue in the 1870s. Author's calculations from state auditors' annual reports. See also Allen W. Moger, *Virginia: Bourbonism to Byrd, 1870–1925*, University Press of Virginia, 1968, 48–49; and Charles Chilton Pearson, *The Readjuster Movement in Virginia*, Yale University Press, 1917, 57. Bond payouts were generally tax-free, and those who could afford to buy the state's debt certificates, which were selling at a deep discount, could use them at face value to pay their taxes. This provision further undermined state revenues, but efforts to close the loophole were prevented by the Virginia Supreme Court, and Governor Holliday was unwilling to contest this ruling. *Journal of the House of Delegates of the State of Virginia for the Session of 1877–8*, 427.

3. Carl N. Degler, *The Other South: Southern Dissenters in the Nineteenth Century*, Northeastern University Press, 1982, 278.

4. *Public Ledger* (Norfolk, VA), October 19, 1883; *Norfolk Landmark*, October 19, 1883.

5. Dailey, *Before Jim Crow*, 32; James T. Moore, "Black Militancy in Readjuster Virginia, 1879–1883," *Journal of Southern History* 41, no. 2 (1975): 171; *Address*

to Virginians. The Eloquent Appeal of the Petersburg State Convention for Harmony Between White and Colored Citizens, and for Earnest Co-operation in Behalf of Common Rights and Common Interests, broadside, 1881, R43, Special Collections, University of Virginia, Charlottesville.

6. Degler, *Other South*, 285–87.

7. Tarter, *Saga of the New South*, 40–41; Degler, *Other South*, 280.

8. Tarter, *Saga of the New South*, 71; Moger, *Virginia*, 48–49; Degler, *Other South*, 282; Pearson, *Readjuster Movement in Virginia*, 144; Carl N. Degler, "Black and White Together: Bi-Racial Politics in the South," *Virginia Quarterly Review* 47, no. 3 (1971): 429; Dailey, *Before Jim Crow*, 69–70.

9. For details of the debt readjustment, see Tarter, *Saga of the New South*, 9, 60, 70–71. For more on Democrats' co-optation of Readjuster issues, see Bryant K. Barnes, "'Are Not Our Interests the Same?': Black Protest, the Lost Cause, and Coalition Building in Readjuster Virginia," *Genealogy* 7, no. 1 (2023): 18fn79; and Moger, *Virginia*, 52. Nonetheless, court cases over the debt continued for years.

10. Barnes, "'Are Not Our Interests the Same?,'" 10; Dailey, *Before Jim Crow*, 75–76; Degler, "Black and White Together," 429; Degler, *Other South*, 283; Moore, "Black Militancy in Readjuster Virginia," 179.

11. *Public Ledger* (Norfolk, VA), October 19, 1883; *Norfolk Landmark*, October 19, 1883; *Staunton Spectator*, October 30, 1883.

12. An 1882 political cartoon of a Black male teacher spanking a white female student, with the word "Coalition" on the chalkboard, captures the sexual preoccupations that underlay the Democratic campaign against the interracial Readjuster alliance. Dailey, *Before Jim Crow*, 98.

13. Dailey, *Before Jim Crow*, 114–16; Degler, "Black and White Together," 435.

14. In poll taxes alone, nearly $1,000 came from Black men in Danville. *Annual Report of the Auditor of Public Accounts to the General Assembly of Virginia, for the Year Ending September 30, 1881,* R. F. Walker, 1881.

15. *Conservative Democrat* (Marion, VA), November 1, 1883, 2.

16. *Fredericksburg News*, November 5, 1883, 2; *Alexandria Gazette*, November 5, 1883, 2–3; *Public Ledger* (Norfolk, VA), December 14, 1883.

17. J. Morgan Kousser, *The Shaping of Southern Politics: Suffrage Restriction and the Establishment of the One-Party South, 1880–1910,* Yale University Press, 1974, 172.

18. C. Vann Woodward, *Origins of the New South, 1877–1913,* Louisiana State University Press, 1951, 59.

19. Lawrence Goodwyn, *Democratic Promise: The Populist Moment in America,* Oxford University Press, 1976, 290.

20. Charles Postel, *The Populist Vision,* Oxford University Press, 2007, 200–201; C. Vann Woodward, *Tom Watson: Agrarian Rebel,* Oxford University Press, 1963; Gregg Cantrell and D. Scott Barton, "Texas Populists and the Failure of Biracial Politics," *Journal of Southern History* 55, no. 4 (1989): 659–92; William Ivy Hair, *Bourbonism and Agrarian Protest: Louisiana Politics, 1877–1900,* Louisiana State University Press, 1969, 273.

21. *Senate Journal: A Journal of the Proceedings of the Senate of the State of Florida, 1877*, C. E. Dyke Sr., state printer, 1877, 37.

22. Paul Ortiz, *Emancipation Betrayed: The Hidden History of Black Organizing and White Violence in Florida from Reconstruction to the Bloody Election of 1920*, University of California Press, 2005.

23. *Recent Election in the State of Florida: Minority Report*, H.R. Rep. No. 44-143, pt. 2 (1877), in *Index to Reports of Committees of the House of Representatives for the Second Session of the Forty-Fourth Congress, 1876–77*, vol. 1, Government Printing Office, 1877, 34–35.

24. *Senate Journal: A Journal of the Proceedings of the Senate of the State of Florida, 1877*, 39.

25. J. Mills Thornton III, "Fiscal Policy and the Failure of Radical Reconstruction," in *Region, Race, and Reconstruction: Essays in Honor of C. Vann Woodward*, ed. J. Morgan Kousser and James M. McPherson, Oxford University Press, 1982, 62.

26. Eric Foner, *Reconstruction: America's Unfinished Revolution, 1863–1877*, HarperCollins, 2002, 588.

27. Woodward, *Origins of the New South*, 59.

28. W. E. B. Du Bois, *Black Reconstruction in America, 1860–1880*, Atheneum, 1972, 664; Hair, *Bourbonism and Agrarian Protest*, 120; Allen J. Going, "The South and the Blair Education Bill," *Mississippi Valley Historical Review* 44, no. 2 (1957): 268; Woodward, *Origins of the New South*, 61–63, 93; Foner, *Reconstruction*, 589; James D. Anderson, *The Education of Blacks in the South, 1860–1935*, University of North Carolina Press, 1988, 31. Spending per pupil would only reach 81 percent of 1871 funding by 1890.

29. By the 1890s, North Carolina spent 60 percent more per pupil on white students than on Black students; Florida, Louisiana, and Mississippi spent twice as much; and South Carolina spent three times more. Robert A. Margo, *Race and Schooling in the South, 1880–1950: An Economic History*, University of Chicago Press, 1990, 21 (table 2.5); J. Morgan Kousser, "Progressivism—For Middle-Class Whites Only: North Carolina Education, 1880–1910," *Journal of Southern History* 46, no. 2 (1980): 178; Francis Butler Simkins and Robert Hilliard Woody, *South Carolina During Reconstruction*, University of North Carolina Press, 1932, 443.

30. Of course, white property taxes were often actually borne by Black tenants through their rents, but this was not taken into account. Paul D. Escott, *Many Excellent People: Power and Privilege in North Carolina, 1850–1900*, University of North Carolina Press, 1985, 184–85; Joan Malczewski, "The Larger Gifts of Taxation: Foundations and Tax Reform in the Jim Crow South," *Journal of Policy History* 34, no. 2 (2022): 154–55; Camille Walsh, *Racial Taxation: Schools, Segregation, and Taxpayer Citizenship, 1869–1973*, University of North Carolina Press, 2018, 17. Black activists seeking equalization of school funding and taxation occasionally found success in the courts when taxes were explicitly defined in racial terms. J. Morgan Kousser, "Making Separate Equal: Integration of Black and White School Funds in Kentucky," *Journal of Interdisciplinary History* 10, no. 3 (1980): 399–428. The demand for racial segregation of school funds often came from white populists, both out of anger that Black Belt white schools benefited from extra funding stolen from the neighboring

Black schools and because the possibility of poor whites' tax dollars funding Black education so consistently undermined mass support for public school taxes. Kousser, "Progressivism—For Middle-Class Whites Only," 181; Andrew W. Kahrl, *The Black Tax: 150 Years of Theft, Exploitation, and Dispossession in America*, University of Chicago Press, 2024, 37. White economic populism usually coincided with deep antipathy to Black schools. Lawrence D. Rice, *The Negro in Texas, 1874–1900*, Louisiana State University Press, 1971, 218; James S. Ferguson, "The Grange and Farmer Education in Mississippi," *Journal of Southern History* 8, no. 4 (1942): 500; Charles Postel, *Equality: An American Dilemma, 1866–1896*, Farrar, Straus and Giroux, 2019, 80; Postel, *Populist Vision*, 60.

 31. Walsh, *Racial Taxation*, 49–50; Malczewski, "The Larger Gifts of Taxation," 159; Rice, *Negro in Texas*, 350.

 32. Michael R. Hyman, "Taxation, Public Policy, and Political Dissent: Yeoman Disaffection in the Post-Reconstruction Lower South," *Journal of Southern History* 55, no. 1 (1989): 55, 65; Foner, *Reconstruction*, 588; Malczewski, "The Larger Gifts of Taxation"; Hair, *Bourbonism and Agrarian Protest*, 60–61; Eric Foner, *Nothing but Freedom: Emancipation and Its Legacy*, Louisiana State University Press, 2007, 70–71; Peter Wallenstein, "Rich Man's War, Rich Man's Fight: Civil War and the Transformation of Public Finance in Georgia," *Journal of Southern History* 50, no. 1 (February 1984): 40; *Okolona Messenger*, August 11, 1881, 2.

 33. Hyman, "Taxation, Public Policy, and Political Dissent," 70; A. A. Taylor, "The Reconstructionists and Their Measures," *Journal of Negro History* 9, no. 4 (1924): 437. Kenneth Stampp finds that, if state and county taxes are taken into account, property taxes actually went up in Mississippi under conservative rule. Kenneth M. Stampp, *The Era of Reconstruction: 1865–1877*, Alfred A. Knopf, 1965, 183.

 34. Kousser, "Progressivism—For Middle-Class Whites Only," 174.

 35. Tipton R. Snavely, *The Taxation of Negroes in Virginia*, University of Virginia Phelps-Stokes Fellowship Papers, 1916; Kahrl, *The Black Tax*.

 36. Ann Patton Malone, "Matt Gaines: Reconstruction Politician," in *Black Leaders: Texans for Their Times*, ed. Alwyn Barr and Robert A. Calvert, Texas State Historical Association, 1981, 70; *Brenham Daily Banner*, May 23, 1877, 1; *Brenham Daily Banner*, October 2, 1889, 3.

 37. Woodward, *Origins of the New South*, 60.

 38. Hyman, "Taxation, Public Policy, and Political Dissent," 61; Merline Pitre, *Through Many Dangers: Black Leadership in Texas, 1868–1898*, Texas A&M University Press, 2016, 45.

 39. Woodward, *Origins of the New South*, 66–74.

 40. *Weekly Pelican* (New Orleans, LA), September 28, 1889, 2; "Louisiana's Stolen Bonds," *New York Times*, October 27, 1889, 3.

 41. *Forest News* (Jefferson, GA), November 27, 1875, 2; *Free Press* (Cartersville, GA), September 18, 1879, 1; Hyman, "Taxation, Public Policy, and Political Dissent," 64. For similar dynamics in South Carolina, see Lacy K. Ford, "Rednecks and Merchants: Economic Development and Social Tensions in the South Carolina Upcountry, 1865–1900," *Journal of American History* 71, no. 2 (1984): 314.

42. Isaac William Martin, "The Shackles of the Past: Constitutional Property Tax Limitations and the Fall of the New Deal Order," in *Capitalism Contested: The New Deal and Its Legacies*, ed. Romain Huret, Nelson Lichtenstein, and Jean-Christian Vinel, University of Pennsylvania Press, 2021, 141.

43. Rodney Harris, "Arkansas's Divided Democracy: The Making of the Constitution of 1874," PhD diss., University of Arkansas, 2017, 59.

44. Charles D. McIver, "Current Problems in North Carolina," *Annals of the American Academy of Political and Social Science* 22, no. 2 (1903): 58.

45. Georgia, for example, devoted its convict-labor proceeds to public education. *Acts and Resolutions of the General Assembly of the State of Georgia, 1880–81*, 98.

46. Matthew J. Mancini, *One Dies, Get Another: Convict Leasing in the American South, 1866–1928*, University of South Carolina Press, 1996, 106.

47. Russell D. Parker, "The Black Community in a Company Town: Alcoa, Tennessee, 1919–1939," *Tennessee Historical Quarterly* 37, no. 2 (1978): 203–21. Chambers would have had to repay the train ticket from his wages, but likely did not know that.

48. *Chambers v. State*, 97 S.E. 274 (Geo. 1918); William Cohen, "Negro Involuntary Servitude in the South, 1865–1940: A Preliminary Analysis," *Journal of Southern History* 42, no. 1 (1976): 41–42; Herbert Roback, "Legal Barriers to Interstate Migration," *Cornell Law Review* 28, no. 3 (March 1943): 286–312. Chambers was presumably freed in November, when the decision was reversed upon appeal.

49. Suresh Naidu, "Recruitment Restrictions and Labor Markets: Evidence from the Postbellum U.S. South," *Journal of Labor Economics* 28, no. 2 (2010): 413–45; Simkins and Woody, *South Carolina During Reconstruction*, 553; Cohen, "Negro Involuntary Servitude in the South," 39.

50. Because local recordkeeping was so lax, the full scope of fees-and-fines peonage is not known. Cohen, "Negro Involuntary Servitude in the South," 55; Christopher Muller, "Freedom and Convict Leasing in the Postbellum South," *American Journal of Sociology* 124, no. 2 (September 2018): 372.

51. Cohen, "Negro Involuntary Servitude in the South," 55; Du Bois, *Black Reconstruction in America*, 175, 179; Theodore Brantner Wilson, *The Black Codes of the South*, University of Alabama Press, 1965, 68, 75; Foner, *Nothing but Freedom*, 50, 68; Brian Sawers, "The Poll Tax Before Jim Crow," *American Journal of Legal History* 57, no. 2 (2017): 166–259; Douglas A. Blackmon, *Slavery by Another Name: The Re-Enslavement of Black Americans from the Civil War to World War Two*, Anchor Books, 2009, 54–55; E. T. Miller, "The State Finances of Texas During the Reconstruction," *Quarterly of the Texas State Historical Association* 14, no. 2 (1910): 91; David M. Oshinsky, *"Worse Than Slavery": Parchman Farm and the Ordeal of Jim Crow Justice*, Simon and Schuster, 1996, 35; Alexander C. Lichtenstein, *Twice the Work of Free Labor: The Political Economy of Convict Labor in the New South*, Verso Books, 1996, 47; Susanne Schwarz, "'The Spawn of Slavery'? Race, State Capacity, and the Development of Carceral Institutions in the Postbellum South," *Studies in American Political Development* 37, no. 2 (October 2023): 181–98; Christopher R. Adamson, "Punishment After Slavery: Southern State Penal Systems, 1865–1890," *Social Problems* 30, no. 5 (1983), 564; Mancini, *One Dies, Get Another*, 120.

52. Oshinsky, *"Worse Than Slavery,"* 63, 71; Ida B. Wells, "The Convict Lease System," in *The Reason Why the Colored American Is Not in the World's Columbian Exposition: The Afro-American's Contribution to Columbian Literature*, ed. Robert W. Rydell, University of Illinois Press, 1999, 24; Blackmon, *Slavery by Another Name*, 67; Cohen, "Negro Involuntary Servitude in the South," 36–38; Muller, "Freedom and Convict Leasing in the Postbellum South," 367.

53. Calvin R. Ledbetter, "The Long Struggle to End Convict Leasing in Arkansas," *Arkansas Historical Quarterly* 52, no. 1 (1993): 6; Adamson, "Punishment After Slavery," 562; Wayne K. Durrill, "Producing Poverty: Local Government and Economic Development in a New South County, 1874–1884," *Journal of American History* 71, no. 4 (March 1985): 769.

54. Blackmon, *Slavery by Another Name*, 55. In all, thirteen states adopted convict leasing. Lichtenstein, *Twice the Work of Free Labor*, 1996.

55. Muller, "Freedom and Convict Leasing in the Postbellum South," 377. Muller notes that Haines was still alive, and still leased to the brick company, nine years later. There is some evidence he survived his sentence; a laborer by the name of Monday Haines worked for the Navy Department in South Carolina in 1901.

56. Wells, "The Convict Lease System," 26.

57. Woodward, *Origins of the New South*, 214; Mancini, *One Dies, Get Another*, 139; Blackmon, *Slavery by Another Name*, 57; Cohen, "Negro Involuntary Servitude in the South," 56; Kirk Spitzer, "The American POWs Still Waiting for an Apology from Japan 70 Years Later," *Time*, September 12, 2014; Anne Applebaum, *Gulag: A History*, Doubleday, 2003.

58. George Washington Cable, *The Silent South*, Charles Scribner's Sons, 1899, 126; Cohen, "Negro Involuntary Servitude in the South," 56; Mancini, *One Dies, Get Another*, 187.

59. Alex Lichtenstein, "Flocatex and the Fiscal Limits of Mass Incarceration: Toward a New Political Economy of the Postwar Carceral State," *Journal of American History* 102, no. 1 (June 2015): 113–25; Woodward, *Origins of the New South*, 212; Adamson, "Punishment After Slavery," 567; Talitha L. LeFlouria, *Chained in Silence: Black Women and Convict Labor in the New South*, University of North Carolina Press, 2015, 74; W. E. B. Du Bois, "The Spawn of Slavery: The Convict Lease System in the South," *Race, Crime, and Justice: A Reader*, ed. Shaun Gabbidon and Helen Taylor Greene, Routledge, 2013, 5; Mancini, *One Dies, Get Another*, 112, 158, 177; Adamson, "Punishment After Slavery," 564; Blackmon, *Slavery by Another Name*, 367–68; Booker T. Washington, "Is the Negro Having a Fair Chance?," *Century Magazine*, November 1912, 54.

60. Oshinsky, *"Worse Than Slavery,"* 42.

61. Derrell Roberts, "Joseph E. Brown and the Convict Lease System," *Georgia Historical Quarterly* 44, no. 4 (1960): 399–400; Mancini, *One Dies, Get Another*, 86; LeFlouria, *Chained in Silence*, 74–77; Peter Wallenstein, *From Slave South to New South: Public Policy in Nineteenth-Century Georgia*, University of North Carolina Press, 1987, 201.

62. Martha A. Myers, *Race, Labor, and Punishment in the New South*, Ohio State University Press, 1998, 14–20; Blackmon, *Slavery by Another Name*, 7,

206; Mancini, *One Dies, Get Another*, 222; Woodward, *Origins of the New South*, 424–25.

63. Aaron Hall, "Slaves of the State: Infrastructure and Governance Through Slavery in the Antebellum South," *Journal of American History* 106, no. 1 (June 2019): 19–46; Alex Lichtenstein, "Good Roads and Chain Gangs in the Progressive South: 'The Negro Convict Is a Slave,'" *Journal of Southern History* 59, no. 1 (1993): 87; Oshinsky, *"Worse Than Slavery,"* 81; Hyman, "Taxation, Public Policy, and Political Dissent," 72; Myers, *Race, Labor, and Punishment in the New South*, 295n6. Georgia's roadwork requirement persisted into the mid-twentieth century. Wallenstein, *Slave South to New South*, 196.

64. Lichtenstein, *Twice the Work of Free Labor*; Myers, *Race, Labor, and Punishment in the New South*, 23; Lichtenstein, "Good Roads and Chain Gangs," 101.

65. Oshinsky, *"Worse Than Slavery,"* 82, 109, 155; Peter Wallenstein, "Slavery Under the Thirteenth Amendment: Race and the Law of Crime and Punishment in the Post–Civil War South," *Louisiana Law Review* 77, no. 1 (2016), 19; Myers, *Race, Labor, and Punishment in the New South*, 21–29.

66. David Zucchino, *Wilmington's Lie: The Murderous Coup of 1898 and the Rise of White Supremacy*, Atlantic Monthly Press, 2020, 175–76.

67. James A. Beeby, *Revolt of the Tar Heels: The North Carolina Populist Movement, 1890–1901*, University Press of Mississippi, 2008, 109–10; Kousser, *Shaping of Southern Politics*, 187; Jeffrey J. Crow and Robert F. Durden, *Maverick Republican in the Old North State: A Political Biography of Daniel L. Russell*, Louisiana State University Press, 1977, 90, 105, 110; James L. Hunt, *Marion Butler and American Populism*, University of North Carolina Press, 2003, 80; David S. Cecelski and Timothy B. Tyson, *Democracy Betrayed: The Wilmington Race Riot of 1898 and Its Legacy*, University of North Carolina Press, 1998, 169; Kousser, "Progressivism—For Middle-Class Whites Only," 178–79. They also created a program of matching state funds to encourage localities to spend more on schools. Hugh Talmage Lefler and Albert Ray Newsome, *North Carolina: The History of a Southern State*, rev. ed., University of North Carolina Press, 1963, 519.

68. Beeby, *Revolt of the Tar Heels*, 8, 172; Joseph F. Steelman, "Republican Party Strategists and the Issue of Fusion with Populists in North Carolina, 1893–1894," *North Carolina Historical Review* 47, no. 3 (1970): 244–69; Ronnie W. Faulkner, "North Carolina Democrats and Silver Fusion Politics, 1892–1896," *North Carolina Historical Review* 59, no. 3 (1982): 230–51; "Propaganda, Passion Across the State," *StarNews*, November 16, 2006; Kousser, *Shaping of Southern Politics*, 187–89; Escott, *Many Excellent People*, 259; Lefler and Newsome, *North Carolina*, 525.

69. Escott, *Many Excellent People*, 254.

70. *News and Observer* (Raleigh, NC), November 10, 1898.

71. As in Virginia under the Readjusters, much of the racist campaign was framed in terms of defending the sexual purity of white women. The Black newspaper editor Alexander Lightfoot Manly had drawn the ire of white supremacists by suggesting that relationships between a white woman and a Black man could be consensual. See also Glenda Elizabeth Gilmore, *Gender and Jim Crow: Women and*

the Politics of White Supremacy in North Carolina, 1896–1920, University of North Carolina Press, 2013.

72. Thornton, "Fiscal Policy," 354; JSC, vol. 7, 923–24; Steven Hahn, *The Roots of Southern Populism: Yeoman Farmers and the Transformation of the Georgia Upcountry, 1850–1890*, Oxford University Press, 2006, 261–62; Kousser, *Shaping of Southern Politics*, 209–14.

73. Tarter, *Saga of the New South*, 40–41.

74. James Hugo Johnston, "The Participation of Negroes in the Government of Virginia from 1877 to 1888," *Journal of Negro History* 14, no. 3 (July 1929): 265–66, fn29.

75. Kousser, *Shaping of Southern Politics*, 63; Snavely, *Taxation of Negroes in Virginia*, 39.

76. Valdimer Orlando Key, *Southern Politics in State and Nation*, A. A. Knopf, 1949, 581; Kousser, *Shaping of Southern Politics*, 65.

77. Woodward, *Origins of the New South*, 336.

78. *Official Proceedings of the Constitutional Convention of the State of Alabama, 1901*, vol. 3, *May 21st, 1901, to September 3rd, 1901*, Wetumpka Printing, 1940, 3381.

79. "Purpose of Laws of 1890, 1954, 1960, 1962 [. . .]," Def.'s Resp. to Pl.'s Interrog. No. 3, *US v. State of Mississippi et al.*, 229 F. Supp. 925 (S.D. Miss 1964), Burke Marshall Personal Papers, John F. Kennedy Presidential Library, Boston.

80. Key, *Southern Politics in State and Nation*, 617–18; Kousser, *Shaping of Southern Politics*, 65–68.

81. Woodward, *Origins of the New South*, 336; Kousser, *Shaping of Southern Politics*, 63, 70.

82. Alexander Keyssar, *The Right to Vote: The Contested History of Democracy in the United States*, Basic Books, 2009, 115; Karin A. Shapiro, *A New South Rebellion: The Battle Against Convict Labor in the Tennessee Coalfields, 1871–1896*, University of North Carolina Press, 1998, 132; John D. Buenker, *The Income Tax and the Progressive Era*, Garland, 1985, 201; Margo, *Race and Schooling in the South*, 21 (table 2.5); Kousser, "Progressivism—For Middle-Class Whites Only," 178; Simkins and Woody, *South Carolina During Reconstruction*, 443. On the causal relationship between representation and government spending, see Stephen Ansolabehere, Alan Gerber, and Jim Snyder, "Equal Votes, Equal Money: Court-Ordered Redistricting and Public Expenditures in the American States," *American Political Science Review* 96, no. 4 (2002): 767–77. Kahrl, *The Black Tax*, 38–39.

83. Quoted in "The Idol of Democracy," *Afro-American* (Baltimore, MD), April 22, 1899, 2.

84. Michael Leachman, Michael Mitchell, Nicholas Johnson, and Erica Williams, "Advancing Racial Equity with State Tax Policy," Center on Budget and Policy Priorities, November 15, 2018.

85. Kim Kelly, "Lawsuit: Alabama Is Denying Prisoners Parole to Lease Their Labor to Meatpackers, McDonald's," *In These Times*, April 19, 2024; Sam McCann, "From Fighting Wildfires to Digging Graves, Incarcerated Workers Face Danger

on the Job," Vera Institute of Justice, July 7, 2018; Robin McDowell and Margie Mason, "Prisoners in the US Are Part of a Hidden Workforce Linked to Hundreds of Popular Food Brands," AP News, January 29, 2024; Jennifer Turner, Mariana Olaizola Rosenblat, and Nino Guruli, et al., *Captive Labor: Exploitation of Incarcerated Workers*, American Civil Liberties Union and Global Human Rights Clinic, June 15, 2022.

Chapter 8. The Federal Income Tax

1. The future French Prime Minister Georges Clemenceau, then a young journalist covering Reconstruction, described Boutwell as "the last survivor of the puritans of a by-gone age . . . too honest and sincere for his opinions to be ignored." Clemenceau called Boutwell's speech summing up the case for President Johnson's impeachment "the longest, weakest, and dullest speech which has yet been made since the opening of the trial" and "better than had been expected of him." Georges Clemenceau, *American Reconstruction, 1865–1870: And the Impeachment of President Johnson*, ed. Fernand Baldensperger, trans. Margaret Mac Veagh, Longmans, Green, 1928, 178.

2. Boutwell left the revenue service within a year to take his place in Congress. He was asked by the Treasury secretary to hold both positions but found this idea improper. George Boutwell, *Reminiscences of Sixty Years in Public Affairs*, vol. 1, McClure, Phillips & Co. 1902, 303, 311–12; Roger Lowenstein, *Ways and Means: Lincoln and His Cabinet and the Financing of the Civil War*, Penguin Books, 2022, 126, 197; Steven R. Weisman, *The Great Tax Wars: Lincoln—Teddy Roosevelt—Wilson: How the Income Tax Transformed America*, Simon and Schuster, 2004, 43; Bennett D. Baack and Edward John Ray, "Special Interests and the Adoption of the Income Tax in the United States," *Journal of Economic History* 45, no. 3 (1985): 608; Sidney Ratner, *American Taxation: Its History as a Social Force in Democracy*, W. W. Norton, 1942, chaps. 4–6; W. Elliot Brownlee, ed., *Funding the Modern American State, 1941–1995: The Rise and Fall of the Era of Easy Finance*, Cambridge University Press, 1996, 44. Confederate Secretary of State Robert Toombs made a similar argument at early as 1863. "Gen. Toombs on the Rebel Currency," *New York Times*, August 28, 1863, 4. C.f. Richard Franklin Bensel, *Yankee Leviathan: The Origins of Central State Authority in America, 1859–1877*, Cambridge University Press, 1990, 171–72.

3. Boutwell was by then treasury secretary under President Ulysses S. Grant.

4. George S. Boutwell, "The Income Tax," *North American Review* 160, no. 462 (May 1895): 601.

5. Boutwell, *Reminiscences of Sixty Years in Public Affairs*, vol. 1, 313.

6. Omer Madison Kem, "Autobiography of Omer Madison Kem Vol. 1," 1937, 67–71, Omer Kem Papers, Creighton University Archives, Omaha, NE.

7. Susannah Broyles, "Vanderbilt Ball—How a Costume Ball Changed New York Elite Society," *Collections Blog*, Museum of the City of New York, August 6, 2013.

8. Ratner, *American Taxation*, 219.

9. Thomas K. McCraw and Forest Reinhardt, "Losing to Win: U.S. Steel's Pricing, Investment Decisions, and Market Share, 1901–1938," *Journal of Economic*

History 49, no. 3 (1989): 593–619; Thomas Piketty, *Capital in the Twenty-First Century*, Harvard University Press, 2017, 439; John D. Buenker, *The Income Tax and the Progressive Era*, Garland, 1985, 28–29.

10. Robert Carroll McMath Jr., *Populist Vanguard: A History of the Southern Farmers' Alliance*, University of North Carolina Press, 2017, 35; Elizabeth Sanders, *Roots of Reform: Farmers, Workers, and the American State, 1877–1917*, University of Chicago Press, 1999, 102.

11. Weisman, *Great Tax Wars*, 219–20, 290; Richard J. Joseph, *The Origins of the American Income Tax: The Revenue Act of 1894 and Its Aftermath*, Syracuse University Press, 2004, 35; Buenker, *Income Tax and the Progressive Era*, 28.

12. Buenker, *Income Tax and the Progressive Era*, 9–10, 32, 239; Ajay K. Mehrotra, *Making the Modern American Fiscal State: Law, Politics, and the Rise of Progressive Taxation, 1877–1929*, Cambridge University Press, 2013, 7; Elmer Ellis, "Public Opinion and the Income Tax, 1860–1900," *Mississippi Valley Historical Review* 27, no. 2 (September 1940): 233; Douglas A. Irwin, "Tariff Incidence in America's Gilded Age," *Journal of Economic History* 67, no. 3 (2007): 582–607, cited in Robin L. Einhorn, "Progressivity and Sectionalism in the United States," paper at the Global Histories of Taxation and State Finances Symposium, Basel, Switzerland, December 1–3, 2016, 8–9; Thomas G. Shearman, "The Owners of the United States," *Forum Extra* 1, no. 2 (April 1890): 12; Charles Edward Russell, *Bare Hands and Stone Walls: Some Recollections of a Side-Line Reformer*, Charles Scribner's Sons, 1933, 23.

13. Baack and Ray, "Special Interests," 614, 619; Sanders, *Roots of Reform*, 218.

14. Weisman, *Great Tax Wars*, 201, 254; Ratner, *American Taxation*, 153; John D. Hicks, *The Populist Revolt: A History of the Farmers' Alliance and the People's Party*, University of Minnesota Press, 1931, 106; Lawrence Goodwyn, *The Populist Moment: A Short History of the Agrarian Revolt in America*, Oxford University Press, 1978, 48.

15. W. Elliot Brownlee, "Progress and Poverty: One Hundred Years Later," *Proceedings of the Annual Conference on Taxation Held Under the Auspices of the National Tax Association–Tax Institute of America* 72 (1979): 228–32; Dominic Candeloro, "The Single Tax Movement and Progressivism, 1880–1920," *American Journal of Economics and Sociology* 38, no. 2 (1979): 116; Ratner, *American Taxation*, 154; Mehrotra, *Making the Modern American Fiscal State*, 76.

16. Buenker, *Income Tax and the Progressive Era*, 385; Ellis, "Public Opinion and the Income Tax," 231.

17. Ratner, *American Taxation*, 49–56; Baack and Ray, "Special Interests," 608.

18. Ratner, *American Taxation*, 148, 152–53, 158, 165; Hicks, *Populist Revolt*, 429, 431; Baack and Ray, "Special Interests," 608; Roy G. Blakey and Gladys M. C. Blakey, *The Federal Income Tax*, Lawbook Exchange, 2010, 9.

19. Ratner, *American Taxation*, 173.

20. 26 Cong. Rec. Appendix 462–67 (1894); 26 Cong. Rec. 1655–58 (1894); William Jennings Bryan, *Life and Speeches of Hon. Wm. Jennings Bryan*, R. H. Woodward, 1900, 237.

21. *New-York Tribune*, January 3, 1894, cited in Blakey and Blakey, *Federal Income Tax*, 15.

22. National Republican Congressional Committee, *Republican Campaign Text Book*, Washington, DC, 1894, 188, cited in Cordell Hull, *The Memoirs of Cordell Hull*, vol. 1, Macmillan, 1948, 48.

23. On requisitions, see Chapter 2; on the three-fifths compromise, see Chapter 4. That the clause was ill-considered is perhaps best demonstrated by James Madison's own notes from the Constitutional Convention. A delegate from Massachusetts "asked what was the precise meaning of direct taxation? No one answd." Mad Farrand, ed., *The Records of the Federal Convention of 1787*, vol. 2, Yale University Press, 1911, 350.

24. *Hylton v. United States*, 3 US 171 (Supreme Court 1796).

25. It was an odd decision in many ways—it took two separate hearings of the case for the court to issue a clear verdict, and between the two decisions, one justice quietly switched sides. Weisman, *Great Tax Wars*, 156–57.

26. More progressive taxes were even less feasible under apportionment. Imagine, for instance, a tax on incomes over a million dollars. Around 2 percent of the US population resided in Kansas during the Gilded Age, so Kansas would have to remit 2 percent of the total revenues from the tax. But while dozens of New Yorkers were making a million dollars a year, Kansas had no million-earners to tax! (Buenker, *Income Tax and the Progressive Era*, 160.) What was Kansas to do? It wasn't clear. Meanwhile in New York, those making a million dollars would be paying a *lower* rate than equivalent earners in other states, since New York had more million-earners per capita among whom they could distribute the tax bill.

27. Boutwell, "Income Tax," 594. If a government were foolhardy enough to enact an apportioned income tax, it would not just be unfair; it would presumably fall afoul of the Constitution's uniformity clause—which, unlike the direct tax clause, is perfectly sensible and requires federal taxes to be "uniform throughout the United States."

28. *Pollock v. Farmers' Loan & Trust Co.*, 157 US 7, 429, 532, 553, 582–83, 607 (Supreme Court 893); "Mark Twain's Little Joke," *Springfield Herald* (Springfield, CO), July 23, 1909. Field's view represented a reversal; he was among the justices who upheld the income tax in *Springer v. United States*, 102 US 586 (Supreme Court 1881). John Marshall Harlan, the other justice on the court during both decisions, deemed the income tax constitutional in both cases.

29. *Louisiana Populist* (Natchitoches, LA), July 26, 1895, 1; Sidney Ratner, *Taxation and Democracy in America*, John Wiley and Sons, 1967, 212–13; *The Advocate* (Topeka, KS), July 3, 1895, 7; Ratner, *American Taxation*, 216; 31 Cong. Rec. 4438 (1898).

30. Ratner, *American Taxation*, 181, 183.

31. Buenker, *Income Tax and the Progressive Era*, 80; Hull, *Memoirs*, vol. 1, 58–61; Sheldon D. Pollack, *War, Revenue, and State Building: Financing the Development of the American State*, Cornell University Press, 2009, 243; Sven Steinmo, *Taxation and Democracy: Swedish, British, and American Approaches to Financing the Modern State*, Yale University Press, 1993, 74; Kimberly J. Morgan and Monica Prasad, "The Origins of Tax Systems: A French-American Comparison," *American Journal of Sociology* 114, no. 5 (2009): 1366.

32. Buenker, *Income Tax and the Progressive Era*, 180. On the measure's defeat in Utah, see 185–86.

33. Buenker, *Income Tax and the Progressive Era*, 160.

34. Charles Postel, *Equality: An American Dilemma, 1866–1896*, Farrar, Straus and Giroux, 2019, 49; Morgan and Prasad, "Origins of Tax Systems," 1364; Sanders, *Roots of Reform*, 387.

35. James L. Huston, *Securing the Fruits of Labor: The American Concept of Wealth Distribution, 1765–1900*, Louisiana State University Press, 2015, 374.

36. Morgan and Prasad, "Origins of Tax Systems," 1364.

37. Buenker, *Income Tax and the Progressive Era*, 167.

38. The Western ardor for big government far outlived the Populist Party. When union organizer Eugene Debs ran for president in 1912 on the Socialist ticket—on a platform that again called for the nationalization of the railroads and a graduated income tax—he received over 10 percent of the vote in seven states: Nevada, Oklahoma, Montana, Arizona, Washington, California, and Idaho. In three of those states, Debs outpolled the incumbent, President William Howard Taft.

39. Steinmo, *Taxation and Democracy*, 73–74.

40. *Brooklyn Daily Eagle*, July 21, 1896, 1.

41. 53 Cong. Rec. Appendix 251–52 (1916); Cyclone Davis, *Memoir*, Courier Press, 1935, 44; Cyclone Davis, *A Political Revelation [. . .]*, Advance Publishing, 1894, 288.

42. Davis, *Political Revelation*, 70, 97.

43. Robinson Woodward-Burns, *Hidden Laws: How State Constitutions Stabilize American Politics*, Yale University Press, 2021, 97–100; Delos O. Kinsman, "The Present Period of Income Tax Activity in the American States," *Quarterly Journal of Economics* 23, no. 2 (1909): 296–306; James A. Beeby, *Revolt of the Tar Heels: The North Carolina Populist Movement, 1890–1901*, University Press of Mississippi, 2008, 130.

44. Buenker, *Income Tax and the Progressive Era*, 191.

45. Robin L. Einhorn, "Look Away Dixieland: The South and the Federal Income Tax," *Northwestern University Law Review* 108, no. 3 (2014): 773; Buenker, *Income Tax and the Progressive Era*, 236.

46. Buenker, *Income Tax and the Progressive Era*, 208; Sanders, *Roots of Reform*, 229.

47. The income tax only passed in Arkansas after a frantic lobbying campaign from William Jennings Bryan. Buenker, *Income Tax and the Progressive Era*, 221.

48. "The Pig-Yoke," *New York Times*, April 13, 1878, 4; "The Communistic Movement," *The Nation*, May 9, 1878; Ellis, "Public Opinion and the Income Tax," 233–34; Buenker, *Income Tax and the Progressive Era*, 242–43.

49. Ratner, *American Taxation*, 217; Michael Kazin, *A Godly Hero: The Life of William Jennings Bryan*, Knopf Doubleday, 2007, 67.

50. Weisman, *Great Tax Wars*, 251; "Attack Income Tax in the Legislature," *New York Times*, April 14, 1910, 5.

51. Memorandum of Joseph H. Choate, William D. Guthrie, Victor Morawetz, Austen G. Fox, and John G. Milburn to the New York Legislature, April 11, 1910, microfilm, Columbia University Libraries, Butler Microforms, 13–14, 18.

52. Memorandum of Choate et al., 13, 16, 18, 20.

53. Weisman, *Great Tax Wars*, 259; Romain D. Huret, *American Tax Resisters*, Harvard University Press, 2013, 138.

54. Edwin Robert Anderson Seligman, *Essays in Taxation*, 1st ed., Macmillan, 1925, 73.

55. Ajay K. Mehrotra, "Edwin R. A. Seligman and the Beginnings of the U.S. Income Tax," *Tax Notes* (2005): 941–50.

56. While the Populist agrarians generally put their faith in legislatures, middle-class Progressive reformers like Seligman tended to focus on building the bureaucracy and civil service. Sanders, *Roots of Reform*, 8–9, 214; Ajay K. Mehrotra, "Forging Fiscal Reform: Constitutional Change, Public Policy, and the Creation of Administrative Capacity in Wisconsin, 1880–1920," *Journal of Policy History* 20, no. 1 (2008): 102–3.

57. Seligman, *Essays in Taxation*, 69, 72–73.

58. Ratner, *American Taxation*, 304; "John D. Rockefeller Discusses Big Questions," *The Sun*, January 11, 1914, 1–2; Weisman, *Great Tax Wars*, 252; Memorandum of Choate et al., 13–14.

59. Buenker, *Income Tax and the Progressive Era*, 273, 276.

60. The threshold was thirty-five states in 1911 and thirty-six states in 1912 (after New Mexico and Arizona became states). Both new states were likely to vote for the amendment, so the ratification threshold was not meaningfully higher.

61. "Corrects Hughes on Income Tax," *New York Times*, May 21, 1911, 12.

62. Buenker, *Income Tax and the Progressive Era*, 149.

63. "Corrects Hughes on Income Tax," 12.

64. Buenker, *Income Tax and the Progressive Era*, 286.

65. "The Income Tax Vote," *New York Times*, July 14, 1911, 6.

66. Weisman, *Great Tax Wars*, 281; Ratner, *Taxation and Democracy in America*, 333–34. Ajay K. Mehrotra, "Lawyers, Guns, and Public Moneys: The U.S. Treasury, World War I, and the Administration of the Modern Fiscal State," *Law and History Review* 28, no. 1 (2010): 180, suggests an even lower figure.

67. W. Elliot Brownlee, "Wilson and Financing the Modern State: The Revenue Act of 1916," *Proceedings of the American Philosophical Society* 129, no. 2 (1985): 175.

68. Author's calculations based on Office of Management and Budget, "Historical Tables," table 1.1, accessed October 2024.

69. W. Elliot Brownlee, ed., *Funding the Modern American State, 1941–1995: The Rise and Fall of the Era of Easy Finance*, Cambridge University Press, 1996, 64; David M. Kennedy, *Over Here: The First World War and American Society*, Oxford University Press, 1980, 16, 112; W. Elliot Brownlee, *Federal Taxation in America: A History*, 3rd ed., Cambridge University Press, 2016, 98; Mehrotra, "Lawyers, Guns, and Public Moneys," 181–82, 186–87.

70. Mehrotra, *Making the Modern American Fiscal State*, 304; William Kingsbury, "Traitors in Disguise," *Railroad Worker* 14, no. 5 (August 1916): 10; Kennedy, *Over Here*, 16; US Congress, House, *A Bill to [. . .] Require That in All Naval and Military Service of the United States, Whether in Time of Peace or War, Wealth Shall Bear and Perform Its Proportional Part of the Service [. . .]*, HR 10663, 64th Cong.,

1st sess., introduced in the House on February 2, 1916. Later versions were HR 10771 (introduced February 3, 1916), HR 14968 (April 24, 1916), and HR 16305 (June 7, 1916).

71. Ratner, *Taxation and Democracy in America*, 374; Kennedy, *Over Here*, 109; "The Conscription of Wealth," *New York Times*, August 24, 1917, 6; "Big Loyalty Conference Is Concluded," *Deseret Evening News* (Salt Lake City, UT), September 8, 1917, 9.

72. "Vrooman Hits War Profiteers," *Nonpartisan Leader* (Fargo, ND), August 2, 1917.

73. Letter from Woodrow Wilson to the Fifteen Thousand Four Minute Men of the United States, November 9, 1917, in Committee on Public Information, Division of Four Minute Men, *Carrying the Message*, Government Printing Office, 1917; Mehrotra, *Making the Modern American Fiscal State*, 323; Committee on Public Information, Division of Four Minute Men, *The Income Tax: An Answer to the Question: Is This a Capitalists' War?*, Government Printing Office, 1918.

74. Kenneth Scheve and David Stasavage, *Taxing the Rich: A History of Fiscal Fairness in the United States and Europe*, Princeton University Press, 2016.

75. "Memorial of Economists to Congress Regarding War Finance," *Bulletin of the National Tax Association* 2, no. 8 (May 1917): 215; Kennedy, *Over Here*, 135; Mehrotra, "Lawyers, Guns, and Public Moneys," 182, 203; Brownlee, *Federal Taxation in America*, 100; Edwin R. A. Seligman, "The War Revenue Act," *Political Science Quarterly* 33, no. 1 (March 1918): 19.

76. Arthur M. Schlesinger Jr., *The Age of Roosevelt*, vol. 1, *The Crisis of the Old Order, 1919–1933*, Houghton Mifflin, 2003, 62–63; "Twelve Ways to Dodge the Income Tax," *New Republic*, May 29, 1935, 74–75; Joseph J. Thorndike, "'The Unfair Advantage of the Few': The New Deal Origins of 'Soak the Rich' Taxation," in *The New Fiscal Sociology: Taxation in Comparative and Historical Perspective*, ed. Isaac William Martin, Ajay K. Mehrotra, and Monica Prasad, Cambridge University Press, 2009, 35. Mellon was not convicted of evasion but was found to have underpaid his taxes by $400,000. Diary of Henry Morgenthau Jr., March 20–March 31, 1937, 184–94, Franklin D. Roosevelt Presidential Library and Museum, Hyde Park, NY; Brownlee, *Federal Taxation in America*, 131. Mellon also approved billions in special tax deals for his own companies, as well as for top Republican donors.

77. Andrew W. Mellon, *Taxation: The People's Business*, Macmillan, 1924, 17, 18; M. Susan Murnane, "Selling Scientific Taxation: The Treasury Department's Campaign for Tax Reform in the 1920s," *Law and Social Inquiry* 29, no. 4 (October 2004): 833–34.

78. Isaac William Martin, *Rich People's Movements: Grassroots Campaigns to Untax the One Percent*, Oxford University Press, 2013, 64.

79. Ratner, *American Taxation*, 400–33; Brownlee, *Federal Taxation in America*, 107; Brownlee, *Funding the Modern American State*, 67; Weisman, *Great Tax Wars*, 343. To the extent Democrats contested this policy, it was to increase exemptions, keeping the tax targeted on the very rich. Joseph J. Thorndike, *Their Fair Share: Taxing the Rich in the Age of FDR*, Urban Institute Press, 2013, 11, 24.

80. Steinmo, *Taxation and Democracy*, 94; Sven Steinmo, "The Evolution of Policy Ideas: Tax Policy in the 20th Century," *British Journal of Politics and International Relations* 5, no. 2 (May 2003): 210–11; Thorndike, *Their Fair Share*, 14–15; Brownlee, *Federal Taxation in America*, 112.

81. On efforts to institute a federal sales tax, see Morgan and Prasad, "The Origins of Tax Systems"; Monica Prasad, *The Land of Too Much: American Abundance and the Paradox of Poverty*, Harvard University Press, 2012; Mehrotra, *Making the Modern American Fiscal State*.

82. Many historians and social scientists have suggested that, for precisely this reason, the federal income tax may have made it harder for the United States to achieve the kind of broad, antipoverty social safety net many European countries developed. Prasad, *Land of Too Much*; Mehrotra, *Making the Modern American Fiscal State*, 17; Molly C. Michelmore, *Tax and Spend: The Welfare State, Tax Politics, and the Limits of American Liberalism*, University of Pennsylvania Press, 2012, 178fn103. Reliance on regressive taxation provides no guarantee of progressive spending, however. Katherine S. Newman and Rourke O'Brien, *Taxing the Poor: Doing Damage to the Truly Disadvantaged*, University of California Press, 2011.

83. Martin, *Rich People's Movements*.

Chapter 9. FDR Turns Americans into Taxpayers

1. Arthur M. Schlesinger Jr., *The Age of Roosevelt*, vol. 2, *The Coming of the New Deal, 1933–1935*, Houghton Mifflin, 2003, 308–9.

2. Lawrence Zelenak, *Learning to Love Form 1040: Two Cheers for the Return-Based Mass Income Tax*, University of Chicago Press, 2013, 71–78.

3. Quoted in Abraham Holtzman, *The Townsend Movement: A Political Study*, Bookman Associates, 1963, 33.

4. Another proposal of the period, the Lundeen Bill, was similarly defined by universal benefits unlinked to contributions. Holtzman, *Townsend Movement*, 17; Molly C. Michelmore, *Tax and Spend: The Welfare State, Tax Politics, and the Limits of American Liberalism*, University of Pennsylvania Press, 2012, 7; Mark H. Leff, *The Limits of Symbolic Reform: The New Deal and Taxation, 1933–1939*, Cambridge University Press, 1984, 125; Jill S. Quadagno, "Welfare Capitalism and the Social Security Act of 1935," *American Sociological Review* 49, no. 5 (1984): 638; Mark H. Leff, "Taxing the 'Forgotten Man': The Politics of Social Security Finance in the New Deal," *Journal of American History* 70, no. 2 (September 1983): 362, 365; Jill Quadagno, *The Transformation of Old Age Security: Class and Politics in the American Welfare State*, University of Chicago Press, 1988, 108; Arthur M. Schlesinger Jr., *The Age of Roosevelt*, vol. 3, *The Politics of Upheaval, 1935–1936*, Houghton Mifflin, 2003, 35; Kenneth Finegold, "Agriculture and the Politics of U.S. Social Provision: Social Insurance and Food Stamps," in *The Politics of Social Policy in the United States*, ed. Margaret Weir, Ann Shola Orloff, and Theda Skocpol, Princeton University Press, 1988, 213; Edwin E. Witte, *The Development of the Social Security Act: A Memorandum on the History of the Committee on Economic Security and Drafting and Legislative History of the Social Security Act*, University of Wisconsin Press, 1962, vi; Daniel Béland, *Social Security: History and Politics from the New*

Deal to the Privatization Debate, University Press of Kansas, 2005, 69; Frances Fox Piven and Richard A. Cloward, *Regulating the Poor: The Functions of Public Welfare*, Vintage Books, 1972, 101.

5. Maris A. Vinovskis, "Have Social Historians Lost the Civil War? Some Preliminary Demographic Speculations," *Journal of American History* 76, no. 1 (June 1989): 51–54. See also Theda Skocpol, *Protecting Soldiers and Mothers*, Harvard University Press, 2009, especially chap. 2, "Public Aid for the Worthy Many."

6. Ann Shola Orloff, "The Political Origins of America's Belated Welfare State," in Weir et al., *Politics of Social Policy*, 67.

7. Franklin Delano Roosevelt, Message to Congress Reviewing the Broad Objectives and Accomplishments of the Administration, June 8, 1934, APP.

8. President Roosevelt's Message to Congress, Transmitting the Report of the Committee on Economic Security, January 17, 1935, APP.

9. Frances Perkins, *The Roosevelt I Knew*, Penguin Books, 2011, 284; Schlesinger, *Age of Roosevelt*, vol. 2, 308; Michelmore, *Tax and Spend*, 5.

10. Kevin Whitman and Dave Shoffner, "The Evolution of Social Security's Taxable Maximum," Social Security Administration, 2011.

11. Leff, *Limits of Symbolic Reform*, 45; Witte, *Development of the Social Security Act*, 74, 148–51; Perkins, *The Roosevelt I Knew*, 293–94; Julian E. Zelizer, "The Forgotten Legacy of the New Deal: Fiscal Conservatism and the Roosevelt Administration, 1933–1938," *Presidential Studies Quarterly* 30, no. 2 (2000): 345; Leff, "Taxing the 'Forgotten Man,'" 366, 368–69; Edward D. Berkowitz, "Social Security and the Financing of the American State," in *Funding the Modern American State, 1941–1995: The Rise and Fall of the Era of Easy Finance*, ed. W. Elliot Brownlee, Cambridge University Press, 2003, 153–54; Orloff, "Political Origins of America's Belated Welfare State," 73.

12. Berkowitz, "Social Security and the Financing of the American State," 154; Leff, "Taxing the 'Forgotten Man,'" 361; Gareth Davies and Martha Derthick, "Race and Social Welfare Policy: The Social Security Act of 1935," *Political Science Quarterly* 112, no. 2 (1997): 217–35. When income taxes were moved to withholding in 1943, domestic and farm laborers were again excluded. Roy G. Blakey and Gladys C. Blakey, "Federal Revenue Legislation, 1943–1944," *American Political Science Review* 38, no. 2 (April 1944): 328; *Economic Security Act: Hearings Before the Committee on Ways and Means, House of Representatives, Seventy-Fourth Congress, First Session on H. R. 4120 [. . .]*, 74th Cong., 1st sess. 901–902 (1935) (statement of Henry Morgenthau Jr., Secretary of the Treasury); Perkins, *The Roosevelt I Knew*, 298; Witte, *Development of the Social Security Act*, 153.

13. Davies and Derthick, "Race and Social Welfare Policy," 221; *Economic Security Act: Hearings Before the Committee on Finance, United States Senate, Seventy-Fourth Congress, First Session on S. 1130 [. . .]*, 74th Cong., 1st sess. 641 (1935) (statement of Charles H. Houston, special counsel for the National Association for the Advancement of Colored People).

14. In explaining the exclusion of domestic and agricultural workers from Social Security, historians debate the relative importance of the incentive to avoid administrative challenges and the desire to exclude Black people from the program's

benefits. See Zelizer, "Forgotten Legacy of the New Deal," 346; Orloff, "Political Origins of America's Belated Welfare State," 77–78; Berkowitz, "Social Security and the Financing of the American State," 167; Finegold, "Agriculture and the Politics of U.S. Social Provision," 212; Robert C. Lieberman, "Race and the Organization of Welfare Policy," in *Classifying by Race*, ed. Paul E. Peterson, Princeton University Press, 1995, 156–87; Jill S. Quadagno, *The Color of Welfare: How Racism Undermined the War on Poverty*, Oxford University Press, 1994. For other efforts by Southern legislators to prevent federal standards from interfering with their states' discrimination, see Witte, *Development of the Social Security Act*, 144–45. Social Security would be extended to agricultural and domestic workers in 1950. By that time, Southern legislators were mollified by the prospect of shifting poor rural seniors off the state welfare rolls and onto the federal insurance program—an early example of the program's remarkable capacity for growth and durability.

15. Schlesinger, *Age of Roosevelt*, vol. 3, 635–38.

16. David T. Beito, *Taxpayers in Revolt: Tax Resistance During the Great Depression*, Ludwig von Mises Institute, 1989; Schlesinger, *Age of Roosevelt*, vol. 3, 635–38.

17. Quadagno, "Welfare Capitalism and the Social Security Act of 1935," 644.

18. 79 Cong. Rec. 7048–50 (1935); Edwin Amenta, Kathleen Dunleavy, and Mary Bernstein, "Stolen Thunder? Huey Long's 'Share Our Wealth,' Political Mediation, and the Second New Deal," *American Sociological Review* 59, no. 5 (October 1994): 678.

19. Alan Brinkley, *Voices of Protest: Huey Long, Father Coughlin, and the Great Depression*, Vintage Books, 1983, 73; Leff, *Limits of Symbolic Reform*, 100; Gerard N. Magliocca, "Huey P. Long and the Guarantee Clause," *Tulane Law Review* 83, no. 1 (2008); James Aloysius Farley, *Behind the Ballots: The Personal History of a Politician*, Greenwood Press, 1972, 249–50; Raymond Moley, *After Seven Years*, Harper and Brothers, 1939, 305; James P. Warburg, *Hell Bent for Election*, Doubleday, Doran, 1936, 72.

20. Joseph J. Thorndike, *Their Fair Share: Taxing the Rich in the Age of FDR*, Urban Institute Press, 2013, 83–88; Arthur M. Schlesinger Jr., *The Age of Roosevelt*, vol. 1, *The Crisis of the Old Order, 1919–1933*, Houghton Mifflin, 2003, 253; John Morton Blum, *From the Morgenthau Diaries*, vol. 1, *Years of Crisis, 1928–1938*, Houghton Mifflin, 1959, 324–25.

21. "Mr. President, Begin to Tax!," *The Nation*, March 6, 1935, 264.

22. 79 Cong. Rec. 7648 (1935).

23. Joseph J. Thorndike, "'The Unfair Advantage of the Few': The New Deal Origins of 'Soak the Rich' Taxation," in *The New Fiscal Sociology: Taxation in Comparative and Historical Perspective*, ed. Isaac William Martin, Ajay K. Mehrotra, and Monica Prasad, Cambridge University Press, 2009, 39.

24. Edwin Amenta, "The Secret Origins of Presidential Polling," *The Conversation*, January 13, 2020; Roosevelt, "Message to Congress on Tax Revision," June 19, 1935, APP.

25. Harold L. Ickes, *The Secret Diary of Harold L. Ickes*, vol. 1, Simon and Schuster, 1953, 384.

26. Thorndike, "'Unfair Advantage of the Few,'" 44.

27. Thorndike, *Their Fair Share*, 165.

28. Schlesinger, *Age of Roosevelt*, vol. 3, 327–28.

29. Franklin Delano Roosevelt, "Address at Worcester, Massachusetts," October 21, 1936, APP.

30. Charles W. Hurd, "President Hits Tax Foes," *New York Times*, October 22, 1936.

31. Leff, *Limits of Symbolic Reform*, 48; Roy G. Blakey and Gladys C. Blakey, "The Revenue Act of 1935," *American Economic Review* 25, no. 4 (December 1935): 673; Warburg, *Hell Bent for Election*, 71; Moley, *After Seven Years*, 310.

32. Joseph J. Thorndike, "Tax History: A Federal Inheritance Tax? We Almost Got One in 1935," *Tax Notes*, January 27, 2020; Blakey and Blakey, "Revenue Act of 1935"; Thorndike, "'Unfair Advantage of the Few,'" 31, 33; Leff, *Limits of Symbolic Reform*, 132–33, 139; Harold Ickes, *The Secret Diary of Harold L. Ickes*, vol. 2, *The Inside Struggle: 1936–1939*, Simon and Schuster, 1954, 272; Schlesinger, *Age of Roosevelt*, vol. 3, 333.

33. Schlesinger, *Age of Roosevelt*, vol. 3, 330–31; Leff, *Limits of Symbolic Reform*, 141, 156, 162–63; "Taxation: 'Hell Raiser,'" *Time*, August 5, 1935, 9; Thorndike, *Their Fair Share*, 131; Zelizer, "Forgotten Legacy of the New Deal," 347; Thorndike, "'Unfair Advantage of the Few,'" 30, 45, 46; Jerome R. Hellerstein, "Federal Tax Policy During the Roosevelt Era," *Lawyers Guild Review* 5, no. 3 (May–June 1945): 161.

34. Leff, *Limits of Symbolic Reform*, 91, 97–111; "Wanted: A Philosophy of Taxation," *The Nation*, July 3, 1935, 4; Michelmore, *Tax and Spend*, 10–11; Blakey and Blakey, "Revenue Act of 1935," 677; Thorndike, "'Unfair Advantage of the Few,'" 46; W. Elliot Brownlee, "Tax Regimes, National Crisis, and State-Building in America," in *Funding the Modern American State, 1941–1995: The Rise and Fall of the Era of Easy Finance*, ed. W. Elliot Brownlee, Cambridge University Press, 2003, 76; "The Tax Fiasco," *The Nation*, July 10, 1935.

35. Ickes, *Secret Diary*, vol. 1, 652, 384.

36. Blum, *From the Morgenthau Diaries*, vol. 1, 326–31; Thorndike, "'Unfair Advantage of the Few,'" 34–35; Ickes, *Secret Diary*, vol. 2, 148.

37. Thorndike, *Their Fair Share*, 7.

38. Carolyn Jones, "Class Tax to Mass Tax: The Role of Propaganda in the Expansion of the Income Tax During World War II," *Buffalo Law Review* 37, no. 3 (October 1988): 716.

39. Beito, *Taxpayers in Revolt*, 116.

40. Carolyn C. Jones, "Mass-Based Income Taxation: Creating a Taxpaying Culture, 1940–1952," in Brownlee, *Funding the Modern American State*, 108; James T. Sparrow, "'Buying Our Boys Back': The Mass Foundations of Fiscal Citizenship in World War II," *Journal of Policy History* 20, no. 2 (April 2008): 264.

41. Advisory Commission on Intergovernmental Relations, *Significant Features of Fiscal Federalism*, vol. 1, *Budget Processes and Tax Systems*, M-197, September 1995; Leff, *Limits of Symbolic Reform*, 233; Joseph J. Thorndike, "The Fiscal Revolution and Taxation: The Rise of Compensatory Taxation, 1929–1938," *Law and Contemporary Problems* 73 (2010): 95–122, 111.

42. Brownlee, "Tax Regimes, National Crisis, and State-Building in America," 74, 91; Ickes, *The Secret Diary of Harold L. Ickes*, vol. 3, *The Lowering Clouds, 1939–1941*, Simon and Schuster, 1955, 76.

43. Roy G. Blakey and Gladys C. Blakey, "The Two Federal Revenue Acts of 1940," *American Economic Review* 30, no. 4 (December 1940): 724–35.

44. George Gallup, "Favor in Plan to Pay Defense Cost Income Tax on Every Family Meets [*sic*]," *Nevada State Journal* (Reno), January 8, 1941; Gallup, "Majority Would Approve of Income Tax for Masses Now Exempt; Dislike Borrowing, Institute Asserts," *Racine Journal Times Sunday Bulletin*, May 25, 1941, 3.

45. Brownlee, "Tax Regimes, National Crisis, and State-Building in America," 76; "Income of Families and Persons in the United States: 1948," *Current Population Reports: Consumer Income*, United States Bureau of the Census, 1950; Leff, *Limits of Symbolic Reform*, 94; Roy G. Blakey and Gladys C. Blakey, "The Revenue Act of 1941," *American Economic Review* 31, no. 4 (December 1941): 813.

46. W. Elliot Brownlee, *Federal Taxation in America: A History*, 3rd ed., Cambridge University Press, 2016, 140–41, 146; Leff, *Limits of Symbolic Reform*, 290–91.

47. United States Treasury Department, *Statistics of Income for 1940: Part 1*; United States Treasury Department, *Statistics of Income for 1942: Part 1*; United States Treasury Department, *Statistics of Income for 1944: Part 1*; Brownlee, *Federal Taxation in America*, 146.

48. Jones, "Class Tax to Mass Tax," 691; Sparrow, "'Buying Our Boys Back,'" 267; Brownlee, *Federal Taxation in America*, 145; Brownlee, "Tax Regimes, National Crisis, and State-Building in America," 92. What happened to the people who owed taxes for one year while also having taxes withheld for the following year? Roosevelt wanted them to pay twice over, but instead, much of the double tax was forgiven. Blakey and Blakey, "Federal Revenue Legislation, 1943–1944," 327–28. So our fictional switchboard operator would have owed only $34 in 1943. On debates over return-free systems during the war, see Zelenak, *Learning to Love Form 1040*, 78–80.

49. Sparrow, "'Buying Our Boys Back,'" 273, 276; Jones, "Mass-Based Income Taxation," 108; Zelenak, *Learning to Love Form 1040*, 83–110.

50. "Berlin Writes Song for Treasury, 'I Paid My Income Tax Today,'" *New York Times*, January 26, 1942.

51. Jones, "Class Tax to Mass Tax," 714.

52. "Crowds Pay Taxes as Deadline Nears," *New York Times*, March 16, 1942, 3.

53. Diary of Henry Morgenthau Jr., March 9–March 11, 1943, Franklin D. Roosevelt Library and Museum, 96; Jones, "Mass-Based Income Taxation," 107.

54. Andrea Louise Campbell, "What Americans Think of Taxes," in *The New Fiscal Sociology: Taxation in Comparative and Historical Perspective*, ed. Isaac William Martin, Ajay K. Mehrotra, and Monica Prasad, Cambridge University Press, 2009, 56.

55. "Income Tax Payers Continue Rush Here," *New York Times*, March 5, 1942, 16; "$22,036,328 Income Taxes Paid in Day, Breaking All Records in Second District," *New York Times*, March 14, 1942, 17; "Tax Offices Here to Be Open Today

as Rush to Pay Income Levy Grows," *New York Times*, March 15, 1942, 1; "Crowds Pay Taxes as Deadline Nears," *New York Times*, March 16, 1942, 3.

56. Sparrow, "'Buying Our Boys Back,'" 271; Campbell, "What Americans Think of Taxes," 53.

57. Isaac William Martin, *Rich People's Movements: Grassroots Campaigns to Untax the One Percent*, Oxford University Press, 2013; Leff, *Limits of Symbolic Reform*, 15; Michelmore, *Tax and Spend*, 176n73; *Constitutional Limitation on Federal Income, Estate, and Gift Tax Rates: Materials Assembled for the Joint Committee on the Economic Report and the Select Committee on Small Business of the House of Representatives [. . .]*, 82nd Cong., 2nd sess. (1952).

58. Berkowitz, "Social Security and the Financing of the American State," 151–67; Leff, *Limits of Symbolic Reform*, 275; Orloff, "Political Origins of America's Belated Welfare State," 78; Finegold, "Agriculture and the Politics of U.S. Social Provision," 215–16; Brownlee, "Tax Regimes, National Crisis, and State-Building in America," 97; Kathleen Romig, "Social Security Lifts More People Above the Poverty Line Than Any Other Program," Center on Budget and Policy Priorities, updated January 31, 2024; Schlesinger, *Age of Roosevelt*, vol. 2, 314–15; Andrea Louise Campbell, *How Policies Make Citizens: Senior Political Activism and the American Welfare State*, Princeton University Press, 2011.

59. See, e.g., Julian E. Zelizer, "'Where Is the Money Coming From?': The Reconstruction of Social Security Finance, 1939–1950," *Journal of Policy History* 9, no. 4 (October 1997).

60. C. Eugene Steuerle, "General Revenue Financing of Social Security," Testimony Before the Senate Finance Committee, February 9, 1999, Urban Institute.

61. Theda Skocpol, "The Limits of the New Deal System and the Roots of Contemporary Welfare Dilemmas," in Weir et al., *Politics of Social Policy*, 295; Zelizer, "'Where Is the Money Coming From?,'" 404; Michelmore, *Tax and Spend*, 27; Berkowitz, "Social Security and the Financing of the American State," 149.

62. Finegold, "Agriculture and the Politics of U.S. Social Provision," 215–16.

63. Skocpol, "Limits of the New Deal System," 295.

64. Michelmore, *Tax and Spend*, 12. See also Julian E. Zelizer, "The Uneasy Relationship: Democracy, Taxation, and State Building Since the New Deal," in *The Democratic Experiment: New Directions in American Political History*, ed. Meg Jacobs, William J. Novak, and Julian E. Zelizer, Princeton University Press, 2004, 120.

Chapter 10. Taxpayers, Tax "Eaters," and the Rise of Reagan

1. Charles C. Robb, "Relief Hike Sought by Recipients," *Pittsburgh Post-Gazette*, June 8, 1966.

2. 113 Cong. Rec. 23508 (1967); Molly C. Michelmore, *Tax and Spend: The Welfare State, Tax Politics, and the Limits of American Liberalism*, University of Pennsylvania Press, 2012, 75–78.

3. *Social Security Amendments of 1967: Hearings Before the Committee on Finance, United States Senate, Ninetieth Congress, First Session on H.R. 12080 [. . .]*, Part 2, 90th Cong., 1st sess. 1467 (1967) (statement of Alice Nixon of the National Welfare Rights Organization).

4. Eve Edstrom, "Irate Welfare Mothers Beset Hearing," *Washington Post and Times Herald*, September 20, 1967.

5. *Social Security Amendments of 1967: Hearings Before the Committee on Finance, United States Senate, Ninetieth Congress, First Session on H.R. 12080 [. . .], Part 3*, 90th Cong., 1st sess. 1649 (1967) (statement of Sen. Long).

6. Martin Gilens, *Why Americans Hate Welfare: Race, Media, and the Politics of Antipoverty Policy*, University of Chicago Press, 2009, 19; Michael B. Katz and Lorrin R. Thomas, "The Invention of 'Welfare' in America," *Journal of Policy History* 10, no. 4 (1998): 405; Thomas Ferguson and Joel Rogers, *Right Turn: The Decline of the Democrats and the Future of American Politics*, Hill and Wang, 1986, 128.

7. Julian E. Zelizer, "The Uneasy Relationship: Democracy, Taxation, and State Building Since the New Deal," in *The Democratic Experiment: New Directions in American Political History*, ed. Meg Jacobs, William J. Novak, and Julian E. Zelizer, Princeton University Press, 2004, 289–90; Rick Perlstein, *Nixonland: The Rise of a President and the Fracturing of America*, Scribner, 2008, 139, 239; Joseph J. Thorndike, "Timelines in Tax History: Guns, Butter, and the Vietnam War Tax Surcharge," *Tax Notes*, January 16, 2023; Keith E. Duke, *Cost of the War in Vietnam*, National Technical Information Service, US Department of Commerce, 1970; *Report of the National Advisory Commission on Civil Disorders*, Bantam Books, 1968, 23.

8. The interviews with the Kalismans and the Burnetts are in *Race: The Power of an Illusion*, episode 3, "The House We Live In," documentary series, dir. Christine Herbes-Sommers, Tracy Heather Strain, and Llewellyn Smith, California Newsreel, 2003; Ira Katznelson, *When Affirmative Action Was White: An Untold History of Racial Inequality in Twentieth-Century America*, W. W. Norton, 2005; Richard Rothstein, *The Color of Law: A Forgotten History of How Our Government Segregated America*, Liveright, 2017.

9. Lisa McGirr, *Suburban Warriors: The Origins of the New American Right*, Princeton University Press, 2001, 14, 25–26; Matthew D. Lassiter, "Suburban Strategies: The Volatile Center in Postwar American Politics," in Jacobs et al., *Democratic Experiment*, 328, 335; Katznelson, *When Affirmative Action Was White*; Rothstein, *Color of Law*.

10. Paul Pierson, "The Rise and Reconfiguration of Activist Government," in *The Transformation of American Politics: Activist Government and the Rise of Conservatism*, ed. Paul Pierson and Theda Skocpol, Princeton University Press, 2007, 21–22; Gary Engelhardt and Jonathan Gruber, "Social Security and the Evolution of Elderly Poverty," working paper, National Bureau of Economic Research, May 2004, 2; Em Shrider, "Poverty Rate for the Black Population Fell Below Pre-Pandemic Levels," United States Census Bureau, September 12, 2023; James Mabli, Jim Ohls, Lisa Dragoset, Laura Castner, and Betsy Santos, *Measuring the Effect of Supplemental Nutrition Assistance Program (SNAP) Participation on Food Security*, Mathematica Policy Research for the US Department of Agriculture, Food and Nutrition Service, 2013; Christian A. Gregory and Partha Deb, "Does SNAP Improve Your Health?," *Food Policy* 50 (2015): 11–19; Stephanie A. Ettinger de Cuba, Allison R. Bovell-Ammon, John T. Cook, et al., "SNAP, Young Children's

Health, and Family Food Security and Healthcare Access," *American Journal of Preventive Medicine* 57, no. 4 (2019): 525–32; Laura Tiehen, Dean Jolliffe, and Timothy M. Smeeding, "The Effect of SNAP on Poverty," in *SNAP Matters: How Food Stamps Affect Health and Well-Being*, ed. Judith Bartfeld, Craig Gundersen, Timothy M. Smeeding, and James P. Ziliak, Stanford University Press, 2016, 55; Douglas Almond, Hilary W. Hoynes, and Diane Whitmore Schanzenbach, "Inside the War on Poverty: The Impact of Food Stamps on Birth Outcomes," *Review of Economics and Statistics* 93, no. 2 (May 2011): 387–403; Michael B. Katz, *The Price of Citizenship: Redefining the American Welfare State*, Henry Holt, 2001, 261; Kim Phillips-Fein, *Fear City: New York's Fiscal Crisis and the Rise of Austerity Politics*, Metropolitan, 2017, 23–24; Ira Katznelson, "Was the Great Society a Lost Opportunity?," in *The Rise and Fall of the New Deal Order, 1930–1980*, ed. Steve Fraser and Gary Gerstle, Princeton University Press, 1989, 197.

11. Gilens, *Why Americans Hate Welfare.*

12. AFDC usage was rising during this period, but the increase was mostly among white mothers and was a consequence of more eligible people receiving the benefits to which they were entitled, rather than rising poverty. Michelmore, *Tax and Spend*, 77; Ellen Reese, *Backlash Against Welfare Mothers: Past and Present*, University of California Press, 2005, 107, 114–15; Katznelson, *When Affirmative Action Was White*, 37; Katz and Thomas, "Invention of 'Welfare,'" 413–14; Gilens, *Why Americans Hate Welfare*, 18–19; Michael K. Brown, *Race, Money, and the American Welfare State*, Cornell University Press, 1999, 186, fig. 5.

13. Gary Orfield, "Race and the Liberal Agenda: The Loss of the Integrationist Dream, 1965–1974," in *The Politics of Social Policy in the United States*, ed. Margaret Weir, Ann Shola Orloff, and Theda Skocpol, Princeton University Press, 1988; Vesla M. Weaver, "Frontlash: Race and the Development of Punitive Crime Policy," *Studies in American Political Development* 21, no. 2 (2007): 230–65; Omar Wasow, "Agenda Seeding: How 1960s Black Protests Moved Elites, Public Opinion and Voting," *American Political Science Review* 114, no. 3 (2020): 638–59; Andrew W. Kahrl, *The Black Tax: 150 Years of Theft, Exploitation, and Dispossession in America*, University of Chicago Press, 2024, 104–5.

14. Reese, *Backlash Against Welfare Mothers*, 117.

15. Katz and Thomas, "The Invention of 'Welfare.'"

16. Perlstein, *Nixonland*, 114–15.

17. *Report of the National Advisory Commission on Civil Disorders*, 26.

18. Heather Cox Richardson, *To Make Men Free: A History of the Republican Party*, Basic Books, 2014, 276; Stephen Hess and David S. Broder, *The Republican Establishment: The Present and Future of the G.O.P.*, Harper and Row, 1967, 267–68.

19. Brad Knickerbocker, "Reagan and Social Issues," *Christian Science Monitor*, October 2, 1980; Rick Perlstein, *The Invisible Bridge: The Fall of Nixon and the Rise of Reagan*, Simon and Schuster, 2014, 410; Rick Perlstein, *Reaganland: America's Right Turn 1976–1980*, Simon and Schuster, 2020, 875–76; Perlstein, *Nixonland*, 184, 282; Monica Prasad, *Starving the Beast: Ronald Reagan and the Tax Cut Revolution*, Russell Sage Foundation, 2018, 46–47.

20. "Task Force on Job Opportunities and Welfare," *Choice for America: Republican Answers to the Challenge of Now, Reports of the Republican Coordinating Committee, 1965–1968*, Republican National Committee, 1968, 125.

21. Wallace Turner, "McGovern and Humphrey Clash on War and Relief," *New York Times*, May 29, 1972; Perlstein, *Nixonland*, 668–70, 734.

22. The maximum benefit under the Family Assistance Plan would not bring a family above the poverty line; it provided much more than AFDC did in the South, but much less than was provided in some Northern cities. Robert J. Lampman, *Nixon's Family Assistance Plan*, Institute for Research on Poverty, University of Wisconsin, Madison, 1969, 19.

23. Warren Weaver Jr., "Nixon Campaigns on Welfare Issue," *New York Times*, October 22, 1970; Daniel P. Moynihan, *The Politics of a Guaranteed Income: The Nixon Administration and the Family Assistance Plan*, Vintage Books, 1973, 11.

24. Vincent J. Burke and Vee Burke, *Nixon's Good Deed: Welfare Reform*, Columbia University Press, 1976, 153–54; Warren Weaver Jr., "Welfare Reform Is Again Rejected by Senate Panel," *New York Times*, November 21, 1970; Brian Steensland, "Cultural Categories and the American Welfare State: The Case of Guaranteed Income Policy," *American Journal of Sociology* 111, no. 5 (March 2006): 1273–1326; Christopher Howard, *The Hidden Welfare State: Tax Expenditures and Social Policy in the United States*, Princeton University Press, 1999, 139, 145.

25. Julilly Kohler-Hausmann, *Getting Tough: Welfare and Imprisonment in 1970s America*, Princeton University Press, 2017, 159; Burke and Burke, *Nixon's Good Deed*, 162; Nick Kotz, "The Political Complexion of the Welfare Reform Issue," *Washington Post and Times Herald*, May 15, 1971.

26. Emmanuel Saez and Gabriel Zucman, *The Triumph of Injustice: How the Rich Dodge Taxes and How to Make Them Pay*, W. W. Norton, 2019, 70.

27. Zelizer, "Uneasy Relationship," 118; W. Elliot Brownlee, "Tax Regimes, National Crisis, and State-Building in America," in *Funding the Modern American State, 1941–1995: The Rise and Fall of the Era of Easy Finance*, ed. W. Elliot Brownlee, Cambridge University Press, 2003, 96; Michelmore, *Tax and Spend*, 51–61.

28. Thomas Byrne Edsall, *The New Politics of Inequality*, W. W. Norton, 1985, 209; C. Eugene Steuerle, *The Tax Decade: How Taxes Came to Dominate the Public Agenda*, Urban Institute, 1992, 24–25; Andrea Louise Campbell, "What Americans Think of Taxes," in *The New Fiscal Sociology: Taxation in Comparative and Historical Perspective*, ed. Isaac William Martin, Ajay K. Mehrotra, and Monica Prasad, Cambridge University Press, 2009, 59, 62.

29. Saez and Zucman, *The Triumph of Injustice*, 23, 43; Michelmore, *Tax and Spend*, 107–8; Edward Cowan, "High-Income Group Gets Almost a Third of U.S. Tax Benefits," *New York Times*, February 13, 1978; Department of Health and Human Services, "Federal and State Expenditures for AFDC," in *Aid to Families with Dependent Children: The Baseline*, National Technical Information Service, 1998, 64, table 4.2; "Money Income in 1977 of Households in the United States," in *Current Population Reports: Consumer Income*, United States Bureau of the Census, 1979; Joint Committee on Taxation, *Estimates of Federal Tax Expenditures* (JCS-10-77), Government Printing Office, 1977, 8.

30. Howard, *The Hidden Welfare State*; Suzanne Mettler, *The Submerged State: How Invisible Government Policies Undermine American Democracy*, University of Chicago Press, 2011; Jacob S. Hacker, *The Divided Welfare State: The Battle over Public and Private Social Benefits in the United States*, Cambridge University Press, 2002. The home mortgage interest deduction represented $4.6 billion in forgone federal revenue by 1977. More than 70 percent of the benefit went to the top quarter of households. Cowan, "High-Income Group Gets Almost a Third of U.S. Tax Benefits"; Joseph J. Minarik, "Who Doesn't Bear the Tax Burden?," in *The Economics of Taxation*, ed. Henry J. Aaron and Michael J. Boskin, Brookings Institution, 1980.

31. Pierson, "Rise and Reconfiguration of Activist Government," 30.

32. Conservatives soon recognized this political effect. Starting in the 1980s, a major conservative argument for tax-advantaged private pension accounts, like individual retirement accounts, was that they would help undercut Social Security. Michael J. Graetz, *The Power to Destroy: How the Antitax Movement Hijacked America*, Princeton University Press, 2024, 79, 178; Steven M. Teles, "Conservative Mobilization Against Entrenched Liberalism," in Pierson and Skocpol, *Transformation of American Politics*, 168–73. President Barack Obama would confront the challenge of entrenched tax benefits during his campaign for the Affordable Care Act.

33. Advisory Commission on Intergovernmental Relations, *Significant Features of Fiscal Federalism, 1976 Edition, vol. 1: Trends*, M-106, June 1976, 41, table 16; Advisory Commission on Intergovernmental Relations, *State and Local Taxes: Significant Features, 1968*, M-37, January 1968, 12, table 3; Joseph A. Pechman and Benjamin A. Okner, *Who Bears the Tax Burden?*, Brookings Institution, 1974, 61; Michelmore, *Tax and Spend*, 92–93; Josh Mound, "Stirrings of Revolt: Regressive Levies, the Pocketbook Squeeze, and the 1960s Roots of the 1970s Tax Revolt," *Journal of Policy History* 32, no. 2 (2020): 105–50; Isaac Shapiro and Danilo Trisi, *Child Poverty Falls to Record Low, Comprehensive Measure Shows Stronger Government Policies Account for Long-Term Improvement*, Center on Budget and Policy Priorities, October 5, 2017.

34. Andrea Louise Campbell and Kimberly J. Morgan, "Financing the Welfare State: Elite Politics and the Decline of the Social Insurance Model in America," *Studies in American Political Development* 19, no. 2 (2005): 173–95.

35. Kahrl, *The Black Tax*, 82; William G. Colman, *Cities, Suburbs, and States: Governing and Financing Urban America*, Free Press, 1975, 62; Kenneth T. Jackson, *Crabgrass Frontier: The Suburbanization of the United States*, Oxford University Press, 1985, 284–85; Gary J. Miller, *Cities by Contract: The Politics of Municipal Incorporation*, MIT Press, 1981, 11; Thomas W. Hanchett, "U.S. Tax Policy and the Shopping-Center Boom of the 1950s and 1960s," *American Historical Review* 101, no. 4 (1996): 1082–1110; Jack Rosenthal, "Suburbs Abandoning Dependence on City," *New York Times*, August 16, 1971; Lassiter, "Suburban Strategies," 331.

36. Kahrl, *The Black Tax*, 206–7; Camille Walsh, *Racial Taxation: Schools, Segregation, and Taxpayer Citizenship, 1869–1973*, University of North Carolina Press, 2018, 163; Robert O. Self, "Prelude to the Tax Revolt: The Politics of the 'Tax

Dollar' in Postwar California," in *The New Suburban History*, ed. Kevin M. Kruse and Thomas J. Sugrue, University of Chicago Press, 2006.

37. Isaac William Martin, *The Permanent Tax Revolt: How the Property Tax Transformed American Politics*, Stanford University Press, 2008, 56, 98; Michelmore, *Tax and Spend*, 112; Kahrl, *The Black Tax*, 212, 230; Nick Kotz and Mary Lynn Kotz, "The Movement for Economic Justice," in *A Passion for Equality: George Wiley and the Movement*, W. W. Norton, 1977; Weusi Tushinde, "Welfare Rights Head Quits to Form Coalition for Poor," *Washington Afro-American*, December 26, 1972.

38. Kahrl, *The Black Tax*. To this day, the property tax remains disproportionately heavy for Black homeowners due to biased assessments and racism in the housing market. Dorothy A. Brown, *The Whiteness of Wealth: How the Tax System Impoverishes Black Americans—and How We Can Fix It*, Crown, 2022; Carlos F. Avenancio-León and Troup Howard, "The Assessment Gap: Racial Inequalities in Property Taxation," *Quarterly Journal of Economics* 137, no. 3 (August 2022): 1383–1434; Mound, "Stirrings of Revolt," 145n123.

39. Kevin M. Kruse, *White Flight: Atlanta and the Making of Modern Conservatism*, Princeton University Press, 2005, 126–30; Lassiter, "Suburban Strategies," 327, 337.

40. Walsh, *Racial Taxation*.

41. Kevin P. Phillips, *The Emerging Republican Majority*, Arlington House, 1969, 32.

42. United States Census Bureau, "Historical Census of Housing Tables: Home Values," USCB, 2000. Taxes rose in part because of the adoption of a new, computerized statewide property tax assessment system that eliminated the traditional informal (and often corrupt and racist) lowball assessments from local tax assessors. Martin, *Permanent Tax Revolt*, 28, 45; Kahrl, *The Black Tax*, 75, 224.

43. David O. Sears and Jack Citrin, *Tax Revolt: Something for Nothing in California*, Harvard University Press, 1982, 32.

44. Martin, *Permanent Tax Revolt*, 81, 102, 107; Mound, "Stirrings of Revolt," 112; Perlstein, *Reaganland*, 306; Eileen Shanahan, "Nader to Press for Tax Reform," *New York Times*, November 8, 1970.

45. Voters defeated Proposition 9 (1968), Proposition 14 (1972), and Proposition 1 (1973). Sears and Citrin, *Tax Revolt*, 20–21; McGirr, *Suburban Warriors*, 237–39.

46. Perlstein, *Reaganland*, 324; Manuel Pastor, "After Tax Cuts Derailed the 'California Dream,' Is the State Getting Back on Track?," *The Conversation*, November 1, 2017; Graetz, *Power to Destroy*, 30; Michelmore, *Tax and Spend*, 135.

47. Peter Schrag, *Paradise Lost: California's Experience, America's Future*, New Press, 1998, 130.

48. Martin, *Permanent Tax Revolt*, 102.

49. Martin, *Permanent Tax Revolt*, 98; Perlstein, *Reaganland*, 326.

50. Sears and Citrin, *Tax Revolt*, 28, 191, 208.

51. Sears and Citrin, *Tax Revolt*, 208–10. Anti-integration measures also benefited from substantial support from the real estate industry. Daniel M. HoSang, *Racial Propositions: Ballot Initiatives and the Making of Postwar California*, University of California Press, 2010. On direct coordination with Jarvis and conservative

political activist Paul Gann, see 120–21. Some scholars have argued that support for Proposition 13 was driven by the *Serrano* decision on school financing; this connection has not been borne out by the data.

52. Perlstein, *Reaganland*, 334.

53. Kim S. Rueben and Richard C. Auxier, "Lessons Learned 40 Years After a Monumental Tax Law," *The Hill*, June 5, 2018; Carolyn Chu and Brian Uhler, *Common Claims About Proposition 13*, California Legislative Analyst's Office, September 2016; Jeffrey I. Chapman, *Proposition 13: Some Unintended Consequences*, Public Policy Institute of California, 1998; California Budget Project, *Proposition 13: Its Impact on California and Implications*, April 1997; Richard C. Auxier, Tracy Gordon, and Kim S. Rueben, "Four Decades After Proposition 13's Tax Revolt, Will California (Split) Roll It Back with Proposition 15?," Urban-Brookings Tax Policy Center, October 26, 2020; Pastor, "After Tax Cuts Derailed the 'California Dream'"; Nada Wasi and Michelle J. White, "Property Tax Limitations and Mobility: The Lock-In Effect of California's Proposition 13," working paper, National Bureau of Economic Research, February 2005; Liam Dillon and Ben Poston, "California Homeowners Get to Pass Low Property Taxes to Their Kids. It's Proved Highly Profitable to an Elite Group," *Los Angeles Times*, August 17, 2018.

54. Alvin Rabushka and Pauline Ryan, *The Tax Revolt*, Hoover Institution, 1982, 2.

55. Perlstein, *Reaganland*, 334.

56. Ferguson and Rogers, *Right Turn*, 18.

57. Sears and Citrin, *Tax Revolt*, 5–6; Robert Kuttner, "The Imitations," in *Revolt of the Haves: Tax Rebellions and Hard Times*, Simon and Schuster, 1980.

58. Tucker C. Staley, "The Impact of Tax and Expenditure Limitations on Municipal Revenue Volatility," *State & Local Government Review* 50, no. 2 (2018): 73; Kim S. Rueben, "Tax Limitations and Government Growth: The Effect of State Tax and Expenditure Limits on State and Local Government," Public Policy Institute of California, 1996; Ariel Jurow Kleiman, "Tax Limits and the Future of Local Democracy," *Harvard Law Review* 133, no. 6 (2020): 1884–1962; Lucy Sorensen, Youngsung Kim, and Moontae Hwang, "The Distributional Effects of Property Tax Constraints on School Districts," *National Tax Journal* 74, no. 3 (September 2021): 621–54; Douglas C. Bice and William H. Hoyt, "The Impact of Mandates and Tax Limits on Voluntary Contributions to Local Public Services: An Application to Fire-Protection Services," *National Tax Journal* 53, no. 1 (March 2000): 79–104; Christine Wen, Yuanshuo Xu, Yunji Kim, and Mildred E. Warner, "Starving Counties, Squeezing Cities: Tax and Expenditure Limits in the US," *Journal of Economic Policy Reform* 23, no. 2 (2020): 101–19; Iris J. Lav and Michael Leachman, *State Limits on Property Taxes Hamstring Local Services and Should Be Relaxed or Repealed*, Center on Budget and Policy Priorities, July 18, 2018; Wesley Tharpe, *Easing State Restraints on Local Taxing Power Can Strengthen Democracy, Promote Prosperity and Equity*, Center on Budget and Policy Priorities, March 28, 2023.

59. Michelmore, *Tax and Spend*, 134; Judith Miller, "Carter and Byrd Ask for Fiscal Restraint," *New York Times*, June 11, 1978; B. Drummond Ayres, "Congress

Responds to Frugality Signal," *New York Times*, June 18, 1978; Michael B. Berkman, *The State Roots of National Politics: Congress and the Tax Agenda, 1978–1986*, University of Pittsburgh Press, 1993, 13.

60. Jacob S. Hacker and Paul Pierson, *Winner-Take-All Politics: How Washington Made the Rich Richer—and Turned Its Back on the Middle Class*, Simon and Schuster, 2010, 118–19; Edsall, *New Politics of Inequality*, 123; Julian E. Zelizer, "Learning the Ways and Means: Wilbur Mills and a Fiscal Community, 1954–1964," in Brownlee, *Funding the Modern American State*, 320; Cathie Jo Martin, "American Business and the Taxing State: Alliances for Growth in the Postwar Period," in Brownlee, *Funding the Modern American State*, 376–77; Mark S. Mizruchi, *The Fracturing of the American Corporate Elite*, Harvard University Press, 2013; Alex Hertel-Fernandez, *State Capture: How Conservative Activists, Big Businesses, and Wealthy Donors Reshaped the American States—and the Nation*, Oxford University Press, 2019; Alyssa Katz, *The Influence Machine: The U.S. Chamber of Commerce and the Corporate Capture of American Life*, Spiegel and Grau, 2015.

61. Edsall, *New Politics of Inequality*, 117–18, 219; Perlstein, *Reaganland*, 280; Binyamin Appelbaum, *The Economists' Hour: False Prophets, Free Markets, and the Fracture of Society*, Little, Brown, 2019; Elizabeth Popp Berman, *Thinking Like an Economist: How Efficiency Replaced Equality in U.S. Public Policy*, Princeton University Press, 2022; Kim Phillips-Fein, *Invisible Hands: The Making of the Conservative Movement from the New Deal to Reagan*, W. W. Norton, 2009; Nancy MacLean, *Democracy in Chains: The Deep History of the Radical Right's Stealth Plan for America*, Penguin Books, 2017.

62. Lawrence Mishel, Lynn Rhinehart, and Lane Windham, *Explaining the Erosion of Private-Sector Unions*, Economic Policy Institute, 2020; Hacker and Pierson, *Winner-Take-All Politics*, 121.

63. Edward Cowan, "Issue and Debate Capital Gains Tax: Wealth, Egalitarianism, the Economy," *New York Times*, June 9, 1978; "Interview with Alfred H. Kingon and Robert I. Weingarten of 'Financial World,'" August 13, 1976, APP; Clyde H. Farnsworth, "Aide to Carter Gives Plan on Tax Revision," *New York Times*, March 25, 1977; "Interview with A. James Reichley and Ann Hengstenberg of 'Fortune Magazine,'" May 1, 1976, APP; "Presidential Campaign Debate Between Gerald R. Ford and Jimmy Carter," September 23, 1976, Key Speeches and Writings of Gerald R. Ford, Gerald R. Ford Presidential Library and Museum; Henry Scott-Stokes, "Business Reacts Hopefully to Carter's Tax Cut Plan," *New York Times*, December 22, 1977; US Department of the Treasury, *The President's 1978 Tax Program*; Joseph Thorndike, "A Cultural Tax History of the Three-Martini Lunch," *Forbes*, January 21, 2021.

64. Ferguson and Rogers, *Right Turn*, 109; Joshua Green, "How 1978 Shifted Power in America and Laid the Groundwork for Our Current Political Moment," Talking Points Memo, January 12, 2024.

65. Phillips-Fein, *Fear City*, 95; Perlstein, *Reaganland*, 260, 279; Elizabeth Popp Berman and Laura M. Milanes-Reyes, "The Politicization of Knowledge Claims: The 'Laffer Curve' in the U.S. Congress," *Qualitative Sociology* 36, no. 1 (2013): 63–64; Green, "How 1978 Shifted Power in America." On the fallacies in the

underlying economics, see Leonard E. Burman and William C. Randolph, "Measuring Permanent Responses to Capital-Gains Tax Changes in Panel Data," *American Economic Review* 84, no. 4 (September 1994): 794–809.

66. Terence Smith, "Bill Cutting Taxes Is Signed by Carter," *New York Times*, November 8, 1978; Karen W. Arenson, "Minimal Impact Seen in Capital-Gains Tax Cut," *New York Times*, April 30, 1979; Perlstein, *Reaganland*, 382; Cowan, "Issue and Debate Capital Gains Tax"; "How to Unsoak the Rich," editorial, *New York Times*, May 19, 1978; Cowan, "High-Income Group Gets Almost a Third of U.S. Tax Benefits"; "Money Income in 1978 of Households in the United States," *Current Population Reports: Consumer Income*. United States Bureau of the Census, 1980; Economic Policy Institute, State of Working America Data Library, "Wages for Top 1.0%, 0.1% and Bottom 90%," accessed October 2024.

67. Hacker and Pierson, *Winner-Take-All Politics*, 122; Edsall, *New Politics of Inequality*, 77; Perlstein, *Reaganland*, 388.

68. Clyde H. Farnsworth, "Momentum for Tax Cut," *New York Times*, July 17, 1978.

69. Perlstein, *Reaganland*, 348. Even so, it took until 1976 for the IRS to rescind Bob Jones University's tax exemption. Randall Balmer, "The Real Origins of the Religious Right," *Politico Magazine*, May 27, 2014; Charles R. Babcock, "School Tax Status: Old Issue Was Heated Up by Courts in 1978," *Washington Post*, January 24, 1982.

70. 43 Fed. Reg. 37296-37297 (August 22, 1978).

71. Perlstein, *Reaganland*, 482; Graetz, *Power to Destroy*, 43; Thomas B. Edsall, "Abortion Has Never Been Just About Abortion," *New York Times*, September 15, 2021; Fred Barnes, "Ronald Reagan, Father of the Pro-Life Movement," *Wall Street Journal*, opinion, November 6, 2003.

72. Robert Freedman, "The Religious Right and the Carter Administration," *Historical Journal* 48, no. 1 (2005): 240; Thomas Byrne Edsall and Mary D. Edsall, *Chain Reaction: The Impact of Race Rights and Taxes on American Politics*, W. W. Norton, 1992, 132.

73. Perlstein, *Reaganland*, 475.

74. Frances FitzGerald, *The Evangelicals: The Struggle to Shape America*, Simon and Schuster, 2017, 303–4; David Von Drehle and Thomas B. Edsall, "Life of the Grand Old Party," *Washington Post*, August 13, 1994; Edsall and Edsall, *Chain Reaction*, 134.

75. Martin Schram and Charles R. Babcock, "Reagan Played Direct Role in Tax Exemptions," *Washington Post*, January 21, 1982.

76. Perlstein, *Reaganland*, 71, 765, 854.

77. Bryce Covert, "The Myth of the Welfare Queen," *New Republic*, July 2, 2019; Gillian Brockell, "She Was Stereotyped as 'the Welfare Queen.' The Truth Was More Disturbing, a New Book Says," *Washington Post*, June 17, 2019.

78. Perlstein, *Reaganland*, 910.

79. Edsall and Edsall, *Chain Reaction*, 145.

80. Rick Perlstein, "Lee Atwater's Infamous 1981 Interview on the Southern Strategy," *The Nation*, November 13, 2012.

Chapter 11. The Triumph of Antitax Politics and the Erosion of American Democracy

1. "Full Transcript of the Mitt Romney Secret Video," *Mother Jones*, September 19, 2012.

2. Lawrence Zelenak, "Mitt Romney, the 47 Percent, and the Future of the Mass Income Tax," *Tax Law Review* 67 (2013): 471.

3. For example, whether an American is enrolled in Medicare, Medicaid, or a tax-subsidized employer health insurance, they are receiving a government subsidy for their health care.

4. Jennifer Epstein, "Obama Attacks on Romney '47 Percent,'" *Politico*, October 16, 2012.

5. Janna Deitz, "Sarah Binder Weighs In: Institutional Hardball—in Congress and the White House—and the Legislative Road Ahead," *Insights: Scholarly Work at the Kluge Center* (blog), Library of Congress, February 24, 2021; Corey Robin, "'The Gonzo Constitutionalism of the American Right," *New York Review of Books*, October 21, 2020.

6. The Democrats' tax cut was more focused on business tax cuts than Reagan's plan. Monica Prasad, *Starving the Beast: Ronald Reagan and the Tax Cut Revolution*, Russell Sage Foundation, 2018, 110, 113, 140; W. Elliot Brownlee, "'Reaganomics': The Fiscal and Monetary Policies," in *A Companion to Ronald Reagan*, ed. Andrew L. Johns, Wiley Blackwell, 2015, 133; Lily Rothman, "Read President Reagan's Best Jokes About Being Shot," *Time*, March 30, 2015.

7. Thomas Ferguson and Joel Rogers, *Right Turn: The Decline of the Democrats and the Future of American Politics*, Hill and Wang, 1986, 121–22, 139; W. Elliot Brownlee, *Federal Taxation in America: A History*, 3rd ed., Cambridge University Press, 2016, 186; Michael J. Graetz, *The Power to Destroy: How the Antitax Movement Hijacked America*, Princeton University Press, 2024, 79; Alan S. Blinder, *A Monetary and Fiscal History of the United States, 1961–2021*, Princeton University Press, 2022, 138; Molly C. Michelmore, *Tax and Spend: The Welfare State, Tax Politics, and the Limits of American Liberalism*, University of Pennsylvania Press, 2012, 146–47. Interestingly, one of the bill's most significant long-term effects was not fully appreciated at the time: the indexing of tax brackets for inflation, which brought an end to "bracket creep" and to the automatic rise of tax revenues.

8. Blinder, *Monetary and Fiscal History*, 133; Binyamin Appelbaum, *The Economists' Hour: False Prophets, Free Markets, and the Fracture of Society*, Little, Brown, 2019, 114.

9. Brownlee, *Federal Taxation in America*, 184–85; Ferguson and Rogers, *Right Turn*, 120.

10. Brownlee, *Federal Taxation in America*, 208; Michelmore, *Tax and Spend*, 142; Ferguson and Rogers, *Right Turn*, 128–30, 138; Martin Gilens, *Why Americans Hate Welfare: Race, Media, and the Politics of Antipoverty Policy*, University of Chicago Press, 2009, 181; Thomas Byrne Edsall, *The New Politics of Inequality*, W. W. Norton, 1985, 17; Matthew Desmond, *Poverty, by America*, Crown, 2023, 109. Some programs, like Medicaid, had powerful enough allies to resist retrenchment. Helene Slessarev, "Racial Tensions and Institutional Support: Social Programs During a Period of Retrenchment," in *The Politics of Social Policy in the United*

States, ed. Margaret Weir, Ann Shola Orloff, and Theda Skocpol, Princeton University Press, 1988, 377. Other programs recovered and grew in succeeding eras. Desmond, *Poverty, by America*, 27–28; Emily A. Shrider and John Creamer, *Poverty in the United States: 2022*, Current Population Reports P60-280, United States Census Bureau, 2023, 23–32, table A-3.

11. Appelbaum, *Economists' Hour*, 117.

12. Irving Kristol, "The Battle for Reagan's Soul," *Wall Street Journal*, May 16, 1980, cited in Mark A. Smith, "Economic Insecurity, Party Reputations, and the Republican Ascendance," in *The Transformation of American Politics: Activist Government and the Rise of Conservatism*, ed. Paul Pierson and Theda Skocpol, Princeton University Press, 2007, 156; Ferguson and Rogers, *Right Turn*, 185–86, 195; Alan Murray, *Showdown at Gucci Gulch: Lawmakers, Lobbyists, and the Unlikely Triumph of Tax Reform*, National Geographic Books, 1988, 34; Fred Block, "Read Their Lips: Taxation and the Right-Wing Agenda," in *The New Fiscal Sociology: Taxation in Comparative and Historical Perspective*, ed. Isaac William Martin, Ajay K. Mehrotra, and Monica Prasad, Cambridge University Press, 2009, 69.

13. The size of the tax cut is measured as a share of GDP. Michelmore, *Tax and Spend*, 148; Brownlee, *Federal Taxation in America*, 190, 207; Murray, *Showdown*, 10, 12; Blinder, *Monetary and Fiscal History*, 155, 158; Graetz, *The Power to Destroy*, 96. The 1986 reform was by most accounts mildly progressive or at least neutral in its immediate effects. C. Eugene Steuerle, *The Tax Decade: How Taxes Came to Dominate the Public Agenda*, Urban Insitute, 1992, 122–23. In the long run, however, the special tax breaks soon multiplied, and the loopholes reopened. Julian E. Zelizer, "The Uneasy Relationship: Democracy, Taxation, and State Building Since the New Deal," in *The Democratic Experiment: New Directions in American Political History*, ed. Meg Jacobs, William J. Novak, and Julian E. Zelizer, Princeton University Press, 2004, 292; Jacob S. Hacker and Paul Pierson, *Winner-Take-All Politics: How Washington Made the Rich Richer—and Turned Its Back on the Middle Class*, Simon and Schuster, 2010, 107; Thomas Byrne Edsall and Mary D. Edsall, *Chain Reaction: The Impact of Race Rights and Taxes on American Politics*, W. W. Norton, 1992, 159, 193.

14. Appelbaum, *Economists' Hour*, 120; George H. W. Bush, "Address Accepting the Presidential Nomination at the Republican National Convention in New Orleans," August 18, 1988, APP; William Safire, "On Language: Read My Lips," *New York Times*, September 4, 1988; Brownlee, *Federal Taxation in America*, 219.

15. R. J. Reinhart, "George H. W. Bush Retrospective," Gallup, December 1, 2018.

16. Julian E. Zelizer, "Seizing Power: Conservatives and Congress Since the 1970s," in Pierson and Skocpol, *Transformation of American Politics*, 116.

17. Graetz, *Power to Destroy*, 89–96; Daniel J. Balz and Ronald Brownstein, *Storming the Gates: Protest Politics and the Republican Revival*, Little, Brown, 1996, 127–28; Helen Dewar, "Republicans Wage Verbal Civil War," *Washington Post*, November 19, 1984.

18. Graetz, *Power to Destroy*, 139–49; Balz and Brownstein, *Storming the Gates*, 139–40; Michael J. Graetz and Ian Shapiro, *Death by a Thousand Cuts: The Fight over Taxing Inherited Wealth*, Princeton University Press, 2011, 26.

19. Jacob S. Hacker and Paul Pierson, "Tax Politics and the Struggle over Activist Government," in Pierson and Skocpol, *Transformation of American Politics*, 267; Graetz and Shapiro, *Death by a Thousand Cuts*, 213–14; Graetz, *Power to Destroy*, 119; Chris Good, "Norquist's Tax Pledge: What It Is and How It Started," ABC News, November 26, 2012.

20. Hacker and Pierson, "Tax Politics and the Struggle over Activist Government," 268; Graetz and Shapiro, *Death by a Thousand Cuts*; Zelizer, "Seizing Power," 116.

21. Richard L. Berke, "Dole Works on Expansion of a Conservative Résumé," *New York Times*, April 12, 1995.

22. Benjamin I. Page and Lawrence R. Jacobs, *Class War? What Americans Really Think About Economic Inequality*, University of Chicago Press, 2009; Vanessa S. Williamson, *Read My Lips: Why Americans Are Proud to Pay Taxes*, Princeton University Press, 2017.

23. Daniel Schlozman and Sam Rosenfeld, *The Hollow Parties: The Many Pasts and Disordered Present of American Party Politics*, Princeton University Press, 2024; Alexander Hertel-Fernandez and Theda Skocpol, "Asymmetric Interest Group Mobilization and Party Coalitions in U.S. Tax Politics," *Studies in American Political Development* 29, no. 2 (2015): 235–49; Martin Gilens, "Inequality and Democratic Responsiveness," *Public Opinion Quarterly* 69, no. 5 (2005): 778–96; Larry M. Bartels, *Unequal Democracy: The Political Economy of the New Gilded Age*, Princeton University Press, 2016; Benjamin I. Page, Larry M. Bartels, and Jason Seawright, "Democracy and the Policy Preferences of Wealthy Americans," *Perspectives on Politics* 11, no. 1 (2013): 51–73.

24. On the decline of working-class politics and the rise of technocracy in the Democratic Party, see Ilyana Kuziemko, Nicolas Longuet Marx, and Suresh Naidu, "Compensate the Losers? Economic Policy and Partisan Realignment in the US," working paper, National Bureau of Economic Research, November 2023; and Elizabeth Popp Berman, *Thinking Like an Economist: How Efficiency Replaced Equality in U.S. Public Policy*, Princeton University Press, 2022.

25. Hacker and Pierson, *Winner-Take-All Politics*, 182, 209.

26. Andrea Louise Campbell, "What Americans Think of Taxes," in Martin et al., *New Fiscal Sociology*, 63.

27. Balz and Brownstein, *Storming the Gates*, 90.

28. Hacker and Pierson, *Winner-Take-All Politics*, 232.

29. Seito Hayasaki, "The Unlikely Heroes of Progressive Taxation: CEOs' Support for Bill Clinton's Tax Increase Package in 1993," *Journal of Policy History* 35, no. 2 (2023): 220; Douglas Jehl, "With Budget Won, Sales Pitch Begins," *New York Times*, August 10, 1993.

30. Graetz, *Power to Destroy*, 159; Brownlee, *Federal Taxation in America*, 245; Dan T. Carter, *From George Wallace to Newt Gingrich: Race in the Conservative Counterrevolution, 1963–1994*, Louisiana State University Press, 1996, 109.

31. Aid to Families with Dependent Children was replaced with Temporary Aid to Needy Families, which did not entitle eligible families to benefits. States could dole out their TANF money as they saw fit—for example, into programs

to encourage marriage or promote abstinence. Desmond, *Poverty, by America*, 29. Today, less than a fourth of TANF funding is distributed directly to the poor. Diana Azevedo-McCaffrey and Ali Safawi, "To Promote Equity, States Should Invest More TANF Dollars in Basic Assistance," Center on Budget and Policy Priorities, updated January 12, 2022. TANF funding has *never been increased* since the program's founding. Inflation has eaten nearly half its value over the past almost thirty years. Gene Falk, *The Temporary Assistance for Needy Families (TANF) Block Grant*, CRS Report No. IF10036, Congressional Research Service, updated April 3, 2024, 1; Hacker and Pierson, "Tax Politics and the Struggle over Activist Government," 273; Brownlee, *Federal Taxation in America*, 235.

32. Graetz, *Power to Destroy*, 177.

33. Sarah Binder, "Challenges of Legislating in Polarized Times," in *Congress Reconsidered*, 13th ed., ed. Lawrence Dodd, Bruce I. Oppenheimer, Ruth Bloch Rubin, and C. Lawrence Evans, CQ Press, forthcoming; Julian E. Zelizer, *Burning Down the House: Newt Gingrich, the Fall of a Speaker, and the Rise of the New Republican Party*, Penguin Press, 2020; Joseph Fishkin and David Pozen, "Asymmetric Constitutional Hardball," *Columbia Law Review* 118 (2018): 915–82.

34. Paul Glastris and Haley Sweetland Edwards, "The Big Lobotomy," *Washington Monthly*, June 9, 2014; Molly E. Reynolds, "What Is the Senate Filibuster, and What Would It Take to Eliminate It?," Brookings Institution, September 9, 2020; David Shribman, "Lament of the Reagan I.R.S.," *New York Times*, April 4, 1982; Jacob S. Hacker and Paul Pierson, *American Amnesia: How the War on Government Led Us to Forget What Made America Prosper*, Simon and Schuster, 2016, 310.

35. Margot L. Crandall-Hollick, *The Earned Income Tax Credit (EITC): A Brief Legislative History*, CRS Report No. R44825, Congressional Research Service, 2018. In another indication of the rightward shift of the party, House Republicans attempted to cut EITC in the 1995 budget—one reason Clinton cited for his veto. Christopher Howard, *The Welfare State Nobody Knows: Debunking Myths About U.S. Social Policy*, Princeton University Press, 2021, 99–100; Paul Kiel, "It's Getting Worse: The IRS Now Audits Poor Americans at About the Same Rate as the Top 1%," *ProPublica*, May 30, 2019; Hadi Elzayn, Evelyn Smith, Thomas Hertz, et al., "Measuring and Mitigating Racial Disparities in Tax Audits," *Quarterly Journal of Economics*, forthcoming; Andrew W. Kahrl, *The Black Tax: 150 Years of Theft, Exploitation, and Dispossession in America*, University of Chicago Press, 2024.

36. Graetz, *Power to Destroy*, 179; Joe Soss and Sanford F. Schram, "A Public Transformed? Welfare Reform as Policy Feedback," *American Political Science Review* 101, no. 1 (2007): 111–27; Vanessa Williamson, "Public Ignorance or Elitist Jargon? Reconsidering Americans' Overestimates of Government Waste and Foreign Aid," *American Politics Research* 47, no. 1 (2019): 152–73.

37. Blinder, *A Monetary and Fiscal History*, 193–95.

38. Suzanne Mettler, "The Transformed Welfare State and the Redistribution of Political Voice," in Pierson and Skocpol, *Transformation of American Politics*, 202; Christopher Howard, *The Hidden Welfare State: Tax Expenditures and Social Policy in the United States*, Princeton University Press, 1999; Christopher Howard, *The Welfare State Nobody Knows: Debunking Myths About U.S. Social Policy*, Princeton

University Press, 2021; Desmond, *Poverty, by America*, 91; Suzanne Mettler, *The Submerged State: How Invisible Government Policies Undermine American Democracy*, University of Chicago Press, 2011; Suzanne Mettler, *The Government-Citizen Disconnect*, Russell Sage Foundation, 2018.

39. *Bush v. Gore*, 531 US 98, 128–29 (2000).

40. The White House, "Announcing the Largest Budget Surplus in History," September 27, 2000; Barry W. Johnson and Jacob M. Mikow, "Federal Estate Tax Returns, 1998–2000," *Statistics of Income Bulletin* 21, no. 4 (Spring 2002): 133–86; Graetz, *Power to Destroy*, 181.

41. Jacob S. Hacker and Paul Pierson, "Abandoning the Middle: The Bush Tax Cuts and the Limits of Democratic Control," *Perspectives on Politics* 3, no. 1 (2005): 40; Peter Savodnik, "Club for Growth May Back Challenger to Chafee in 2006," *The Hill*, May 18, 2005.

42. So much so that the Republicans took the unprecedented step of ousting the Senate parliamentarian. Nick Anderson and Janet Hook, "Lott to Oust Senate Parliamentarian Who Ruled Against GOP," *Los Angeles Times*, May 8, 2001.

43. Hacker and Pierson, *Winner-Take-All Politics*, 214; Graetz and Shapiro, *Death by a Thousand Cuts*, 122–23; Hacker and Pierson, "Abandoning the Middle," 38; Larry Bartels, "Unenlightened Self-Interest," *American Prospect*, May 17, 2004.

44. Isaac William Martin, *Rich People's Movements: Grassroots Campaigns to Untax the One Percent*, Oxford University Press, 2013, 183; Bartels, "Unenlightened Self-Interest"; Larry M. Bartels, "Homer Gets a Tax Cut: Inequality and Public Policy in the American Mind," *Perspectives on Politics* 3, no. 1 (March 2005): 15; Hacker and Pierson, "Tax Politics and the Struggle over Activist Government," 258; see also David Hope, Julian Limberg, and Nina Weber, "Why Do (Some) Ordinary Americans Support Tax Cuts for the Rich? Evidence from a Randomised Survey Experiment," *European Journal of Political Economy* 78 (June 2023): 102349, 1–15.

45. Bush was not concerned about reducing spending either. Zelizer, "Seizing Power," 132; Graetz, *Power to Destroy*, 196; Blinder, *Monetary and Fiscal History*, 237–38; Edith Rasell and Christian E. Weller, *The Perils of Privatization: Bush's Lethal Plan for Social Security*, Economic Policy Institute, May 1, 2000.

46. Hacker and Pierson, "Abandoning the Middle," 33, 40, 43; Andrew Prokop, "In 2005, Republicans Controlled Washington. Their Agenda Failed. Here's Why," *Vox*, January 9, 2017; Graetz, *Power to Destroy*, 193; Larry M. Bartels, "Homer Gets a Warm Hug: A Note on Ignorance and Extenuation," *Perspectives on Politics* 5, no. 4 (December 2007): 786; Blinder, *Monetary and Fiscal History*, 233; Graetz and Shapiro, *Death by a Thousand Cuts*, 206; Hacker and Pierson, *Winner-Take-All Politics*, 215.

47. Bartels, "Homer Gets a Tax Cut"; Joel Slemrod, "The Role of Misconceptions in Support for Regressive Tax Reform," *National Tax Journal* 59, no. 1 (2006): 69; John Sides, "Stories, Science, and Public Opinion About the Estate Tax," working paper, George Washington University, July 2011, 31; Carole V. Bell and Robert M. Entman, "The Media's Role in America's Exceptional Politics of Inequality: Framing the Bush Tax Cuts of 2001 and 2003," *International Journal of Press/Politics* 16, no. 4 (October 2011): 548–72; Hacker and Pierson, *Winner-Take-All Politics*, 214.

48. Neta C. Crawford, "The U.S. Budgetary Costs of the Post-9/11 Wars," Costs of War Project, Watson Institute for International and Public Affairs, September 1, 2021, 1.

49. Brownlee, *Federal Taxation in America*, 262–65.

50. Hacker and Pierson, *Winner-Take-All Politics*, 199.

51. Sixty-four percent of the public supported aiding homeowners. Blinder, *Monetary and Fiscal History*, 299.

52. Kate Zernike, "In Power Push, Movement Sees Base in G.O.P.," *New York Times*, January 14, 2010; John Barry, "Stirred by Deficit, Mad at Both Parties," *Tampa Bay Times*, updated April 5, 2010.

53. Theda Skocpol and Vanessa Williamson, *The Tea Party and the Remaking of Republican Conservatism*, Oxford University Press, 2016.

54. Also because of a special 2008 tax rebate, an effort to stimulate the collapsing economy. Blinder, *Monetary and Fiscal History*, 261.

55. Carl Davis, Andrew Boardman, Neva Butkus, et al., *Who Pays? A Distributional Analysis of the Tax Systems in All 50 States*, 7th ed., Institute on Taxation and Economic Policy, 2024, 5.

56. "The Non-Taxpaying Class," *Wall Street Journal* editorial, November 20, 2002; Zelenak, "Mitt Romney, the 47 Percent."

57. When Florida Republican Rick Scott made such a proposal some years later, he was immediately excoriated by Republican leadership and on Fox News for planning to raise taxes.

58. Zelenak, "Mitt Romney, the 47 Percent," 474–75.

59. Thomas B. Edsall, "Hill Vote Is Milestone for Forces of Government 'Containment,'" *Washington Post*, June 30, 1995.

60. Zelenak, "Mitt Romney, the 47 Percent," 475.

61. William G. Gale, "What the Kansas Tax Cut About-Face Means," Brookings Institution, June 13, 2017; Michael Mazerov, *Kansas Provides Compelling Evidence of Failure of "Supply-Side" Tax Cuts*, Center on Budget and Policy Priorities, January 22, 2018, 11–12; Russell Berman, "The Brownback Backlash," *The Atlantic*, October 26, 2015.

62. City of Ferguson, Missouri, *Annual Operating Budget, Fiscal Year 2014–2015*. See also United States Department of Justice, *Investigation of the Ferguson Police Department*, Civil Rights Division, March 4, 2015, 10–13; Bruce Katz and Elizabeth Kneebone, "On Ferguson, Fragmentation, and Fiscal Disparities," Brookings Institution, April 2, 2015; Thomas Luce, "Reclaiming the Intent: Tax Increment Finance in the Kansas City and St. Louis Metropolitan Areas," discussion paper, Center on Urban and Metropolitan Policy, Brookings Institution, April 2003.

63. Emma Pierson, Camelia Simoiu, Jan Overgoor, et al., "A Large-Scale Analysis of Racial Disparities in Police Stops Across the United States," *Nature Human Behaviour* 4, no. 7 (2020): 736–45; Magnus Lofstrom, Joseph Hayes, Brandon Martin, and Deepak Premkumar, *Racial Disparities in Traffic Stops*, Public Policy Institute of California, October 2022; Matthew Menendez, Michael F. Crowley, Lauren-Brooke Eisen, and Noah Atchison, *The Steep Costs of Criminal Justice Fees and Fines*, Brennan Center for Justice, 2019, 6; US Commission on Civil Rights,

Targeted Fines and Fees Against Communities of Color: Civil Rights and Constitutional Implications, US Commission on Civil Rights, September 2017; Vesla M. Weaver and Amy E. Lerman, "Political Consequences of the Carceral State," *American Political Science Review* 104, no. 4 (2010): 817–33; Jonathan Ben-Menachem and Kevin T. Morris, "Ticketing and Turnout: The Participatory Consequences of Low-Level Police Contact," *American Political Science Review* 117, no. 3 (August 2023): 822–34; Ariel White, "Misdemeanor Disenfranchisement? The Demobilizing Effects of Brief Jail Spells on Potential Voters," *American Political Science Review* 113, no. 2 (2019): 311–24; Gabriella Sanchez, "In Florida, the Right to Vote Can Cost You," Brennan Center for Justice, September 7, 2022; Kristen M. Budd, "Florida Bans Voting Rights of Over One Million Citizens," Sentencing Project, January 2023.

64. Sierra K. Thomas, "I Yelled 'Black Lives Matter!' at a Trump Rally. This Is What Happened Next," *Washington Post*, March 18, 2016; Jenna Johnson and Mary Jordan, "Trump on Rally Protester: 'Maybe He Should Have Been Roughed Up,'" *Washington Post*, November 22, 2015.

65. Amber Phillips, "'They're Rapists': President Trump's Campaign Launch Speech Two Years Later, Annotated," *Washington Post*, November 25, 2021. See also Trump's earliest forays into politics. Jan Ransom, "Trump Will Not Apologize for Calling for Death Penalty over Central Park Five," *New York Times*, June 18, 2019.

66. Breaking with tradition, Trump had refused to release his most recent federal income tax forms. But some previous years of Trump's taxes, available from business filings related to his casinos, showed no federal income tax liability.

67. Philip Rucker and Rosalind S. Helderman, "Romney: I've Paid at Least 13 Percent Tax Rate in Each of Past 10 Years," *Washington Post*, August 17, 2012.

68. Vanessa Williamson, "The 'Tax Cuts and Jobs Act' and the 2018 Midterms: Examining the Potential Electoral Impact," Brookings Institution, August 27, 2018.

69. Charles Homans and Mark Peterson, "How 'Stop the Steal' Captured the American Right," *New York Times*, updated July 28, 2022.

70. Vanessa Williamson, "Understanding Democratic Decline in the United States," Brookings Institution, October 17, 2023.

71. Christina D. Romer and David H. Romer, "Do Tax Cuts Starve the Beast: The Effect of Tax Changes on Government Spending," working paper, National Bureau of Economic Research, October 2007.

72. Emmanuel Saez and Gabriel Zucman, *The Triumph of Injustice: How the Rich Dodge Taxes and How to Make Them Pay*, W. W. Norton, 2019, xi, 23; Appelbaum, *Economists' Hour*, 127.

73. Saez and Zucman, *Triumph of Injustice*, xv, 7, 98.

Conclusion

1. *Pollock v. Farmers' Loan & Trust Co.*, 157 US 531–32 (Supreme Court 893).

2. Bill D. Moyers, "What a Real President Was Like," opinion, *Washington Post*, November 12, 1988.

3. Evan S. Lieberman, "The Politics of Demanding Sacrifice: Applying Insights from Fiscal Sociology to the Study of AIDS Policy and State Capacity," *New Fiscal Sociology: Taxation in Comparative and Historical Perspective*, ed. Isaac William Martin, Ajay K. Mehrotra, and Monica Prasad, Cambridge University Press, 2009, 101–18; Evan S. Lieberman, *Race and Regionalism in the Politics of Taxation in Brazil and South Africa*, Cambridge University Press, 2003, 4; Alberto Alesina, Edward Glaeser, and Bruce Sacerdote, "Why Doesn't the U.S. Have a European-Style Welfare System?," working paper, National Bureau of Economic Research, October 2001; Rourke O'Brien and Adam Travis, "Racial Change and Income Tax Policy in the US States," *Socio-Economic Review* 20, no. 2 (2022): 585–609.

4. Noel Ignatiev, *How the Irish Became White*, Routledge, 2012; Jennifer L. Hochschild and Brenna Marea Powell, "Racial Reorganization and the United States Census 1850–1930: Mulattoes, Half-Breeds, Mixed Parentage, Hindoos, and the Mexican Race," *Studies in American Political Development* 22, no. 1 (2008): 59–96.

5. Daniel N. Posner, "The Political Salience of Cultural Difference: Why Chewas and Tumbukas Are Allies in Zambia and Adversaries in Malawi," *American Political Science Review* 98, no. 4 (2004): 529–45.

6. See, for example, President Biden's and Kamala Harris's rhetoric about the price gouging of consumers, or Elizabeth Warren's statement "There is nobody in this country who got rich on his own."

7. The amount of revenue that can be raised from the rich is more limited than you might imagine; there are not very many extremely rich people. Sven Steinmo, *Taxation and Democracy: Swedish, British, and American Approaches to Financing the Modern State*, Yale University Press, 1993, 18. The revenue limitations of highly progressive taxation decline somewhat as the wealthy come to have an increasingly obscene share of wealth and income. But presuming that one intends to reduce the concentration of wealth, it is wise not to make one's social welfare system dependent on highly progressive tax revenue. When Senator Bernie Sanders proposed Medicare for All in 2016, the financing included a payroll tax.

8. Vanessa S. Williamson, *Read My Lips: Why Americans Are Proud to Pay Taxes*, Princeton University Press, 2017. For recent decades, see Gallup poll questions on which tax is the "worst tax—that is, the least fair." For earlier data, see Advisory Commission on Intergovernmental Relations, *Public Opinion and Taxes*, annual reports, 1972–1994. LBJ understood that you could tell people about taxes. When he described his Medicare proposal, he led with the costs: "Now, here is how the plan will work. During his working years, the worker pays about $2.50 a month. This, plus a similar amount from his employer, will provide the funds to pay up to 60 days hospitalization for each illness. It also provides adequate nursing home care." Lyndon B. Johnson, "Remarks to the Press Following a Meeting with Congressional Leaders to Discuss Medical Care Legislation," March 26, 1965, APP.

9. Michael J. Graetz, *The Power to Destroy: How the Antitax Movement Hijacked America*, Princeton University Press, 2024, 79, 178; Steven M. Teles, "Conservative Mobilization Against Entrenched Liberalism," in *The Transformation of American*

Politics: Activist Government and the Rise of Conservatism, ed. Paul Pierson and Theda Skocpol, Princeton University Press, 2007, 168–73.

10. Daniel R. Alvord, "The Triumph of Deficits: Supply-Side Economics, Institutional Constraints and the Political Articulation of Fiscal Crisis," *Sociological Quarterly* 61, no. 2 (2020): 206–30.

11. Charles Tilly, "War Making and State Making as Organized Crime," in *Bringing the State Back In*, ed. Dietrich Rueschemeyer, Peter B. Evans, and Theda Skocpol, Cambridge University Press, 1985; Sheldon D. Pollack, *War, Revenue, and State Building: Financing the Development of the American State*, Cornell University Press, 2009; Richard Franklin Bensel, *Yankee Leviathan: The Origins of Central State Authority in America, 1859–1877*, Cambridge University Press, 1990; Steven A. Bank, Kirk J. Stark, and Joseph J. Thorndike, *War and Taxes*, Urban Institute, 2008; Kenneth Scheve and David Stasavage, *Taxing the Rich: A History of Fiscal Fairness in the United States and Europe*, Princeton University Press, 2016.

Index

Galloway, Abraham, 109
Gallup, George, 197–198
Gardner, Henry, 3
Garrison, W. C., 99
Gary, Martin W., 112, 113(fig.), 120, 129
gas tax, 209
George, Henry, 162–163
George III (king), 24
Georgism, 163
German American voters, 110
Gerry, Elbridge, 52
gerrymandering, fiscal, 141
GI Bill, 204, 233
Gilded Age, 7, 143, 159–164, 248
Giles, William Branch, 58
Gingrich, Newt, 228, 229, 231–232
Gold Ring scandal, 131
Goldscheid, Rudolf, 8
Goldwater, Barry, 206, 214, 221
gonzo constitutionalism, 225
good-roads movement, 148–149
Gore, Al, 231
Gould, Jay, 131
government shutdowns, 231–232
Grange, 163
Gray, Daniel, 49
Gray, Harrison, 3
Great Britain. See Britain
Great Depression, 182–183, 187
Great Society, 201, 203
Great War, 177–179
Greenback-Labor Party, 163
Green Tree Tavern, 61
Gregory, John H., 151
Grenville, George, 25, 28, 31
Griffin, June, 220
Griffin's Wharf, 1–2
Gulick, Luther, 181–182

Haines, Monday, 146
Hamburg Massacre, 113, 126
Hamilton, Alexander
    Constitutional Convention, 52–53
    taxation as economic stimulus,
        45–46, 58

as treasury secretary, 57(fig.), 57–60, 67
    Whiskey Rebellion defeat, 60, 67–72
    whiskey tax, 56–60
Hampton, Wade, 113–115, 114(fig.),
    128, 133
Hancock, John, 29
Harding, Warren G., 179
Harmar, Josiah, 62
Hayes, Rutherford B., 114(fig.), 115, 131
Hearst, William Randolph, 189
"Heart of Oak" (Royal Navy anthem), 27
Helper, Hinton, 75–78, 76(fig.), 90
Helperism, 75, 88
Henry, Patrick, 78
Henry III, 23
Hewes, George Robert Twelves, 1–2
Highgate, Edmonia, 98
Hodges, William A., 103
Hofstadter, Richard, 79
Hogeland, William, 60
Holliday, Frederick W. M., 135
Holman, Edward E., 118
Holmes, Oliver Wendell, Jr., 15
Hood, Oliver Roland, 151–152
Hoover, Herbert, 179
Hopkins, Harry, 184
housing segregation, 204–205, 210–212
Howard, Christopher, 209
Huggins, A. P., 107
Hume, David, 45
Humphrey, Hubert, 207
Hunnicutt, James, 103
Hunter, Margaret, 98
Huston, James, 169

Ickes, Harold, 189, 191
immigrants, 238
The Impending Crisis of the South
    (Helper), 75
import duties, 2
The Income Tax (Seligman), 175
income taxes
    bracket creep, 208–209
    calls for reinstatement of, 163–164
    Civil War, 130, 163, 165, 166

Lenape, 62
Letters of a Farmer in Pennsylvania
    (Dickinson), 28
Levittown, 204
Lewis, John, 123
liberty, 3, 42, 248, 250
Lincoln, Abraham, 100, 102, 157
literacy rates, 86–87, 97, 108–109, 141
Little, Finis H., 123
Little Turtle, 62, 70
Livingston, William, 45
localization of taxes, 141–142
Logan, Trevon, 105, 106
Long, Huey, 186–189
Long, Russell, 202–203, 207, 218
Los Angeles Times (periodical), 206
The Louisiana Populist (periodical), 167
Lynch, John, 118
Lynchburg Christian Academy, 219

Madison, James, 44, 51–53, 85
Magna Carta, 21–23, 30
Mahone, William, 136, 137, 138, 252
Mancini, Matthew, 144
Manning, John L., 112
Manning, William, 66–67
marginal tax rates, 65
Martin, Isaac, 180
Mason, George, 78
Massachusetts Bay Colony, 26
McFarlane, James, 68
McGary, Dan, 109
McGovern, George, 207
McKinley, William, 172
Medicaid, 205, 226, 244
Medicare, 11, 199, 205, 209–210, 231,
    233, 240, 251
Mehrotra, Ajay, 162
Mellon, Andrew, 179–180, 187, 198
Mettler, Suzanne, 233
Miami (tribe), 62, 69, 70
Michelmore, Molly, 199–200
military-industrial complex, 204–205
Militia Act, 69

militias, 37, 39, 49, 55–57, 62, 68–70, 113,
    120, 150
Miller, Thomas E., 96
Mills, Wilbur, 201–203
Mingo Creek Association, 56, 70, 71
Mississippi State Normal School for
    Colored Youth, 98
molasses tariffs, 24
Mondale, Walter, 227, 230
Moral Majority, 221
Morgan, Albert T., 89
Morgan, J. P., 160, 187
Morgenthau, Henry, 185, 187, 190, 193,
    194, 197–198
Morris, Richard, 85–86
Morris, Robert, 40, 41, 44–46
Moses, Franklin, 101
Moss, Francis, 103
Movement for Economic Justice, 211
Moynihan, Daniel Patrick, 207
Murphy, Liam, 14

NAACP, 185
Nader, Ralph, 211
Nagel, Thomas, 14
Nash, William Beverly, 102, 105
The Nation (periodical), 125, 126, 130,
    188, 191
National Gazette (periodical), 65
nationalism, 46, 79
National Review (periodical), 239
National Tax Reduction Week, 179
national wealth tax, 6–7
National Welfare Rights Organization
    (NWRO), 201–202, 207–208, 211
Native confederacy, 62, 70
Neville, John, 55–56, 60, 68
New Deal, 162, 183, 189, 190, 192, 200
"New Purchase," 61–62
Newsom, Matthew T., 99
The New Spirit (film), 192–193
The New York Herald (periodical), 130
New-York Journal (periodical), 63
New York Taxpayers' Association, 131

redistribution of, 12, 96, 236, 245
suburban concentration of, 210–211
tax, 6–7, 103, 187–192
taxation of Black, 142
Webster, Noah, 42
The Weekly Pelican (periodical), 143
welfare programs
  AFDC, 201–203, 206, 209, 224, 226
  associated with Blackness, 205–207
  block-granting aid, 231
  demonization of, 205–207
  dichotomy with earned benefits, 199
  effects of Proposition 13 on, 215
  FAP, 207–208
  fraud accusations, 206, 232–233
  "hidden" in tax code, 209
  land grants, 71
  opposition to, 12, 17
  Reagan's rhetoric, 206–208
  recipient portrayals, 201–202, 204,
    223–224, 238
  as redistribution of wealth, 12
  Republican opposition to, 207–208, 222
  stigma of, 238

"welfare queens" and, 204, 221
  work requirements, 201–202
Wells, Ida B., 97
westward expansion, 63, 71
Whately, Thomas, 31–32
Whipper, William J., 109
Whiskey Rebellion, 55–63, 67–72
whiskey tax, 55–57, 59–63
White League, 113, 116
white supremacy, 7, 17, 96, 107,
    149–150, 248
Wiley, George, 211, 212
Wilson, Woodrow, 176, 178
Wilson-Gorman Tariff Act, 164
Winchell, Walter, 196
women's rights, 5–6
Wood, Barry, 197
Woodward, C. Vann, 139
World (periodical), 167
World War I, 177–179, 187
World War II, 181–182, 192–198, 252
Wyandot, 62, 69

Yorkville Enquirer (periodical), 119

Vanessa S. Williamson is a senior fellow in governance studies at the Brookings Institution and a senior fellow at the Urban-Brookings Tax Policy Center. In addition to her previous books, her writing has appeared in *The New York Times*, *The Washington Post*, *The Atlantic*, *The Nation*, and elsewhere. She lives in Washington, DC.